# WE WERE CHILDREN THEN · VOLUME II

Stanton & Lee Publishers, Inc.

*This book is gratefully dedicated
to all of the men and women
who have
so generously shared
their memories and wisdom
with us*

# WE WERE CHILDREN THEN · VOLUME II

## Stories from the Yarns of Yesteryear Project

Edited by CLARICE DUNN & GEN LEWIS
Illustrations by MARIAN LEFEBVRE
Introduction by BEN LOGAN

All of the stories appearing in this book
are drawn from the Yarns of Yesteryear Project,
the program sponsored to preserve the recollections
of Wisconsin's senior citizens.

All royalties from this book go toward the continuation
of the Yarns of Yesteryear Project.

First Edition
Copyright ©1982 by Stanton & Lee Publishers, Inc.
All rights reserved.
Illustration Copyright ©1982 by Marian Lefebvre.
All rights reserved.
Introduction Copyright ©1982 by Ben T. Logan.
All rights reserved.
Direct all inquiries to:
Stanton & Lee Publishers, Inc.
44 East Mifflin Street On the Square
Madison, Wisconsin 53703

Library of Congress Cataloging in Publication Data          (Revised)
Main entry under title:

We were children then.

  Vol. 2: edited by Clarice Dunn & Gen Lewis;
published by Stanton & Lee Publishers.
  1. Children—Wisconsin—Collected Works.  2. Wisconsin—Social life and customs—Collected works.  3. Wisconsin—Biography—Collected works.  I. Gard, Robert Edward.  II. Lengfeld, Fred.  III. Lefebvre, Mark E.
HQ781.W38          305.2'3'09775          76-22961
ISBN 0-88361-041-8 (v. 1)          AACR2
ISBN 0-88361-085-X (v. 2)

Edited by Mark E. Lefebvre
Copyedited by Diana Balio
Designed by Marian Lefebvre
Typeset by Total Type
Printed in the United States of America
by Straus Printing & Publishing Company.

# Acknowledgments

Grateful acknowledgment is made to University of Wisconsin-Extension Arts Development and the Wisconsin Regional Writers Association, sponsors of the Yarns of Yesteryear Project.

Special acknowledgment is hereby given to the persons who, in addition to the editors, gave generously of their time to read and judge the manuscripts: James Batt, Frank Custer, Jill Dean, Howard Kanetzke and Doris Platt.

Acknowledgment is also made to the following publications where certain of the stories have appeared: *The Milwaukee Sentinel* and *The Grand Forks Herald* for "August," "Mrs. Sadler" and "Grand Forks Days" by Robert G. Anderson; *Italian Americana* for "With a Baby in My Arms" and "White, Gray and Purple-Ribboned Wreaths" by Anne M. Dunst; *Exclusively Yours* for "The Big Save" by Ann Baumgard; *Madison Select* for "The Culoch" by Roderick MacDonald; *The Capital Times* for "Worms but No X-Rays" by Cecelia Howe; *The Milwaukee Sentinel* for "The Murder of Eleanor: A Story to Melt Your Heart" by Wanda Aukofer; *Wisconsin Trails* for "The Old Fourth" by Marion Clapp; *Farm Wife News* for "The Sears Order Box" by Jean Bunker Schmidt; *This Is Madison* for "The Corner Grocery Store" by Margaret Kennedy; *The Milwaukee Sentinel* for "The Roll Basket" by Edna Hoeller and *The Gazette* for "The Center of Our Home — The Dining Room" by Catherine W. Lewis.

# CONTENTS

# 3. Born Before 1890

# 4. Hard Times

## 11. Going Home

## List of Participants, 1976-1978

Introduction

To talk of "then" is to acknowledge that "then" wasn't so very long ago. As a Nation we remain very young, especially there in the Midwest of my childhood. It was then new land, settlers still coming in, older generations being left behind in the East or farther yet, so there are grandparent stories aplenty in this book, but very few about *great*-grandparents. We did not know them.

Many of the summer-night voices of my childhood, including the voice of my own father, had the strong accents of "the Old Country." For Father those words always meant "home,"and I forever saw him as two persons, only one half belonging to us, his loyalties and memories shared with a world I had never seen. True, I had images of his running along the edge of the cold North Sea as a child, but he still remained illusive.

Now I find added glimpses of my father here in stories about those like him who came to "the New World." I have a new feeling of how strange it must have been to land in New York, speaking no English, having little money, with only a vague knowledge of destination of a place somewhere to the west, called Wisconsin. There are glimpses here of the courage and determination of such searching people and a realization of how often they were helped and how much they owed to people whom they had never met before and would never see again.

There are glimpses, too, of how accidental life is. I remember the story of a non English-speaking immigrant who was trying to get to Detroit. Someone misunderstood what he said and mistakenly sent him to Beloit instead. The immigrant worked there until he had enough money to try again. This time someone mistakenly sent him to DePere, so there he stayed and lived out his life, never seeing Detroit.

To talk of "then" is also to acknowledge that "then" is not a separate time buried deeply in the past. Our childhood goes on being a part of us, and we are every age we have ever been. These stories are written by persons who understand that. They reach back to feelings and details of their earlier years and bring them alive to be experienced again. By means of their memory we partake in a rich tapestry of our own past.

I keep referring to what is collected here as "stories." That is not the right word. These are bits and pieces of real life, sometimes born of remembered happiness and laughter, sometimes out of sadness and tears. Real people reach up from these pages, authentic in a way that characters from fiction rarely are.

Occasionally a few words can capture an intriguing reality. For example: "A tan dress that my sister refused to wear because it looked like a baseball suit." Or a woman who would walk three miles to catch the train to Madison, and on the way home "as the train pelted past her farm she would reach across her startled seatmate, open the window and hurl a loaf of bread into her backyard." Or a rather determined person who used to say, "I am always right. Even when I am wrong I am right."

Recalled too are the little losses that forever haunt us. "Where are the sliding doors of my childhood?" "What happened to the missing serving bowl that went with Mama's footed dishes, red ones trimmed with gold?" These are described by people who know that we need to hold tight to the reference points of our lives — the rituals, the persons, the lovely things that helped glue life together into something that made sense, despite hard times.

Distances were more frightening then. It took a different kind of bravery to go out "on one's own" in a time when goodbyes were more likely to be forever. And small pleasures were bigger — like the feel of your first pair of silk stockings, part of the thrill coming from knowing that silk worms in some far-off country had created the thread. And the "I'm-a-big-person" feel of going to the store for the first time as you are trusted to remember what is needed and to bring back the proper change. One boy (his story is here) could not resist temptation, and his mother found him outside the store, the money gone and his mouth stuffed full of chocolate.

Such incidents allow me to be part of them. I even find myself making my own additions, saying "Hey, I used to do that!" Or "I had one of those." Or "Say, he sounds just like my Uncle Lou!" I think this is proof that I shared a childhood with more persons than I realized. I value that knowledge, though I can't tell you why this sense of linkage with those who lived before me feels so important and right.

In one of the yarns there is a description of someone cutting thin shavings from a bar of Fels Naptha laundry soap, something I also did on wash days. In another a boy is embarrassed at wearing a dust cap, reminding me of a time I decided a boy my age should not be seen hanging up the washing. When anyone passed by on the road I would hide between the billowing sheets, not even racing out to meet George Holliday, the mailman, who came sometimes with mail but almost always with a story. (He was the father of Lloyd Holliday whose tale of Rattlesnake Tom is included here.)

These writers keep letting me in on my own past, triggering memories of a long-ago me. A mention of those incredible cookies in the tin boxes with glass tops transports me through time to a store in Gays Mills. The rest of the scene begins to fill in — the feel of "going to town" from the farm, several pennies in my pocket, sidewalks hot underfoot, the bustle of strange people, a runaway team of horses racing down Main Street. But none of those sensations can compete with the cookies. Overhead fans whirr in the silence as the white-aproned storekeeper lets me alone to press my face against glass after glass. It's odd, but I always remember the rich chocolate smell of those cookies while I looked at them much better than I remember the taste of those I usually chose, the ones with a pretty design and a white marshmallow underneath the chocolate.

There were other agonizing choices. Sometimes I had a whole nickel. Should I break it up into pennies and make it last or should I use it all at once for an ice cream cone, bag of salted peanuts, or one of a dozen different candy bars?

Once, Ralph Henderson, an older neighbor boy who was working away from home, found me trying to make my choice at Ackerman's drugstore. "What are you going to have?" he asked me.

Suddenly my decision was made. I paid a reluctant goodbye to candy bars and peanuts and selected rich, strawberry ice cream piled high on a cone.

"I'll treat you," Ralph said, jingling a few coins.

I hesitated, pulled out my lone nickel and showed it to him. "I can't treat back."

"That's all right," he said. "I got lots of money."

I let Ralph buy me the cone (I don't know if I ever treated him in return) and even returned later for the salted peanuts.

That was almost a half-century ago, and the feel of the hot summer night, the sounds of the drugstore and Ma Ackerman's shuffling walk are all there, made part of today again by someone's simple words about the cookies of their childhood.

I keep meeting in these pages persons who are new to me, yet I know them instantly. There is the man who remembers the Depression forcing people into travel and new adventure: "As I watch the trains go by I often think of the days I rode the steam locomotives and boxcars to the West Coast and back," he writes. And there's a woman remembering a doll named Betsy, taken out after sixty years, her lovely smile still able to captivate and reassure. And there's the memory of a marvelous act of liberation and revenge — a small girl, banned from the cool water where the boys swim in the nude, can still hear the screams resulting from the crabs she dumped into their swimming hole.

The reality of life and death unfolds in the fragile scene of a small boy standing with a goose egg (the first one he has ever seen) in his hands, as he says to his older sister, "Cook this for me." A person who now is old remembers that particular scene, and must now go on to remember how soon that boy was to die.

Such a scene is real and exists without sentimentality. It is the way life is — something to be lived as it happens and not fought against. It is people stubbornly standing up for their rights and for the "right thing," all the while accepting the power of what they cannot control. It is picking up the pieces and moving on with the only life we are granted to live.

And, finally, there is the rousing, living epitaph of a forever-young seventy year-old woman saying, "An old swinging bridge still lifts me, a whistling train bears me on. I skim over the pond, ride too fast, and court danger anew. 'I dare you' and 'fraidy-cat' still needle me . . . And I still want to move on and up and away. I ask of flying time, What next?"

I ask the same. And I am proud that I too was nurtured by this same Midwestern land, proud that such people as these are part of my heritage and of history. We were not just children *then,* but children *there* as well.

Ben Logan
Author of *The Land Remembers*

# 1 Family Album

## MY NEW COUNTRY
*Hugo Drechsel*

Dear Great-grandson:

This is an abbreviated account of my arrival in the United States as an immigrant from a very small town known as Thalheim, Germany. I will attempt to describe the wonderful sights and events which I encountered from New York to Milwaukee, Wisconsin.

The steamship *Cleveland* docked on February 26, 1926, at Pier 88 in New York. After a minor inspection I left the ship with the other passengers. Instantly, I recognized my brother, Max, who lived in Dover, New Jersey. He wanted to visit with me before I continued my travel to Milwaukee.

With a great deal of astonishment I looked at the improved change in my brother's appearance. I could always recall him as being dressed in conservative clothing, but today he wore a modern gray overcoat, pressed pants, a white shirt, and a necktie. Even more surprising, when he smiled I noticed that in place of his brown, tobacco-stained teeth, he exposed clean white upper and lower dentures.

After a handshake and a few words he hailed a taxi for the drive to the ferry landing. This was my first ride in a taxi and I felt rather dignified.

Along the way I noticed some fruit stands which displayed piles of apples and oranges, boxes of every kind of vegetable, and bunches of bananas which dangled from hooks. Never in my life had I seen such an abundance of fruit and vegetables, especially in the month of February.

On the ferry everyone seemed to be wearing their Sunday clothing. Some ladies even wore fur coats. How beautiful they looked with their faces slightly made up and their shapely legs enveloped in silk stockings.

In Dover, my brother lodged in a rooming house, and we talked until late at night about families and friends.

The next morning, much to my disappointment, my brother went to work. Before he left he told Frank, the lodging house caretaker, to purchase a railroad ticket for me.

Frank and I left the house some time after nine o'clock. Outside of a store Frank stopped. Inside were two elevated chairs with two sticks in front of each one. He said, "Let's have a shoeshine."

"A shoeshine? A shoeshine in a store?" I thought. Not me.

He opened the door. A bell tinkled. He climbed onto a chair and glanced outside through the window, saw me still standing, jumped down again, opened the door, and called, "Come on, have your shoes shined, and don't worry about the pay."

Even my old German shoes must have wondered about the polished treatment.

At the railroad station Frank bought a ticket for a Pullman coach for the thirty-four-hour ride. He thought he had done the right thing; however, in my mind I reflected on the many times I had traveled on hard wooden benches in the old country.

At noon my brother escorted me to the railroad station. Not many passengers were waiting for the train. When it arrived we said good-bye to each other. It was the last time I saw my brother. For family reasons he returned to Germany.

In the coach, as I searched for a seat, a black, uniformed man approached me. His cap had the word Porter. He said something, then he smiled. Because I didn't answer, and noting the sight of my clothes, he knew that I was a foreigner. In sign language he indicated that he wanted to see my ticket. He glanced at it, lifted my suitcase, and motioned to me to follow him. It was the first time I had seen a black man in nature. He placed my luggage under a seat in the middle of an elegant coach and pointed to the upholstered velvet-covered place.

Captivated, I stared at the round, brown, highly polished ceiling, the shiny bronze light fixtures, and the high class of passengers.

At the next stop a distinguished-looking man took the empty seat across from mine. Nonchalantly, he said hello. Then he inspected me closely. *"Sie sind sicherlich ein deutscher Einwanderer"* (You must surely be a German immigrant"), he said in perfect German. His name was Schaller and he was a businessman. During the conversation that followed we forgot about time until a white-uniformed young man walked along the aisle ringing a soft bell.

"Dinner time," said Mr. Schaller, and without delay he reached into his briefcase. "My wife wrapped two sandwiches for me, because I don't like the diner," he said. And as if it were a daily occurrence, he handed me one of his two sandwiches, which was richly covered with ham. "And no thanks. Just eat and enjoy them," he remarked.

One of my problems, a visit to the men's room, was solved by Mr. Schaller after lunch when he guided me to this place. I could hardly believe my eyes when I saw the clean washroom and the three snow-white washbowls with the glistening faucets.

Then he led me to the observation car. It is impossible to describe my delight about the train and the informative, friendly businessman.

It was dark when we returned to the coach. With amazement I noticed that on a few places the round ceiling had been lowered to form berths.

Mr. Schaller had to get up early the next morning and soon suggested we retire.

"We probably won't see each other again by the time you get up, but I can assure you that I enjoyed your company," he declared, and sincerely I too extended my appreciation.

Before I slowly dozed off in my upper berth I compared this certainly prosperous man who had conversed with me, a plain immigrant, against the class differences in Germany.

The next morning Mr. Schaller had left. I went to the washroom, then took a look from the observation car, and returned to my place. A new passenger occupied Mr. Schaller's place. He was a man in his thirties, of strong build and a healthy complexion. In only a few minutes he noticed my German origin and, surprisingly, he also spoke German.

"Call me John," he said without any formality. John, who was a cattle dealer, told me everything he knew about farming and animal husbandry. He was a jovial fellow who seemed to be without financial worries, because at noon he invited me to lunch and ordered a delicious meal for us. As if his generosity meant nothing, he waved his hands when I thanked him. He departed in Buffalo where we had a one-hour layover. I decided to walk a little and casually sauntered toward the depot. Suddenly I thought, why not try my school English, which I had learned fifteen years ago.

Gamely, I approached the newsstand and now, thinking about it, I probably said, "De shu have a tscherman newbaber?"

The older man behind the counter stared at me and

replied, "Whaaat?"

"I vont a nuwsbaber. A tscherman baber?"

His eyes switched as if facing a nut, and quickly I returned to the coach.

Again the train moved, and darkness fell. Time: eight o'clock, nine o'clock. Then there was light in the distance. Signs appeared and one of them said Chicago.

The train slowed down. Would I be able to find my train to Milwaukee? But my fears were groundless. When the train stopped, the porter again helped me. Carrying my luggage, he led me to my train. I knew he deserved more than a one-dollar tip. Smiling, he accepted. What a great black man!

Sitting alone on a bench I was puzzled how the conductor on this train also knew who I was, because close to my destination he motioned me to get ready.

When I got off the train, a big sign said Milwaukee. My heart bounced faster. I looked for my sister and her husband. Had they received the telegram my brother promised to send?

Slowly I stepped with my suitcase into the depot. In just a few seconds a pretty young lady came toward me. She was obviously a street girl, I thought, like the ones I noticed in some railroad stations in the old country. But her approach and her manner nullified my apprehension. Courteously she addressed me in English, and, noticing my embarrassment, she switched to a fluent German.

"I am from the Travelers Aid Society," she said. "Can I help you?"

Wavering, I told her of my predicament. With assurance she mentioned that I should not worry and that she would find a way to get me to my sister's house.

While we talked, the station door opened and my sister and her husband walked in. It was a happy reunion with smiles and smiles. I was grateful to the compassionate lady and she, wishing me good fortune, stepped back.

No one can imagine the deep feeling I had for my new country, and in all these many past years that feeling has never faltered.

## OF THEE I SING
*Esther V. Smith*

The children in the neighborhood used to gather in her kitchen as she worked, and they would listen, openmouthed, as she told them stories of her childhood on the little island of Öland, off the southeastern coast of Sweden.

One day her four-year-old son embarrassed us all by innocently asking, "Mama, who is the pretty lady standing by Papa in that picture?"

When she laughingly told him that it was herself, incredulity showed plainly on his face. And as we all looked at the large framed photograph that hung high on the wall, it was hard to believe. The lady who stood beside her seated husband in the typical pose of the 1890 era was truly beautiful. There was a cameo perfection to her features that so many Swedish women seem to have, and she smiled down at us with her large beautiful eyes and very generous mouth.

In contrast, the woman working in the kitchen before us seemed quite old, although I realize now that she was only in her early thirties. One of her eyes and the right side of her mouth had become twisted with a facial paralysis. Some of her teeth were missing, and her stomach protruded from much childbearing. Yes, it was hard to believe.

But she had an inexhaustible store of anecdotes about the Old Country that we were always teasing her to tell and retell.

She had been the youngest child in a very large family, and they were always hungry. She said she had never known what it was to be really sated until she came to America. Almost everyone found it "hard scratching" on this little island where fishing seemed to be the main industry. Johann Johannson, her father, worked in a kiln as an experienced brickmaker, and his family could have been more prosperous than the rest of the islanders if he hadn't been so addicted to the bottle. The quenching of his insatiable thirst seemed to be the only thing that mattered to him. Often he was too drunk to go to the kiln, and when he did work, the biggest part of his wages went for whiskey. This no doubt accounted for Eleanora's abhorrence of liquor, and many were the sermons she preached to us on the sins of drinking.

There were no free public schools in Sweden in the 1870s, so parents paid a schoolmaster to teach their children. It is easy to see that with the kind of father the Johannson children had, there was very little money for education. Consequently the number of weeks that Eleanora spent in school were very few. Instead, she was hired out to farmers by her father before she was even in her teens, and he promptly collected her wages as soon as they were payable. At three o'clock in the morning, she would start on a round of milking cows, which was followed by hour after hour of other laborious chores. She used to tell us that when she finally tumbled into bed at night, her little arms ached so much that she was unable to sleep.

One "landgreve," or landowner, must have appreciated her efforts, for he told her she was doing so well that he was going to raise her wages. She said she was almost afraid to ask, but finally picked up the courage to request that the additional money be given to her instead of her father, and to her surprise he consented to do so. Every ore of this precious money was saved until finally she had hoarded enough to buy her passage to Denmark, for she was determined to get out of the reach of her father's grasping hands.

Here, her wages were somewhat higher, and with her father unable to collect them, she had soon saved enough to buy a steerage ticket to America, the Promised Land, where everyone was rich—or so she had heard.

Her brother Ernst, who had become a sailor, was already in America, so with great difficulty she wrote a letter to let him know when she was coming, and requested that he meet her in New York. Since she had addressed her letter to "Herr Ernst Johannson, United States of America," it is not surprising that when her boat docked her anxious eyes could not see her brother anywhere. Her clothes were in a roll, which she carried with her as she walked—she was afraid to let them out of her sight lest they be stolen. Since she had no more money and couldn't speak a word of English, she didn't know what to do. When it began to rain and both she and her bundle of clothes were getting drenched, her courage forsook her, and she began to cry. A kindly policeman discovered her plight and looked up a city employee who could speak Swedish. They found out that she was penniless, that somehow her brother had failed to meet her, and that she needed work at once. The Swedish-speaking lady had a friend who was looking for a domestic, so Eleanora was taken there and engaged on the spot.

Mrs. Reynolds, her new mistress, must have been a remarkable woman, for she more than went out of her way to be kind to her little "greenhorn" maid. She taught her the value of American money. She found an old primer, and every day there was a lesson in reading and a new word to learn to pronounce and use. When she learned that Eleanora's ultimate goal was Menominee, Michigan, where an aunt was now located, she looked up a map of the United States and showed her where Menominee was. When she boarded a train at last for her final destination, tears came to her eyes as she bade this woman good-bye. Mrs. Reynolds had become to Eleanora the symbol of American kindness, and she knew that she was really leaving a true friend behind.

In Menominee she fell in love with and married Gustav Salem, a Swedish shoemaker, who had already, as he proudly stated, "taken out his first papers." As they raised their family, they never failed to impress on their children that America was the land of opportunity and that they were very lucky to be born Americans.

When Eleanora's husband received his second papers, their pride knew no bounds. All the neighbors were invited in, and Swedish *kringlar* and coffee were passed time and again, for as they proudly put it, "Now ve are really Americans."

If the children started to converse in Swedish, as they sometimes did, they were stopped at once with this admonition: "Yu are American. Yu must taalk American."

Eleanora had no singing voice, but as she rocked the cradle, which was never empty, with her foot, and at the same time worked the churn dasher up and down, these are the words with which she lulled her children to sleep:

*My countree, tis of dee,*
*Sweet lend of libertee,*
*Of dee I seng.*

In a community that was made up largely of foreigners, most of the children were put to work, either in a factory or as an apprentice, as soon as they had finished grade school. But not Eleanora's children. In a land where education was free, they were going to have an "eddication," and an "eddication" was what they got. No sacrifice on her part was too great to provide her children with the advantages she had never had.

I marvel now to think that anyone with so little formal education could have provided her family with such a well-balanced diet, and with so little money, but she seemed to have an uncanny instinct for what her children needed to make them strong. The cow she cared for daily furnished plenty of milk, homemade butter, and cottage cheese. The chickens provided eggs and an occasional fowl. The pigs that were raised through the summer and the yearly calf gave them many meals of pork and veal. The butcher was always glad to give away liver, since in those days no one would buy it anyway. She could get an enormous basket of fish for a dime by walking out to the shacks when the fishermen were coming in from Green Bay with their catches. Her garden, which she miraculously found time to keep weeded, kept them in fresh vegetables throughout the summer, and what was left in the fall was garnered and placed in the "root cellar." From this, during the winter, great kettles of vegetable soup, thick with Swedish dumplings, provided many a hearty meal.

She and her children gathered wild strawberries, raspberries, gooseberries, blueberries, and cranberries, which she canned over a wood-burning range in the evenings, all after having tramped for miles through woods and marshes to gather them. But there was always plenty of canned fruit to last through the winter. All this was in the days long before vitamins were discovered, and no doubt Eleanora had never even heard of proteins, carbohydrates, and minerals. But all these things were free in this wonderful new country, and this mother, who had known so much deprivation in her youth, accepted it all gratefully.

When World War I broke out, Eleanora had no sons to lend to Uncle Sam, since her oldest boy had a withered right arm from early childhood and her other two sons were ten and twelve. But she hobbled on arthritic feet for over a mile to the Red Cross rooms where her fingers made the knitting needles fairly fly. I'm sure she never missed a meeting. To her, it wasn't a chore—it was a labor of love. Now she could do something for her Uncle Sam, who had already done so much for her.

How do I know all these things? Because Eleanora Johannson was my mother. It was to me, my sisters and brothers, and our little neighborhood playmates that these stories were told and these songs were sung. And long before the words of that beautiful anthem were written, she was fervently praying, "God bless America."

## FRUEHLING BRINGS A FAREWELL
*Ruth Allschwang*

My awareness of life began when I was old enough to join the family for meals in the dining room. I don't remember exactly how old I was—perhaps seven or eight—but there I was one evening, and every day thereafter, assigned to my own chair facing my brother Klaus. He was three years older and had been eating with the grown-ups for some time.

With joy I discovered my own silver napkin ring, initialed with the scrolled letters of R.G. (Ruth Galinski). To the right of the simple white china plate was my very own silver, with the traditional large soup spoon, gleaming and reflecting in the soft evening candlelight.

Father believed in and adopted the strict German relationship between children and parents. The law was to be punctual and to speak only when spoken to. The timing of the meals during the day was lax, but the evening meal, except for the Sabbath or holidays, was served precisely at the same time every day. This caused a conflict when we were playing with friends, but the desire to share the warmth, love, and belonging around the dinner table always won out.

Soup preceded every meal, and as Anna, our cook, ladled the steaming broth into the deep white soup plates, it was an announcement of the kind of day it had been—a workday, holiday, Sabbath, or company day. The steaming soup tureen placed in the center of the table, shared by loved ones in the spirit of warmth, was a symbol of our way of life.

*Fruehling*, the German word for spring, to me is one of the most melodious sounds in the German language. Just say *Fruehling*, and immediately thoughts turn to blue skies, soft warm breezes, gay sounds of birds chirping, and trees alive and budding.

It is the same feeling of excitement and joy running through your whole being when opening a special gift package from a loved one. Your impatient and eager fingers want to tear it open, but you hesitate, deliciously prolonging this moment, the moment you might find your wish.

The *Fruehling* in 1928 started with the same glow and

excitement, but the package I opened held nothing I wanted or ever wished for; I never thought it could happen. It was the year my beloved grandfather died. It all happened so suddenly. Klaus and I were working hard at school. Spring brought the end of a school year and we buckled down with studies for exams and a special last effort for good grades. We had heard Grandfather cough a lot during a few nights; also we were awakened by the low-kept voices of Father and Mother and a narrow strip of light coming from behind the door of Grandfather's room. There also were the frequent visits of our doctor, Herr Lichtwitz, and Grandfather's best friend, Herr Pinkus.

It was April 30, the final day of school. We were let out early, and with Easter vacation and a new semester starting, I hurried home full of plans and joy. Grandfather was the first I wanted to show my report card to. Not noticing the unusual silence as I rushed into the house, my feet stopped abruptly on the threshold of Grandfather's room, for I had never seen so many visitors there before. They were standing around his bed. My heart began beating in panic as I moved closer to his bedside. I did not dare look up to the familiar faces of Father, Mother, the doctor, or my good friend the Hebrew teacher, the Rabbi Herr Winterberg, for fear of what I might find.

"Grandfather, I passed my exam." His once-pink cheeks now were hollow and pale. When my eyes fell on his prayer shawl folded across his hands, tears jumped into my eyes and I felt a big lump in my throat.

"Where is Klaus?" he asked in a whisper. Just then Klaus walked in. There was a look of fear on his face. I stepped back to let Klaus take my place. My heart began to beat fiercely again, for I was afraid Klaus would break down completely. He was always so soft-hearted and kind;

never once had he fought back against his three-years-younger sister, no matter how much abuse I gave him. But there he stood, all of a sudden a grown man of fifteen years, my heart loving him very much at the moment. He placed his new school cap on Grandfather's prayer shawl without a word of explanation. The previous year's had been a deep red velvet. Now it was green. There it lay on the prayer shawl, green like the spring outside, full of life, its secret not yet unfolded. Grandfather's hand touched the soft velvet, and he knew that Klaus had passed his exam.

His eyes closed and his lips began to move into a prayer. Herr Winterberg started to pray loudly in Hebrew, and when I heard Father's voice repeating after him, I left the room, blinded with tears, finding refuge in the alcove in the living room with its windows looking out upon the marketplace. The sun shone brightly on the ivy leaves that climbed and almost covered the church across the way with golden hues. Glints of light twinkled from the Rathskeller windows. The farmers noisily pulled their tents up, driving away with their horse carts and wagons. I wanted to shout, "Stop! Let everything stop. How can you talk?" How could life go on as though nothing had happened?

Herr Winterberg walked into the living room and put his arms around me. I cried on his chest long and hard. I have never cried like this since. "You loved him very much, Ruth," he comforted me, "but he ended his days, just like there has to be a beginning. This is God's will."

The rest of the day and the next day were in a turmoil and disorder, but nobody cared. Relatives and friends filled every room of our house. The funeral had to take place within twenty-four hours, since, according to Jewish laws, the body becomes unclean once the soul has departed.

Father and my five uncles were sitting in mourning on low benches in the room with Grandfather, who was now dressed in a white shroud, covered by his prayer shawl, and lying in a wooden coffin, with a candle placed at his head. The clothing of father and the uncles was cut and torn, a ceremonial showing grief. There was much weeping when the hour came for having the coffin carried out of the house and placed onto the waiting horse-drawn wagon. Each of the four horses was completely covered with a black cloth with just their eyes showing.

The procession began. It was a long, slow, and silent walk. The cemetery was at the far end of town on a high hill. At last Grandfather came to rest. The coffin was lowered into the grave, our rabbi saying prayers in Hebrew, then placing a small sack of earth from the land of Israel on his coffin. We waited until the grave was covered with earth and all the men repeated the Kaddish after the rabbi—the prayer for the dead.

On arriving home, we found our three maids, Anna, Frieda, and Imgard, waiting in the long entrance hallway. Anna, our cook, with red, swollen eyes and still crying, grasped Mother's hand and told her that she had taken it upon herself to prepare the food and set up the tables. Mother linked her arm gratefully into Anna's and, with me closely behind, walked through the double doors to the dining room, living room, and library. In each of the rooms Anna had put up tables covered with shiny Damask cloth. Dishes and silver sparkled. On the buffet were Mother's largest crystal platters, covered with meats of tongue, beef, and jellied veal. The soup tureen stood on the marble serving board. Mother's boat-shaped crystal bowl now held a shimmering red liquid with pieces of fruit floating in it, the first time it had ever held food.

"I made fruit soup for the ladies and farina dumpling soup for the men," Anna said anxiously, looking at Mother, but Mother nodded approvingly. Then while tears must have choked her voice, in her loving fashion, she simply kissed Anna.

For seven days the rooms were crowded with relatives and friends. All the while, Father and the uncles sat on low seats on the floor in mourning (a custom called sitting shive). In these seven days I came to know a new father. The wall that he had built around himself, his authority, his ability never to show emotion, the face of strictness crumbled away and I found within me a feeling of compassion and tenderness for him that brought us closer from then on.

He who always was so vain about his appearance suddenly did not care. He was unshaven, and his suit looked as if it had been slept in. For seven days he did not set foot in the store or even ask the bookkeeper about the accounts. Anna would take his food to him, mostly while he was sitting in Grandfather's room, and Frieda brought us meals in our room, not at a specified time, but whenever we were hungry.

The nightmarish seven days passed. The household continued in the regular time pattern, but the cloud of hushed silence and sadness would not leave. We were talking, moving, doing things, but it seemed like some force kept pulling the strings to keep us performing. The living room looked like a strange guest with an impersonal cold face. Instead of the chanting prayers coming from Grandfather, there was a great silence.

The Friday which I never wanted to come again, came. I was afraid to open my eyes, to face this day without Grandfather. It used to be such a happy day, right from morning on, both of us baking the challah. I got up, for I knew Grandfather wanted me to carry on and to keep our traditions alive. When entering the kitchen I was glad to find Mother and Anna busily kneading a huge yellow mass of dough on the floured, wooden board. The tile stove glowed like a sunset; on it the black iron soup kettle gave out the fragrance of chicken soup.

Suddenly the cloud of sadness was gone, lifted like magic, a forceful gay wind blowing it to pieces. There was laughter taking its place, and the laugh was on me. I must have looked funny, because I had put on one of Anna's aprons which covered me like a tent, not even my feet showing. My hands and face were covered with flour as I had so seriously a minute ago started to roll the dough into four braids, the way Grandfather had taught me. I looked up at Mother and Anna, down at myself, joining in their laughter, wiping the tears with the back of my hands, the only unfloured part of me.

The day passed in the usual preparations for the Sabbath, peace and tranquility again taking possession all around and within us. Father and Klaus came home from the temple, this time bringing our Rabbi Herr Winterberg along as our guest. Father said the prayer over the challah, then handed me a small piece. I swallowed it fast, not wanting to remember all the other Fridays.

There was an empty chair across from me and a full goblet of wine on the table in front of this chair. This was Grandfather's place. As we lifted our goblets in prayer, a shadow fell on the side of his chair, and the wine in the goblet rippled as if someone had taken a sip. *He is still with us*, I thought. He always will be. Whenever I am happy or sad, when holidays come, or when I bite into a piece of challah, especially on Friday nights, even though I have drifted away from the kosher laws, forgetting the Fridays, the candles and the prayers, I know that he

knows in his simple way. He also knows that life made me compromise, but he knows too that I have paid dearly. We all have.

He is here with me at this moment, David, as I fight my way back to my true belief in Grandfather's religious ways, which I have never really abandoned inside of me. He is with me, and with his help I shall find myself walking in his ways. Farewell, my sweet grandfather, dearest friend.

## GRANDPA'S FAMILY
*Helen Schlough*

Grandpa would have understood and sympathized with the young men who went to Canada to avoid the draft. At seventeen he came to Wisconsin to escape four years of military service in his native Austria. I think Prince Otto Edward Leopold von Bismarck had something to do with it because Grandpa named his succession of male dogs Bismarck. Grandpa would look at his current dachshund and say, "Bismarck, you are a son of bitch." Russel and Rachel would run around chanting, "Bismarck is an S.O.B." When Aunt Jennie protested, the little innocents would say, "But Mama, Bismarck's mother was a bitch." Bismarck grinned and squirmed. Grandpa laughed and laughed.

When Grandpa was ninety, Peter Faber took him along with some visiting firemen to a burlesque show in Chicago. The men never forgot that evening. Grandpa had more fun than anyone.

Grandpa sired six noisy, rambunctious children: Albert, Frank, Joseph, Minnie, and the twins, Mary and Jennie. Minnie was baptized Amelia; my father called her

Runty, the smallest in the litter. Aunt Jennie was baptized Johanna. I think all the children were baptized in the Catholic church, but they lived their lives and died "freethinkers." When St. Barnabas Church in Mazomanie was built, Grandpa's feelings were hurt. He and his sons had helped quarry and haul the sandstone for the building, and then the priest expected a contribution equal to that of less active parishioners. Grandpa rebelled and took the whole damned family out of the church.

Grandpa was an authority figure. His children and grandchildren deferred to him until the day he died at ninety-seven. In their moments of affection he was Papa, but when he put his newspaper or book down, looked over his glasses, and gave an order, it was, "Yes, Father." He spanked Jennie when she was a married woman because she sassed him. When Minnie told him she had got in trouble, he asked, "Do you want that fellow?" Minnie said, "Yes, Father." Grandpa got his buggy whip. The marriage was as happy as most and endured for nearly fifty years until that fellow held the dying Minnie in his arms, calling to her not to leave him.

As the grandchildren came along, we learned we had a friend in Grandpa. He had time for us. He made swings for us. He made boxes and trunks, painting them red and blue, for us to store our junk in. He lifted us to the backs of horses and led the horse when we were scared. He took us to circuses and tent shows. He was always ready to go fishing, gathering nuts, or just walking over the hills.

His wife died when he was in his sixties. He found a nice widow lady he thought he would marry, but his children said, "No, Papa. You live with us." So for thirty years he lived in his children's homes, rotating from one family to another.

On holidays the whole tribe gathered, filling one of the homes to bursting with food and hearty eaters. There was little drinking—oh, perhaps a little homemade wine with the meal. This family didn't need outside stimulation. They were self-propelled. They shouted, they quarreled, they scolded, they complained that Grandpa didn't love them. They joked, they teased, they laughed. Grandpa had the loudest laugh of all.

At one gathering, the women were sitting around Aunt Minnie's living room. In those days ladies wore skirts to their shoetops and sat with crossed ankles. Uncle Joe took Grandpa's cane and said, "We are going to have a contest to see who has the prettiest legs. Frank will be the judge." They circled the room, Uncle Joe hooking the cane under the ankles and lifting the legs. The women yelled and giggled. My dad gave the prize to my mother. Mother stood, blushing, and lifted her skirt to her knees. During the clapping, Grandpa kissed my mother. We kids loved to see the adults at play.

The family went places and did things. When home became boring, they traveled. Mother said there was a little gypsy in them. Aunt Jennie's husband was a railroad man; she rode the rails on a pass, taking Aunt Mary with her. When Aunt Mary went to bed for a few days saying, "It's my heart," Aunt Jennie came along and said, "Come on, Mary, let's go to Chicago." Aunt Mary jumped out of bed, grabbed her hat and coat, and they caught the first train out.

Min and Bill went to Yellowstone Park with the first wave of tourists. They built a bed in their Model T Ford; they loaded a two-wheeled trailer with cans of gasoline and water, spare tires, fishing gear, and a tent. Camping out, they traveled gravel roads, and got stuck in the Dakota gumbo, but they made it there and back, having a wonderful time fishing where no white man had fished before.

Before my father married, he worked in the lumber camps and followed the harvest from the Dakotas to the Montana wheat fields. When I was a child, Dad went to Mexico where he was caught in a revolution. From his hotel room in Veracruz, he watched the war going on in the streets. He heard the shooting and saw the dead men in the streets. He didn't know who was fighting or why. He didn't stick around to find out. He boarded the first ship out of the port.

One fine September day, the day I was born in the Dover farmhouse, Dad was gallivanting. Leaving his horse and buggy at Aunt Minnie's barn in Mazomanie, he took a train to Madison. About three o'clock in the afternoon, Mother sent her oldest son with a note to a neighbor, Loveday Hottmann; she and Dr. Brown assisted at my birth. When Dad came back to Aunt Minnie's, he had a new carpet sweeper. He scattered sand on Aunt Minnie's carpet and demonstrated how well the sweeper cleaned. Aunt Mary arrived to say, "Go home, Frank. You have a baby girl at your house. I'm going to the farm with you." Dad grabbed his carpet sweeper and ran shouting, "Oh, hell, it won't live anyway." Twenty-five years later, on a cold January day, Dad fell dead with a heart attack as he was hurrying to catch a train out of Madison.

When Grandpa decided to live with his children, he divided his property and money, including a gold mine in Montana, among his children—five of them anyway.

Albert, his oldest son, had had his share. Albert left Mazomanie to go to St. Louis, leaving his debts, a wife, and three children. Grandpa took care of the family, but for Albert no more.

For thirty years, his children paid him interest. Three of the five sent Albert his share, paying his interest. The twins continually challenged the three: "Papa is looking to you for Albert's interest."

In dividing the property, Aunt Jennie got the gold mine. In 1923 my father bought the Madison property that had been owned in common. Two at a time the children took turns renting the two houses. The twins found a buyer. Grandpa said, "Hold on to the Madison property; it will be worth something someday." Dad met their price, around six thousand dollars. In 1966 Mother sold the property for fifty-six thousand dollars minus taxes.

Grandpa paid board to his children. He had money for travel and simple pleasures. He was always available to his grandchildren for a short loan or an outright gift.

At long intervals Albert visited his father, bringing his new wife, Emma. Emma had a tendency to turn up her nose at the Schlough tribe. During one of Albert's visits, the tribe gathered at Aunt Jennie's home in Merrimac. The men and boys went fishing all day, returning at sundown with their catch. The women said, "You caught 'em, you clean 'em and cook 'em." The men did produce a gargantuan fish fry at midnight. Uncle Albert was chief cook and bottle washer.

A few months before Grandpa died, a letter came from Emma saying Albert had died and was buried in St. Louis. Grandpa said nothing as tears slid down his cheeks.

Uncle Joe's last trip was from California to Minnesota. He had a heart attack in Los Angeles. He was taken by ambulance to a hospital-equipped railroad car. A nurse traveled with him; at intervals she was relieved by other nurses who boarded the train along the way. When the train was to cross the Continental Divide, a doctor came on board and rode through the night with him. The passengers knew a dying man traveled with them. Uncle Joe was aware of their concern. He arrived home where he was cared for by two nurses. Easter Sunday was coming. To pass the long, sleepless hours, the night nurse made an Easter bonnet for him with feathers, flowers, and veiling. At dawn he sat up in bed, wearing his Easter bonnet, to surprise the day nurse. Before sunset that day he died. Uncle Joe didn't die laughing, but just about.

Grandpa went to Europe several times. He wrote to friends and relatives in Vienna and sent them money. During World War I, a delegation called on Grandpa and told him to cease giving aid and comfort to the enemy, to get rid of all those German books and magazines, and to stop speaking German. From that time on, German was not spoken. After the war, Grandpa went to Vienna and came home saddened. Vienna without a hinterland was unable to feed her starving people. Their hero was Herbert Hoover because he sent them food.

The family remained close even though at times they fought bitterly. In the heat of an argument, one sibling would yell, "You talk like a sausage." Sudden anger would dissolve in sudden laughter. They bore no grudges. There was nothing furtive or secret in their relationships. Everything was open and aboveboard. If you didn't like it, you could yell. In days of trouble, they shared the time, the money, the sorrow.

When Grandpa died at Aunt Mary's home, his children shared the deathwatch. Granddaughter Rachel read to him from the Bible that had the names of his children, his grandchildren, and his great-grandchildren. He lay quietly, listening, resting for the long journey. His past middle-aged sons held his hands, kissed him, and wept. Grandpa wept too; he didn't want to go.

They are all gone now, the whole lively bunch. None lived to the age of the father. Like their mother, they died young. Something vital went out of my life with their going.

# PICTURES OF THE PAST
## *Clara Erb Cline*

Things didn't always turn out the way they were planned, even in the good old days. There were people then, too, who didn't accept what happened without making at least one modest effort for improvement.

My father was one of these helpful people. When he first came to this country he noticed that everyone's table knives were not sharp and would not cut meat. Evidently they were too busy to sharpen them, and he thought his employer's wife would be very pleased to find that someone had done the job for her. So one day when the boss and his wife were gone to town he took all the table knives out to the grindstone wheel and was almost through sharpening them when they returned. He looked up, expecting a surprised and happy greeting, but instead heard a horrified scream from the woman. Needless to say, my father was as surprised as she was, but for a different reason, and after that he didn't sharpen any more table knives.

They were practical people, these Wisconsin settlers, and usually attacked a problem at its source. We heard of one husband who, upon observing his wife's extremely pointed-toe shoes, took them to the chopping block and shortened the offending shoes with two whacks of the ax. Fortunately, he was good enough to let her get her feet out first.

There was yet much uncleared land on our farm, and Papa needed some extra acreage for a potato patch. He had the idea that this virgin land would produce extra-good potatoes. So after much stump blowing and rock removing he asked his daughters, who happened to be my sister and myself, to help plant these potatoes. The ground still had many roots in it, and he only slightly lifted a clod of soil and we would quickly throw a seed potato into the opening. It was a dry year, but the potato plants emerged and were green and thrifty-looking all summer in that rough, young field. That they had potato bugs on them didn't matter. We girls periodically picked them off.

We all wondered how the potato crop would be. Papa finally couldn't stand the suspense any longer, so one day he took a spade and dug the first two hills. He was overjoyed at the two huge potatoes he found. They were so large that he displayed them in Koch's General Store in Mt. Vernon where everybody was astonished at their unbelievable size. Expecting a bumper crop, he relaxed and busied himself with cutting corn and doing other farm work. When the potato vines were brown and dry he started to dig the potatoes, and imagine his consternation when no potato in the whole field was bigger than a walnut. It was as if all the strength of the soil had gone into the first two potatoes. He could hardly face Mama with the earth-shaking news. We learned from this that one cannot always judge what one cannot see by what one can see.

Wildflowers grew in abundance in those days. The spring woodlands were covered with sweet-smelling violets, buttercups, snowdrops, shooting stars, honeysuckle, and a host of other beautiful plants. One could pick handfuls of them. They grew mostly, but not always, on cutover timberland that had not been trampled by cows. Sometimes, deep in the woods, we would find a new flower of which we didn't know the name. A brilliant orange lily would suddenly come into view at some unexpected place, and maidenhair ferns would be hiding in a deep shady nook where the sun just filtered through the trees.

One day while exploring the woods, we came upon a large patch of quaint golden flowers that looked to us as though they could be fairy shoes. They had a wonderful and unusual scent. We had never before seen such strange, beautiful flowers. Later we learned they were called lady's slippers. We had to pick every one at once and run home to show to Mama. These lasted a long time when put in a vase of water. How we loved them, and the next spring we returned to the same place, expecting to see more of them, as we did the year before. But there was not one flower, not even one plant. Where did they go? What had happened? Maybe someone else had found this place and had even dug and taken them home. Yes, this is what must have happened. We thought of neighboring children and accused them in our minds. We were so unhappy. And so it was the next year and the next—not even one plant was ever there.

It was not until we were grown up and no longer on the farm that we found out who was responsible for the disappearance of the lady's slippers. We learned that a lady's slipper is a plant that will not live if it is picked when in bloom. In later years, they were classified as an endangered species, not to be picked by anyone.

The winter of the 1918 epidemic of Spanish influenza was a cold one and the snow was deep. People who needed a doctor often had to shovel the snow so he could get through with his horse and cutter. Our good Dr. Sharp was busy day and night, making calls to whole houses full of sick people. My father was one of the lucky ones, at least for a while. He did not get the flu, while many farmers were unable to milk their cows or do their chores. Papa would do his own work, then go first to one and then the other place and milk and feed the cattle, and after that go to the houses and keep their fires going and maybe cook some soup or heat some milk for those in bed.

The worst was about over, but at Christmas all of us except Papa were still confined to either a bed or the couch in the living room. Looking consolingly at us, Papa said, "Just because Mama can't bake anything doesn't mean we aren't going to have some Christmas goodies." So after supper he started to make French pastry and fancy Swiss rolls. He loved to cook and bake, and he was in his glory. He would come in from the kitchen from time to time to show us what he was doing and let us admire the "leaf" dough and the "twist" rolls and "doves" he made, with raisins for eyes and with golden, shining backs. He had flour all over his overalls from the bib to the knees. It was about midnight when he had finished. Then he said he was feeling a little dizzy, but if it should be the flu coming on he would fix that, by golly, so it would not get him down.

He fixed the fires for the night and then mixed himself a good stiff drink or two of heated red wine and a generous amount of brandy sprinkled with cinnamon. Then he lit the lantern and started to climb the stairs. We could hear the lantern banging against every step as he unsteadily made his way up to his bedroom.

In the morning it was very quiet for too long, and finally Mama was able to get out of bed long enough to call upstairs to Papa. Papa said he was not able to get up because he had the flu. Our faith in hot wine with plenty of brandy was considerably weakened. Now it was our turn to get help, and those who were able to do so came and milked our cows, made us cocoa and soup, put mustard plasters on our chests, kept the fires burning, and did all those things that needed doing. But as for Mama, she never changed from her "temperance" and held firm to her faith in the healing powers of hot lemonade, goose grease, and skunk oil.

# JUST PLAIN MA AND PA
*Albert A. Dobrient*

Prosperity ended at the close of World War I. At our house, there was no end of prosperity, only a continuation of poverty.

Pa's two brothers lived with us to make ends meet. Our house was a four-room, one-bedroom unit. A bed added to the dining room and the parlor changed it into a three-bedroom unit. The attic was converted into a two-bedroom unit, with "built-in" features, to house our two boarders. Plywood from old piano crates was nailed up as the separator walls for each bedroom. Packing crates were added to make closets. A lock and a hasp gave it the final appearance of security as a safety deposit vault. A thunder pot was provided under each bed and a tin pan as a wash basin.

Pa bought our little house with the two-hole outhouse attached to the summer kitchen—adding class to *our* house—for a fifty-dollar downpayment and fifteen dollars a month to pay off the mortgage.

Pa weighed 135 pounds, which matched his five feet four. Ma was five feet even, even wider than that at times. My three brothers and my sister were undoubtedly the reproduction of Ma. I was the exact duplicate of Pa. "Skinny, like a wiener," as Ma so aptly put it.

Pa continued to lose weight; he went down to ninety pounds. Ma tried to find a doctor who would barter for a physical examination. The trade would be two chickens and two dozen eggs (worth about a dollar and a quarter). The result disclosed that Pa had consumption, the dread disease of the times. He was sent to a hospital in Denver for two years.

Uncle Izydor did leave shortly after Pa was taken to the hospital. There was a strange sadness when Uncle packed his two straw suitcases and two wooden apple boxes on the top of an old promenade buggy used as a delivery wagon. He was moving to a basement room that he was sharing with two men. He would pinch pennies and save as much as he could to hurry the day when he could book passage for his wife and four children from Belgium to the "U.S. of A.," as he stated. The tears flowed freely and shamelessly as he began the slow, tedious departure, three miles from our house, with my older brothers lending a hand to support the overload. The wrist-length sleeves were conveniently used to pick up the overflow of tears and excess discharge from the nose.

Uncle would have made a fine replacement for Pa. Ma would miss him the most. There was always a special glow in her eyes when she spoke to him. His patience, love, and attention to all of us were unheard of during those times when "children were to be seen and not heard." His leaving left a deep void in our lives. I think his main reason was to avoid any possibility for gossip.

Uncle Sam would leave a few weeks later. Knowing Sam, Ma recognized the feverish excitement that was developing in him at the thought of meeting his family after a three-year absence.

"Sam, don't forget your money belt. You have different colored socks! You forgot to button your shoes! Do you have your train tickets?" Long after he was out of hearing range she kept up these warnings, until finally to herself, "I just know something will happen." Ma was like a mother hen constantly clucking her warnings to her chicks. A two-hour wait at the depot was in store for Uncle. As he wandered around he came upon the washroom. After consideration and a deep study he decided to use the warm indoor facilities made available for five cents. He very carefully unhitched his money belt and laid it on the floor alongside, slightly toward the back of this public convenience. To himself, he kept repeating, "When I get rich, there will be two such conveniences in my house!" Sad to say, Uncle walked out of this "pleasure parlor" without the thought of the money belt. Halfway through the depot, he remembered it. The wailing and moaning could be heard all the way to New York. The thought of facing Ma was worse than the loss of twenty-five dollars. Ma made a quick withdrawal from her personal bank: ten dollars from the double-pinned area of her bra and fifteen dollars from the triple rolled upper part of her stocking, locked in by a garter.

Uncle Sam was on his way to New York after the final good-bye, which was preceded by a tongue lashing. He had also left a void in Ma's bank account.

The two boarders left when they found out we were going to lose the fine house with the two-holer built so close for convenience. We returned the house to the loan company. Ma said they were very kind to rent us another house for five dollars a month. They did not return any part of the equity for being honest.

As we were viewing the new place she had rented, all her inner strength exploded to release two geysers of tears. "Are you crying because you're sad, Ma?" "No, I'm just happy they found such a nice house for me," she lied! The dictionary describes a slum as a low dirty street inhabited by the very poor. It could be classed as a disaster area but never as a slum. The structural design was called the shotgun house, three very narrow rooms in a row.

Moving day brought out a variety of vehicles to be used to transport our furniture. A borrowed two-wheeled pushcart for the heavy pieces, like the wood-burning kitchen range that weighed five hundred pounds. A parlor stove that almost ruptured all of us, including Ma. I just couldn't understand why my brother screamed so loud when he was pinned by it. I was really amazed how well Ma and her two boys manipulated the heavy pieces.

The second vehicle was called a coaster. That was the word printed on the side. It had two large "English promenade" rubber-tired buggy wheels on the rear and two very small stroller wheels in the front, which gave it an appearance of tipping forward.

The third vehicle was an old buggy. The body was missing. Two apple crates standing on end allowed us to lay the large asbestos plate from under the stove on top of the crates to act as a platform body. The job was well done without scratching any of the vehicles!

After the first month, the floor began to take on the well-scrubbed look. The daily newspapers served as our runner rugs after each scrubbing. When Ma got her job sorting out rags at the junkyard, she was allowed to make the first selections. The charges were deducted from her pay. After all, she did receive second-shift pay, ten cents an hour from six o'clock at night until midnight.

Ma got an additional job plucking feathers in the unheated basement at the butcher shop from five to nine in the morning. She earned ten cents per hour and was allowed to keep the soft goose down.

Ma went to the "Abraham Lincoln" house, the senior center of that day, for advice.

She got up at five on Sunday mornings and went to the farmer's market to select fruits and vegetables that were only partly rotted. With a quick slash or cut of the rotted part, she could recycle and reclaim a variety of health foods.

Sunday afternoon was reserved for a trip to the dump site to gather up chocolate that was turning white, hardened sugars that were cleaned out of the vats and thrown out. Ma gathered these for our hot chocolate.

The commercial baking company sold week-old bread at a penny a loaf. The pound cakes were also sold for a penny a loaf, if they were ten days old. These were supposedly bought for our horses. Rudy, Art, Dave, and I were quite healthy little horses!

Late Sunday afternoons were set aside for Ma to select and wear her very best recycled clothing. She would cook a fine meal from chicken necks, wings, and gizzards, donated by the butcher, and fix a vegetable salad or fruit salad. The toasted pound cake was topped with jams or jellies made from recycled apples or plums, then served with hot chocolate.

The best salvaged scarves and doilies were used under the candelabra. When the candles were lit, a glowing reverence would turn our five-dollar-a-month house into a palace. Ma's face beamed the brightest as she smiled. She was making it on her own, with her five "pootzies," as she whispered, "Denks Gott!"

## MY PROHIBITION AUNT
*Dorothy B. Haas*

In 1924, I had the unique privilege of voting for my father's sister, Marie Caroline Brehm, as the vice-presidential candidate of the Prohibition Party. To the best of my knowledge, she is the first woman to run for that office in a national election.

My aunt was a remarkable woman. She was not beautiful by classical standards, being rather buxom, but had dark, expressive eyes and a crown of snowy hair. She was tall and carried herself like a queen. She dressed with exquisite taste. There was something about her that commanded attention, and she knew how to hold an audience.

Born in Sandusky, Ohio, she was educated at home by her father (according to *Who Was Who*). Her first important role was her election to the General Assembly's Permanent Committee on Temperance of the Presbyterian Church of America. That led to becoming a prohibition lecturer, working closely with Frances Willard. During her career she visited Europe at least eight times and Japan once. As a child I was greatly influenced by her letters and gifts. She sent edelweiss from Switzerland and a book of legends and customs from Japan. When I was still very young, my one aim in life was to visit Europe and see the wonders she wrote about.

Occasionally she visited us, and it was always an event. My first remembrance of her was when she came to Springdale, Arkansas, where we were living. I was about five at the time and was taken to a church auditorium to hear her speak. I remember quite well how beautiful she looked in a lovely yellow gown, made for her, of course. In spite of her rich, resonant voice, I'm afraid I went to sleep before she finished her address.

When we moved to Racine, Wisconsin, she visited us two or three times. She always announced she would arrive on a certain date. My mother would immediately be in a tizzy, for we lived in a rather old-fashioned house. There was a large spare bedroom, but there was no closet. In fact, closets were in short supply throughout the house. As a result, the bed in the spare room held the out-of-season clothing. The bed was piled with coats, dresses, hats, and spare bedding, all carefully protected by a sheet. Under the bed were numerous boxes filled with letters too precious to be thrown away and elegant fans and ornaments from bygone days. When Aunt Marie was coming, our first task was to clear off the bed and pull out the boxes and somehow get them and the clothing stored wherever we could find room for them. It was a day's work, and, being the only girl in the family, I was a major part of the hustle and bustle. There was cooking to be done and great effort spent to have every inch of the house in shining order.

When Aunt Marie arrived, she took over. She always brought a large trunk, and it had to be dragged upstairs to her room. After she was settled she would descend to the living room and begin to pontificate. She had promoted a "cause" so diligently for so many years that she would unconsciously make the simplest sentence sound like one of the Ten Commandments. My father, one of the most tolerant of men, would begin to squirm. He would take it with fairly good grace for the first day, but come the next, he would unobtrusively disappear, seeking out the cronies with whom he could talk on equal terms. When Aunt Marie had left he would say, "I can take just so much of Mame, and then I get a bellyful and I have to get out before I tell her I think she is a bag of wind."

My aunt was the president of the Illinois WCTU for two terms. She was a true crusader. She believed passionately in her cause and could expound endlessly on the dangers of alcohol, the curse of mankind. Nor did she tolerate smoking. Tobacco was second only to alcohol in her list of the evils that destroyed men and wrecked homes.

I once crossed swords with her, to my sorrow. I was a sophomore at the University of Wisconsin and had the temerity to write to her saying that politics was a dirty business and no place for a woman. She came to see us a few months later. We were having breakfast when she turned to me and said in her most authoritative voice, "Dorothy, how dared you write to me as you did? Don't you know that politics are dirty because there are no women in government to clean things up? Just give us a chance to hold office and we will show what women can do to make the country free from graft and corruption." My father suddenly had a coughing spell and beat a hasty retreat. That was all we saw of him that day except at mealtimes. As for me, I was crushed. I wished avidly that I could suddenly become invisible.

She was not elected to office, of course, so she retired to her home in Long Beach, California. But she stuck to her guns. On her front porch was a container not unlike the sand-filled pots near elevators in hotels. No man entered her home smoking. He was politely invited to deposit his vile stogy in the proper place.

Nothing about Aunt Marie was ordinary, not even her death. On New Year's Day, 1925, she attended the Rose Parade at Pasadena, sitting in the grandstand. The contractor must have cheated on material or workmanship, for the stands collapsed, injuring many people. My aunt was badly hurt with a broken kneecap and internal injuries. She died two months later.

When her estate was settled I was given a beautiful watch, which she had worn with great pride. It was presented to her by the Illinois WCTU in 1906 when she retired as president. The watch was especially designed by Peacock's of Chicago. A bow, representing the white ribbon, the badge of the WCTU, and a sprig of lilies of the valley, their flower, are etched on the cover of the watch. In the center of the bow is a handsome diamond. This watch is one of my most prized possessions. It is a precious gift from an aunt of whom I am justly proud.

# THE CHINABERRY TREE
*Ann C. Haller*

To say they don't make women like my grandmother anymore would be absurd. They never did. She was, I think, unique.

When others wax nostalgic about their grandmothers' kitchens I can go along—up to a point. Certainly her kitchen contained all the ingredients for nostalgia. There was the usual massive black iron range from which rose the mouth-watering aromas. There was the coffee grinder for the freshly roasted beans, the egg basket, even the old soapstone sink above which hung the communal dipper. The dipper was germ free, of course. Grandmother did not believe in germs. What she did not believe in did not exist, at least not in her house.

Unfortunately for me, the kitchen also frequently contained my grandmother.

For many years I thought that my grandmother disliked me. Through a rather erratic process of reasoning in my later years I have come to believe that I may have done her an injustice. She was very much a person of absolutes: black and white, good and evil, your way and her way. Her first grandchild, my older sister, could in her eyes do no wrong. I was her second. It may have been simply a matter of balance.

Grandmother rarely raised her voice. If something annoyed her it was banished immediately, mentally and/or physically from her presence. And no matter how hard I tried to practice the virtues expected of me, inevitably I erred. Her pale blue gaze would sweep over me, she would point with a full-armed swing to the back door, and she uttered one word, "*Heraus!*" I spent a great deal of time under the old chinaberry tree in the backyard, counting my sins like a doleful rosary.

It was small comfort to realize finally that she applied this tactic impartially. Aunts, uncles, cousins, the iceman, the milkman, my grandfather, even my own mother, at one time or another suffered banishment. No one ever argued. They departed quickly and quietly.

The results were not all bad. I became a very well-behaved and obedient child. Thin and nervous and fast on my feet perhaps, but most certainly obedient. Even today, half a century later, if someone said "*Heraus*" in my ear in the proper tone of voice, I would probably scuttle mindlessly for the nearest exit and the comforting shelter of the chinaberry tree.

Grandmother's use of the word *heraus* stemmed from a firm if mistaken belief that she spoke fluent German. Brought to this country at the age of six months, she developed over the years a language all her own, one understood only by her immediate family. At one gathering a puzzled European asked which German dialect she was speaking. "My own," she answered, and courteously continued a polite social dialogue intelligible only to herself.

As I grew old enough for comparisons I began to admire and envy her superb sense of her own worth. She would not have understood today's women with their liberation movements and fights for equal rights. If she thought about it at all, which I doubt, I am sure she considered herself the equal if not the superior of most of those whom she encountered in her lifetime. Her creed was summed up in the remark with which she ended one minor skirmish with my grandfather. "I am right and I know I am right. Even if I am wrong I am still right," she said. Nobody laughed.

When I was twelve we moved to another city.

Returning after an absence of several years, I was shocked when I saw my grandmother. The head of the woman I remembered as ten feet tall came barely above my shoulder, and I am not a tall woman. We chatted pleasantly for a while, my grandmother was quite charming, and I became vaguely uneasy. Either my memory was totally at fault or someone had switched grandmothers on me.

It was, of course, merely a lull. At dinner my grandmother announced that she had decided to attend a movie that evening. A nod in my direction told me who would accompany her. A grandson hurriedly called his girl and told her he would be a little late. I began to feel more at home.

At her appointed time Grandmother was tenderly handed into the car and carefully driven the two full blocks to the neighborhood theater. It was obvious to me that she had been there before. The young woman selling tickets turned pale and gave us an overly cordial greeting. The ticket taker snapped to attention as we entered. The odd behavior of the flashlight in the hand of the usher was explained when I realized he was trembling, although Grandmother spoke kindly to him as we followed him down the aisle.

Where a wide aisle bisected the theater our small cortege halted. Stabbing with her cane in the direction of the two end seats, my grandmother uttered the single word *"Heraus!"* A large bag of popcorn supported by two small boys immediately arose from the seats and vanished into the darkness.

Grandmother's hand on my arm guided me firmly toward the second seat. I had the strangest feeling that if I looked down I would find I was wearing the ruffled organdy, the white silk socks, and the gleaming patent leather slippers of my long-vanished childhood. Whoever said you can't go home again had obviously never known my grandmother.

The people who ran the movie theater just as obviously did. Settled comfortably in her chosen seat, Grandmother waved away the hovering usher and glanced back over her shoulder. The house lights promptly dimmed. Nodding regally in the direction of the screen, Grandmother allowed the movie to begin.

## CATS, LILACS, AND PEPPERMINT CANDY
### Elaine A. Gardner

My grandma was apron strings tied around a middle that wasn't there. She was floating breasts resting on her stomach. She was blood-marked chin where Grandpa's straight-edge nicked instead of smoothed away graying stubble. Cataracts were beginning to cloud her pale blue eyes. She worked with shaking hands. Warnings against using the razor went unheeded. Fresh nicks appearing regularly clearly proved Grandma took orders from nobody.

She was pink scalp peeking through strands of gray hair, yellowing, too thin to hold a proper pug. More than that, she was the cluttered shanty built onto the back of the house directly off the kitchen that smelled of cats, garden tools with earth left on them, ripening and overripe vegetation, stuff left for the compost pile. Mostly, it smelled of cats. She was lilacs in the yard and spicy peppermint candy.

Grandma loved her cats and her garden, too. That's why the shanty never offended her. I got caught once holding my nose against the smell. I might have been boxed across the ears but that time I escaped it. Grandma's hand flew free with little provocation. After that I went through the shanty by gulp-and-hold method—a gulp of air, swallow, and hold my breath until I got outside. Out there I could breathe the lilac air. Pale lavender spirals on a tree so high I thought it might reach the sky dropped curly flowerettes on the ground for me to scoop in tiny fistfuls, and sniff up my nose until I felt dizzy.

There was a way to the garden through the side door, a better-smelling way, but Grandma used only the shanty.

It was while the aunts were kaffeeklatsching over thick slices of bread spread with homemade jam that Grandma would say, "*Komm*," and stoop her heavy frame toward the shanty, scruff-scruffing felt-slippered feet heavily against the bare wooden floor.

"Grandma likes you better'n us," the cousins would accuse.

"That's 'cause she's so little," my sister would supply. "That's 'cause she never grew up!"

Sibling rivalry. Antagonism. I *was* small for my age, but more to the point I was the only one who followed. The others never understood about her passion, never guessed about her pleasure. They never saw Grandma smooth her wrinkles, relax the scowling pout, unveil her steely eyes. Out in the garden she seldom rubbed them. Neither did she jammer, "Ya, ya," mournfully. She sighed only from habit. They didn't know Grandma, soft, sensitive, kind.

We communicated by gesture. Grandma never learned the English language; she never tried to understand it. She felt isolated but was stubbornly independent.

When Grandma set her jaw, rubbed hard across her eyes with fisted hand, wound her long full apron 'round her arms, I was dismissed. I ducked through the bushes, avoiding the shanty. At the side I could smell lily of the valley, heliotrope, or peony, whichever bloomed that season. I heard a long, slow, "Ya, ya," a quivering, deep-drawn sigh, and then the shanty screen door bang. Grandma returned her other self to her common world.

With kaffeeklatsch over, everyone clearing the table, rinsing heavy dime store mugs under cold water, setting the kitchen back to rights, Grandma sometimes managed a hard-fisted knuckle-nudge against my head. Her stare warned, "Be quiet," but "*Komm*."

This time it was her bedroom, a tiny cubbyhole crowded with a high, hand-carved dresser that she and Grandpa had brought from Germany and a double wooden frame piled high with featherbedding. There was one narrow window, which I don't believe opened. The closed-in musty smell squeezed me, made me feel chokey.

Between the dresser and the bed was the big porcelain slop jar that scared me to death. (I was quite old before I learned to call it a chamber pot.) Grandma with all her bulk, her full long skirts, and her blundering feet never so much as touched it, but I could only believe I'd someday fall right into it, kick a crack in it, or, Lord save me, even upset it! So I stayed at the door unless Grandma pulled me in.

She knew just how far to pull out the top dresser drawer before it squealed and wheezed. She knew exactly how to insert two fingers to grab the paper sack—which always was there because Grandpa brought a new one every Saturday—without letting it crackle. No one was to know we were there.

If all went well I got one piece of white peppermint candy. If a snooping cousin foiled the conspiracy, I got instead a crack across the head and a shove out the door with a rough, *"Raus! Raus!"* so genuine that even I thought I might have been trespassing.

"Grandma's pet got caught, ha! Grandma's pet got caught!"

Snickers behind cupped hands, wrinkled noses, protruding tongues, silent clapping hands behind grown-up backs. But I knew all I had to do to get the delayed peppermint was to find some excuse for coming back after everyone had gone home. The only drawback was that I could never come alone. It wasn't too far for me to walk; I wasn't too young to know the way; I was only "too small" to do anything on my own. My sister had to "take" me.

Grandma knew why I came back. Before long she went to her room. The dresser drawer squealed but I never heard the paper sack. I never heard jingled coins. But always Grandma came back with a nickel for Irma and, from under her apron, a sticky peppermint for me along with a palm-warmed silver dime.

Irma wasn't fooled. I think Grandma knew that. All her methods clearly said she did things the way she pleased; anybody want to contest it?

"What did Grandma give you?" This was the first thing Irma said when we were out of earshot. The peppermint didn't matter but she coveted my dime.

"Grandma always gives you the little one." She was so sympathetic. "But I'll trade you if you want."

A dime or a nickel made no difference. I had peppermint juice sucked through my teeth sliding down my throat. I blew hot vapors up my nose and cooled it with a breath of air. I had spicy peppermint sweetness!

Somewhere it all faded into time. Grandma was gone. Her house is still there, not much changed on the outside. Strangers have owned it for years.

I have lilacs in my own yard now. Sometimes I have white rounds of peppermint candy on my cupboard shelf. My cheek used to get fuzzy raw where I held a piece to make it last. My breath was spicy cool.

A tear on my cheek? It's a happy one. It's for cats, lilacs, and a piece of peppermint candy.

## AUGUST
### *Robert G. Anderson*

The year was 1930. I was fourteen and my brother Carl eleven when my mother, who had been divorced for several years, remarried.

His name was August Damlin and he blew out of the Minnesota woods to bowl us over with the force of his vitality. Big, gangling, gaunt—his features must have been hewn with an ax—he was an ugly, exuberant Finn with a terrific zest for life.

He knew he was ugly, with cheekbones wide and high as a Mongolian warrior's, fierce blue eyes, and a skin mottled by too many storms and too many blast furnaces. His tangled eyebrows worked like opposing pistons whenever he became excited. This forty-year-old former sailor, steel puddler, copper miner, and lumberjack had come to South Milwaukee and now worked in the foundry of Bucyrus-Erie Company.

He and my mother met at a lutefisk supper given by the ladies of the Norwegian Lutheran Church. Ma helped in the serving line while August helped himself at the tasting end of the line. After they were married, a weekend at Wisconsin Dells served as honeymoon because August couldn't take off from work.

He soon became dissatisfied with living in a fifteen-dollar-a-month flat; he wanted a home of his own. Buying a lot for two hundred dollars on the outskirts of South Milwaukee, near the bluffs overlooking Lake Michigan, he had Northwestern Building Company put up a four-room cottage at a cost of fifteen hundred dollars.

There was gas and electricity but no running water and no basement—August, Carl, and I dug out the basement later that summer. With the help of a good neighbor August sank a well and struck sweet water at sixty feet. In back was a privy that soon became home to mud-dauber wasps that droned ceaselessly through the door's half-moon but never stung any of us. Good thing—exposed as we were.

August possessed hidden resources of strength. He proved it when he needed some timbers to shore up the basement wall. Scouting together, we found a discarded dye vat half buried on the beach below the Newport Chemical Works in Carrollville.

"That's it!" August exclaimed.

After returning home for the car and a heavy maul, we drove back along the bluff and scrambled on foot down the steep path. August used the maul on the vat, soon reducing it to a pile of four-foot timbers, creosoted and heavy as teak. I struggled with two of them, their sharp edges knifing into my shoulder, while August carried five and used a sixth as a staff! He climbed steadily upward, singing some wild Finnish song, and I stumbled after, clutching at prickly juniper to keep from sliding back. At the top I had to rest to get my wind back.

After the last strenuous trip we relaxed in the car. Gazing over the choppy indigo expanse of Lake Michigan, August recalled his copper-mining days. "I worked in the deepest copper mine in the world, Rob," he said with quiet pride. "Tamarack Number Two in Victoria, Michigan. It can be zero above ground but down in the mine it's so hot

we strip to the waist. And you should've seen the copper! It gleamed like gold!" But then he sighed, "Funny thing, when it gets close to the surface the color fades. I had a big chunk of pure copper but it was too heavy to carry around. I left it with a landlady." We sat in silence for a few minutes, then he drove us home.

August was very fun-loving and at a party would insist on dancing with all the girls. They in turn, confronted with his mixture of the Charleston and a lumberjack hop, shrugged helplessly and tried their best to follow. Meanwhile, August had a ball.

But he had his quiet moods also, especially when soft rains fell. At those times he urged my mother, "Come, Maria. We will go for a ride in the Starry." Starry was his nickname for his 1925 Star automobile.

They took roads leading out past drenched farmlands, and August would grow unusually quiet. My mother respected his mood and refrained from small talk. She told me that sometimes they traveled for miles in a close and friendly silence, content in their snug cocoon to watch the rain-washed fields slip by.

One of the shortcomings of the Starry was that it was a coupe—a little car with room for only two passengers. It did have a tiny trunk space, or "turtle," in the back but the lid opened the wrong way. August took the trouble, because he knew how much "his boys" enjoyed auto rides, to remove the lid and turn it around.

Bouncing on a makeshift seat with a blanket to cushion our backs, Carl and I were happy to ride in this homemade rumble seat. Wind whipping our hair, we waved at everyone we passed. What matter if tire chains and old tools scraped at our ankles?

August brought joy another time. We boys hungered for a tent to put up in a nearby sand pit. But the

Depression was worsening—no money and no materials. August told us about two six-by-eight-foot sections of a dismantled billboard he'd seen lying on the Cudahy dump and we clamored to be taken there. August tied the sections on the top of the car and slowly—very slowly—he negotiated the five miles home. Luckily, there was no wind.

Arriving at the sand pit, we leaned the tin sections together in an A-shape and closed the ends with burlap sacking. Presto! Instant tent! My brother and I were kings of the neighborhood for a while.

One time August landed in the doghouse. On a Saturday morning we were all dressed to go visiting friends north of Chicago, but August said he had an errand to attend to first. "Wait," he told us. "I'll be right back."

We waited and waited—hours crept by. Finally, all thoughts of the trip were abandoned and Ma changed back into her housedress, her face a storm cloud as she prepared our meal.

August returned late in the afternoon wearing a sheepish expression. His explanation? He'd met a friend who invited him into the basement to sample some home brew. Soon several more fellows drifted in and suggested a poker game. One player, a truck driver for the Johnston Candy Company, quickly ran out of funds. "Listen, guys," he pleaded. "I'm short of cash but I've got boxes of chocolates outside in my truck. How about one box, one buck?" The others agreed.

"It took a while," August finished. "But I finally hit a winning streak." He went out to the car and returned with twenty-two boxes of candy.

That softened Ma up. We gorged ourselves on chocolates for days—even gave some to the neighbors.

In a few short years our happiness was shattered. August suffered a stroke. It seemed incredible that a tiny blood vessel bursting in the brain could cut down so vital a man. For two days he hung in limbo at Milwaukee County General Hospital. Then early on a sparkling May morning, when everyone should have been singing, a man came to our door and mumbled a few words to my mother. With a cry of anguish she rushed into our bedroom.

"He's gone! August's gone!" she sobbed and threw herself across my brother and me. Being half asleep, the full impact of the news didn't quite register. In a few minutes, however, we boys realized our loss, and tears came while Ma pulled herself together.

Now it is many years later and my mother is gone also. When the soft rains fall I go driving in my "Starry." I think of them and see August's homely, earnest face in the million lighted drops zigzagging down my windshield.

You will note I did not call him my stepfather; August was a real father. While showing love and respect for my mother, he accepted Carl and me as if we were his natural sons. And he treated us like men.

We loved him, we remember him, and we miss him.

2 People

# THE END OF AN ERA
*Marjorie Van Ouwerkerk*

I grew up in the unique small world of the iron mining country of northern Minnesota called the Mesabi range. It was a wild, somewhat desolate area, dotted with small towns leaning south to the big city of Duluth, which began at the top of a long range of hills and spilled downward in a startlingly steep manner to the icy waters of Lake Superior. The huge mines, which for fifty years reluctantly yielded their treasure, took their toll of deaths in cave-ins and of broken skulls. We children took all this for granted and hardly glanced at the huge gaps in the earth, which were often a mile across and just as deep.

This was the era of the hired girl, and I look back on it with nostalgia. Automatic dishwashers and self-cleaning ovens are great, but housework is a lonely job and appliances can't talk back. Our hired girls not only washed the dishes and cleaned the house, but they also considered themselves part of the family and often lived with us for years. We shared our troubles and our joys and, in the process, became good friends. Mother called them maids, no doubt feeling she was keeping the wilderness at bay and at the same time propping up the standards of the family. Whatever it was, I liked it. I could read for hours undisturbed while the hired girl did the housework. She was also a biased referee in the numerous fights my older brother and I had. "Give 'im hell, Margie!" she'd yell. We women stuck together.

As the mines employed men mainly of central and southern European origin, our hired girls were the daughters of families who had recently "come over" and in whose homes they spoke their native tongue. They were bilingual and, sadly, ashamed of it. They became passionate Americans and tried to speak English correctly. This was a wonderful heritage for me, as I grew up completely unprejudiced. I loved to listen to the soft Italian, spoken with great rapidity and many gestures, the equally limpid, musical cadences of Hungarian, Slovenian, or the harsher Russian. My school friends taught me songs in Finnish or Norwegian, and I sang them with gusto until our current maid, who was Finnish, told me I was singing a dirty song. Then I sang it constantly, especially in front of my parents.

One particular hired girl endeared herself to me. Her name was Pearl. She was rightly named for she was an unpolished Slovenian gem. In the three years that she lived with us Mother succeeded in smoothing only a few of the rough edges. But Pearl was kind to us kids, had a heart bigger than life, and lived her philosophy of *che sarà sarà* to the hilt. She loved our indoor plumbing and Mother's cooking, especially the Cornish pasties, which Mother, being English, made to perfection. Nothing was ever too hard or too menial for her to do for us.

Her deep brown hair had reddish highlights and was so frizzy it coiled like fine springs ready to snap to attention. Her dusky olive skin and slanty black eyes revealed that way back in time a Tartar had slipped into her family. Her conversation was powdered with pithy oaths that I immediately added to my vocabulary and used on the playground until my brother tattled on me to Mother and I was severely reprimanded. But I followed Pearl around like a puppy, waiting for a new word to pop out.

We had a summer cottage at one of the untouched, seldom-fished, and quietly beautiful lakes north of town. Each spring when school ended, we moved to our lake home, along with two dogs, a cat, numerous household necessities, and, of course, Pearl. Down the sandy road about a mile, through the woods of tall Norwegian pines that smelled so deliciously in the hot sun, was a CCC camp. These were depression years and young men who couldn't find work in the county were mercifully employed in this camp. They built roads, planted trees, and hacked out the underbrush. It was a large camp, all tents, settled on level ground and exploding in all directions like a vine gone wild. Mother forbade me to go near it because *men* were there, but once Pearl discovered it, she knew fun city was only a few skips away.

Underneath that riotous hair and faded dress beat a romantic heart. Every night after the work was done and the dinner dishes quickly washed, Pearl would put on her reddest lipstick and longest earrings and hurry down our winding driveway to the gravel road that led to the camp. The CCC, besides teaching the boys which end of an ax could cut off a foot, believed strongly in entertainment. They had no trouble getting a makeshift band together, so every night was dance night. The hired girls from every cottage around attended, tired or not. We always knew when Pearl had found a new boyfriend because she whistled while she served the breakfast pancakes and jiggled a new identification bracelet on her wrist, no doubt wrestled from some muscular arm the night before. When a romance took a disappointing turn we knew without being told. Pearl would say, "My God, Miz T., ain't you got no wood to chop?" and off she'd go, frowning, to the woodpile. Every swing of the ax echoed her frustrations and seemed to say, "And that for you, and you, and you!" After an hour of strenuous chopping, back she'd come, panting but smiling. Oh, for the simple solutions of the woodpiles!

One June my mother's favorite brother came to visit.

My brother and I were warned that quarreling would not be tolerated. This put a strain on us, as the lack of discipline in the summer undid what the school year had just tied up. In preparation the cottage was polished and shining. The bright sun oozed through spotless windows. Bats were fished out of the water tanks and pried off porch cushions. A few snakes sunning themselves on the warm stones of our rock garden were disposed of, and we were ready.

The first night we sat down to a delicious dinner of pasties and strawberries with Devonshire cream, strictly English, typically Cornish to the last mouthful. The conversation was lively and spiced with "Do you remember?" and we kids listened appreciatively to the stories until I noticed, and soon everyone did, that the person laughing the loudest was Pearl. As she served dinner she got such a kick out of "her" family that she could barely take time out to go to the kitchen for refills. I noticed Mother's apprehensive eye on her. Pearl stood in the doorway with a bowl of hot gravy, her head thrown back in a hoot of laughter, exposing a few teeth missing. The gravy was sloshing back and forth as if gathering speed to jump out.

Dinner finally ended without mishap and we trailed into the large, comfortably furnished living room where my uncle established first rights in a cozy rocking chair next to the fireplace. Pearl came right along in with us, one of the family and to heck with the dishes. Mother hadn't noticed this but when she went to sit down in her favorite chair and found Pearl there first, our gem was sent to the kitchen. We all started to laugh, but stopped at the expression on Mother's face. After listening to plates being banged together and the unusually loud clatter of silverware, I slipped unnoticed into the kitchen to keep

Pearl company and wipe the dishes. She knew this was a great concession on my part, as I hated that job, and she gave me a thank-you hug.

After living with us for three years, a few of the rougher edges had been trimmed, but only a few. She remained the same outspoken, cussing, hard-working hired girl, devoted to us to the last sweep of her broom. When I left home to go to college, I kissed and hugged her good-bye, never dreaming that I'd never see her again. I later found out that she left our home to get married to a CCC man, who, I hope, had a wonderful supply of jokes, liked to dance, didn't mind cussing, and had a big woodpile for Pearl when life became too much for her.

The iron mines have long since coughed up their last ton of rich ore. Trees now grow right up to the edge of the pits. The company houses, which all looked alike because the paint was a gift of the owner of the mine, have been sold and moved to other towns. It is still lonely country between mining locations, but it was a special place in which to grow up. As I look back I realize that there is no area like that left in this country. The era of the hired girl is gone, but I remember these girls with love and appreciation. They worked so hard to better themselves, and they succeeded. No matter where I live, and I have lived many places in my life, that little mining town on the Mesabi range with its precious memories will forever be home to me.


## MRS. SADLER
### Robert G. Anderson

When I was a boy in the early 1920s in the small prairie town of Grand Forks, North Dakota, most families had no money to spare for sports equipment. But that was all right with us kids. We had Mrs. Sadler.

A tiny widow on the sunny side of fifty, her brown hair pulled back in a bun, she usually wore long dark dresses with a touch of white at throat and wrists. Her plain face was saved by a wide, good-humored mouth and dancing gray eyes. She had a sixteen-year-old son, Frank, a handsome boy and a fine athlete.

Early on a summer morning Mrs. Sadler would emerge from the rear door of her neat cottage, her arms a cornucopia of balls, bats, gloves—even beanbags and checker games. Around her skirts jumped a clamorous army of neighborhood kids too poor to buy bats and balls of their own. I was one of them.

Not only did she generously supply us with athletic equipment (which she had paid for) but she also found time to supervise many of our games. And this was before the day of planned playground activities.

At that time all the buildings on our block were private homes except for Landom's Grocery on the corner, Shave's Secondhand Store, and The Laundry. A few vacant lots dotted the block like gaps in a schoolboy's grin, and all the back yards ran together. Fences were rare. Thus an inner court was formed that provided space for play.

In this area our coach had her son and the other boys hang volleyball nets, put up basketball hoops, and lay out a softball diamond. Softball was a curtailed affair, however, and the older boys batted opposite their natural stance at the plate because of the nearby windows.

Mrs. Sadler possessed a keen insight into the young mind. Be gentle but firm was her credo. Trust without being a patsy. Whenever a loud argument arose, her soft words and common sense smoothed feathers. If these did not prevail, the presence of Frank and his buddies cooled the hotheads.

Although gentle and soft-spoken, she insisted on a few simple rules:

1. No fighting or swearing;
2. Be responsible for your equipment—don't lose it;
3. Return it after you have finished;
4. If something gets damaged or broken, fix it.

There were additional facets to Mrs. Sadler's character. A story is told about Amos Alonzo Stagg, the old University of Chicago warrior who continued to coach football at age ninety-five. One day during practice one of his giant tackles accidentally collided with Stagg and sent him sprawling. Calmly picking himself up, the venerable coach quietly asked the young man, "Did I hurt you, son?"

Mrs. Sadler exhibited a similar toughness. Chuck Jondahl learned that when he tried to stretch a triple into a homer. Rounding third base too wide where our tiny coach stood cheering on the sideline, Chuck barreled into her and down they went in a windmill of arms, legs, and petticoats. Unruffled, Mrs. Sadler got to her feet, patted her hair into place, and ordered the game to continue.

As time went on she discovered my brother Arvid could run like a startled gazelle, and she put his talent to good use running errands. He eagerly volunteered, not because of the nickel, the Eskimo Pie, or the Tootsie Roll reward, but because she "timed" him.

"I need a box of Mother's Oats," she'd say, handing him the money. "I'll time you."

Arv grinned, dancing like a boxer warming up.

She drew a big, thick Illinois railroad watch from her apron pocket, frowning in mock concentration at the dial. Slowly her free hand rose. Arv crouched, tense as a sprinter in the starting blocks.

"Go!" And her hand fell.

Arv was off, a missile arrowing toward its target.

In a surprisingly short time he returned, pink-faced and panting, as he clutched the white china knob of her screen door. Inside the mellow gloom of her kitchen, Mrs. Sadler gasped incredulously, "My! Only four minutes and eighteen seconds. You beat your old record by five seconds!"

Arv swelled with pride and gloried in her praise but tried to sound casual. "I'd have beat it by more if old man Landom wasn't so darn slow in hookin' the box down from the top shelf."

Thereafter, whether it was downtown for an early *Grand Forks Herald*, to the dime store for a bag of milk chocolate chunks, or to Redwing and Elstad's Hardware for a nickel's worth of nails, Arv's twinkling feet were pitted against the bulbous railroad watch as Mrs. Sadler timed him. Western Union's bicycle boys had nothing on the fleetest courier in town.

In the same way she boosted Arv's ego, Mrs. Sadler used creative imagination in dealing with smaller kids. Their quiet games palled sometimes, and they looked to her for excitement. She didn't disappoint them.

Carrying a bulging bag of peanuts into her yard, she tossed handful after handful on the ground, laughing as the yard became a melee of dervishes who scrambled and squealed like warthogs.

On another occasion she surveyed the usual ring of kids crowding her back door. It was tar-melting weather, and a hot wind blew chafing dust onto perspiring bodies and grimy faces. Mrs. Sadler told those who owned swimsuits to go home and change; the others stripped to their shorts.

After Frank uncovered the twin rain barrels that

stood at the corners of the house, both son and mother proceeded to dunk us in the cool, leaf-dappled water. She was forced to stand on a sturdy milk-bottle crate to reach, but we felt safe. Her strong grip kept us buoyant and enabled us to clamber in and out. Later, after our dips, we water spaniels chased each other dry.

Mrs. Sadler never missed a chance to talk up for us, thus opening another avenue of enjoyment. One occasion stands out.

The young son of a farm friend delivered some fresh eggs to her door. Tom was thirteen and drove a red, two-wheeled cart drawn by a brown Shetland pony, a lively animal with choppy gait and a mane like flowing wheat.

We were familiar with the common workhorse, such as the heavy-footed team that hauled Fuller the drayman's sledge in winter and wagon in summer. But this smaller edition of horse with its dainty cakewalk seemed especially created for kids.

We drew close to admire, poke the pony's hide, and watch the skin quiver. We stroked the dark velvet nose. And when Mrs. Sadler noted our fascination, she asked Tom to give us a ride.

He was willing and agreed to take us two at a time. Perched on the gaily painted seat on either side of the driver, we took our allotted spin around the block. During my turn I know I was transported in more ways than one—listening to a merry click of hooves and inhaling the heady perfume of pony sweat. Surely, my cup runneth over.

Our family moved to Wisconsin when I was still a boy. New days—new ways—and gradually a different phase of life took over, demanding attention. Mrs. Sadler was gone but bright in memory. Sometimes across the years I see her clearly, frowning over a fat railroad watch as my brother shouts, "Time me! Time me!" Her arm swings down and the race is run.

Scattered around the country are men like me. We were children then. Do they remember their benefactor? Do they recall the tiny, unheralded woman who cared enough to provide gloves and bats and balls unstintingly; who cared enough to dunk little kids in a rain barrel and scatter peanuts in a dusty yard; a real lady who parleyed for pony rides and lavished love as a supreme gift to childhood?

Rest easy, Mrs. Sadler. I remember. You were my friend, coach, guide, teacher, and unanimous All-American. I'll never forget you.

## HUBE
### Ralph Potter

A goat or a wet collie dog would have smelled better than that seventh-grade classroom, whose door I opened about ten o'clock that cold December morning. The stench of thirty bodies that were bathed certainly no more often than once a week, all of them now in long underwear (this was even before the advent of B.V.D.'s), which doubled as pajamas, struck me almost as a blow might have. Some of these kids weren't housebroken, and along with the odor of unwashed bodies and asafetida, which some kids wore about their necks in a little bag to ward off diseases, was the acrid smell of urine.

The steam radiators were protesting with a great clanking, hissing, and gurgling the heat they were being forced to produce. The bare walls were a uniform dirty tan with here and there an occasional pencil mark and, lower down, black heel marks. My desk, to which I now sidled, was like all the rest much carved and scarred—carved better than some because in the upper right-hand corner just below the hole for an inkwell was a crude figure of a nude woman. I had many a time rubbed my finger over those marks. Right in front of me sat Hube Warttreu.

Hube was not my friend nor was he my enemy. He was just another guy, a social misfit he would be called today. He was sixteen and still in the seventh grade—not exactly the honor roll type. If you said, "Good morning," to Hube, he would in a few minutes think of the answer. He was big with large, brown, protuberant eyes. He wore a heavy coat despite the heat, and in his pocket, I knew, was a big knife that he used for whittling and for skinning the animals he trapped.

About him during the winter months was always the pungent aroma of skunk. A star skunk, one with a single white spot on its head, was worth three dollars, a fortune, and Hube had told me about trapping this one.

"Ketched it by the hind leg," he said, "but afore I could get to it, that goddam dog of mine made a rush at it. That skunk pissed right in his face—got him right in the nose and eyes—and if you ever saw a dog puke! He was sicker 'n a dog." And Hube slapped his thigh and laughed at his witty saying.

But this morning was no time for trapping stories. Carranza was teaching us grammar. Carranza, typically Hoosier-mispronounced Carranzy, was really Walter Hurley, and like Carranza, the dictator of Mexico after whom we had named him, he was the dictator of the seventh and eighth grades. He was a big fellow—not fat, but big; at least to me he appeared so, and he was a stern disciplinarian with an unstable temper. Boys and girls alike who incurred his displeasure he flogged.

We were studying parts of speech and had progressed from noun, pronoun, and verb to modifiers and were now ready to tackle the adverb.

"What the hell's an adverb?" Hube said and turned to me as he did so.

But he needn't have, because Carranzy was already defining it: "An adverb is a word that modifies a verb, an adjective, or another adverb."

"Now, Hube," he said, "what is an adverb?"

Hube stopped picking his nose. "An adverb," he said through that newly cleaned nose, hanging on longer than necessary for each syllable and stalling for time. But he was stuck; he could go no farther.

Carranzy repeated the definition. "Now, Hube, what is an adverb?"

And Hube started again in a nasal monotone. After he had said, "An adverb," and had stalled, I did a foolish thing. I prompted him with "is a word," which Hube laboriously repeated. And I added, "that modifies."

"That modifies," said Hube.

And then perversity struck me. Without thinking of the possible consequences, I said, "a noun."

And Hube duly repeated, "A noun."

Carranzy looked up from his textbook, surprised and irritated. "No, it does not modify a noun. It modifies a verb, adjective, or another adverb. Now, you say that, Hube."

Again the laborious process, and when we got to the "that modifies," I whispered "a preposition," and Hube said, "a preposition."

I should at that moment have had an irresistible urge to go to the bathroom, have induced myself to vomit by sticking my finger down my throat, or at least have desisted. All the eighth graders, who sat on the other side of the room, were by now an interested audience. But I was on a one-way ride, and when Carranzy, now standing, face red and very menacing, again repeated the formula and when Hube arrived at his impasse, which was "is a word that modifies," I whispered these words and then added "a conjunction."

Well, things happened so fast they were a blur. For a big man Carranzy moved like lightning. He was on Hube in a split second, seizing him by the shoulders, lifting him from the seat as though he were a throw rug, and then shaking him like one. I was so scared I jumped over three rows of adjoining desks.

I didn't go out for recess that day to play Fox and Geese in the big ring trampled in the snow, although I would have liked to. And when school closed, I was reluctant to leave with the rest of the kids. I didn't know whether Hube knew what had happened to him or not, but I wasn't taking any chances.

For two days I hung around after school. "You want that blackboard washed, Mr. Hurley? Kin I pick up the papers from the floor?" The Brownie points I earned! But I knew that I would eventually have to face my victim.

On the third day I ventured forth, and the first guy I saw was Hube, holding that big knife in his hand, whittling on a piece of pine.

There were two things I could do: I could run or I could throw myself on his mercy. But paralysis had set in. "Hube," I said, "Carranzy . . ."

"Yeah, that son-of-a-bitch, what about him?"

"But, Hube?"

"You wanta see that skunk I ketched this mornin'? Only it ain't a star, just a broad stripe. Oh yeah, say, thanks for tryin' to help me."

## RATTLESNAKE TOM
*Lloyd M. Holliday*

The Kickapoo area has always been the home of the rattlesnake, and there's almost as many at home now in the hills as there were in the heyday of the snake hunters who took them for bounty.

This is a story about one of those hunters.

Rattlesnake Tom was a long, lean man. His unsmiling face was creased by his ugly disposition. Pale blue eyes stared from under bushy eyebrows. His lumpy Adam's apple had plenty of room to bob up and down in his long scrawny neck, and he had the strength of seasoned hickory. I was told that his crooked nose had gotten its ugly hump from being shoved into other people's business.

If you had had the impertinence to ask Tom in his later years—he lived past ninety—what he'd accomplished in his long life, I'm sure his answer would have been either "None of your damned business" or "I was the champion liar, thief, fighter, boozer, dynamiter, troublemaker, and rattlesnake hunter of my time, and if anyone else has outchampioned me it's because I can't get around anymore."

He wasn't even honest in his bounty hunting! He'd carefully cut off the rattles short of the body and turn the snake loose to live and raise more snakes. "I don't want to destroy the main source of my income," he'd say.

Without his rattles a snake was a deadly menace. Many of these derattled snakes were taken by other hunters who let it be known that another one of Tom's pets had been killed.

Tom's moniker, "Rattlesnake," came from an incident that only he could have hatched.

The local saloon was Tom's first home. There he was

himself. A few drinks would add more big devils to his already devil-saturated character. One day the bartender remarked that he'd rather have Tom's rattlesnakes turned loose in his place than the man himself—at least they didn't lie.

Some old crony carried the words to old Tom.

He just grinned and said, "The hell, ya say. I'll oblige."

Late that afternoon when the saloon was full up, he walked in and dropped a live gunny sack on the bar, gave a few jerks at the bottom of the bag, and out rolled a slithering mass of rattlesnakes.

"Barkeep," he said, "here's your rattlesnakes."

But the barkeeper had joined the mob trying to escape through the one lone door.

Tom had the place to himself and proceeded to get drunk—one of his singing, shouting, cursing, fighting drunks. He could be heard all over town. He yelled, "Come back in here, you lousy good-for-nothings. That was just a bag of happy rattlesnakes. Can't ya hear 'em singing?"

"You're sure missing lots of good liquor—there's no one in here to take your money."

"Hey, barkeep, your rattlers are all over the place. I just saw one go through a knothole; some of 'em are trying to crawl up the wall. You might as well crawl around on your belly in here as out there, you varmit."

But no one went in. Most of them were more afraid of the snakes than of him. Everything had been pretty quiet for maybe twenty minutes when Tom staggered out the door, the bag of snakes in one hand and a bottle of whiskey in the other.

"I'm going home, barkeep, and finish off this bottle. I've got all the snakes but one. You can have him for a pet."

The barkeeper and a few friends carefully turned the place upside down, looking for one lone rattlesnake. It couldn't be found.

Tom came in the next morning and offered to find the snake—for a pint of whiskey. He got the whiskey and proceeded to sit down and enjoy it.

"You've got your whiskey. Why don't you start looking?"

"Because I'm a liar," said Tom. "You said so yourself. What did I say when I left here?"

"You said you had them all but one."

"That's right." He got up and left.

"Tom, come back and find that snake."

"What snake?" Tom asked, and kept on going.

The barkeep got the message—all for nothing. He'd get a lot of ribbing over it.

He went to the door and yelled out, "Tom, you're nothing but a stinking, dirty rattlesnake."

Word got around. That night in the saloon everybody wanted to know where the pet snake was. What do you feed him? Goin' to cut his tail off short? Want any more pets? When Tom walked in, someone shouted, "What do you know, fellows, here comes 'Rattlesnake Tom'!"

Tom was grinning, his revenge was sweet, and to him, the moniker was a gleaming halo.

People in the valley miss the old rascal.

# MY MOST UNFORGETTABLE CHARACTER
### *John R. Peckham*

It would be fair to state that few if any of Ed's contemporaries would have agreed with my evaluation of him as an unforgettable character. I know how most of his neighbors in that community of sand farms, ringed in by the bluffs of Juneau County, Wisconsin, saw him. The impunity with which his autocratic wife, Net, scolded, berated, and low-rated him was not lost upon the neighborhood, and his son-in-law, my Uncle Earl, who farmed the home place, referred to him continually as "the little man," half contemptuously, half affectionately. Aunt Ardis defended him desultorily, but she did so automatically and without conviction. Only to me, and to a lesser extent to the other youngsters who grew up around the farm (I say to a lesser extent because their regard was necessarily tempered by their parents' lack of sympathy with him), did he have stature. I was an occasional dweller in the household. While there I was his admiring satellite; when away I looked forward to my return and another delightful interim of story and song.

In retrospect, it seems strange that Ed should loom stronger in my memory and my affections than Net. Net was the one who babied me, who bought me clothes, gave me shiny dimes to save or to spend. Her name appears as godparent on my baptismal certificate, and she accumulated the savings which were intended for my college education. (That she lost them, and more too, in an acquisitive attempt to multiply them mightily in a blue-sky venture with the notorious Elmer Huckins had no effect on my feelings. I was too young to be concerned at the time.) Her appearance was imposing. Her fine, sharp features, topped with thin white hair drawn severely back and tied in a knot in back, her erect angular frame, and the affection which shone from her face when she regarded me are among my treasured memories.

But Ed was different somehow. Short, broad, mustachioed—to me he was the singer of songs (some ribald, to be sure), the fiddler (though how those gnarled fingers contained that magic I never fathomed), and the quiet island of strength in that rather contentious household. When we sat milking adjacent cows in the cool of morning or the sultriness of a summer evening, the chores were no longer chores. The pail filled and the strippings fell off to nothing without my knowing it as he mocked the cats until they were frantic, looking for the intruder in their midst. His repertoire of anecdotes about logging and lumbering was limitless, and his voice still rings in my ears as I recall the ditties that he sang for my amusement. Was it a cracked voice, not true in tone? I don't know. To me it had appeal and depth never equaled by the likes of Lanzo or Crosby.

Ed's strong points, the qualities which could cause a boy's face to reflect worshipful respect, were not learned from his lips. Winnowed from the chaff of criticism for his seeming complaisance in the face of familial badgering, I learned of his prowess as a swimmer: that in his youth he continually astounded his lumberjack companions by his fearlessness in that element which claimed the lives of so many as the big rafts were floated down the spring-swollen streams. How he could swim completely around and sometimes under those broad accumulations of fodder for the sawmills. That he was utterly without fear I knew. That nemesis of many a farmer, the herd sire, was no object of terror for Ed. The bull never lived that could cause him a moment of concern. The one that caught Uncle Earl in the barn and broke his leg was kept from completing the job by the bare hands of "the little man." He disdained the conventional ring staff with which most bulls were moved from place to place. I've seen him walk up to a bellowing, earth-pawing animal which was straddling the baseball which had eluded me, and with nothing more than his voice and the flat of his hand cause him to retire in muttering confusion.

Ed was no longer young when I appeared on the scene, shortly before my third birthday. My first real memories of him date from my high school years, the early 1930s, and he was probably in his sixties then. His hearing was going, and those "new-fangled hearing aids" never seemed to make things any easier and were all eventually relegated to the cigar box on his dresser. After my marriage, my visits to the old farm became more infrequent. In his eyes, of course, I never grew up, and his greetings were always the same as the ones I remembered from my earlier visits. When all of the others had had their fill of words and handshakes, Ed would retire to the porch and wait for me to join him. He loved a "story" and expected me to have one for him and would have been disappointed if it were too well laundered. In order to make him hear, I shared my fund of jokes with his neighbors as far away as Sheep Pasture Bluff, to the obvious discomfiture of my family and his.

Ed died at the age of eighty-eight, and I saw him the summer of his passing. An incident occurred that day that epitomized the quiet, indomitable courage of this little-understood man. Maybe it won't affect you as it does me, and maybe that will be due to my poor faculty for telling the tale properly. You'll have to see the poor, blinded eyes straining to perceive a well-known face out of a cataract-caused haze, the deaf ears tuned to catch the phrase that might be directed his way, the arthritic joints that imprisoned him in the darkened bedroom, if the story is to mean something. As we left my cousin's adjoining farm to make this visit, which we sensed might be our last one, we were accompanied by my cousin's small son, who had been Ed's shadow for the past two or three years. David was the sickly one of the family, and the pace to which he was limited by his asthma and tricky heart was accommodated well by that of the old man. But the last month, during which Ed had failed so badly, had been spent by David in the hospital and this was his first trip away from the house. When the group left Ed's bedside, the old hand reached out and David stayed on as the rest filed out. The cracked and labored voice, meant only for those young ears, carried out into the parlor. "David," he said, "I've missed ye, boy. Hear ye've been sick." "Yes, sir," said David, "and I've missed you. But I'm all right now." "Tell you what then, Dave, you come over to see me Wednesday for sure, because that's my birthday. You come over and we'll go and sit on the front porch and *raise hell*."

## TOM
### *Alvina A. Floistad*

Come along about maple sugar time I, in twirling my memory ring of the early 1900s, remember a gentleman who lived near my childhood home, a little settlement named Nasonville in central Wisconsin. His abode was a twelve-by-fifteen wooden house with black tar paper tacked to the walls with shiny discs. The walls appeared studded with silver where the rays of the sun lingered.

Tom was a slow individual. He arose with the sun and retired at its setting, unless there were doings at the MWA Hall a bit up the way. He always said, "Daylight is better for human beings than nightlights."

He owned two vehicles, one a single-seated top buggy and the other a fringed surrey. The latter was used for Sundays and special occasions. Two or three times a week he found the occasion to pass our place on the way to see his sister Mary, who lived just over a wooded hill. As he rounded the bend in the road, nearing her house, he whipped up his two big bays, who were fat to the dappling stage, and arrived there with expectation of tea and pones or whatever she had on hand.

When we, who were not yet in our teens, saw Tom approaching, buggy top tipped back and Tom peering over his reading glasses (which he usually forgot to remove before starting out) and clucking to his bays with the kind voice they knew so well and heeded little, we wore our best smiles because Tom would say, "Whoa," very softly, smile at us, and say, "Well, well, you don't forget Tom. Here is a nickel to use next time you go to town with your dad." He beamed and we ran to put away the coveted nickels. Dad would wander down the driveway and visit with Tom before he drove on. We came back and lined up with Dad, saying nothing because we had been taught not to interrupt when older folks were conversing.

What a heyday it was when Tom drove by in the surrey and stopped to give us a ride. Our bare toes fairly wiggled with enthusiasm for that surrey, Tom, and his bays. Tom would be dressed in a white shirt and his best dark suit, neatly brushed, and the bays were curried.

Tom was shaped like an egg. His thinning red hair was always parted in the middle—where there was hair enough to part, that is. But that didn't make any difference to us, for wasn't he always supplied with maple sugar and nickels whenever he came to call! A smile from Tom with a gentle pat on the head was a very satisfying experience.

Tom's shoes were always so long that there was room for a crab apple in the back. He said, "I wear them long 'count of the bunions," and he would sometimes explain how important it was for us to wear well-fitting shoes, for he didn't want us to have the "uncomfort" of bunions. They pained him at night.

He didn't do much road walking, but now and then he would walk the short distance to our school yard. When he turned into the yard there we'd be ball playing. We circled around him. We didn't talk about much except the weather and the last rain. If it were spring he'd say, "The mayflowers, spring beauties, and some other flowers are out. If you wanta pull 'em up by the roots, and if the schoolmarm will let you, you may go to my woods tomorrow." Then he would leave and we would inform the marm of Tom's invitation. I remember one of those marms. She was game for a walk with us no matter how busy she was. We couldn't all walk next to her, for there were nearly fifty of us, so we took turns holding her fingers. Maybe the first time we went Tom would come along so we wouldn't miss the patches of flowers newly blooming. He showed us where to walk so we wouldn't trample the young roots of other plants. He knew every square foot of his ten acres. Now and then he would stop, put his foot on a log, and tell us of the many wonders of his woods. Believe it or not, his trees were all maple. He would tell us to look for the tiny trees. We noted the color of the bark of the old trees and of the young. He would say, "See how wrinkled the old bark is. See how smooth the bark of the young trees is. It reminds me of your young faces."

Sometimes Tom would be too busy cooking to go with us. Then the teacher would ring the bell a little early. I remember Ruel, a ringleader for mischief. Tom would be in his house, napping or reading. Smoke would be curling out of the stovepipe. That kindled Ruel. Once he shinned up the ladder and placed a shingle on the pipe. We hid in a thicket. Ruel hid in a corner where he could see us. When Tom came out we motioned, and Ruel shinned up the ladder and removed the shingle. Once Tom caught us. He winked and gave each one a maple sugar lump. With a twinkle in his eye, he looked us all over. Someone told, and we all laughed, including Tom.

Once I asked him where he had come from. He said that he was "Pennsylvanie Dutch" and proceeded to tell how he had had a hankering to go west and Wood County was where he finally "landed."

At the end of the maple sugar season Tom invited us to his sugar house for after school. We heaped snow into our hands. Tom would wiggle a stream of hot sugar from his ladle into the snow in our hands. We marveled at the curious shapes as the snow fell away. Oh, the *taste* of that sugar!

Years afterward when I was many miles away, one of the men of the community sent me a whole big box full of maple sugar that he had made in Tom's woods. On the package was written, "For old times' sake from Tom and me." That was the sweetest package I ever got. Not only was the sugar sweet, but sweet was the memory of Tom's woods and of the wonderful parties and trips to his woods.

One spring Mary's daughter, Ella, was to graduate from the Wood County Normal and to become a teacher. Tom was in a gala mood. A *teacher* in the family—that was really something! Tom drove the twelve miles to town in his surrey and purchased a white embroidered dress for his niece. My father met him on the road. Tom stopped, unwrapped the package, laid its contents on the side of the road, and said, "Golly, Andrew, did you *ever* see the like of that dress! Won't Ella look like a queen!" There was evidence that the package had been unwrapped and rewrapped many times. I heard later that Mary had washed the dress, Ella had worn it when she got her diploma, and Tom had been there to see her get it. He stopped to tell us the whole story of the event and ended with, "Can you beat it, Andrew! A *teacher* in the family!"

As time went on, I too taught in the little district school near Tom's place. I liked to stay late putting on assignments and planning. Tom didn't like it; neither did Dad. One evening right after school as I was clapping erasers outside, I saw Tom coming down the road, carrying something unwrapped. He turned in the driveway and greeted me and walked so fast I was afraid he would stub his toes. What was he holding? A big glass lamp! "Now," he smiled, "your Dad can bring you a bed, and you won't need to go home." He was looking over the reading glasses that he had forgotten to remove. I was glad for the lamp. But the days were getting longer, and school would soon be out, so I didn't have occasion to light the lamp very often. Tom thought little of himself and much of others and of his little piece of land.

I moved miles away to teach at other places. One day Mother, in one of her letters, wrote that Tom had "gone home." That evening I didn't stay at the desk very long. I went for a walk in the woods along the bank of Hemlock Creek in Vesper, Wisconsin. I thought about Tom and how he had instilled in me the love of the woods. Now, as I drive past where Tom used to live, I look up the side hill and see Tom's trees. Somehow, his woodlot is still preserved. I think God had a hand in that. Tom, although he seldom went to church, is one of His, I'm sure.

# THE HERMIT OF SOUTHWEST WISCONSIN
*Ruben W. Mauer*

Nearly all of the pioneer communities of Wisconsin had one person who was different. The town of Liberty in Grant County had a real hermit.

Sometime in the 1860s a German Jew came to Liberty and became a pack peddler, which was then a common way of merchandising. He made his regular trips through northern Grant County, especially in the German settlement.

He was a short, broad-shouldered man, dressed in black, and wore a long coat and a broad hat. He was very different from the local men. People looked forward to his coming; he was well educated and kept up with the news of the world. He was welcomed into the homes as a visitor from the outside world.

His pack was a miniature variety store. He prospered and was able to buy a horse and cart. He now had bolts of calico, gingham, wool, and silk. His business grew and he bought a farm and built a house. He had reached his goal.

He announced he was going back to Germany and would bring back a wife. He was gone only a short time and returned alone. The girl had married and had several children. She had written to him all this time and let him think that she was waiting for him.

He came back home broken in spirit, a completely changed man. He gave up his peddling, retreated into his house, and was only seen when he had to get supplies. To anyone who asked him questions, he would answer, *"Ich bin kein Mensch,"* a German idiom meaning "I am nobody."

From the best-dressed man in the area he became the worst. He used no soap or water. He never changed

clothes. He wore them until they became so worn and tattered they practically fell off. His beard and hair, of which he had been proud, were mats of dirt. He lived from his garden, and the rent paid for his farmland.

Children were afraid of him, but he never harmed them. Occasionally there would be tales that he was having one of his spells, which I know now were just too much of his homemade wine. One day he gave a stranger a drink of his wine—no native would have touched it. The man said, "That is good wine. How do you make it?" He invited the man into the house to show him. All the dirty kitchen utensils were scattered around on the floor; in fact, everything was on the floor. The man was no longer interested in his wine.

He had a method of storing the fresh grapes in dry cane sugar, keeping them until after Thanksgiving. He gave my Dad some once and they were beautiful to look at but—*ugh*.

I was one of the few people who ever saw the inside of the house. My dad, who was town treasurer, went to collect the taxes and I went along. I was about six years old and I have never forgotten the sight and smell of that house. He finally sold the farm and moved the house with all its debris to the nearby village. That couldn't happen today with all of our environmental restrictions.

He grew his own tobacco, and when he came to the post office with his large-bowl German pipe filled with home-cured tobacco everybody left except the postmaster. He received a lot of mail, answered ads, took some German newspapers, and was on the mailing list of all the wildcat mining companies. He bought shares in Colorado gold and silver mines for a penny a share. My dad tried to discourage him but he insisted they were paying dividends, never in cash, just in more shares. He lived to be over eighty years old and had two large trunks full of beautifully printed mine shares—all worthless.

Frank Hessler, who had come to this country a bright, ambitious young man with high hopes, lived here about thirty years as a hermit and an outcast. He was buried in a Gentile cemetery far from his Jewish homeland or any relatives. He made no intimate friends but neither did he make any enemies. *"Ich bin kein Mensch."* "I am nobody."

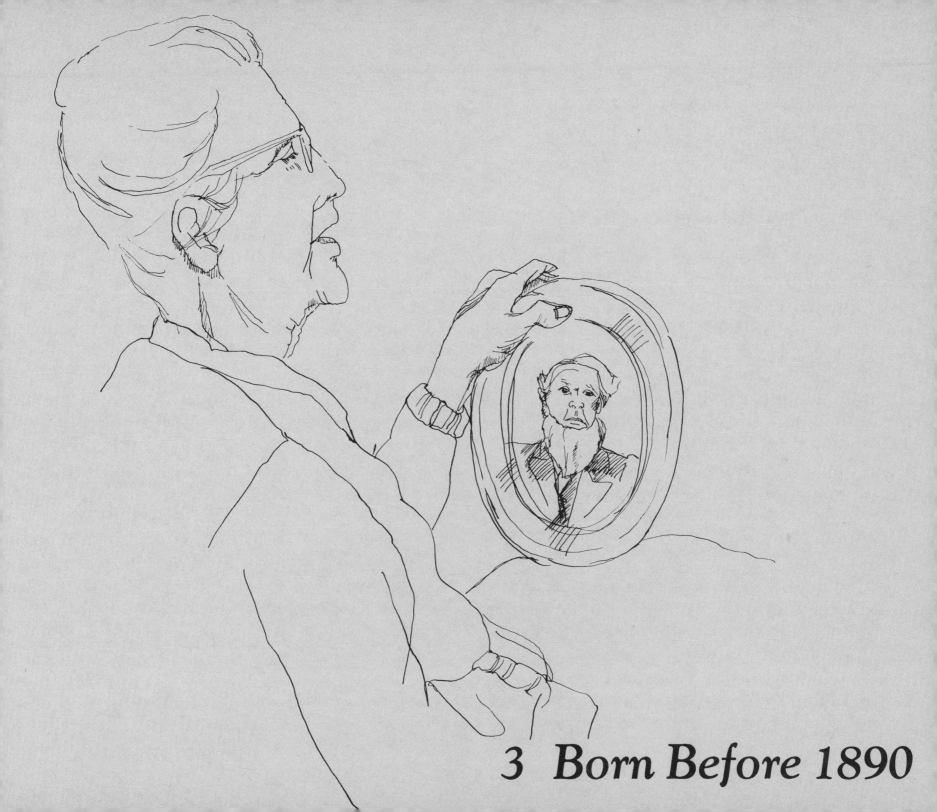

**3  Born Before 1890**

# I REMEMBER A WILDERNESS
## *Lydia Doering*

When I first came to Athens in April of 1883, everything was all woods. I was only five years old at the time, but I remember it well. My family took the train from Milwaukee to Dorchester, which was as close to Athens as the Wisconsin Central could take us. Keel, the land agent for Rietbrock, took us by horse and wagon to Brookerville. We had to walk the rest of the way to Athens. I remember that it was getting dark and we were tired. We finally came to Victor Stremer's shanty, where we spent the night.

The next day we walked on to our land, where my father had built a shanty for us. You see, my father came here first. We had originally come from Saxony, Germany, to Milwaukee. Once in Milwaukee my father contacted the Rietbrock Land Office. He bought 107 acres from Rietbrock for nine hundred dollars and began to clear it before we came. And, oh, that shanty! It wasn't made so sound, and it leaked water. We had to set pots all around inside to catch the water.

There was such fine timber on the land, but we were here to farm the land, so we had to clear it. There was no market yet for timber, so we had to burn it. The logs were pushed together and a big fire was started. The green wood did not burn well, so my father had to get up during the night to make sure that it was still burning.

After the trees were cut down, we had to dig out the stumps. We used a lot of dynamite for this. We had to pick stones and pull roots, too. When the land was cleared we could plant such crops as rye. Everything was hard work then; we had no machines. Do you know how we harvested grain then? The wheat was first cut by a scythe and put into bundles. Then the wheat was beaten with a flail to separate the grain from the stalk. Finally, the grain was thrown up into the air to separate the wheat from the chaff. The chaff would blow away.

We did have oxen right away. We had bought them in Poniatowski. There were no fences or pastures then, so the oxen ran loose in the woods. They were a lot of trouble. When you needed them, you had to go and look for them. Sometimes they would get into a turnip field and dig up the turnips. A little later we bought two cows. They too ran loose in the woods. The cows wore bells; you could recognize your cow by the sound of its bell. We had a house and a barn by this time.

My mother planted a garden right away so that we would have food to eat. She fixed sweet and sour pumpkins and dill pickles. Oh, they were so good! We tapped the trees and made maple syrup. We also got our "gum" off the trees—we chewed the hardened pitch. We picked berries in the woods and dried them for the winter. People also shot deer for meat. At first, we didn't have cows or pigs, but when we did we had veal and pork to eat. My mother fried the pork with lard on a wood stove that had been ours in Milwaukee. After we got more land cleared, we planted potatoes. They grew so well that we sold them for ten cents a bushel to the lumber camps.

Oh, everything grew so well then! I remember that bull thistles grew well, too. They were huge. It was my job to dig them out of the ground and to take the soft white part and stamp it fine. It was then mixed with bran and fed to the pigs.

Ladd School was the first school in the area. It was taught by Mr. White, who came from Manitowoc. All of our teachers were men then. The teachers and the children walked to school. If the teacher wasn't there on time, Frank Stremer and Charles Behrendt taught the classes. The school was heated by a big wooden stove. In the winter we would put our mittens and other clothing underneath it to dry. These school days were good days. I went there until I was twelve years old.

We worked hard, and before we knew it, Athens began to change. Rietbrock built a sawmill, which brought many people here. Pine logs were cut because they could float down the creek to the sawmill. The train ran farther now—in 1887 there were stations named Athens, Corinth, and Milan. More churches were started. By the early 1900s we had electricity to replace kerosene lanterns. In 1906 or 1907 we had a telephone put in.

We worked hard, and before we knew it much of the land was cleared. I often think of all the big and beautiful trees. Oh, that was a long time ago.

## THE STORY OF MY LIFE
### Nettie Blair

I was born January 23, 1880, in the Village of Hatton, Town of Lind, Waupaca County, State of Wisconsin.

My earliest memory is when I was between three and four years of age. Then my father owned an eighty-acre farm one-half mile north of the Crystal Lake Four Corners. I said Father had eighty acres, but one acre had been sold at the southwest corner. There was a house and a building housing an old-fashioned country store and the post office.

We lived in a shanty that was higher in front than back and the roof sloped down to the back. It contained the kitchen, pantry, and closet for work clothes. The front room and bedroom were in the front. A district school house was close to our place, and when I was four years old I used to run away and join the school children at play in the yard. When they went back in after recess, I would go with them and right into classes also. The teacher, who had been a former scholar here, told my mother I was ready to go to school regularly; she would bring her sister who was the same age as I. From then on we worked together until we graduated from the eighth grade.

When I was about six years old Father bought the eighty-acre farm adjoining ours. The buildings were much better and the house larger, but a one-hundred-sixty-acre farm meant he had to hire men, one by the year and one by the month. I had to do my share in the field. When I was only ten years old I had to currycomb and brush my own team of horses. I was not tall enough to get the collars on without getting on top of the manger, but I did it without any help.

I cut all the grain and had to have a three-horse team hitched to the binder. When the grain was dry enough to stack, I had to do that too. When I asked my father why one of the men could not do it, he told me I could make a better stack. I knew that was not so, as they had never tried since working for him. I think I knew then but it made no difference. I know he was disappointed because I was a girl instead of a boy, and he won out by making me do the work of a man. Mother never said anything to make it any easier.

We always had a large field of sugar cane. Twice during its growth each season I had to have several boys and girls from the neighborhood to help me cut the suckers off. If they were not off, the sorghum molasses was bitter. We always made from a hundred to a hundred twenty-five gallons. A sorghum mill was half a mile from our farm. Mr. Packard, who owned it, had an old white horse that pulled what they called a sweep around in a circle, which turned the rollers that squeezed the juice out of the sugar cane and into vats where it was cooked. It had to be skimmed constantly.

I was about twelve when I started high school. I went only one year because my father said he could no longer afford to pay tuition and board. One of the young men graduating that year, who was going to teach at our country school the following year, wanted to arrange for me to take charge of the classes up to third grade. In return he would help me with second-year high school work and with arithmetic, which was my weakest subject but one I needed for teaching school. I was determined to teach. I brushed up on first-year high, got second year, and received help all through decimals and fractions so I would have no trouble with either of those.

When I was sixteen I was supposed to go to summer school before I could teach, but my father said he did not have the money and I would have to borrow it myself. I already had a school and was to get eighteen dollars a month. I would have to pay my board, but that was taken care of. A farmer and his wife who lived near the school and were old friends of mine said they would charge me only five dollars a month if I would take apart the milking machine, wash it, and put it back together again in time for night milking. She had been a city girl and knew nothing about things on the farm. He kept the grass cut on the school yard in summer and built fires and shoveled snow in winter. I decided not to teach anymore because the pay was so poor and I always had to go five weeks to summer school and pay for that.

I had a good job at the hotel—good pay, room and board, and furnished uniforms—but when my father needed me on the farm, I had to go. The second day I was home a gentleman and his daughter came to see me. He was school clerk of the second school from us, and she was a chum of mine. She thought she could persuade me to take their school, but I told her that it had a bad name. I would not take it under any conditions. For the last three years each young teacher had left halfway through the term because she had to go outside to get all the wood and water, and the boys and girls would lock the door, leaving her out in the cold. After such treatment three teachers quit, and no one applied. I advised them to look for a young man. The next day the county superintendent came to see me and told me he wanted me to take the school. He said I could handle it and would finish the year. "We will make or break the school," he told me. He was going to lay down a number of rules with the school board, which must agree to them. I finished the term. By Christmastime the scholars and I were on the best of terms and they gave me a surprise party.

I was soon back working in the hotel. Then I was offered the job of night operator in the telephone office. It was in the back of the millinery shop and a milliner took care of it until eight o'clock, then I would work until closing time at midnight. It worked out very nicely for me.

I was twenty years old when the Central Railroad started an elevated track through town (Waupaca). My mother boarded six of the men who were building it, and I got up early enough to pack six lunch buckets while Mother was preparing the men's breakfast. Then I had to get to the hotel in time to wash the breakfast dishes.

One day during an electrical storm the kitchen door was open and Mother was standing by the stove when lightning struck an apple tree close to the door, hitting Mother at the same time. The doctor said she would be in bed several weeks, so I had to quit the hotel and do the work at home. The railroad work would soon be done and Mother able to be up and around again and could manage with a little help.

When I was married on October 30, 1901, we had our house rented and most of our furniture paid for. A couple of years after we married I went into a nursing class, kept up with it for two years, then took two more years with a retired doctor. He taught me to give first aid in case of broken bones or burns and how to make and apply several bandages. One, especially, I found very helpful, the cone bandage for eye operations. My work as a nurse in hospitals was increasing, and I was being called by doctors to help with births in homes and hospitals. About that time the midwife that I had helped several times offered me the chance to work with her in all cases. She said she was old and she would help with the birth and turn the cases over to me to finish up as long as the mother and baby needed help.

We had a son in 1905 and a daughter in 1908. The son contracted flu in 1918, was only sick a few hours, and died just before the armistice ending World War I was signed.

In 1928 my husband, daughter, and I started three years of night school. I took up sewing, cutting, and fitting, so I could make coats, suits, dresses, and men's shirts. My husband took up repair of furniture and fixing doors, windows, steps, and racks. My daughter took cooking and baking.

When my husband and I were in our late seventies we decided to enter the Shady Lane home for the aged, so we disposed of our furniture except for what we would use to furnish our room at the home. Instead of taking a large bed, we bought two chair beds; each unfolded and made a comfortable bed or could be put together for a double bed. They made nice-looking easy chairs for daytime and gave more space in the room. We were there about twelve years. We both liked it, but the doctor asked me to find a couple of rooms and do light housekeeping and try to keep my husband more quiet. By then he was both blind and deaf. The same evening I found an ad for a partially furnished three-room flat on the first floor. Rent was reasonable, so we moved in the next day and lived there five years. Three doctors said my husband must go into the county hospital. He was there two and a half years and died of flu at eighty-five years.

After that I went back to Shady Lane and was there about fifteen years when I had to have more nurse care. Now I am at Park Lawn Nursing Home where I expect to spend the rest of my life. I am happy and satisfied for I know God is with me.

## MY EARLY DAYS
*Beulah Bowden*

I was born at Brodhead, Green County, Wisconsin, on July 20, 1883. My first memory has to do with an incident occurring in South Dakota when I was three years old. My father was not at home, and while Mother cared for my baby brother I wandered away. Mother could not find her little girl and in her desperation she raked the well—a hole in the ground into which a bucket at the end of a rope was lowered to secure water.

What I remember was sitting alone playing with what seems to me now like an egg yolk, which it may well have been. A man came along on horseback, picked me up, and took me to my mother. She laid me on the bed, lay down beside me (I doubt she could have sat up any longer), and talked very seriously. I understood little of what she said but kept wondering, "Why does Mama feel so bad?"

Before the well was dug my father had to haul water several miles, and Mother was so in the habit of conserving water that to the end of her life she never used half enough water for anything.

We left South Dakota after a few months for a farm eight miles from Wisner, Nebraska. On the way there we ran into travelers with (to my mind) very peculiar-looking vehicles. Years later in my school book I saw pictures of the covered wagons used in the westward movement and knew then what I had seen.

We moved into a new one-room building just erected for a barn. There was no insulation—just a single layer of wide lumber nailed to the outside of two-by-fours. We could see out through the cracks. Before the next baby came Mother pasted newspaper over some of the cracks near her bed to keep out some of the wind. There was no covering over the wide lumber that constituted the floor but left cracks between. Our feet were cold. I can well remember snow sifting in onto our pillows in the night. Here two of my brothers were born without the aid of doctor or midwife.

I remember the big blizzard of the 1880s. It had been a balmy day, when all of a sudden the storm struck, blowing the door open. I can yet see both my parents struggling with all their might to get that door shut. My uncle would have perished in the storm had not his folks kept calling and calling while he walked toward their voices. The snow was so thick one could not see his hand in front of his face. The next morning a snowdrift much higher than the house was piled in such a way that a path was left between it and the house. I can remember going right over fences on a handsled after the snow became crusted.

This handsled was the only plaything we ever had. There was no money for toys and we never missed them. On the prairie we gathered buffalo bones and strung them together to make fences for our animals, which might be represented by other bones or by chicken feathers. We learned the fun of developing our imagination. And we had each other.

Remember, we had no telephone, no TV, no radio, no daily newspaper, no mail delivery. Population was sparse and neighbors far away, and ours were Bohemians who knew almost no English. When rarely my father went the eight miles to Wisner he used a lumber wagon and a team of draft horses. I remember Father took us all to town one summer day after none of his family had been off the place for a whole year nor seen anyone aside from our own family. Trees were a great rarity on the prairie. But on our way this particular hot day we drove for some distance beneath a long row of cottonwood trees. Oh, the welcome shade!

When Father occasionally went to town Mother could get letters from her parents. She must have lived for it. Money was scarce, but when Mother wrote she could get a whole letter on a penny postal card. A sealed letter would have cost two cents!

Mother had to work in the field, and by the time I was six I had to be left in the house to diaper babies and care for them otherwise. A carefully brought up child can assume responsibility early.

One fall all the potatoes froze in the ground before they could be dug. That meant that for months our diet was the bread our mother baked. She set the yeast at night, wrapping the big breadpan in several quilts to keep it from freezing. While she was molding the dough the next day the fire would be sure to get low and she would have to get her hands out of it to supply the necessary cobs or "cow chips." Wood was very scarce, and we had never heard of oil or electric heat. That winter one cow was giving some milk for the little children, the others having gone dry. That meant we had no butter, and for a month we had only sorghum for our bread. To this day I do not want to hear of sorghum.

When I was eleven we left the Nebraska farm and returned to the then small village of Brodhead. At my grandmother's home one night I watched her get ready to go about half a mile to the business district on an errand. When my aunt dressed to go with her I innocently asked, "Why must two people go?" I was told, "It is not nice for a lady to be on the street alone at night." Such was the ethical standard of those days. Being the oldest child, I had at times to be sent downtown at night, but never till after I left to teach school did I ever go on the streets after dark without one or two brothers with me. I never resented it, for I well knew: "It is not nice for a lady to be on the street alone at night."

In Brodhead in the 1890s there was no running water, to say nothing of hot water from the tap. We got our water from an outdoor pump, which would have to be thawed out in winter. Of course there was no bathroom. You visited an outdoor toilet even when it was twenty below zero. (On the Nebraska farm there had been not even that. You went behind the barn or some shrub.) Water froze in your sleeping room. You wrapped a hot flatiron to take to bed with you. In the morning you grabbed your clothes and dressed behind the only stove in the house.

We had no washing machine or clothes dryer. We got out the big boiler, filled it with water, and heated it over the cookstove. Then we put warm water in a tub and with soap rubbed all the soiled garments up and down on the washboard—a long, back-wrecking process. Next, all the white clothes were put into the boiler with more soap and boiled and boiled. Then they were rubbed on the board again. Eventually they were well rinsed and hung on the clothesline. In winter your thumbs got numb and the clothes froze to the line.

We never went to school in Nebraska, as the distance was too far. Mother did try to teach me some things from a child's primer. My schoolroom experience started when I was eleven years old. I always hurried home the moment school was out to help care for the younger children as well as with necessary housework. And I never thought that I was abused.

I would have had it no different. There was nothing on earth I did not do for my younger brothers except to bring them into the world. I was happy caring for them and having them trustingly appeal to me. I could have loved them scarcely more had they been my own.

Precious, holy memory!

## THRASHING VIA THRESHING
*Gustave Telschow*

Thrashing and threshing. How many reminiscences of former years and present time do those two words call up. There are perhaps four billion people evenly distributed over the face of this big earth, and some of them are still thrashing, as their ancestors did. When the Puritans arrived at Cape Cod, Massachusetts, in 1620, they didn't find anything in this country that they could thrash, and naturally they thought often of the agricultural activities in England. During the early winter, some of the men returned to England on the *Mayflower* and came back the following spring with more immigrants, grain, and other things that were needed. That same year they started to thrash some grain.

As year after year went by, more and more people arrived in the eastern states of this country and many of them went west. Many located in the big forests, where it was easy to build a home. A portion of this woodland was later called Wisconsin, admitted to the United States in the year 1848 as the thirtieth state. Fifteen hundred years ago this area was almost treeless, with hills and valleys covered with grass and other vegetation. Only a few trees grew here and there. The blue flags had large beds in the meadows, where also the Turk's-cap lilies bloomed during the summer, and asters, sunflowers, and the goldenrods made the autumns beautiful. Bobolinks made their nests in the meadows, and the redwing blackbirds located their nests near the edge of the rivers and brooks.

In 1870 my parents arrived from Germany and purchased eighty acres of that great woodland in Juneau County, where other pioneers had located. They built a log cabin and two barns so near each other that the roof covered a driveway between them. This driveway was later used as a thrashing floor. Later when cutting the biggest trees in the woods, they counted segments in the trunks, left by the yearly growth of the sapwood, and none of those big trees was a thousand years old. These men were all agriculturists and thrashed their grain by flailing it.

When I was six years old the farmers cut their golden grain field with cradles, leaving long swaths of grain on the ground behind them. On our farm my mother and my oldest brother raked and tied the grain into bundles. On the other side of the golden wheatfield I heard the bobwhite whistle its cheerful notes. Not far away was a field of bearded barley, just starting to change its color. Those were beautiful summer days, and it now seems that nowhere else did the summer sunshine fall so softly. The wheat bundles were placed in shocks and, when dried, conveyed to the barn or stacked near the driveway. This made it handy at thrashing time.

Until I was twelve I had the task of providing my parents with spring water for drinking when they worked in the fields. I had really kind parents. My father never hit me when I was naughty or gave me a thrashing. He would talk to me sternly and give me good advice to become a better boy. My mother's nature was somewhat similar to Dad's, but she also believed in providing some discipline when I was naughty and once made me sit on a footstool for a long time. Being thus disgraced when I was naughty I felt bad and cried bitterly. I didn't get angry, as I knew I deserved it. When I went to her, trying to regain her confidence and love, it seemed she tried to ignore me. I clung to her apron but gave no attention to the pockets that sometimes contained candy for me. She soon clasped me in her arms and there was extra moisture in her eyes as she said, "Now be a better boy." Who can fathom the depth of a mother's love?

On some farms after the grain was stacked near the barn, it was thrashed during the autumn days and sometimes throughout the winter, but no straw stacks were made. Sometimes when the supply of flour got low in the kitchen flour bin, the thrashing of wheat began. The bands of the sheaves were removed to loosen the contents, and two rows were generally made on the thrashing floor, the heads of the grain intermingling. The flails generally are slender and some had a leather lash attached to one end, and the beating the straw received seemed like whipping it. It never took long to remove the grain from the hulls. Then the grain was cleaned with a fanning mill to remove the chaff and large items. Finally it was conveyed to the mill and made into flour.

For a long time the word thrashing served its purpose, but about a century ago the word thrashing was changed to threshing when the threshing machine was invented. The machine was a great help to the farmers, and how they appreciated it. At that time they were operated by horse power. Four teams of horses went in a circle around a power unit that had a tumbling iron rod near the ground and extending to the threshing machine. One autumn morning when I was twelve years old I saw two teams of horses pulling a threshing machine along the main highway. They then entered our farm road and placed the machine between four stacks of grain not far from the barn. Soon other men came with two teams and started to get the power unit and the machine ready for thrashing.

My mother had to prepare dinner for the thrashing crew, about fifteen men. I went to the hen house and selected five nice young roosters, put them into a gunny sack, and took them to the wood chopping block that was located near the kitchen back door. My mother came out to help me. I took a rooster out of the sack, held it by the legs, and offered the hatchet to my mother, who refused to take it, saying, "I can't do it. You cut off their heads." For an instant I looked at her face with those mild eyes closed. Now cutting off those roosters' heads, I for a few moments divided their spirit. I tossed them on the ground. They couldn't walk but leaped up in the air a few times and while their wings fluttered, I noticed two of them opened their eyes twice before they died. I helped my mother take the roosters to a big iron kettle of boiling water that hung on a crossbar between two posts with a bed of red coals beneath it. Thus the feathers were soon removed. Our

neighbor's wife helped my mother prepare the big dinner. A few of the dishes were new potatoes, carrots, fried onions, bread, cake, two kinds of cabbage salad, and pumpkin pie.

It was a wonderful day for me, watching the men work and listening to the hum of the threshing machine while it was being fed with the bundles of grain. Later in the afternoon the men, horses, and machines went to another farm and the place where the stacks of grain stood looked so dismal. The only interesting thing that remained was the fluffy straw stack that would almost defy any intruder. Later we boys had fun climbing and playing around it, but we sometimes felt sorry that the threshing season was gone.

## REMINISCING
### Gustave Telschow

Far away on a farm among the hills near Elroy, Wisconsin, stood a large log cabin, and around it, many years agone, a group of boys and girls played. At that time I was twelve years old and loved the meadows and tree-covered hills where the singing birds built their nests and wild animals had free range. I had no books on birds; thus I gave them names that seemed to suit them. The red-breasted grosbeak was called a parrot, as it somewhat resembled a parrot the city shoemaker kept in a cage in front of his shop. The bobolink was called a fiddler on account of its merry notes. The song sparrow had the name teacher, as my teacher's name was Maggie Murfey. Early in the morning I would listen to the bird singing, "Miss, Miss Maggie Murfey is my teacher." I am sure that if you paid special attention to the bird's song, you would get the same sentence. My parents told me the name of the robin and bluebird.

Some of the meadows and all the woodlands also were beautiful when decked with flowers of blooming spring: snowdrops, bloodroots, hepaticas, violets, lady's slippers, jack-in-the-pulpit, and dutchman's-breeches. The last had deep nectar cups; insects with short tongues couldn't reach the nectar. Twice I saw honeybees cut a hole in the breeches near the cups and remove the nectar.

The log cabin on the farm was a wonderful place; it was my home. It was a story and a half high. The upper portion was for storage and sleeping lofts. The roof's rafters were poles from the woods; boards placed on them and the pine shingles nailed on the boards completed the roof. It was a cozy place to sleep, and sometimes in the winter I could hear the snow drift across the roof. During the summer when a thunderstorm approached, I heard the big drops fall first and then the downpour. It made me appreciate the wonderful protection the log cabin provided. Some nights when lying awake for a while, I heard the owls hooting and it gave me a sad or weird feeling.

To me there were many interesting things on the farm. The haying and harvest time in autumn was productive and beautiful with its long rows of corn shocks and the ripe pumpkins lying between them. All this was wonderful, but summer was the most wonderful season; often I would sit outdoors in the moonlight, sometimes watching a thunderhead far away in the distance, flashing and lighting up its billows as it slowly moved along above the horizon. There were always things that drew a person's attention, and how interesting it was to watch the moon waxing from crescent to full phase. Now that I am ninety-two years old, I often think of the beautiful evenings on the farm when the full moon was really queen of the night. It is our nearest neighbor in space, many thousands of miles away.

Perhaps my reminiscences will bring pleasant memories of the days when you were young, when you left home and wandered far and wide to mingle with others in this busy world, and now are enjoying a nice position. I am sure fond memories come to you occasionally of the time when you perhaps were on a farm or in a village or small city. Sometimes the winters on a farm were quite pleasant with plenty of sleighing, skating, and skiing to pass the cold season. Then in March came the maple syrup time. Trees were tapped by boring holes in the trunks and inserting spiles that had a deep notch cut the full length. The sap was collected with wooden buckets and then boiled to make the syrup and candy. They were very delicious and easy to preserve.

When I was twelve we went to the Fourth of July celebration held in the city park, now called the fairgrounds. After a ball game in the forenoon, many families served a nice picnic dinner and there was plenty of noise made with firecrackers. I purchased a package and had a small portion hanging from my hip pocket, so as to take one occasionally. Unnoticed by me, a big boy evidently came up behind me and lit the package and they started to explode. I immediately grabbed the package and was successful in extinguishing the fire and lost only a few.

The afternoon entertainment had horse races and running contests for men and boys. The last event of the day was the balloon ascension, and Art Tayler, a well-known man, was going up with it. Four ropes were attached to the bottom of the balloon, held open and the right distance from the ground with four posts. With an oil fire burning on a small cart, the balloon was inflated by smoke and hot air. When the big balloon showed signs of getting filled, four men took the ropes to keep it from ascending. As soon as the balloon was almost completely inflated, it was difficult to keep it from ascending. Soon the fire was removed and a parachute capsule having a closed parasol was immediately attached to the bottom of the balloon.

The parachutist eagerly entered the capsule, and as the balloon was ascending, only his face, chest, and hand holding on to the release rope were visible.

It was a quiet day and the balloon ascended to a great height, then slowly started moving east. Fearing that the balloon might stop over or above the millpond, the parachutist immediately pulled the release cord and the parachute fell with increasing speed to our great alarm. Then the parasol opened and stopped the rapid descent. The large celebration crowd cheered joyfully as the parachute and man landed softly in a cornfield southeast of the Stabler farm.

Now my two younger brothers and I started for home. We went south of Elroy on the main highway for about a mile and then took a side road that went through a meadow and woods. It guided us to the old farm, and then in the distance we saw the large log cabin, our Home Sweet Home.

## HOW IMPORTANT SOCIAL DEVELOPMENTS SINCE 1900 HAVE AFFECTED MY LIFE
*August J. Christianson*

As I recall some of my experiences during these ninety-one years I have lived I can think of nothing very spectacular, but I do find some which are at least interesting to me personally. Some of them follow.

My memory seems to go back as far as my fourth or fifth years. I can definitely establish that these experiences were during these years, as I know positively that I left Chicago, with my parents, before I was six years of age. I recall very vividly one day when I was playing alone in the gutter in front of the house in which we lived at 67 Cornell Street that a drunk man was leaning on our front gate. I was terribly frightened and I ran around the block to the back entrance to our home. I also recall another instance when my mother took me along one afternoon to visit with an aunt of mine. I noticed a shiny musical instrument on the table in the center of the living room and I was very much interested in this item, which may have been a trumpet of some kind. During the afternoon I presume that I talked about it, and from what my aunt said I got the impression that she intended to let me take it home when we left. But when the time came for leaving she said nothing about it and I left there very much discouraged. Although I know very little about psychology I have learned from the above incidents that in order to impress anything on a child's mind it must be made spectacular and if you succeed he will never forget it.

In my early teens I was very much interested in lawyers and I often went to the courthouse when I knew that there would be a plea to the jury. I wished very much at those times that I could be able to make speeches like the ones I heard when these men made their dramatic appeals. But during those days I was employed by one of the local telephone companies as night operator at the switchboard. There was strong competition between the two companies in their attempt to get the public to give them their long distance telephone calls. One day the long distance line between our village and another about twenty miles away, separated by a river about midway, was out of order. That meant that the opposition company would be receiving all the long distance business. A couple of days passed by and the line still had not been repaired by the troubleshooter who lived in a village across the river. Then I got the bright idea that I might go out on the line and see if I could find the break and maybe repair the line. Early on Saturday morning I got busy and got a small coil of wire, a hammer, a few spikes, and a pair of pliers. I started out on foot and I found the wire broken. It was still fastened to the insulator on the twenty-two-foot pole and the other end was on the ground. I spliced the wire and tied it to my waist, and with the hammer I drove in the spikes on the pole and was able to reach the insulator and made the splice which cleared the line for service. We had no local troubleshooter.

A couple of weeks later Mr. A.C. Bowe, the general manager who resided in Minneapolis, came to the office when I was on night duty as switchboard operator. He said, "I have been wondering how our long distance line became repaired a couple of weeks ago when our Pine City man was too busy to take care of it." I told him that I had repaired it because I knew we were losing business. Then he said, "If you are that much interested in the company, I am now raising your wages from the eight dollars a month to thirty-five dollars. Now when you know of any telephone trouble you go and see if you can fix it." So in

this way I became the local troubleshooter and later took a short course in telephony and it became my life's work. As a result, I eventually purchased a small company from the local farmers and later sold it at a good price. This experience indicates that some incident can change the direction of your life.

When living in a small village, during the administration of President Calvin Coolidge, I received a letter that said his campaign committee for the state was looking for someone interested in conducting his campaign in our county. I answered the letter, was appointed county campaign chairman, and the campaign turned out very successfully. I took the postmaster examination and was among the three highest contestants. After some political maneuvering I finally received the appointment and served as postmaster for nine years but then lost out when the other political party won the election. When the county judge was obliged to resign, the county chairman asked me to submit my name to the governor for the appointment to finish the unexpired term. I received the appointment and completed the term. Then I ran for election and served two terms, sixteen years in all or until I reached the age limit. I was not an attorney, but the law did not require the judge to be one for a county of our population.

Back when I worked for the local telephone company, the method of transportation was the horse and buggy. One of the two livery barn owners in the village let me have a team and buggy for my own personal use. On one of these occasions I drove out to meet my girlfriend, who lived about thirty-five miles away, but the horses caused me some trouble. One of the horses had a way of maneuvering so he could get the rein under his tail and he would clamp down on it so you could not do anything but let the team run down the road. On the way out this happened but I was able to get the rein loose and by being very careful I could prevent this from happening. After arriving at the girl's home we decided to go out for a drive. I was standing by the buggy with the reins in my hand and was helping the girl get into the buggy. She had just put her foot on the step and to my surprise the line was under the horse's tail and they ran away in such a hurry that we hardly knew what had happened. They ran out the driveway and across the highway and into the woods but had to stop when each horse was there with a tree between them and the tongue of the buggy broken. I was obliged to call the livery man and he had to bring out a new team and make the repairs and give me a good team so that I could get back to town. By the way, an older brother of mine told me that I was being bribed when they let me have a free team for my personal use. The way this turned out I believe I had my punishment for accepting a bribe. There were no automobiles in those days but I eventually was able to buy a gentle gray mare and a buggy. My girlfriend and I went out quite often, and since she was a schoolteacher I took her to her school and back to her home every week.

My memory goes back to the kerosene wick lamps and sawing wood on a sawbuck with a bucksaw. I remember mornings when I would go to the kitchen for a drink of water and find the tin dipper frozen in the ice in the water pail. I remember wearing knee pants the first year in high school. We wore long knit stockings above our knees. I have often been glad I had these experiences.

When I was eighty years old I worked in the sheriff's department as part-time jailer and radio traffic dispatcher. As I sat at the desk one morning someone pounded on the cell block door, which was a signal that a prisoner wanted cigarettes. I took the big iron key and unlocked the first iron door and stepped back, as was our custom, but when I opened the door there stood the prisoner. He had managed to come through an eight-by-fourteen-inch opening through which we passed the meal trays. He was a man of twenty-three years and short in stature, a marine who had been picked up because of being AWOL. He looked bewildered but grabbed the key out of my hand and turned his back to me, intending to unlock the second door and push me in the cell block, lock it, and make his escape. I did some fast thinking, and with both of my hands I grabbed him around his neck until I felt my fingers around his wind pipe. He sank slowly to the floor as I called for help, and a man in a nearby room came to the rescue. We put the young man back into the cell block. I was very happy for if the prisoner had escaped it would have been a bad reflection on the sheriff for having an old man like me as a jailer. As it turned out, it was good publicity for the sheriff and it did a lot for my ego. The local paper made a big deal out of the fact that at my age I was able to control the situation.

### THE STORY OF MY LIFE
*Josephine Brozek*

I was born in Rumania in 1885 and was the seventh in a family of ten children. My father was an assessor for thirty years in Rumania, and he also owned a bowling alley. When the neighbors came to bowl, my youngest brother and I set the pins—only nine pins were used in my time. When all pins were knocked down, we would holler, "Aller niney," and we received a grietzer (a penny). When we had ten grietzer, we thought we had a lot of money and we would fight over it.

Rumania did not have any modern conveniences at the time I lived there. We had lamps for light, a hand pump outside for water, and an outdoor privy. I was baptized and confirmed in a Lutheran church. When I was seventeen years old my brother and I did a lot of singing together. We went different places to entertain people with our singing. Around this time we lost our mother, who was forty-three years old. It was not easy for us. My oldest sister, who had lost her husband, moved back home with us, and we all lived together. My father lived to be ninety-six years old. I learned dressmaking and made ten cents an hour, but I did not stay long there. I got myself a different job, giving massages after steam baths. My salary was four dollars a week, but I made more in tips than wages. After I had some money saved I went traveling and visited Mother's relatives who lived in Bucharest. There life was not like I was used to, so I left and went to an agency to inquire for a job. He recommended me to some people with two children, whom I was to take care of. I did not like the work, so I returned to the agency and they asked me if I would like to go to Budapest in Hungary. I thought it over, went back to the agency, and told them I would accept the job. There were three people in this family. The mother was an opera singer. It was very hard for me until I became used to the work. I had to dress her and go to the opera with her. I stayed with them until I came to America. By the time I left Rumania for America they had electricity and running water. The outdoor pumps were all closed.

I had two brothers who had come to America before me and settled in Cincinnati, Ohio. So in May of 1909, when I came to America at age twenty-four, I went to stay with one of my brothers. He had electricity, an icebox, and gas for heating and cooking. It was very hard for me the first few months as I could not speak English, but I could speak four other languages. Because I had a sister-in-law who could understand German and speak English, I could learn the English language. While staying with my brother I worked at the Colonial Inn as a waitress. One day there was a fire at a house about a block down from where I lived, which was a Rumanian settlement. While I was at the fire a young man by the name of Carl Brozek came running from the building that was on fire. He stopped and talked to me for a while and then asked me to marry him. I was very undecided, but I did accept later. He told me that he took me for an actress and was afraid I would marry another young man from Rumania who lived there also.

Mr. Brozek and I were married in September 1909. We lived in Cincinnati for four years, then moved to Milwaukee. We had two lovely boys, Carl and Ben. My husband was a sheet metal worker all his life. Both boys went into sheet metal work also and had businesses of their own. My husband passed away in 1952. After his death I went to live in Florida until 1967, and then I came back to Wisconsin to live with my oldest son who then lived at Crooked Lake. I lived with him until 1972, when I had the misfortune to fall and dislocate my hip. I then came to the Gillett Nursing Home and have been here for five years. The personnel is so good to me and I like it here very much. For my pastime I still do crocheting and knitting. I also think of all the traveling I have done in my lifetime. I have been to Rumania, Turkey, Hungary, Austria, Germany, Canada, Mexico, and several states in America.

## HELPING PEOPLE
*Emma Larson*

I'm ninety-two years old and I have lived a very interesting life. When I was young I traveled all over the United States. I did a lot of charity work in my time, helping the poor families, young people, and the handicapped. If I heard about a family that needed help I would visit them and report it.

Once I went into a house and found a woman lying on a bed with a young child. The house was dirty, and much dirty clothing was lying about. It turned out that she had eight children and was very poor. I reported the situation, and they got the oldest daughter a job and helped her with money to keep the children in school. I didn't get paid for this but I guess I did it because I felt sorry for them.

I lived in Spokane, Washington, and in Madison and helped the people around there. In Madison I helped the young people. There was a small organization that helped juveniles with problems. One boy was so mean and caused so much trouble that they were going to close the organization. I told them that nobody in the world is so mean that they don't have some good in them. Everyone does but you just have to find it in them. I told the boy just that and after that he changed and was one of the nicest boys you'd ever want to meet.

Once around Christmastime I went to a house and found the husband in bed with typhoid fever. The little girl said to me, "Mama left us, but she'll be back, she'll be back." It turned out she had taken off with another man and left her husband sick with eight children to care for. I reported this, and they got medicine for the man and even a small Christmas tree and presents for all the children. They were very happy about this.

Most people who are poor won't ask for help because they are too proud. When they are dressed so poorly, they don't want to be with people who are well dressed.

I helped many people who were elderly. Some of them were poor and needed money badly. I reported poor children and they were given clothes so they could go to school. Some of the people I reported were helped to get jobs so they could support themselves. I did all of this before I was married.

After my marriage we moved back to Waupaca and adopted four foster children. If we hadn't taken them they would have been sent to the reformatory. One of them was going to be sent to the reformatory for hunting out of season. I went to court and I said, "I am not defending this boy for what he did, but the same man who is supposed to be protecting this wildlife also hunts out of season." The man admitted this and I got to keep the boy. This boy is now the chief engineer at one of the reformatories in Wisconsin. He is married now and has a fine family.

All my foster children turned out well. I hear from them all around Christmastime. They are all just wonderful. I am glad I did these things for people in my life. I still feel sympathetic toward people who are poor, have problems in their youth, or are handicapped.

## THE STRANGERS
*Maude M. Becker*

I was born in south central Illinois in 1886, the same year in which the Haymarket Riots occurred in Chicago.

Though there were many personal events that were as unsettling to me as the Haymarket Riots were to Chicago, I am sure I had many happy experiences in my childhood. But as I think back over the many years that have passed since then, it seems that loneliness and fear were my constant companions, my predominant feelings. I believe this was largely because my father died in 1886 when I was an infant, and my mother, who was the sole support of seven young children, must have felt harassed and very lonely, and this feeling somehow transmitted itself to me. Living in the country and having no close neighbors also doubtless contributed to my loneliness.

We were three miles from the nearest town, Enterprise, Wayne County, Illinios. It was a very small, quiet, sleepy little town with a population of perhaps fifty or seventy-five. Its streets were tree lined, and I can still hear the cheerful chirping of the sparrows as they flitted about the branches.

There was one general store, owned and operated by Mr. Barth, and it carried everything one might need—groceries, clothing, hardware, patent medicines, toys, stick candies. Always there was a large, round cake of cheese on the counter, a knife lying beside it, and close by an open container of crackers. No one need go away hungry—it was all free! The town also boasted a blacksmith shop and one church, which served the spiritual needs of the community. In the quiet country the church bell could be heard for miles, and I thought it the most wonderful sound in the world.

The summer evenings were especially difficult times for me. As it grew dusk we usually sat out of doors to get whatever breeze there might be. I am sure the rest of the family enjoyed this greatly, but to me it was very depressing. I listened to the eerie hooting of the owl, the plaintive call of the whippoorwill interlaced with the hoarse croaking of the bullfrog in a nearby pond, or the harsh, grating cry of the screech owl, the sleepy twitter of birds, and the varied sounds of the insects, and the whole symphony of night sounds filled me with a deep loneliness, sadness, and even fear.

In the days of Coxey's march to Washington with his five hundred unemployed midwesterners, we had many tramps, men who wandered aimlessly over the countryside without purpose or destination. Their clothing was old and ragged; they were dirty and unshaven, and an old battered felt hat might cover scraggly, uncombed hair. They slept in strawstacks, haylofts, or anyplace where they could find shelter, and went from one farmhouse to another begging food. They were a sight to inspire fear in a child, and even an adult.

Peddlers also were a common sight. These men traveled over the countryside selling their wares. They were quite typically swarthy, short, and of stocky build and spoke in very broken English. As they appeared at our door their heavy shoes, clothing, and the bulky packs on their backs were white with dust from walking on the country roads. Very infrequently my mother would permit one of them to come into the house and open his pack. We children gathered around to see the treasures displayed. There were brightly embroidered linens, sparkling, gaudy jewelry, and all sorts of trinkets, and we gazed in rapt, open-eyed wonder at these bright and to us unfamiliar treasures. Mother, of course, could not afford to buy any of these things. The peddlers were not slow in showing their disgust, even anger, at the fact they could not make a sale, and they muttered their disapproval as they went on their way.

Alarming and disquieting as these occasions were, they could not begin to compare with the fear I felt at the arrival of a Gypsy caravan, which usually made an appearance several times during the summer months. Gypsies, as is known, are a migrant, vagabond race and are found in Europe and parts of Asia, Africa, and America. They are considered to be descendants of some obscure Hindu race. We found them to be clever and cunning and not at all concerned as to the methods they used to gain their food and other supplies.

In the large wooded area just across the road from our house, there was a space that had been cleared of trees and shrubs, and this made an ideal camping spot for these travelers, for there they had easy access to both food and water, all of which they obtained from us without permission.

The appearance of the Gypsies was always quite an alarming experience for us. The caravans were easily recognizable. Even at a distance there was no mistaking them. As they drew nearer, one could clearly see the covered wagons with their dirty, torn, and tattered canvas covers flapping in the breeze, with dirty, uncared for children bursting out of every opening. On the driver's seat was a Gypsy man with a red band tied around his head and long earrings dangling from his ears. The tired, plodding, half-starved horses wearily pulled the load. Two or three dogs with drooping heads and tails, and looking as tired and starved as the horses, followed along behind the wagons.

It was only natural that the Gypsies would not pass by such a wonderful camping area as this clearing afforded them, and—to our dismay—they stopped and made camp for the night. In a very short time two, sometimes three, of the women appeared at our door. They were tawny of skin with long, very black hair hanging down over their shoulders. Their eyes were large and a brilliant black; there was an air of boldness about them that brooked no opposition or refusal. Their skirts, made of a very bright colored fabric, were long and very full and partially covered their bare feet. Blouses were low necked and sleeveless. They also—as the men—wore long, dangling earrings. There was an "unwashed" look about these Gypsies, as if soap and water were not an important part of their daily routine.

Without knocking at the door or waiting for an invitation, the women would walk into the house and begin exploring all the rooms, doubtless with the idea of finding some article that would be useful to them. Next they made their way to the kitchen where Mother was preparing our supper. They examined all the food, immediately decided they wanted some of the dishes, and did not hesitate to say so. Their manner was so demanding and threatening that Mother, afraid to refuse, would comply with their demands even though this meant she must prepare something else for our supper.

Meanwhile the Gypsy men, who were slight of frame but lithe and agile, had invaded the barn, the corncrib, and hen house and carried away their spoils to the campsite. The water that they got from our very deep well had to be drawn with a bucket fastened to a long rope, without the aid of winch or pulley.

During all this time the children stayed at the camp and did not cause any trouble. They were doubtless roaming the woods and enjoying their freedom from the tiresome ride in the small, cramped confines of the Gypsy wagon.

At dusk the Gypsies built a big bonfire with logs and small twigs they had gathered in the woods, and there they cooked their supper over the open fire. After this was finished they danced and sang and were very gay and noisy. While all this activity was taking place in the Gypsy camp, we watched and waited, wondering what might happen next, always fearing they might come back and demand something else.

It grew late, but still the Gypsies continued their merriment. We would grow so very tired, yet be afraid to go to sleep, until finally weariness overcame our fears and we slept. During the night we were often awakened by the noisy flapping and squawking from the hen house, and we knew the Gypsies were making sure they would have plenty of chicken to eat the following day. Finally it would grow quiet in the camp, and we would rest.

Our first thought on awakening the next morning was to look across the road to the campsite to see whether the Gypsies were still there. What a joy and relief it was when we found on occasion they had already packed and gone on their way.

Now we could be unafraid until another tramp, peddler, or Gypsy caravan came our way. But who could foretell when that might be!

# TO WHOM IT MAY CONCERN
*Mrs. Perry James*

I am ninety years old and will be ninety-one in May. After a stay of four months in a hospital and nursing home, I can do most of my work now but have to use a walker at times. I wear glasses only to read and do handwork.

I had plenty of time while lying there to review my whole life. We had a happy home life—my father, mother, and seven of us children. I always liked music and it comes to my mind now. My father and mother both sang. Papa sang tenor; Mama sang a beautiful alto and played the organ well. They told me many times how, as a child, I would stand beside them and listen to them sing together. One song seemed to interest me more than the others. Its title was "Far up in Heaven's Blue." I learned the words of it also. I was four years old at that time. My grandparents knew I could sing it. They went to church in the old German Settlement Church; in fact, my grandfather preached there. They asked my parents if I could sing at the Christmas program. Papa and Mama said I could. Mama played for me.

The day I was to sing, we drove to Grandma's house and we had supper. After supper one of my uncles stood me up in my chair and asked me to sing my song. I refused and no talking or coaxing made me change my mind. He told me I would not be able to sing it at church if I did not practice.

We went to church. When I was called to sing, I ran up on the platform and turned around and said, "Now who is afraid, Mama White?" She got so nervous when she tried to play for me that she could only give me the key with one hand. I remember it all so well. I got a big doll on the

Christmas tree, and I was very happy. I never knew who gave me the doll. That was the beginning of my loving music and singing and hearing my parents sing.

When I was thirteen, our choir leader in the Methodist church in Elkhorn started a children's choir. My sister and I joined it. She sang a beautiful alto that our mother had taught her. I had taken music lessons on our organ and soon learned to play the hymns. We sang together all our lives until we were married and she moved to Minnesota. We had sung at funerals, basket socials, and church for so long. I also taught a Sunday School class of boys thirteen to fifteen years old. I loved it all.

I asked Papa to sing with me for the last program I had in school. We sang "Red Wing." He sang the verse and I put in the alto in the chorus. I was so happy I could hardly breathe. He was applauded loudly. But I had the surprise of my life when he got up to sell the picnic baskets. He was an auctioneer and had cried a sale all that day, but his voice was so clear. He got up and then gave one of the most wonderful speeches I have ever heard. He compared the school of our day to the schools of his day. I wish I had a copy of it. I was so proud of him. The applause was terrific. I could have cried I was so happy.

My husband and I lived on a farm—in fact, in the house he was born in—and we have two lovely daughters. Both are musical; one plays the piano and the other the violin. We have seven great-grandchildren. We celebrated our sixty-fourth wedding anniversary last December 6. We are still able to care for ourselves in most ways and enjoy having been together so many years.

# MY NORWEGIAN GRANDFATHER
*Mabel Longley*

In the early 1800s my great-grandfather, Christopher Oleson, sold his small farm near Oslo, Norway, and purchased tickets to Palmyra, Wisconsin. Relatives who had preceded him to Wisconsin had written him that here was not only a land of freedom but a country that would provide him and his family a wonderful living. These Norwegians had built not only their homes but a Lutheran church and school.

Christopher had sewn enough money into his woolen underwear to make the down payment on what he hoped would be their future home in the Wisconsin territory. Before they reached the port of sailing, his wife died. After burying his wife in Norway, brokenhearted Christopher and his son, Chris, and daughter, Ann, proceeded on their journey to America.

On the boat a woman made friends with Chris and Ann and convinced Christopher that she would take care of the two children and him. Christopher, who knew little about the care of children, married her. Before they reached the American shore, Christopher died and was buried at sea.

The stepmother took the money that Christopher had sewn in his underwear and continued the journey to Palmyra. When they reached Palmyra, she took them to the town pump, gave them a drink, and told them to wait until she returned. They never saw her again.

Mr. Wilson, the hotel owner, found them. He went home and said to his wife, "There are two children out at the town pump. They are frightened and can't understand English." Mrs. Wilson, a kindhearted woman, went out and brought Chris and Ann into her warm kitchen where she fed them and gave them her love. Soon the children began to love and trust her.

Mrs. Wilson bought new clothes for them, taught them to speak English, and sent them to school. Chris became adept at learning and at making friends.

Mrs. Wilson was not a Lutheran, but she knew the people who lived in the Lutheran settlement, and Chris grew up in that faith. By the time he was eighteen, he had grown from an undersized boy to a six-foot tall, broad-shouldered man.

Though very strong, he was always gentle. The person who said, "Nothing is so strong as gentleness; nothing is so gentle as real strength," must have had people like Chris Oleson in mind.

At twenty-two, he married a Lutheran girl and together they purchased a farm. It had hills and a lovely stream near the house. It reminded them of Norway. Together they raised eight children, all of whom went to high school, and those who wanted it had college training.

Time passed and many grandchildren joined the clan. We were a close-knit family, and at all holidays and in between we gathered at Grandfather's house for a sumptuous dinner where Mrs. Wilson was the guest of honor. It was a Norwegian custom that all men and boys be served first, but Grandfather insisted that Mrs. Wilson sit at his right and be the first one served. She was the spirit of goodness and his first love.

At one of those early Easter dinners, someone remarked, "Father, you certainly have a tall family," so Chris, my mother, and her three younger brothers stood up, and two other sons stood on chairs and held a board just six feet from the floor. All five heads touched the board.

Chris was a fast-working man and he always wanted a fast-traveling road horse. When his wife or daughters wanted to go into town, he would harness Nora to the buggy and bring her to the door for them. He would give Nora a pat on the hip and say, "Don't let anyone pass you on the road." Nora had been well trained. She went off at a brisk trot. If anyone tried to pass her, she broke into a gallop and the driver had to hold a tight rein.

Chris Oleson enjoyed life, God, his family, and all people. They made his life complete. The kindness of Mrs. Wilson was always in his mind. We, of the third generation, called her Grandma Wilson. She was a much-loved guest at my wedding, and when each of our two sons was born she came to see that all was well.

As Chris grew older, it was his delight, after a family dinner, to gather the children about him and throw pennies to them. If a small child didn't get his share, he would throw a handful directly at his feet.

He never forgot how people had helped him when he was in need. Although his purse was often nearly empty, he never refused a few coins to someone who had less than he had. Often, if a hungry man came to his farm, he would go to the kitchen door and say, "Put on an extra plate, Mother. There is a hungry man here who will eat with us."

Chris Oleson was not only a thrifty man but a devout one. Each day began with Bible readings, and before each meal he gave thanks to God for His continued care and guidance.

Goethe once said, "We are shaped and fashioned by what we love." Chris Oleson loved God and his fellow man. If Abou Ben Adhem's vision comes true, the Angel writing in the Book of Gold will write Chris Oleson's name, with Abou's, as "one who loved his fellow man."

## REMINISCENCES OF AN AMERICAN INDIAN
*Melissa Cornelius*

I went to Carlisle Indian School when I was thirteen years old. A number of Oneida Indian children were sent there, including my older sister. When we arrived they left us alone for a while. No one told us where we had to be. All of us Oneidas used to get together and have crying spells because we were so homesick.

When I arrived at Carlisle, I was examined and tested to find out how much I had learned in previous schools, and they decided to put me in the fifth grade because I had studied history, geography, and mathematics. I was there just a short while before they put me back in the second grade because I could speak no English at all. I noticed that there were some other older children there in the second grade, and it seemed that we were all put back because we did not know English. From that moment on I was determined to learn the English language. I worked very hard and in a few weeks was put back in the fifth grade. My other friends from Oneida were surprised and asked me how I was able to learn so fast since I had been there only a little while and could already speak. I told them I did not know if I spoke correctly or not, but that I was trying very hard to learn English because I believed that was what a person should know. At that time the most important thing in the school was to have a good command of the English language. We studied Shakespeare and many other things and learned to debate and to express ourselves dramatically.

During the regular school session we were required to work at some assigned job for five hours each day and to attend classes the other four hours. The girls were taught home economics, including cooking, dressmaking, and even hospital work.

The superintendent of Carlisle, General Pratt, was always careful about who we were with and decided that we should always be with highly educated and influential people. And it happened that way. When I was at the school, my summers from June until September were spent with important families. I was sent to live and work with these people. That was part of my education. Once I was sent to Cape Cod in New England, and I was very interested because I knew some of the history by then. I went to see where the Pilgrims first landed in this country. The poet Longfellow had said that it was a rockbound coast. I noticed that it was. But there was only a small marker to show where they had landed and the rocks had since been washed away.

Education at Carlisle was first class and the boys were required to learn military discipline. They wore the uniforms of the Civil War. The girls wore white blouses with navy blue skirts and black stockings with high-topped shoes. It was all a wonder, something to think about: This was the way we should live and the way we should learn.

Every morning we were marched to the dining room in groups. There were about eight hundred students in the dining room for breakfast, lunch, and dinner. We would have a prayer and sometimes we would sing at noon and in the evening. We always had a prayer in the morning. Sometimes the superintendent would come and talk to us, and of course every time he came he talked a very long time. We all got very anxious because we were supposed to be at work at half past seven. We always had to wait until he finished speaking and then run as hard as we could to straighten our rooms and fix our beds for the inspection. If everything was not just right, it was reported and counted as a demerit against us. We had to be very quick.

At Carlisle we all knew what we had to do. We had to be ready for school when it started or we had to go to work. We did not go to school all day because we worked five hours and went to classes only four. We changed every month from morning to evening school and we had a study hour every evening for one hour. When we worked in the morning it was from half past seven until noon and we went to school from one o'clock and were out by four. At four o'clock we went to the gymnasium and did calisthenics. It was all very interesting.

They had a West Point cadet who was the disciplinarian for the boys. He used to come around and we saw him marching. He kept himself so that he was something to look at. A West Point cadet has a special way of walking because he is so physically self-disciplined. It was always interesting for me to see a West Point cadet walking.

The boys were required to march in military parades, and of course the boys were more military than the girls, but we girls too lined up in three company groups and marched here and there, to the dining room, to the school, and if we went downtown, we always had to line up and march. Company A were the taller girls, Company B the shorter, and Company C were the really young ones.

We appreciated this very strict education. That was the wonderful part of it. If there were no real regulations, then the students would be free to do this and that. The rules had to be. For instance, when we were learning English, we always had to report when we were lined up each day if we had spoken any Indian. When they called our names, instead of saying "Here," we would say "Indian" if we had spoken it; if we had spoken only English, then we would answer "no Indian." Many times I had talked Indian nearly all week and I would report that, but then on the fifth day I would speak only English and I would say "no Indian" so that I never got the fifth demerit, otherwise I would have had to do some kind of extra work for my punishment.

The girl I roomed with at Carlisle started coughing and I thought she had the flu. She coughed and coughed, then after a while I started coughing too. It was an awful cough and my chest hurt so that I could hardly cough any more. They took the girl out of the room and to the hospital, but I do not remember if I lay there or if I got up. They took me to the hospital too and took samples of my blood and I had to spit into a glass. I heard a dragging noise in the next room and I asked what the noise was in the other room. The nurse said that the girl I had roomed with had died. She died of quick tuberculosis and that is what I had.

When I left to go to Carlisle my mother told me that if anything happened to me to try to get to the Quaker people. I was fortunate enough that after I was in the hospital for quite a while, I got better and was sent to the country to live with a Quaker family. It was a beautiful place. They lived in a great stone building three stories high. It was located somewhere in Pennsylvania and it had a creek passing by. Children from the college took their boats there at vacation time. There were other Indian girls there too. Because I had TB when I came there, I was generally out of doors. I was tired and sleepy a lot but my cough had stopped. I still did not realize that I needed to be active and to get outside because I wanted to rest so badly. So they made me do things like planting strawberries. I had quite a garden of strawberries—I think it was two hundred plants.

We used to have commencement in the spring in

March. So many Indians graduated and some member of the graduating class would have to say something to let people know that education meant something to the Indian. We always had a wonderful speaker there. I did not have time to graduate because a few days before the commencement I got a telegram that my mother was very sick and I had to go home. And that is the way it was with that kind of life.

## MY FIRST YEAR OF TEACHING
### Ellen O'Brien Wagoner

My first term of school opened in October 1901. Sixteen curious scholars came early, all decked out in new clothes. They ranged from primary and intermediate to advanced stages. At nine o'clock it was time to start the day. I stood in the open doorway and rang the handbell vigorously. The pupils came in and got settled in the seats they had previously selected. Textbooks were distributed and a few lessons were assigned, as I listed their names. Peace and quiet seemed to be the order of the day.

In 1901, the nation was at peace. There was no pollution. Millions of stars were to be seen. Northern lights danced over our homes. There was no shortage of food, fuel, or water. Lady Moon was a virgin. "Everything was lovely and the goose hung high," as the old saying goes.

I had signed a contract to teach seven months, do the janitor work, build a fire, and keep order. My salary was twenty dollars per month. I had found a boarding place near the school. The folks I lived with were kind and helpful. The food was wholesome, organically grown, and served lavishly.

My room was all cozy and warm. The furniture consisted of a good bed with a high headboard, a dresser to match, a bowl and pitcher, and a kerosene lamp. All this was for six dollars per month providing I went home over the weekends.

The school building was small. It had two shuttered windows on either side. A narrow hall across the front contained a bench for dinner pails. Some hooks were placed in the wall for caps and coats. Factory-made seats and desks accommodated long and short legs. The teacher's desk was homemade, rough, and roomy. The library books—about 150 of them—were kept in a wooden box. I found copies of *Black Beauty, Little Lord Fauntleroy, Agonac the Eskimo Girl, Little Brown Brother,* and *Easy Bible Stories.* A large round oak stove occupied the middle of the room.

I posted my daily program showing fifteen-minute periods for reading, arithmetic, grammar, geography, spelling, and penmanship. Agriculture and physiology were to be worked on occasionally. The beginners learned from a large chart on the blackboard.

The teacher was supposed to furnish the timepiece, which I did with my gold watch. (My father had purchased it at Eckern's Jewelry Store at Black River Falls.) Also missing, along with a clock, was a hickory stick.

During the good weather everyone played outside such games as Andy Over, Come Away or I'll Come and Fetch You, Wood Tag, and London Bridge Is Falling Down. There was no such game as Cops and Robbers.

Our pump was a real luxury. Every morning an older pupil would bring in a bucket of water. At noon a fresh bucketful was brought. Everyone drank from a long-handled dipper. The yard was large. A creek trickled along the east end. Two "comfort buildings" were placed sixty or seventy feet apart. Their entrance was screened by panels made of boards placed horizontally.

At the end of the month it was time to collect my salary. First, I had to obtain an "order" from the school board. Next, the order had to be signed by the director. When I returned from those errands, my mother, with Irish the driving horse and buggy, was waiting to take me home.

I unlocked the school door and picked up my lunch bucket. We were on our way to the home of the treasurer of the school board. How grateful I felt. I was doing my part of the world's work and being paid for it.

The fall term lasted three months. At Christmas we put on a program in the town hall. A Christmas tree was trimmed with strings of popcorn and cranberries. At the top of the tree a star covered with tea-lead shone brightly. The program consisted of songs, recitations, and dialogue. The concluding act presented the three wise men kneeling on the stage with a nervous dog. After the lights were turned down and the flare behind the wise men was lighted, the dog jumped from the platform and ran barking to the door. The curtain was drawn, the lights were turned on, and Santa arrived. He distributed the gifts. Each child got a mosquito-bar bag filled with candy, nuts, and a popcorn ball. The school district furnished plenty of good Wisconsin apples. Everyone seemed happy! A three-week vacation had begun.

Vacation went by too quickly. As the days got longer the cold got stronger. School opened the third week of January. Attendance was poor. My beginners did not return until the first week of February. They seemed to have forgotten all they had learned. I had to be patient. I knew they were as anxious to learn as I was to help them. In a month they were promoted from the chart to Appleton's beginners' reader.

Spelldowns were quite the thing that winter. We decided to challenge the Coon Valley school. They came, along with their parents. Our parents came too. The little room was crowded to the seams. Coon Valley lined up on one side of the room, we on the other. The visiting teacher pronounced the words from the familiar speller. Sorry to say, they spelled us down with the word "kerosene." You can believe me, after that spelling was important. Our school received a challenge from a neighboring school. We accepted with a feeling of assurance. A parent offered to take us over there. We met at the school building. It looked like a big evening. The good man with his team and sleigh came. The box was half filled with straw, which was covered with blankets. Some fur robes were there to cover our knees. How happy we were! We climbed in nimbly as squirrels. While sleigh bells jingled we sang "Jingle Bells." The moon made it almost as bright as day.

Having arrived at our destination our challengers ran to help us out of the sleigh and conduct us inside. Everyone was laughing and singing. Inside all jollification stopped. The serious challengers lined up. We lined up as usual, eager to start. As the visitor, I had the honor of pronouncing the words. We put them down with the word "Mississippi." After that night we were firmly cemented. It seemed we all realized the importance of the old saying "Put your best foot forward." May I add, "Keep walking."

Late in March 1902, the spring term began. My fourteen curious scholars were not curious anymore. We understood each other. The schoolroom and its furniture had gained personal respect. The surroundings were something that had been a part of their daily life.

Spring was flirting with us. April showers brought

May flowers. The grass was springing up. Green leaves were showing. Some birds had returned. Again, "Everything was lovely, and the goose hung high." The girls were flitting around in calico dresses, some trimmed with ruffles, some with lace. They all had changed to lighter shoes and stockings. The boys wore bib overalls and lightweight shirts. We left the door open for the fresh air. The program I had posted was getting to show the winter's wear and tear. President Lincoln's picture needed a washing. Several new library books had been added and numbered. Our enthusiasm for spelling had shifted to grammar.

I was determined that my hopefuls would speak and write good English. My intermediate and advanced classes were combined. I put stress on number, person, and cases. They understood singular and plural and how to form possessive plurals. They liked to diagram. Now in 1977, I am surprised to hear so many grammatical errors in conversations on TV and radio. I feel something important has been lost along the way.

The beautiful trailing arbutus had sprung up in the woods. Some children brought a bunch of them that scented the whole room. Later there were sand flowers. Later still came lilacs, apple blossoms, and lady's slippers. The pussy willows were turning into elder bush leaves. The last day of school was drawing near. Arbor Day was observed without classes. The yard was raked, the woodpile was put in order. It was customary to plant a tree. We planted a sturdy pine and named it Evangeline.

One Monday morning the county superintendent dropped in and heard some recitations. The children did not seem nervous, which is more than I can say for myself. He made observations and made notes in a little book. He gave two advanced boys an examination that decided if they were ready for high school. Their papers were placed in a folder he had. He bade us good-bye with no criticism or compliment. A week later we received notice that the boys had passed.

The last day arrived. There were classes until noon. We ate our lunches. By that time my mother came with homemade ice cream and crackers. Two of the girls helped us serve. Then all the texts, slates, and copy books were placed in boxes. While the children played, Mother and I drove to the home of the school clerk to get my order. He surprised us by having my pay there. I gave him the register, took my pay, said good-bye, and left. The children were ready to leave. They took their dinner pails and said good night and good-bye. I did not hear "See you in the morning." I could have cried. The door was locked, the key given to the clerk's son, and Mother and I left for home. That's the way it was. I would not have missed it.

## VISITING GRANDMA
### *Alice Converse*

One time eighty years ago when I was a little girl I went to visit my grandparents. There were no autos, of course, as they hadn't been invented, so I had to go on the train, which was a big thrill. My father walked down with me to the depot. I had on my Sunday dress and carried my everyday dress and some aprons in a bag. (Grandma called my aprons "pinafores.") When the train came my father talked to the conductor, who told father not to worry because he would see that I got off at the right place. He took me in and showed me where to sit. The train seats were all covered with red plush. They looked beautiful and I felt very important. In just a little time the conductor came along and said, "Here is your station, little girl." He helped me down the steps and there was my grandfather. We walked along a wide boardwalk to where the hitching posts were, and Grandpa untied his horse and buggy and we drove out to the farm.

Grandma was glad to see me, and after dinner took me to see her flower garden. She had some flowers she called snapdragons; when you pinched them, they opened their mouths, ready to snap. She had some hollyhocks, and if you cut off the stems and turned them upside down they made pretty doll hats. Later in the afternoon Grandma said she was going to feed the chickens and gather the eggs. She had a big basket to put the eggs in, but she let me carry a couple that I found and I put them in my apron pocket. On the way back we stopped to look at the pigs, and when I leaned over the fence to see better those eggs in my pocket squashed and began to run down my apron. What a mess! I didn't know what to do and stood there looking at what I had done, but Grandma said "No matter." She took off my apron and we went on to the house. She put the eggs from her basket in a box and would sell them later for ten cents a dozen.

The next day was Friday and the day my grandma made butter. In the back yard there was a little stone house called the spring house, and it was always cool in there. Inside was a table that had a long row of milk tins on it. They put the milk in the pans and let it set till the cream all came to the top. Then Grandma would skim the cream off and put it in a churn that had a paddle on a long handle. You had to plunge up and down many times until the butter separated. Then she put the butter in a jar and mixed in some salt. Saturday was always baking day, and my grandma would make bread and baked beans and pies so she wouldn't have to work on Sunday, as that was the Lord's Day.

On Sunday we wore our best clothes and went to church. Grandma had a velvet dress with little buttons down the front. We all waited on the porch till Grandpa drove up with the surrey and two horses, and everyone got in. We had a special pew in the church. People could pay rent on a pew to reserve it. We had a big Sunday dinner and the folks usually took a nap after that. But I went outside to play with the dog on the lawn. There I saw a patch of clover and found a four-leaf clover, which meant something lucky would happen to me.

The days went fast and it was time for me to go home. My father met me at the depot, and as we started the short walk to our place he said, "We have a surprise for you. While you were gone we got a new baby at our house." I could hardly believe it and said, "Are we going to keep it?" He laughed and said, "Oh, sure, your mother wouldn't part with that baby for anything." Then all of a sudden I remembered my four-leaf clover and the good luck it was going to bring me, but I never dreamed it would bring a baby.

## A MEMORABLE PARADE
### Wilma J. Meyer

Now if you can relax for a few minutes I'll tell you an interesting little story about a political torchlight parade that took place in our city of Sheboygan in the year 1892. That was a long, long time ago, but, strangely, the memory of that parade stayed with me all through the ninety years of my life.

First, try to picture our city when it was young, when there were no automobiles, no televisions, no radios, or

70

countless other conveniences we now take for granted. Instead of garages, there were barns and woodsheds. Only two of our streets were paved, and they were paved with cedar blocks. Yes, there was electricity, but it was then used only for lighting purposes. That was Sheboygan in 1892.

Many people have never seen a torchlight parade and do not know what a torchlight really is, so I'll describe it as I remember it. It is a long, slender pole that has a tin can suspended from its top. These cans contain a wick and kerosene. When lighted they produce a bright flame and sometimes some very undesirable smoke.

There is a possibility that the torchlights for this parade were made right here in our own city because at that time we had quite a few industries making furniture and other wood products.

The parade was scheduled to go up Eighth Street and down Sixth Street. This gave us the chance to see it twice because our grandmother lived on Sixth Street and we lived on Jefferson Avenue where the parade formed.

Fortunately the evening the parade took place was a beautiful one. There was great excitement in the air. The streets were decorated with flags and the stores were draped with red, white, and blue bunting. After all, this parade was a political one. James G. Blaine, a Republican, was running against Grover Cleveland, a Democrat, who was seeking a second term in the White House in 1892.

In the distance we could hear music. The band was coming closer, and before long we heard that old familiar shout, "The parade is coming!" First, we saw some men on horseback. They were not the trained horses you see so often in today's parade but horses that had probably already done a day's work delivering groceries, paint, or possibly milk (which was then only five cents a quart).

Next was a carriage that contained notables, then our American flag, and a band with a long procession of Republicans carrying torchlights. It was a beautiful sight to see all those lights flickering in the dark. It was such a simple parade compared with the elaborate parades of today, but for us it was a wonderful event. Everyone seemed in a jolly mood. The Republicans were chanting as they marched, saying, "Blaine, Blaine, James G. Blaine," while enthusiastic Democrats yelled, "Grover, Grover, run him over."

Well, that's exactly what Grover Cleveland did. He ran over James G. Blaine politically in the election that followed, and he then became the twenty-fourth president of the great United States of America.

*Now at last my little story is finished,*
*My stock-pile of paper is greatly diminished,*
*One gathers, through the years,*
*memories galore,*
*But to put them on paper is a miserable chore.*

## 4  Hard Times

# THE FIRST ARMISTICE DAY
*Russell J. Devitt*

November 11, 1918, was an Indian Summer day in Wisconsin. Although the trees had been stripped of their leaves by driving rains and cold fall winds, there was a hint of summer past in the air. The temperature was forty-five degrees, the sun shone, the sky was a deep blue with a haze near the horizon, and silky cobwebs drifted in the sky.

And there was a stir of excitement in the air, even for a six-year-old boy. Rumors were that the war to end wars would soon be over, that the Kaiser wanted to quit, and that our victorious boys would soon be marching home.

Because of an erroneous cable from Paris by a United Press reporter, there had been a false armistice celebration on November 7. But now the world waited breathlessly, in the cities, in the country, and in the small towns like Delavan where I lived.

Then, flashed by cable and wireless around the world came the news everyone was hoping and waiting for. The Germans had accepted the armistice terms laid down by Marshal Foch on November 8, and on this day, November 11, 1918, at 11 A.M. the guns became silent. And although we lacked the communication media of radio and television we had the big city newspapers with their extras with massive headlines like "War Ends, Kaiser Quits," "Armistice Signed," "Yanks Victorious," "Democracy Saved as Huns Run."

And like wildfire the celebrations began. History being made was more important than studying history past, and the schools closed. The town's major industry, Bradley Knitting Mills, closed for the day. In that era of no unions the workers would lose a day's pay, but who cared? The world was saved for democracy.

The fire whistle blew but there was no fire and no fire engines for small boys to chase. The mill whistle joined in, followed by the school bell and those of the Methodist, Congregational, and Baptist churches around the school park. And from across town the bells of St. Andrew's Catholic, Christ Episcopal, and St. Mark's Lutheran joined the cacophony.

Young and old, everyone who could walk, run, or hobble hurried to the business district on Walworth Avenue. Sure enough, someone had strung a straw-stuffed Kaiser Bill to a lamppost. And the saloons were doing a land office business.

This was indeed the real thing, not like the false alarm of November 7. An impromptu band was organized, and there was dancing on the brick pavement, together with unrehearsed and unasked for speeches by the mayor, captain of the home guard, and others, mostly drowned out by spontaneous shouts and cheers.

As the golds and reds faded and twilight fell there was a torchlight parade headed by the town band playing John Philip Sousa's "Stars and Stripes Forever."

The band, resplendent in their blue uniforms with gold braid, formed a circle under the streetlamp in Tower Park and played and played. There were the foot-tapping, spine-tingling patriotic marches, mostly Sousa's. And of course there were all the war songs like "Over There," "It's a Long Way to Tipperary," "Beautiful K-K-Katy," "My Buddy," "Oh, How I Hate to Get up in the Morning," "Good-bye Broadway, Hello France," and the haunting "There's a Long, Long Trail A-Winding."

Then with the chill of the November night people began to drift away, the band stopped playing, and it was over.

Many of the townspeople had not joined in the wild and tumultuous celebration. Wives and mothers of the servicemen gathered at the various churches of their faith to give thanks that the holocaust was over and that soon they could take down from their windows the service flags with the blue stars. And there were others at the churches, mothers and wives who proudly displayed the service flags with the gold stars in their windows, praying but also remembering the better days.

But for a youngster like myself this had been a day of both joy and pride. And as I slowly scuffed my way home through the dark streets a chill wind rattled the branches of the big maples and I knew that Indian Summer as well as the first Armistice Day was at an end.

## THE PENNY AUCTION
*Verna Maassen*

Today was the day they would lose their farm and everything they owned after twenty long years of hard work. Ruth reached over to awaken Hans. He was gone. The sheets were cold where his warm body had been. She bolted up in terror and eased quickly but cautiously out of bed, trying not to touch the squeaky boards in the wide, pine flooring. A faint streak along the horizon showed it was nearing dawn. From habit she didn't light the kerosene lamp. You didn't waste precious kerosene in this depression year of 1934; besides, it might awaken the boys. No use making them suffer the misery of the coming day a minute longer than necessary. Then too, if—if—something had happened to Hans, she didn't want the boys to see. She'd get a neighbor to help.

"Oh, God!" she breathed. "Please, save Hans for me."

Apprehension swept over her. Nothing went right. The tip was gone from the shoelace. The last ten cents of the egg money had gone for John's school tablet.

They had held their little private wake the night before, mourning the death of their dreams. They had sat and talked in low tones, almost as if the walls could hear and would later report their bitterness. The boys had been thrust into a cruel, merciless adult world that was snatching their chance for high school away from them. The boys sat and talked and watched their buoyant, enthusiastic parents turn into middle-aged, disillusioned, desperate people.

Their farm was being foreclosed. Today was the auction of the personal property. Everything was to be sold except the household goods and their clothes. The bank had renewed a neighbor's loan, but when Hans walked in, he had been turned down. Why? Why could one man get a loan renewal and not Hans? The banker said he didn't realize that so many would be coming in. If he gave more loans it might start a run on the bank and he'd have another 1933 bank closing on his hands.

"Sorry, Hans. You're a good risk. You keep your place up. Even in these drought years, you've built wing dams to stop flooding. You've culled your herd down to the best producers. Your wife has sold vegetables, eggs, and dressed chickens in town so the boys could go to high school." He paused. "I don't dare overextend the bank," he ended lamely.

Too lamely, Hans had thought. Now beaten and discouraged, he talked to his family. Bitterly he muttered, "It's the end of the rope for me!" Angrily he added, "If the bank officials want a better price for the stock they can come out and curry them. No way will I clean them up."

The April chill had roused them. The wood fire in the stove had long since gone out. Stiff and exhausted they rose. Hans and the boys went up to bed. Ruth moved about the kitchen, stirring down the cold ashes and laying the fire for morning.

Now, Hans's bitter words seared her memory. "This is the end of the rope for me!"

Tiptoeing downstairs, she called softly, "Hans, Hans!"

There was no answer. Grabbing her denim jacket, she fled outside. Mick, the dog, rose and stretched as he greeted her. Impulsively she glanced toward the machine shed. No sign. The horse barn. No one there. Then she caught a glimmer of light from the cow barn. Frantically, she tore open the door.

"Hans, Hans, are you there?" she screamed.

A head popped up from behind a cow. "Ruth, what are you doing down here at four o'clock?"

"Hans, you weren't in bed—I—I—Hans, I was so scared."

Gently he took her by the shoulders and tenderly kissed her forehead. Softly he whispered, "I don't blame you, Ruth. I talked like a fool last night. When I couldn't sleep, I thought, my neighbors aren't going to see my stock shaggy and dirty, so I came out here. I've got them all curried."

"Hans, shame! You know the neighbors will stick with us. Remember how they said not to worry, it'd be all right."

"Let's be realistic, Ruth. They are as broke as we are. One more year of drought and depression, and they'll lose their farms too."

"Hans, it won't last that long. Farm programs are going through, our cooperatives are growing, and President Roosevelt even talked about electricity for every farm!"

"You're the best tonic a man could have. I'm through here. Come on, let's have some breakfast."

After eating, the boys put fresh straw in the stalls. Ruth scrubbed the floor, and Hans took down a granary door to rest on sawhorses for a table in the empty machine shed. The Ladies Aid would be serving lunch there. Then, washed and dressed in clean clothes, the family paused in the kitchen for a doughnut and a glass of milk.

They heard the auctioneer and the auction clerk drive up. They had been assured that the mortgage holders' claims would be legally satisfied by the proceeds from the sale of this property. They would be out of debt. Nothing would be left. Nothing but their strength, just as they had started out twenty years before.

Ruth and Hans smiled. They had much more! Two fine sons, worth all the twenty years of hard work. They joined hands a minute, straightened their shoulders, and lifted their chins.

The boys felt their chests nearly bursting with pride. Dad and Mom weren't despondent, middle-aged failures, but the same buoyant, industrious people who had been community leaders all their lives. Together the four of them stepped out into the April sun.

A much larger crowd than expected was gathering in the yard. Feelings had run high among the neighbors when they had heard of the foreclosure sale. Hans had sensed something sinister, almost as if they would boycott the sale.

Hans sighed, "Of course, poor devils, they had to come. No one dared antagonize the chattel mortgage holders." A wave of hopeless futility surged over him.

The auctioneer had set up the sales ring and the

clerk's table on one side of the big oak tree. On the other side, directly under the large overhanging limb, lay a coil of three-quarter-inch hay rope. The crowd stared at the rope, remembering the threatened hanging of a reluctant judge in Iowa, who had refused to accept the proceeds of a penny auction. This was the technique that the farm friends had decided upon to save Hans and Ruth's personal property.

The first horse went up—eighteen hundred pounds, sixteen hands high. Curried and groomed by Hans in the wee hours of the night, it gleamed in the sunlight, despite its thinness for want of oats.

The auctioneer boomed, "What am I offered? Twenty-five dollars?"

Silence.

"Twenty dollars?"

Silence.

"Ten dollars? Come now, spring work's just beginning."

A man reached down, picked up one end of the hay rope, coiled it into a noose, then threw it contemptuously to the ground.

"Twenty cents!" came from one side.

"Twenty-five cents!" came from the back of the crowd.

A director from the bank yelled, "Thirty dol—"

Four husky men pressed menacingly close to him.

The auctioneer didn't hear. "What's your bid?"

One of the men reached down and picked up the hay rope.

"Thirty cents," the director's faltering voice ended in terror.

On and on the auction went. The best cows for twenty-five cents. The poorer ones for fifteen and twenty cents.

Pigs for five and eight cents. A plow for one dollar. A grain binder for two dollars. The "10-20 tractor" for five dollars.

The sale was ended. The auction sales clerk paid the proceeds of the sale to the bank officials, legally satisfying the mortgage. Then the auctioneer and the clerk, the bank officials and moneyed people got into their cars and drove swiftly out of the yard.

One by one, the neighbors led the stock they had bought back into the barn. This was the way they would handle foreclosure sales all over the Northwest. Ruth, Hans, and the boys thanked their neighbors with tears streaming unashamedly down their faces. They'd all be in the Town of Dunn come Friday. Ole Thompson's sale would be held at 10 A.M.

Ruth Olsen's reminiscence stopped abruptly. Then she chuckled, "You know, penny auctions went on all over the Northwest. A man on our school board was one of the early pilots carrying United States mail. He had engine trouble one day down in Iowa and landed near a farm where a penny auction was in progress. As he was examining his plane, he was surrounded by men with pitchforks. Nearly scared him to death. They thought he was a government agent sent to stop the sale."

Her hands folded in unaccustomed quietness just for a moment, then energetically she pointed to two large trunks. "Those trunks are full of newspapers, programs, and records of the past fifty years. I'm going to sort them out, label them, and file them."

We smiled indulgently. "No way," we thought, "will Ruth Olsen sit quietly at a desk."

We were right. The next Cooperative paper showed a picture of Ruth, at eighty-three, directing the "Green Thumb" program for retired farmers.

## RIDING THE RODS, 1933
*Edmond J. Babler*

Depression days found many young men from the Middle West going west in search of employment, and that was the situation of two of my cousins and myself after graduation from high school.

We heard we could obtain jobs picking fruit in the Yakima valley in the state of Washington and earn several hundred dollars in one season. One week my uncle from Milwaukee was visiting in Door County, and he offered to take us to the freight yards in Milwaukee. Our mothers fixed us about a dozen sandwiches and we each packed trousers, a shirt, underwear, socks, soap, and toothbrush in a blanket, tightened a belt around the roll, and swung it over the left shoulder.

My uncle dropped us off near the railroad yards where we confronted hundreds of railroad cars and tracks. A friendly yard switchman informed us which train was headed for Minneapolis.

When we heard two short blasts from the locomotive we climbed topside an empty boxcar. We were rather chilly that night in our light summer jackets and caps. As the train pulled out of the city headed toward La Crosse, we each lit up a cigarette to calm our nerves, and we began to realize we had a long way to go with only a few bucks in our pockets. A chill runs up your spine when you leave home for the first time.

Our ride to Minneapolis was very enjoyable as we followed the Mississippi River almost all the distance, sitting topside and viewing the scenery all the way to Minneapolis.

We soon found that St. Paul-Minneapolis was more or less a terminal where trains were assembled to travel to various parts of the country. As soon as we hit the yards I looked for a friendly yardman to inquire whether there were any "hot shot" freights that traveled faster and made fewer stops en route to Spokane, Washington. When we learned which train was the hot shot we checked the departure time and hurriedly bought three loaves of bread and two rings of bologna. Upon hearing two short blasts from the locomotive we hopped aboard a comparatively clean cattle car and stayed at the far end of the car until we were out of town, otherwise the railroad bulls may have kicked us off.

Once we were out of the Twin Cities we sat in the doorway, dangled our legs, and enjoyed the scenery as we listened to the steady clickety-click-click of the wheels passing over the joints in the railroad tracks. There was also the steady rattle of the couplings that kept the cars together.

After a few hours we became sleepy and spread our blankets on top of some paper usually found on the hardwood planks of empty cars. We slept for hours as the train traveled rapidly along, passing through town after town and state after state and stopping for coal or water.

Brief stops were made at such cities as Fargo and Bismarck, North Dakota, and Lewiston, Idaho, towns that had only about twelve thousand people in those days. This train traveled steadily for five days, and whenever the stop was long enough we would get some bread and bologna, with an occasional bowl of hot bean soup and coffee, which we found in the hobo jungles.

On a bright sunny morning we pulled into Spokane. We were dirty and hungry, so we washed up and shaved in a creek at the edge of the city. We changed our pants and shirts, attended mass, and had a good meal.

Bright and early the next morning we hopped on a

freight that was headed toward Yakima. En route we passed through many small towns, and the engineer just blew several blasts at the road crossings. The train never stopped except for coal or water.

Our next stop was Pasco, Washington, as some hoboes had told us that at the transient camp located there we could get a few good hot meals and showers and sleep on mattress and springs. A doctor checked us over; we were given pajamas and a hot meal of stew, potatoes, bread, and coffee; our clothes were steam cleaned; and we took hot showers and slept between clean white sheets. At 6 A.M. lights went on and we received hot toast, oatmeal, prunes, and coffee.

We dressed and hopped on a freight to Yakima and as soon as we arrived we learned that we were a month too early for the apples. Luckily we found jobs picking peaches at fifty cents an hour. To get there we walked nine miles into the country, but we were told to stop after four hours. Why he didn't want us he did not say.

Next we picked hops for a month and had a good time as we had our own tent and cooked our own meals.

We didn't get jobs picking apples so we hopped aboard a freight headed toward Los Angeles. There were no jobs available so I walked up to the Main Street gym to try and get a few fights to enable us to eat. I was all lined up to fight once a week, but in the meantime my two partners went back to our fifty-cent room in a flophouse. When I awoke the next morning my partners were packed to leave for home, and I decided to stay with them.

It was rough trying to get out of California as there were railroad bulls at every station armed with .38 revolvers and clubs. We would get on a train and were soon threatened with a .38 and were on and off trains for one whole day before we finally managed to get out of the city. It appeared as though they wanted no one to come in and no one to leave.

We finally reached Yermo, California, and had a hell of a time leaving. One night we pulled in about ten o'clock and we were sitting quietly on top of the car waiting for the train to pull out when two bums scrambled up the ladder and sat alongside of us. Almost immediately two railroad bulls climbed topside and ordered us all to get off the car at once.

They took the two bums to their squad car and marched us to the railroad station office where they shook us down to see how much money we were carrying. As a rule we carried only about two dollars in change in our pockets and three or four bucks in our shoes. When they found we had a little change they made us buy a ticket to the next town and we rode the cushions, which we did not want to do.

When we arrived at the next town the bulls were there waiting for us and they promptly said to get out of town. "You bums hit the road or we will lock you up for vagrancy," they said, so we had no choice but to hit the road.

We walked out of town about a mile and a half to a spot where there was a long grade, and we figured the train would slow down at least enough for us to hook a ride. As the train approached the grade we grabbed a rung and swung onto the cars. After climbing to the top we were met by a railroad bull with his .38 and a club, and he motioned us off.

There wasn't much choice but to jump off. We began a long hike down the road that turned out to go through a stretch of Death Valley. Believe me, it was hot, and we had no access to water. About ten miles down the road we came to a house where some Mexicans gave us water.

The next train we caught made all short stops at Provo, Cheyenne, Rock Springs, North Platte, and Omaha.

At Council Bluffs, Iowa, I decided to travel faster so I looked at the schedule board at the depot and found a special, the "Corn King Limited," that would get to Chicago in eleven hours. As the train pulled out, I grabbed a bar and swung on between two mail cars. I stood there for the entire trip. The couplings rattled, the cars swayed, and the smoke hit me directly in the face. When I jumped off the train I was in downtown Chicago's Loop.

## THE SUMMER OF '32
*James Andre*

In 1932 times were hard. Money was scarce, and it was impossible to find work. On a warm sunny day in early May I met my friend "Wabeno Joe" Enders in Kewaskum. He asked me to join him on a trip to Livermore, California, to visit his uncle. We agreed to meet at the depot at 6 P.M., ready to ride on the coal tender of the Chicago Northwestern passenger train. During the afternoon I packed some extra clothes, warm jacket, soap, towel, and so on in my packsack. I had $2.25 in my pocket. My partner was waiting for me, and at 6:30 P.M. we were on our way to Oshkosh. Six others were riding for free on the coal tender. At Oshkosh we got off to get a Soo line to Minneapolis. A policeman would not let us get off until we convinced him we would leave town at 10:30. He was at the Soo station to see that we got on the train.

Stevens Point was a difficult place to get through. The railroad detectives were tough and checked all trains for riders. The friendly engine crew let us ride in the engine. As the fireman filled the water tank he told the detective, "No riders tonight." Early the next morning we got to the Twin Cities, jumped off the coal car, and walked out of that big depot with the paying passengers. How we got away with this I will never know. This was our last ride on a passenger train. We always rode on freights after that.

At the Great Northern railroad yards we found a place to wash and clean up. Quite a few men were waiting for a ride west. Some time in the afternoon about fifteen of us got into an empty boxcar just as the train started to leave the yard.

Riding through the western states was an interesting experience. In several places there were fenced graves of workmen killed in the building of the railroad. The graves were well taken care of by the section crews. We stayed together until we got to Washington. Whatever food we could get we shared. Milk was always available at dairies. Sometimes we would eat at the Salvation Army. Some days we were hungry. At Wolf Point, Montana, our train was in a side track to let a passenger train go by. One of our group came back to the train with a large, very hot ham that he must have taken from an oven. We hid it until the train left town. With some day-old bakery goods we had a really hot dinner. He never did tell us where or how he got the ham. After we got to Spokane we headed south to Pasco. Along the Columbia River at Pasco there was a camp called Hooverville of about five hundred men. They lived in shacks made of tin and old lumber. Most of the men fished, trading what they caught for other food.

Leaving Pasco, we headed for San Francisco on the Western Pacific. For many miles the track was built along the Feather River. Many men were panning for gold on the sandbars. Very little gold was found. There were many large sawmills, most of them closed, at Tracy, California. We were in an engine graveyard. Several hundred railroad engines were parked there. Some were very old and had diamond stacks.

We finally got to Pleasanton and had to walk the last seven miles to Livermore. My $2.25 was still in my pocket. We met Joe's uncle, Jack Harter, in town. He had brought in the eggs from his flock of a thousand hens.

Mr. Harter had about eleven acres of grapes and apricots. We helped him pick his apricots and build a shelter for another eight hundred chickens. We cut the apricots in half, removed the pit, and dried them in the sun on large trays. While there he gave each of us five dollars, which we spent in San Francisco. Riding the cable cars and the bay ferries was a new experience. Joe's uncle tried to find work for us in town, as he did not want us to leave. No jobs were to be found, so we decided to head for home. Mr. Harter gave each of us five dollars when we left.

Mojave, Barstow, and Las Vegas were the next places to visit. We stayed in Las Vegas for ten days. Legalized gambling was just a year old in Nevada in 1932. The "lucky strike" Golden Nugget and Apache Club were the only gambling places in Las Vegas at that time. Even at that time they were open twenty-four hours a day. Free food and drinks were passed around and nobody was hungry. With the building of the dam it was a boomtown and wide open. We lived like kings without spending a dime.

Finally we left Las Vegas and rode the freight trains to Ogden, Utah, and then east to Chicago on the Union Pacific. Going east there were no empty boxcars. Most of the time we had to ride on top of the cars. At Cheyenne, Joe and I somehow lost each other and we looked for one another in the yards on the way home. I arrived in Milwaukee on a Saturday afternoon. I was hungry and spent the first of the five dollars I had when I left California on two large hot beef sandwiches in the Red Room of the Plankington Arcade. I rode a passenger train from Milwaukee to Kewaskum, arriving home at 10:00 P.M. Joe Enders had come back on the 6:00 P.M. train.

Later my friend Joe went to Alaska and died there. He was found in the woods—someone had shot him. I am now retired and live near the Chicago Northwestern track north of Kewaskum. As I watch the trains go by I often think of the days I rode the steam locomotives and boxcars to the West Coast and back.

## SOLO CROSS-COUNTRY
### Ruth C. Lembke

Wide awake at dawn on this December Sunday, I bolted out of bed, jumped into my flying slacks and sweater (wearing apparel which was not in vogue in 1941), and dashed into the kitchen. This was to be my solo cross-country flight. I was more excited than I had been on my first solo. Myriad times I had mentally traveled the triangular trek that today I would really fly alone.

"You've got to eat breakfast or we won't let you go!" My father's words broke into my reverie. He believed that flying was for birds and maybe men, but not for his daughter. Mother smiled, but I knew worry-tears were close to the surface. They always were when I left to fly.

Once at Curtiss Wright field (now Timmerman Airport, Milwaukee) I helped to push the Taylorcraft I was about to fly out of the hangar and onto the apron, put shocks under the wheels, and climbed up to check the gas. All the men stood around giving useless advice that was intended to bolster my courage.

"Don't land downwind," John shouted. Everyone laughed. A woman flier, particularly a "schoolmarm," was a novelty. She had to take good-natured tormenting.

"Get in. I'll give you a prop." George was helpful. "Remember, Cokes for all when you get back, if you get back." That was the typical celebration for a solo cross-country flight.

I taxied down the bumpy grass runway, turned into the wind, revved up the motor, and checked the gauges. Pushing in the throttle, I took off. The thrill of feeling the plane lift into the air exhilarated me as nothing else could do. Below, everyone, even the mechanics, stood watching.

With a bank to the right I left the pattern. Holy Hill came into view quickly. At five hundred feet the church was at eye level, a strange sensation. I glanced at my instrument panel. It held an altimeter, an air speed indicator, oil gauge, and tachometer. No compass graced this plane. I used contact flight and "dead reckoning."

Beaver Dam was the first stop. I could feel that the velocity of the wind was increasing. As I landed, the wind whipped under my left wing, almost upsetting the plane. I dropped down with a thud. Grateful that the plane was right side up, I taxied slowly to the hangar, cut the ignition, and climbed out with log book in hand.

The manager raised an eyebrow when he saw me.

"Are you alone?" he asked.

"This is my solo cross-country," I beamed proudly.

"It's pretty windy for flying today." As he spoke I froze. Would he ground me here? Hesitantly he signed my log book and walked out with me to the plane.

"You'd best take off quickly, for this wind will increase, I'm afraid." Then he propped the Taylorcraft and I took off, happy to be aloft again. The tail wind blew and Fond du Lac loomed ahead of me faster than I had expected.

The landing went well, but I had trouble taxiing. Strong head winds lifted the tail and the plane kept trying to take off. It was an eerie situation. When I finally made it to the office, I found no one there. Small airports just closed up on days that were poor for flying. I needed a signature to prove I'd made my landing there.

While I wondered what to do next, a woman appeared.

"I hope you don't need gas," she said. "We don't have any and my husband, the manager, isn't at home."

"No," I breathed with relief. "I need your signature for my logbook." She signed.

"Will they question my signature since I am not a pilot?"

"It's just to prove I did land here." She smiled and left in a hurry.

Another first stared me in the face. I had never had to prop my own plane alone; I had done it under supervision. I found shocks and put them under the wheels, set the throttle, and carefully pulled the prop through. Although Taylorcrafts were not noted for easy starting, it caught on the first turn.

After takeoff I looked back and knew that had the woman's husband been there, he would not have allowed me to take off in this high wind. I looked down to see cars traveling faster than I. The plane seemed to be standing still in the air. I wanted to push the panel to help. This would be the longest trip back from Fond du Lac that I had ever encountered. At times I seemed to be traveling backward. I had plenty of time to think. I knew there would be men on the field to catch the wing tips as I landed to prevent the plane from flipping over on its back or ground looping.

Confidently I flew on, now eager to end this flight. As I entered the Curtiss Wright pattern to make my landing, I glanced down. No one was on the field. Not a single soul lounged on the apron. Not a person leaned against the office wall. Absolutely nobody was there to herald my victorious return. Even the manager wasn't there to see that his rented plane was whole. Strange! This was unlike any other solo cross-country I had witnessed.

Deflated, I landed with only a slight bounce and taxied to the hangar at a snail's pace. Not a mechanic worked on a plane. Tools and parts lay about as if men had left in a hurry. I dragged the plane into the hangar myself, took my logbook, and walked to the office.

Opening the door, I found everyone there, backs to me, huddled around the one small office radio. It was so quiet that the squeak of the door hinge sounded like a burglar alarm. No heads turned. The voice on the radio rang through the office, "I repeat, the Japanese are bombing Pearl Harbor!" Petrified, my glorious flight forgotten, I couldn't believe the message my ears received. In a daze I turned, too overcome to talk to anyone, and drove home.

No one ever did ask about my solo cross-country flight. I'm not sure they knew I returned at all. That feat was lost in the magnitude of the events that had occurred elsewhere. I shall always remember Sunday, December 7, 1941, for I was in the air, several thousand miles away, at the very moment the Japanese were bombing Pearl Harbor.

## MOMENT OF FEAR: OKINAWA, 1945
*Gordon P. Hoard*

A faint dull gray on the eastern horizon gave the sleepy eyes of the 0400 watch a glimpse of scudding, low-flying clouds. A pale streak fought its way up from a shadowy horizon. Dark and angry clouds sprayed a mist on the already slippery decks. The 0400 watch rubbed the sleep from their eyes as they sipped coffee and grumbled as they prepared to scrub the oily decks of LCI(L) 353. A smoke-making assignment had kept everyone on alert until midnight and dumped a film of oil on the decks.

Since the initial landing at Okinawa when we shelled the beach with mortar fire, our only duty had been to make smoke to cover the larger ships. This week it was our turn for duty at Ie Shiana, the nearest island to Japan. Our introduction to the action here had come early the evening before. At about 1700, an alert sounded and all hands feverishly dashed to their battle stations. Our first class signalman, perched atop the conning tower, was the first to spot the enemy. As the plane broke out of the overcast sky above us a wayward beam from the setting sun darted through the low-hanging clouds and reflected the emblem of the rising sun on the wing of the plane. The pilot fought for altitude to start his dive as the tracers from the 20 mm laced the sky around him. Only when he had reached the desired height and started his descent did we realize what his target was. A large Dutch freighter, riding gently at anchor about a hundred yards from us, was what he had set his sights on. All the watchers gasped as the seemingly grotesque form in the cockpit hurtled the projectile at the waterline of the freighter. The cessation of the yammering 20s caused a deathlike stillness, cut only by the high-pitched shriek of the descending plane. The flash and the jarring blast that followed shook everyone from his lethargic state. The officer of the deck was the first to regain his composure and started barking orders to dispatch the men from the railing where they were straining their eyes, trying to penetrate the cloud of steam and smoke rising from the scene of the crash.

A cheer went up as the smoldering cloud drifted away. No gaping hole greeted the disbelieving eyes, only an oil slick and floating debris. The kamikaze had either stopped a bullet on his way to eternity or misjudged his dive.

I raced for the engine room to supervise the starting of the engines while the coxswain started the anchor winch. The skipper had decided that until we had to make smoke to cover someone, we would be better off farther away from such a prime target. The smoke-making assignment came shortly, and we moved into a position to cover the same Dutch freighter that had so miraculously escaped destruction earlier. Some five hours and eleven barrels of fog oil later, we received an all clear. Weary, oily, slime-coated crewmen collapsed in their bunks.

Now as dawn came slowly, the ominous stillness was broken by a seaman's curse as he slid about the deck in the half light. It seemed that the events of the evening before had been a harbinger of evil. At 0800 everyone who had stomach enough had eaten breakfast. The main engines were warmed up and the anchor hoisted. The 0800 watch on the starboard was on duty. Continuous alerts had drained the efficiency of the crew so badly that the skipper had split the crew in two sections, starboard and port. Only in extreme danger was the crew at rest to be called.

Action was not long in coming. At 0845 a clatter of gunfire at the northern end of the island was heard, condition red was signaled over the ship's radio, and the battle was on!

A black cloud of smoke came pouring up from the place where we had heard the gunfire. One of our destroyers had been hit by a kamikaze. A moment later, four Japanese fighters appeared out of the overcast sky. The first plane spotted a minesweeper on patrol about a thousand yards south of us and circled over it. Horrified, we watched as it made one circle, then dove straight for the center of the main deck. We were soon to get a closer view of the disaster. A call came over our radio to get our doctor over there to help the wounded. As we pulled alongside the stricken minesweeper a few dazed crewmen who had escaped the blast grabbed our lines and secured them. The Japanese plane had pierced the main deck, and the bomb he carried had exploded in the engine room, killing or maiming all of the men on duty. With feverish haste, we struggled to get the broken bodies on the stretchers and over the railings onto our ship, all the time trying to keep an eye on the other three Japanese planes. From the corner of my eye, as I was lifting a stretcher over the railing, I saw one plane disintegrate as it dove on a destroyer escort. Some sharp-shooting gunner had saved their ship.

One more disaster and the most humiliating, hair-raising experience of my life were yet to come. An LSM (landing ship medium) with a deck full of oil drums was between us and the island. This amphibian had the conning tower and crew quarters on one side of the ship. Another Japanese plane deliberately crashed into the conning tower and exploded, setting the oil drums afire and nearly blowing the LSM apart. We could see survivors of the blast jumping off both ends of the ship.

We had nearly finished our task of removing the minesweeper's wounded when I heard a cry of alarm. The destroyer escort, emboldened by their previous kill, had moved over by the LSM to pick up survivors and were engaging the last plane in sight. We were now within range for our 20s but too much in line with our own ships to fire.

Suddenly the Japanese pilot turned from the destroyer and headed for our ship. I was on the gun deck getting ready to cast off our lines when I heard the warning cry "He's coming for us!" I stood rooted to the spot momentarily, not knowing what to do. The oncoming pilot seemed to be aiming directly at me. I glanced back at our fantail. The officer's steward and a seaman were diving off the ship. This roused me to action. I dashed for the ladder to the fantail. I wanted to jump overboard with the others. Mostly, I wanted to get out of line and out of sight of the oncoming destruction. When I reached the fantail, I glanced up at the starboard 20 mms. The gunner's mate had frozen to the gun and I literally ripped his fingers from the gun and hooked myself in. Maybe the resultant blasting of the 20 mms diverted the pilot or he may have been only trying to scare us. My dazed and incredulous eyes watched as he zoomed over us. I swung the 20 mms around and the tracers followed him into the low-flying clouds surrounding us.

Moments later, a group of Navy Corsairs arrived on the scene and began circling the area. With trembling limbs, we cast off our lines and started scouting the area for survivors. It was some consolation to know I was not the only one who was frightened. We picked up our own deserters and two from the destroyer who had jumped when the first plane was diving at them.

Never before or since have I known such appalling, demoralizing, petrifying fear. This is what I ashamedly call my "moment of fear."

5 Survival

## WITH A BABY IN MY ARMS
*Anne M. Dunst*

A woman I could not identify handed me a small, wrapped bundle and told me to hold it. I cradled it gently in my arms. She seemed surprised. "How naturally you handle it," she cried.

Quickly I answered, "I was born with a baby in my arms!"

Those words kept ringing in my memory as I woke up with a start. It had been a dream but a very vivid one, for in my dream I had expressed a truth that went back to my early childhood.

I was the first daughter born to my parents, after three sons. The oldest son died in early infancy. I was followed by another brother, and in time there were ten living children. Shortly before my fifth birthday, I came home one day to find a brand new baby, born at home while I was at school. Surprise and delight were my immediate reactions. I had a sister!

They were happy days that followed. When Mother was busy with her cooking or other work, she sat me down on the kitchen floor with my little sister in my arms. She would say, "Hold your little sister while I finish my work."

I was proud to be considered capable of taking care of the baby and watched over her carefully. As the oldest girl in a Sicilian family, I had, without a question, the duty of being responsible for the care of the younger children, to be, in fact, a second mother. I did not realize then what the future was to hold for me.

My sister was followed by another brother. His coming was another happy event for me. He was born late in November, a few days after the delivery to our home of a handsome, nickel-plated, isinglassed heating stove with an impressive dome. Shortly before, my mother had purchased two pairs of high-button shoes for me, the first in all my six years.

I was overwhelmed with all these events coming so close together. I found a scrap of muslin and decided to make a cap for my baby brother. Proudly I brought it to my mother and said, "I made this for the baby."

I spent many hours caring for my little brother. I changed, washed, and dressed him and took him for walks, holding him carefully in my arms. I can recall walking to his godmother's house with him in my arms, a shawl wrapped around both of us.

Two years later I welcomed a second little sister. Again I was happy. I delighted in embroidering little dresses for her. I was proud when Mother decided that for her first photograph when she was two she should wear the little white dress I had embroidered. She was photographed with the baby brother who was four months old.

My youngest sister slept with me, and I took complete care of her the summer she was two years old. She followed me everywhere, adoringly. I never questioned or minded caring for her or the younger brother.

By the time I was eleven, we were eight, five boys and three girls. I was used to the routine of washing dishes, scrubbing floors, making beds, and helping my mother with the washing, boiling, rinsing, and hanging up of the family's clothes and laundry. School made up for the hours spent working at home and caring for my younger brothers and sisters. Nothing could keep me at home. Fortunately, I was sturdy and strong. My unhappiest moments came when Mother made me stay home from school to take care of the little ones while she did some shopping. I cried and tried to convince her that I could not

miss school. I complied, of course, but not without bitter tears and reproaches to my mother.

It was that same year that Father and Mother decided to go into business full time. For some time they had been selling olive oil, tomato paste, olives, salami, legumes, and other articles imported from Sicily. Now their customers and their business demanded more space and merchandise than one room of our rented flat offered.

They decided to rent a store with living quarters above it in the center of our community. Father gave up his work as a tailor. With his growing family, he needed to earn much more money if he was to realize his ambition and dream of sending all his children to school beyond elementary and high school.

My two older brothers were in high school when Father and Mother opened the new grocery store. A few months later, my oldest brother entered Marquette University as a freshman. He was going to be a doctor.

I had followed my older brothers' high school studies with fervent interest. I echoed their practice of German, repeating the numbers, words, and poems they memorized. To this day, I remember the "Lorelei," which they sang.

There was no question in my mind: I was going to high school and to college, too. I read voraciously and enjoyed all my schoolwork. My report card was always stamped with "Special Merit." This pleased my father. He took great interest in our schoolwork and urged us to take advantage of our opportunities. Because his father had died at an early age, he had only two years of schooling in his native Sicily. His natural ability and uncommon interest spurred him on to self-improvement. He wrote correctly and beautifully in Italian despite his brief schooling.

The grocery business flourished. Father and Mother worked long hours. The older boys took over the delivery of grocery orders after school and on Saturday. Mother spent less and less time with the housework and the care of the younger children. It was my responsibility to take her place.

I was thirteen, in my last semester of elementary school, and looking forward to attending high school. Three months before I graduated, my mother gave birth to her second to the last child, another son. Now we were nine.

I was kept home from school to care for Mother and the new baby. With foreboding of trouble to come, I refused to look at the new baby until the day after he was born. I was uneasy. How was Mother to manage with the new baby and the dry goods store she and Father had recently added close to the grocery store?

Undaunted, I signed up for high school. That summer I had the complete care of the new baby. Several times a day, I took him to Mother for his feedings. I recall my bitter words to Mother one day, "It's a good thing I can't nurse him, or you would have me do that, too!"

I had complete charge of the house, the younger children, and all they entailed. I washed mountains of laundry, ironed, cleaned and scrubbed, cooked, and washed dishes with the reluctant, occasional help of my eight-year-old sister.

My maternal grandmother, who was visiting a daughter in California, had promised she would come to live with us when she returned home. She did come home before school started, but her youngest daughter, who had a baby a month or two younger than ours, prevailed upon her to change her mind and live with her instead.

I was crushed. I knew I would not go to high school.

Ironically, my parents were able to afford hiring a woman to take care of the baby. But I was doomed. As the oldest daughter, it was simply, and unquestionably, my duty.

For two years I wept at the mere mention of school. The final blow came when I was fifteen. My youngest brother was born. Now I had the care of another infant brother, in addition to all the other work. A public library across the street was my great solace and comfort. I read every moment I could spare.

My oldest brother was then in medical school, the next one in college, and the brother two years younger than I in high school. I asked my father, "If I were a boy, would you keep me at home?" He answered simply, "But you're not a boy."

My tears and pleadings and the urging of my oldest brother finally bore fruit. When the youngest child was eighteen months old, my father gave in. I finally convinced him to allow me to attend school only in the morning. Mother protested, "You love school more than you love me!"

I went to high school. There were no more babies to keep me at home. I still carried the brunt of all the housework. I went to summer school, and after a year and a half I was allowed to go full time. I graduated in three years and realized my dream of going to college, too.

I was privileged to have six children of my own to love, to cherish, and to hold. I have one sadness. One child was stillborn, a beautiful little son I never held in my arms.

## UPS AND DOWNS AT THE LEAD MINE CHEESE FACTORY
*Jennie Erb Joos*

An American immigrant's first few years were often a time of on-the-job learning while making his living doing the job. By trial and error he learned what and what not to do. Children had the same experience, although what not to do was taught with immediate discipline.

My parents came from Diemtigen, Switzerland. In summer, cheese became the product of the alpine-grazing cows' milk. In America, Papa soon became a cheesemaker, a somewhat nomadic life, as the permanency of the cheese factory residence depended on the one-year contract made with the group of farmers. If the cheesemaker didn't perform satisfactorily—or all perhaps depended on the whims of some powerful farmer—the contract would not be renewed, and the cheesemaker had to find another factory.

The cheesemaker usually received a fixed percentage of the receipts from cheese sales. He had to buy the machinery, usually from the former cheesemaker. He could have all the milk he needed, a reasonable amount of cheese for family consumption, and free living quarters. There was usually a chicken house, a large garden patch, sometimes even a pigpen. The arrangement was really quite nice—a roomy home, most of the food, privacy, one's own business—and quiet. Back in 1910 we saw an automobile on the road for the first time and excitedly watched its progress. Occasionally some farmer might grumble about an inordinate amount of cheese being consumed or complain about the finished product, overlooking the fact that sometimes farmers brought in spoiled milk or skimmed milk or even added water to their milk to make it weigh more.

It was fun to "help" my father make cheese. He stirred the milk in enormous, shiny, copper-lined kettles, adding the rennet extract to make it set into a solid curd, then cutting it with a large wire-tined knife, lengthwise and crosswise. After sufficient cooking, handfuls of curds would squeak as we chewed them. Occasionally a fly was rescued from the caldron. Eventually the whole was lassoed into a large cheesecloth, the cheesemaker holding the front end with his teeth, while using both arms to fling the banded cloth to the opposite side to embrace the kettle's entire content. Finally managing to get the whole curd-filled cloth up to a point where he could make a large stout knot, he attached it to an enormous hook, hauled it up high, and had it trolley away into its flexible mold. There more whey would be squeezed out as the mold was drawn tighter. After many weeks of salting, washing, and curing at various temperatures in different brines and cellars, the cheese was ready for sale.

Cheesemaking was done twice daily, morning and evening—cheesemakers often worked until midnight. In his spare time, my father made the wooden boxes for shipping cheese, sawing and hammering for days for "block" and "Swiss." The cheese buyer would come and look over the cheese. Inserting a boring knife, about three-fourths inch in diameter and three inches long, he pulled out a chunk, looked it over for texture and holes, broke off the inside end for taste, and then reinserted the specimen piece so the test opening was barely visible. On this ritual depended the "grade" (and the price) of the cheese— no. 1, no. 2, or perhaps a poor no. 3.

My earliest recollection of cheesemaking life goes back to the year 1910 at the "Lead Mine" factory, located on the Charles R. Collins farmland, near Blue Mounds, Wisconsin. I was three years old, having been born at Mt. Vernon, Wisconsin, in June 1907. My sister Clara, a year younger, was born at a factory near Cross Plains. Another sister, Paula Angelina, was born at the "Lead Mine" factory in 1910 and baptized by Pastor G. Nitardy of Verona. Her godparents were her aunt and uncle, Frau Catherine Erb and Herr Friedrich Erb, after whom there is now a road named Erb Road, which leads south off Highway 18-151 about four miles west of Verona. Paula died within three months of whooping cough. I well remember the tiny gray casket in the parlor and wailing loudly while riding with neighbors, instead of with my parents, to the Blue Mounds Cemetery.

The Lead Mine factory got its name from the area's lead mine pits. They were deep and abandoned with water on the bottom. People threw junk into them—barbed wire, broken glass, and other debris; they were probably also infested with rats and rattlesnakes. Our parents constantly warned us to stay away from these dangerous holes. But to an adventuress of three, what could be more tempting than to get just as close as possible, peer down, and see for oneself just what *was* down there, disregarding the warning that she might fall in? No, I couldn't resist, and the hole didn't resist me. Down I went, pigtails flying, dress flying, my screams drowning out the screams of Clara who witnessed my sudden disappearance. My descent was stopped by a barbed wire catching my dress. There I precariously hung while Clara ran screaming to Ma and Pa that Jennie had fallen into a lead pit.

My father rushed to the rescue but could not reach me. He ran to neighbor Collins for ladders, while I fortunately remained dangling by a thread. Finally they succeeded in hauling me up, not too much the worse for wear. But when

I got home, my derriere became considerably worse for wear. I stayed away from lead mine pits forever.

Everybody makes mistakes—even fathers. Chicken houses often have mites. They come out of the woodwork and wood roost cracks at night and torture the poor chickens until they are thin and scrawny and lay no eggs. No amount of hand-powdering each chicken with louse powder seemed to help, so Papa decided to de-mite the entire chicken house. He went at it with a hoe, removing all debris, removing all roosts and egg-laying boxes to get into every crack. Then he washed and drenched everything with a pail of kerosene. Finally, satisfied that no louse or mite could still be alive and that the worst of the job was over, he contentedly lit his tobacco-pipe before beginning to replace the roosts and boxes. Wham!! The whole chicken house caught on fire and burned to the ground. My father got out in time and lived to build again, using a carbolic acid solution in future chicken house cleaning.

My mother—a very careful lady—also made a bad mistake at this factory. One day she and Pa had to go to town, leaving their two small girls alone. In those days people kept fascinating things—dried peas, beans, lentils—in the jars now used for "antique" display. The last thing Mama said when leaving was, "Now don't do something idiotic while we're gone, like sticking peas up your nose!" That did it! Such an exciting new game had never occurred to us. No sooner had she left than we rushed to find a jar of dried peas and proceeded to experiment which one could put the most peas up her nose. I won—more peas came back out of my nose than out of Clara's. For a while everything seemed well. Mama noticed nothing amiss. But about a week later my little sister's nose began to get bigger and bigger and purple, almost closing her eyes. It got so bad that neighbor Collins drove us to a doctor who excised from the poor little (now big) nose a pea that had sprouted roots and fought being dislodged from that nice garden of cozy moistness. I think Mama learned to omit suggestive warnings.

My father, however, had not only learned a lesson about kerosene, but that same year received recognition for his skill in cheesemaking. In 1910 he received a certificate that said, "The National Dairy Show Association awards this diploma to Jacob Erb in recognition of superior merit—brick cheese score 94½—by authority of the Board of Directors." He also received a gold medal fixed to a watch fob, with a dairy cow embossed on the front and an inscription on the back awarding first prize. Mama bought him a gold watch to accompany it. After Papa's death in 1954, we discovered another certificate: "Diploma of Excellence awarded by the International Dairy Show Association, Milwaukee, Wisconsin, to Jacob Erb, Monroe, Wisconsin, in official recognition of superior merit in drum swiss cheese as exhibited at the International Dairy Show held at Milwaukee, Wisconsin, October 22nd to 31st, 1912—Score 94.00." It was still in the original tube wrapper with its three two-cent stamps.

## LOOK, MOM, NO SCARS!
*Verna Maassen*

The greatness of the American pioneers, in their ability to accept and cope with emergencies, was often demonstrated in their use of common materials to save lives. In most communities there were women who could birth a baby and men who could set a broken bone. Their close contact with animals taught them simple methods of healing and of dealing with pain. To such neighbors I owe my life. The scene, of a day long ago, is indelibly etched into my memory.

This day I had slept past the time my older brothers and sisters readied themselves for school. Now I hurried to lace my high shoes. This was a hard job for my three-and-a-half-year-old fingers, but at last I ran into the kitchen.

The folks took one look and rebuttoned my dress, then noted that my shoes were on the wrong feet. "Change them," they said.

"They are not wrong," I protested. "I hid them the right way last night."

My folks laughed, "Guess Glenn found them again. You'll have to change them or they will hurt your feet."

I sat down next to the kitchen range and started the long, hard job over again. Dad left for outside. Mom started to make beds. I was alone with the ticking of the big wall clock and the crackling of the oak wood as the fire burned hotter.

The folks were cooking bran mash and water to coax a few more eggs before the hens went into a winter molt. The stove lid had been removed, and the mash, in an old three-legged kettle, was set directly on the fire. Hotter and hotter the fire burned. Faster and faster the mash bubbled like a small Yellowstone Park mud pot, until one large bubble burst forth with such force it dislodged the three-legged pot, which tipped sidewise, sending the boiling mass down over me.

My screams brought not only my folks but the neighbor, Mrs. Stevens, too. Dad grabbed me up, set me in his big rocking chair, and began pulling my clothes off. As he pulled off the long sleeve of my union suit a strip of cooked flesh tore loose and clung to the cloth.

Mom was on the phone calling Dr. Hess. He was fifteen miles away in the hills with his team. The heavy, early November snow made it impossible for a car to get through. He would not be able to come for hours.

Gently, Mrs. Stevens spoke. "We put poultices of honey and flour on my grandson when he spilled boiling gravy on his hand."

Dad's jaw was set as he said, "I'll get the honey!" He walked out of the door, putting his jacket on as he went toward the neighbors. Mom opened the tablecloth drawer so Mrs. Stevens could start ripping bandages, and then went into the bedroom for the big jar of Vaseline.

When a party line phone rang, everyone listened. It could be a fire or an accident. It could save a life and it certainly beat waiting for the weekly paper to get the news. Women who had listened soon entered the kitchen bearing white linen tablecloths for bandages, which they had tucked into freshly ironed pillowcases to keep them sterile. Efficiently they moved about, taking the teakettle from the stove to the washbasin to be sure that their hands were thoroughly clean, then refilling the kettle. Latecomers moved in, slipped a big jar of beans to bake in the oven, and set some unbaked bread to finish rising by the stove. The men outside as quickly set about cleaning barns and feeding the stock.

Dad returned and set the two half-gallon Ball jars of honey on the table. A bowl was scalded and dried to mix the honey and flour. The rolls of bandages were smeared with Vaseline to put against my burns. The honey and flour mixture was spread on the other side. More bandages were wound around to keep the poultice from oozing out.

The pain made me sick. People seemed to wobble and to float around the room. On the little shelf on the side of the big wall clock were medicines. No child would dare touch them! Camphorated oil for earache, peppermint for upset stomach, aconite for fever, and laudanum for pain. Dad put a drop or so of laudanum in a spoonful of sugar and told me to swallow it. The world slowly faded away.

The doctor's voice wakened me about eight o'clock that evening. "She would not be alive if that much burned area was left exposed." Carefully, he pulled the sheet over me. "You did just right," he added. "I'll be back." Like many another country doctor he quietly accepted the homemade remedy since his limited supplies were little better.

Silently, the neighbors left as my folks shook their hands and murmured thanks. My crib had only a six-inch rail and suddenly I was afraid of falling out. Mrs. Stevens said she would sit with me until midnight so my folks could sleep a few hours. For the next several weeks someone was with me day and night.

My brother, Glenn, who had changed my shoes from left to right, tried to make up for my getting burned. He read to me as soon as he had finished chores after school. But as days lengthened into weeks, the weeks to a month, his teen-age halo wore thin. He decided to teach me to read so he would be free to slide and skate with the others. By Christmas I could read the small stories in my books.

Because my fingers had been protected under my hands, they weren't bandaged and I could turn the pages.

The doctor came time and again to change bandages and check for infection. There wasn't a dry eye when they heard my screams from the excruciating pain. Neither were there many white linen tablecloths. Day after day neighbors and friends came with freshly sterilized cloths, bearing gifts of pies, cakes, jars of baked beans, homemade sausage, or soup. A few sacks of flour and jars of honey were also left. Somehow, it seemed, my older brothers and sisters ate far more honey on biscuits and pancakes than was used on my poultices. The neighbors would sit by my bed or wash clothes, mend, churn butter, or chop wood so my folks could rest.

As the healing progressed and the pain lessened, I remember events less vividly, but it was well into February when Dad carried me to the living room. There on the red plush couch with the raised head, I could look at pictures with the stereoscope. My favorite one showed a guardian angel hovering over a little girl in bed, just like me. I didn't know the little girl had died and the angel had come to take her.

More and more of the bandages were removed. Miraculously, there were no scars. Finally, one bright, cold March day I was allowed to get up. In the four and a half months my feet had grown so those pesky shoes would not go on. I padded around in my black cotton stockings. The next day as the doctor made his rounds, he stopped. Someone had sent me a brand new pair of shoes. Buttoned ones!

The kindness of the neighbors to our family over those long winter months was often talked about. This is the real strength of America, people caring for people.

## VIGNETTES: 1919 AND 1921
*Mary S. Bruce*

In the winter of the blissful fourth year of my life, 1919, it did not disturb me that influenza was sweeping the country and people were "dropping like flies," as Papa said. Mama rarely allowed me to play outside. When I did I had to wear cumbersome leggings, heavy galoshes with hard-to-clasp buckles, and scarves wound around my neck so that my mouth and nose were completely covered. I was not allowed to play with my friends on Lathrop Street in Madison, neither inside nor outside.

But I was not concerned. Schools were closed so my older brother, Gerald, and my sister, Madeline, could give me unusual attention. Madeline spent hours reading to me, playing make-believe, and helping me care for my family of twenty-one dolls and stuffed animals.

Almost simultaneously, Mama and Papa, my brother and sister, became desperately sick—too sick to move from their beds. They all had the flu! For ten days, I cared for them—alone. I answered the phone, answered the knock on the door, and made them toast and tea, which they were too sick to touch. Luckily, Papa had made me a crude little stool so I could reach the top of the stove. How I managed to make toast (in a tent-shaped holder placed directly over a gas burner) and boil water without burning myself, I'll never know. It was as though I had been inspired by this new role, given some innate knowledge I did not know I had.

I never worried about my family during those days. I was never lonely or afraid. I delighted in running up and down the stairs to wait on them, delighted in repeating phone messages. Much of my time was spent with Betsy, my most-loved doll. She had an exquisite china face (made

in Germany) and blue glass eyes that "listened" to and understood everything I said. "They'll all be well soon, you'll see," I reassured her. "Don't worry, Betsy." And she smiled, perpetually, showing her four tiny, perfect teeth.

Someone (I don't know who) tended the furnace, entering and leaving through the always-unlocked back door. The floor registers were havens of warmth, so Betsy and I played close to them. Friends came to the door, knocked, and handed me baskets of food. They held their scarves over their mouths with one hand, thrust the food toward me, and departed hastily. I was glutted with food. There was no one to say, "That's enough!" Betsy and I thrived.

Finally the wonderful day came when Mama, gaunt-eyed and thin, decided that everyone was well enough to be up, dressed, and downstairs. (Mama was like that.) She was appalled by the sight of wasted food and clutter of dishes. With the help of my equally pale and gaunt Papa, brother, and sister all was put to rights in a few hours.

That night, near my usual seven o'clock bedtime, I said to Mama, "I don't feel just right." She laid her smooth, cold hand on my forehead and said, "Oh, my!" I remember little of the next few days. I was put to bed in my parents' big bed, between icy sheets. Though I was twitching with fever and drifting in and out of delirium, I do remember the doctor coming in the middle of the night and saying, "Don't bite this thermometer, girlie!" Then he told Mama, "Verge of convulsions! Wrap her in cold, wet sheets."

During those hazy days, I dreamt about Uncle Roland (Mama's brother) who had died in a cold, muddy field in France. I cried for him. I made hideous rasping snorts just as Papa had done when he was sick—and which I had ignored.

One morning I awoke to bright sunlight and knew that I was almost well. Mama said, "You're going to be good as new." Madeline looked deep into my eyes and said, "Dearest little girl, you've come back to us." She assumed an almost-around-the-clock vigil at my bedside.

One lovely day, Betsy and I came downstairs together. Nothing had changed. My brother and sister took up their play-tease game of putting my stuffed monkey into my doll bed after I was asleep. In the morning I would apologize to Betsy and fling monkey *out*! My world was good again.

In the sixth year of my life, 1921, I became aware of people, places, and things with a clarity that surprises me now. It was as though, in that year, my mind let in the whole world.

We moved from Lathrop Street to Warren Avenue, a more densely populated area with stores only a block away. Mother frequently gave me a penny and I would run up the hill to the Piggily-Wiggily on the corner. Mr. O'Neil, the proprietor (with wax-twisted moustache, squinty eyes behind gold-rimmed glasses, and long white apron) knew what I wanted: a huge dill pickle. He lifted the wooden lid off the small barrel on the floor and with wooden tongs plucked out and held up one pickle after another. Finally, I shouted, "There! That's the one! Thank you, Mr. O'Neil." I walked home slowly, trying to make the luscious pickle last and last.

On one of those dill-pickle trips, I watched Mr. O'Neil's sons, Sam and Tom, unload a crate of bananas from a wagon. Tom unpried the top of the crate with a crowbar, and Sam lifted the three- or four-foot bunches from the straw and hung them on three huge hooks attached to chains hanging from the ceiling. When they had finished, I looked at the green bananas. I marveled at how tightly they were pressed against each other and wondered how huge the tree must have been to hold them.

From one of the bunches crawled a large, brown-furred creature. "Mr. O'Neil, come, look what came with the bananas," I cried. He came running, looked at the creature, scooped me in his arms, and deposited me on the sidewalk outside. "Don't you come back in the store till we've killed that thing," he shrieked. "That's a tarantula!" It looked like a furry spider, but spiders were part of our lives and nothing to be afraid of. From the doorway I watched Mr. O'Neil and the boys, each broom-equipped, chase the creature around the store until it was finally smashed.

Mama thought the incident "horrible." Papa laughed, "They are harmless. People just make up stories about tarantulas. Don't you ever be afraid again."

Next door lived three "old maids"—all very stout and rosy-cheeked—and their elderly father. They'd put their papa on the front porch, snugly wrapped, and go about their business. Their "business" was making pots, vases, and pencil holders out of a concretelike material slathered onto any tin can or jar they could scrounge and embedded with bright chips of broken glass, marbles, and shiny pennies. They made vases, too, by gluing triangular pieces of paper onto containers, outlining each piece with India ink, then shellacking the whole thing. I was entranced with their creations, brought them many pieces of colored glass and bright paper, and even sacrificed some of my marbles. They fed me cookies and gave me tea but never offered me one of their creations.

How they sustained themselves and their father with the twenty-five cents apiece they charged for their wares, I'll never know.

Oh, so many things happened on Warren Avenue!

One icy winter day we heard the clang-clang of the fire wagon and felt the shaking thunder of four sets of hooves. As they turned our corner, one of the stallions slipped and fell. The wagon came to a sliding, smashing halt on the curb. The three firemen jumped from the wagon, unhitched the fallen horse, and examined him. They talked, shook their heads sorrowfully, then nodded at one another. They had reached an agreement. While I watched from the window, one of the firemen shot the horse. "Mama, Mama," I screamed, "why did they do such an awful thing?" Mama explained that a horse could not sustain a broken leg, but there were tears in her eyes, too.

That year there were many small tornadoes. How often we all huddled together in the coal bin—praying—while the wind shook and rattled our little house. Strangely, that salmon-colored house remained untouched. It still is there today, dingy and decayed, but alive.

I took Betsy out of the storage room today. She is as beautiful as she was in 1919. The bright blue eyes and lovely smile captivated me and reassured me as they did during the years of my childhood.

# WHITE, GRAY, AND PURPLE-RIBBONED WREATHS
*Anne M. Dunst*

There was nothing macabre or even unusual about my going to "view the remains" that eventful day, for whenever I learned that someone of our community had passed away, I always paid my respects to the dead.

I was just past nine when I took to this seemingly unusual pastime. Most of the children in our section of the city, known as Little Italy, trooped in and out of homes where a white, gray, or purple-ribboned wreath silently proclaimed the loss of a loved one.

The white wreath was the saddest one. That was for a child. The gray was for a young adult, and the purple for the old.

It was amazing how quickly the word was spread from one child to another that a departed member of our community was lying in state. Our section was about seven square city blocks. Yet, in the space of a few hours, a stream of children could be seen coming out of the bereaved home.

We lived in an era when children made up most of their pastimes and entertainment. We were children of people who had less than those of most of the sections of our city. We played many of the usual children's games, but not in a well-equipped playground or on a pleasant green lawn. Our section with its houses with practically no space between them, in front or in back, rarely offered more than the busy streets and sidewalks to play in.

The boys managed to find a few spaces, here and there, where they could play ball. For the little girls like me, there could be no playing beyond one's doorstep. Sometimes I went down our own block to jump rope or play jacks, but that was a rare privilege. Usually, I was sewing or embroidering while hanging on to a toddling brother or sister in my care.

Well-disciplined little girls among our people were seldom seen playing, skating, climbing, or indulging in any game more strenuous than jumping rope or ball and jacks.

I remember vividly that hot July afternoon when my mother's Aunt Peppina stopped at our house on her way home after she had delivered a baby at a neighbor's home. She was one of the midwives who attended the women of our section. Naturally she knew more about the local happenings than my mother did.

I was all ears when Aunt Peppina stopped in for a visit with my mother, busying myself with some task that kept me within hearing distance. I took in the news Aunt Peppina's quavering voice related. Mother had just put the baby to bed for her afternoon nap.

"A terrible, terrible shock! That's what it is," Aunt Peppina repeated as she twiddled her thumbs in nervous excitement.

"That poor mother, losing her only daughter!" Mother sympathized with glistening eyes. She always cried when she heard sad news.

I listened carefully for more details and soon learned that a little girl just a year younger than I had died suddenly from a mysterious ailment.

"She was sick less than a week," Aunt Peppina told Mother.

Mother sighed deeply, then asked, "Will she be buried tomorrow?"

Aunt Peppina nodded, "Yes, at nine."

I made up my mind immediately. I would leave while Mother and Aunt Peppina were still talking. Mother would be too busy to raise any objections to my going out.

"I'm going outside for a while," I announced casually.

Mother nodded. Her attention was focused on Aunt Peppina and her news. Outside I noticed happily that my younger sister was playing house with her friend Angelina. My brothers had gone to play ball, taking our three-year-old brother with them. Everything seemed to be tailormade for my contemplated visit to the bereaved home.

The home I was going to was on our street but almost at the other end of it, some five blocks away. At that time, that short distance seemed very long to me, for I seldom went farther than two blocks away from home. The area I was going to was unfamiliar, as were many of the people who lived there.

I skipped along with measured step, as befit the occasion. My long braids bobbed up and down as my mind busied itself with the memories of similar excursions.

I remembered the tiny baby of a relative, Don Nicola, one of our most influential men, and the unfortunate, elderly man who was found murdered, the day before he was to return to his native land.

Most vividly, I remembered going to the home of a young unmarried man who had died in an accident. He was laid out in a room that was filled with flowers, candles, and people. I had been impressed by the numerous relatives, their copious weeping, and the loud blowing of their noses. Most impressive was the stricken mother who mourned her son with eerie wailing, passionate beating of her thin chest, and resounding bangs of her head as she hit it repeatedly on the wall behind her. As she wailed, she clawed at her face and pulled the hair that hung about her bent shoulders. Other relatives took up her wailing, and their loud laments filled the crowded room. Coughing and sneezing added to the blood-chilling sounds of mourning. Everyone had agreed that Donna Annuzza had properly mourned her son.

I arrived alone at the home of the dead little girl. Quietly, with properly subdued steps, I entered. The little girl's body lay in the front room, which had been stripped of all furnishings except for a number of chairs, holy pictures, family pictures, and calendars on the wall. Directly over the casket there was a picture of the Sacred Heart, with a sheaf of palms over it.

After a quick glance at the grieving people in the room, I gazed respectfully at the body of the little girl. I remembered her. She was a year behind me in school. Her hair was in two long braids and as dark as mine. Her small face had my pale olive coloring.

I knelt in front of the coffin and began to pray. I prayed for the young departed soul, and as I prayed, I could feel the warm tears welling in my eyes. I lifted my head and brushed away the tears.

Suddenly, the quiet wailing in the room was broken by a piercing shriek, "My daughter! That's my daughter!"

Startled, I turned, facing the bereaved mother. My knees shook, and I gasped in fright as the little girl's mother lunged toward me, her black shawl dropping unheeded to the floor, and her long hair hanging about her black-clad figure.

For a moment I froze. Then quickly I made a dash for the open door. As I rushed out, I could hear the commotion and the mother's agonized shriek. "My daughter! That's my daughter! Come back to me!"

I hurried home as fast as my legs could manage. My cheeks were blazing, and my breath quick and agitated. The loud thumping of my heart almost frightened me. I was home in a few minutes. Our second-floor flat looked heavenly to me. I slipped into our dining room unnoticed.

Mother was cooking. As casually as I could, I started setting the table, and gradually I felt better. Only the occasional loud thump of my heart gave me moments of troubled thoughts, as my mind persisted in returning to the experience and shock of that afternoon.

The following afternoon, Aunt Peppina stopped in again. She couldn't wait to settle her plump person in the chair Mother offered. "The strangest thing happened yesterday," her voice rushed on to relate. "Mrs. Brunetto, the mother of that little dead girl I told you about, had a terrible shock!"

"No!" Mother answered.

"A terrible shock!" Aunt Peppina repeated, her quavering voice rising.

I left the room, but remained within earshot. My cheeks flamed as I listened to Aunt Peppina's vivid account of the visit of a little girl who so resembled poor Mrs. Brunetto's dead daughter that it had given the broken-hearted mother a shock that had almost killed her, so Aunt Peppina claimed.

"Who in heaven's name could it be?" Mother asked.

I breathed easily when I heard Aunt Peppina reply, "Who knows!"

But I, who knew, never told anyone how a grief-stricken mother mistook me for her dead daughter.

White, gray, and purple-ribboned wreaths on doors, thereafter, lost all their attraction for me. It was a long, long time before I could view the remains of another departed neighbor, friend, or even a relative.

## THE BIG SAVE
### *Ann Baumgard*

There comes a time during everyone's life that fear for personal safety envelops him like a dark cloud. Then through that darkness comes a ray of light by way of a great trust in one who is considered a protector. Such a time came to me when I was very young, but that incident of many years ago remains indelible in my mind.

I was seven years old. Grandpa had recently passed away, and my Pa assumed full charge of Grandpa's farm. The old farm was run down. Repairs were needed everywhere. Hinges were loose, window glass in outbuildings needed replacing, fences needed fixing, paint was needed everywhere, rotted boards needed replacing.

It was mid July, a beautiful day, and Ma decided to let the baby ducks out of the coop to nibble grass and to paddle in the old dishpan full of water that sat near the old well by the house.

The afternoon passed, and in the evening Ma collected the ducklings in her ever-ready apron and took them back to their coop for the night.

As she took them out of her apron to put them back into their shelter, she counted them. There should have been nine.

Tenderly lifting them out of her apron, she counted in her soft, gentle voice, "One, two, three, four, five, six, seven, eight—eight—eight." She shook her apron, looked carefully on the ground, and began to search for the missing little one.

The whole family was enlisted in the search. We looked everywhere. We searched under burdocks, behind bushes, in the long grass—everywhere.

At length Ma said, "He'll come out when it's dark." I was delegated to watch and listen.

I sat outside on the bottom step of the kitchen stairs and listened and listened and listened. Then I heard it!

I followed the sound. Louder and louder it became as I approached the well. Then I heard it plainly. "Peep-peep!" The sound came from down inside the well!

"Ma! The baby duck's down in the well!"

Panic!

Ma called Pa and rescue efforts began. Pa examined the flooring over the well, and sure enough, there was a rotted-out hole as big as his hand.

Foolish little Peep had fallen through it and was bobbing like a cork in the standing water, deep down in the well.

Pa removed the entire well covering and looked down. Total darkness! Then he got a lantern from the barn, tied a rope to it, and let it down into the depth of blackness. Little Peep, evidently encouraged by the light, began a series of soft peep-peep-peeps, and seemed less frightened.

"Yup, he's down there," Pa said.

Now, what to do?

Ma held the lantern rope and Pa let down a small bucket. By shaking the rope, he hoped to tip the bucket enough to scoop up the little vagabond.

Failure. Ma was almost in tears.

Then Pa looked at me.

"If I let you down with a rope, do you think you could pick up that little feller?" Pa asked.

Torn between the loss of Little Peep and saying no to Pa, I hesitated but answered, "I guess so."

Then with all the ingenuity of a master craftsman, Pa fashioned a harnesslike contraption onto me. One strong rope was tied under my arms and another around the lower part of my body.

Pa made sure all was super-safe, and while Ma held the lantern rope, Pa let me down into the well. As I was let down, hanging like a four-legged animal, Ma recited the Hail Mary.

Everything looked blackish—the stones lining the wall, even the air itself. The darkness was broken only by the circle of light surrounding the lantern.

I tried to be brave—but, what if the rope should break or a knot come untied? I whimpered to myself, but then I remembered Pa was holding the rope. He would not fail me. He never did. Trust overcame fear.

I descended ever so slowly, and soon I could see the yellow fluff ball clearly.

"Come on," I said in my kindest tone. Little Peep made no effort to avoid me, so catching him was no problem.

I cradled the little fellow in my hands, gently but securely, and yelled, "I got him!"

Then slowly the whole contingent came up—petrified child, peeping duckling, glowing lantern.

As everything came into the all-safe area, Ma knelt down, made the sign of the cross, whispered, "Thank God," and then came and embraced husband, child, and duckling.

Pa covered the well promptly and securely and nailed the hole shut.

While Pa worked late into the night, Ma held the lantern. I slept safely in my bed. I dare say Little Peep, cuddling among his eight brothers and sisters, dreamed of his experience.

## SQUEEKY
### *Roderick MacDonald*

Squeeky was a little pig, a very little pig at first, but he grew fast and lively. He was what they call a runt, which is a little pig that is pushed aside at mealtime by the other, not so little, little pigs.

One morning when my sister Flora and I were milking the cows, she said, "We must do something about that little runt pig. I truly don't think he is getting anything to eat at all. Look at him—he can hardly walk." As she said this, she squirted some milk toward him, and he at once sat down on his haunches and drank, or rather gargled the milk, at the same time making a peculiar noise. It wasn't a grunt like the kind pigs usually make but more of a groan. We laughed at the way he drank the milk and the funny sound he made.

As he grew older he would come closer, and sometimes he would put his front feet on Flora's knee while she squirted milk into his mouth until he had his fill. Then he would wander away, making that noise, which sounded something like a bagpiper trying to get his pipes started. First a squeak, and then a heavy groan, lasting several seconds. He was the busiest animal on the farm and the most mischievous.

It wasn't long before he learned that one of the older cows would stand for his getting milk from her udder. After that he would follow her around as if she was his mother, that is, until she wandered off the farm and down the road a half mile or so, eating the tall grass that grew along the side, and got killed when she wandered onto a railroad track.

For a few mornings after this happened, he would watch the cowbarn door where she usually appeared, but he soon forgot, as there were altogether too many activities to keep him busy to remember his foster mother for very long. Soon after that he discovered he could, by watching closely, get into the milkhouse when the door was left open or not closed properly. So quite often that summer he would show up at our low dining room window, place his front feet on the ledge, and make one of those bagpipe noises, his whiskers and nose being covered with our best heavy cream. Then it would be Flora's and my task to chase him back to his pen. One of us couldn't do it alone for he could run like a deer. At such times, my father would say, "I don't like that pig's eating habits, and it seems to me he is getting rather big for a pet." This remark worried Flora and me, as we had come to like the little rascal, though not so little now. We doused him good with a pail of water when we got him into the pen. This he seemed to like. He kept making that crazy noise like a bagpipe all the time Flora was trying to clean him with the barn broom.

One day several of our family were admiring Fanny's new colt (Fanny was the pet of all our horses), a very beautiful colt, just able to get around on its shaky long legs and seemingly anxious to be petted by the womenfolk. We were all in the lane between the barn and our house and had just come out of a small potato patch where we had dug some early potatoes. The women were having fun making a fuss over the colt, and my father and I were feeding Fanny some new potatoes, which she seemed to like, when a row started right back of us in the potato patch.

Our dog Lad was a big, good-natured dog, but he liked to tease Squeeky. This time Squeeky didn't run as he generally did, however, but lunged at Lad, and Lad, completely surprised, jumped back barking sharply as he did, while Squeeky kept making that bagpipe noise and lunging at Lad. This went on for some time, then Squeeky slowly got to his feet and started for the barn, staggering sideways as he went, while Lad, never getting too close, kept on barking, with Squeeky not paying the least attention. It looked as if he had all he could do to make any headway.

My father, who had been watching all this, said, "I know what is wrong with that pig. I dumped a half barrel of hard cider in the corner of the potato patch, and that's where he has been busy the past hour. In addition to getting some small potatoes, he must have gotten a whole lot of hard cider. That pig is drunk." Now Squeeky was becoming a real problem, and Pa was taking a definite dislike to him. This worried Flora and me.

We had to put the hens' nests up high or he would eat the eggs. He was always hanging around the milkhouse. If an apple dropped from one of the many apple trees around our house, we would have to sprint to beat him to it. He always seemed to be right close by when one dropped. It took some swift kicks to break him from feeding from the udders of several of the cows, or rather, trying to, for the younger cows didn't want him near them.

We never did find out how he got up in the straw mow. We learned that he did, though, one afternoon when my father and I were cleaning some wheat. We had cleaned and swept a place on the barn floor, large enough to accommodate several hundred bushels which we planned to put into bags when we had it cleaned. I turned the crank on an old-fashioned fanning mill for several hours, until we had what looked like more than two hundred bushels in a big heap, when we heard that bagpipe noise, and down came Squeeky from the mow above, with about a half ton of straw and chaff, covering us, the fanning mill, and our newly cleaned wheat.

This put my father in a very bad mood. He grabbed a flail that was leaning against the wall nearby and raised it over his head for a good whack at Squeeky. But the loose end hit him a resounding blow on the back of his own head instead. This stopped him for a few seconds, and in the meantime Squeeky got away. Now it was plain to be seen that my father was fed up with Squeeky, but strange things can happen on a farm.

One day my oldest sister Christina, who was married and lived some distance away, was visiting us. With her was her little son, about a year and a half old. She and some neighbors were having a midday dinner with us. Her little son Lawrence was playing back of the house on a flagstone walk that ran from the house to the milkhouse. The grass was high on both sides of the walk, tall and heavy all the way to the milkhouse, a distance of about thirty feet. A little neighbor girl of about ten was supposed to be watching little Lawrence, but apparently she had gone chasing butterflies. We were just finishing our meal when we heard a scream from the back.

I was the first to reach the door and stood there for a moment, transfixed. There was Squeeky, standing over little Lawrence and chewing on a good-sized rattlesnake. Squeeky had the snake just back of its head, and its head was not more than six inches from the baby's head. While I stood there in a sort of trance for half a second, Squeeky moved away. I ran and picked up the baby. As I did I could see why the little fellow had screamed. Squeeky had been standing on his leg. All the folks were out of the house now. I gave the baby to Christina, and she ripped its clothes off to see if there were any marks of fangs, but the marks were those made by Squeeky when he stepped on the little fellow's leg, no others; the marks the pig made

hadn't broken the skin. Squeeky ran when I picked up little Lawrence. I guess he thought I might take the snake away from him. However, he didn't go far; he stood off a ways, chomping on his catch.

Our neighbor from across the road, Allen Whitney, said, "The snake was attracted by the milk house." We sold the farm not long after that. We were all terribly afraid of rattlers. Squeeky went with everything else. Flora and I felt pretty bad; in fact, so did all the family.

## SISTER FLORA AND ME

*We ran through green fields,*
*Tumbled high in the mow.*
*We romped with old Rover*
*And rode every cow.*
*Stole eggs from the chickens,*
*Climbed high the oak tree*
*While chasing a red squirrel,*
*Sister Flora and me.*

*We hid in the manger*
*So our mare Black Bess*
*Would nip at my britches*
*And nuzzle her dress.*
*We gathered wild flowers*
*Got stung by a bee*
*And cured it with blue clay*
*Sister Flora and me.*

*At the old swimmin' hole*
*We encountered a frog*
*Majestically seated*
*On a half submerged log.*
*He winked at us gravely,*
*Great round eyes had he;*
*And croaked a "good morning"*
*To Flora and me.*

*We corralled our stray sheep*
*In a stiff winter gale*
*As the wind stung our faces*
*With pellets of hail.*

*We forded a swift stream*
*That was swelled to its crest,*
*While she held a stray lamb*
*Leaning close to her breast.*

*Then in the warm sheepshed*
*All safe from the storm,*
*She fed it by bottle*
*Like a child newly born;*
*Then we bed them all down*
*Just as snug as could be*
*With great billows of straw,*
*Sister Flora and me.*

*To the old district school*
*We went each school day*
*With kids of our neighbors*
*Playing games all the way.*
*In summer we'd linger*
*'Neath a great apple tree*
*And eat harvest apples,*
*Sister Flora and me.*

*But now I have lost her,*
*The Flora I loved.*
*But I am sure*
*She's in heaven above.*
*And I hope and I pray*
*That together we'll be*
*In that happy place,*
*Sister Flora and me.*

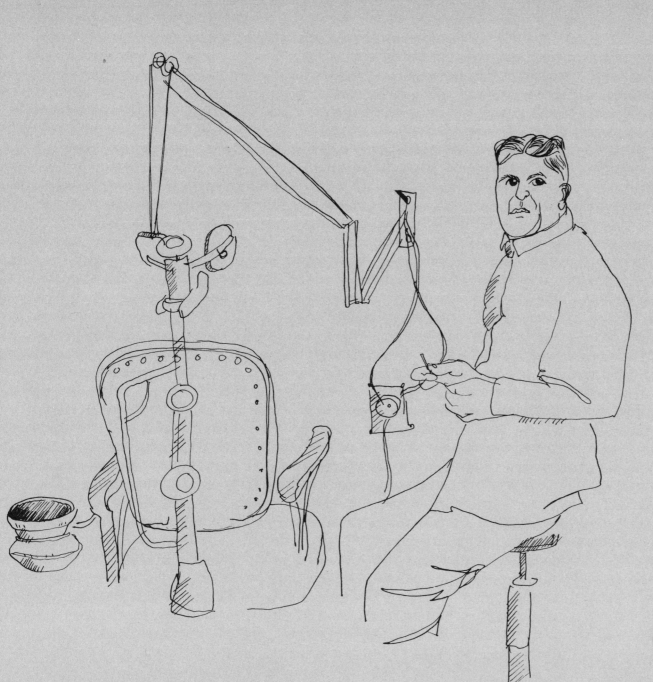

**6 Medicine**

# THE MISERIES
*Thelma Davies*

Do you remember, many years ago, that quite often in the winter months you would wake up some mornings with a runny and stopped-up nose, ears plugged so that when you talked it sounded like you were talking in a drum, throat sore and swollen shut, a raspy voice? You ached all over and you felt so miserable, you couldn't even be interested in getting up and playing?

I'm sure we've all experienced that feeling many times in the past. The wonderful part of it was that, when you were young, you had the comforting knowledge that your mother would soon be there with her expertise in bringing you out of your "miseries," and you *did* feel so miserable.

Around the turn of the century, the incomes for many small-time farmers averaged between three and four hundred dollars a year. Large families were very much in evidence then, often averaging from eight to twelve children per family—and ours was an average family. With that income, and that many people to care for, it is no small wonder that each family unit *had* to be as self-sufficient as possible, making do with what they had and improvising.

Diseases, plus the various childhood ailments, were very prevalent in those days, and many children died in infancy. For one thing, they didn't have our modern day miracle drugs. Sanitation facilities were very different from now, and people often just didn't know many of the basic rules of health.

Even today, much isn't really known about how to prevent and treat the "common cold." The medicine and methods used now help make the patient more comfortable until the cold finally wears itself out. The progress in medical care and diagnosis and treatment during the past fifty or more years has been fantastic; one just has to look about to realize that or visit a neighboring cemetery and see what the average life span of our earlier settlers was. The cost of this medical knowledge has risen just as much, and that factor alone would have been prohibitive in those years. They just had to be self-reliant.

Below are some of the home remedies that my parents used to treat the colds, croup, and sore throats that were so prevalent in pioneer families.

Winter colds and sore throats were very common. This recipe for a good cough syrup was taken from an old cookbook of my mother's (she had handwritten this remedy on the flyleaf): "Gather new tips of the pine tree branches. Cover these tips with cold water, bring to a boil, and cook till the water has partly evaporated. Then strain and add the juice of two or three lemons and sugar to make a syrup and cook until proper consistency. Put the above mixture in a bottle and add ten cents worth of menthol crystals; shake well to mix, and it is ready to use." I remember the cough medicine well, and it couldn't have tasted too bad or I would have remembered that. Whether it did the trick in curbing coughs, I don't remember.

Smartweed was also used for relief from colds. It was gathered just as it was coming into bloom, then spread on a screen or hung in small bunches to dry. After a small bunch of the blossoms was steeped for half an hour in water and strained, you had a redolent liquid to drink as a tea. Dosage was about one-half cup at a time if the cold was bad. Some of this brew could also be added to hot water to soak the feet in.

Another product of the day, Raleigh's Liniment (good

for man or beast), was a good remedy for colds. Take half a glass of hot water, add a little Raleigh's Liniment, a little sugar, and some milk. Drink this mixture as hot as possible and hop into bed. It really didn't taste so bad!

A combination of honey, melted butter, and a dash of black pepper was used as a cough medicine. Another cough medicine was made by boiling vinegar, butter, and sugar together long enough for the cooked mixture to form a hard ball when dropped into cold water. This product was then poured out onto a greased platter and, when cold, was broken up into small pieces to be held in the mouth to help relieve coughing—a forerunner of today's cough drop. We didn't have much candy in our house, so we thought this was a real good medicine.

The most popular sore throat treatment of the day was a bad one. The remedy was almost worse than the ailment, especially after the pork got cold and slipped from under the wrapping around your neck (which had to be a wool sock or piece of old wool underwear) and down onto your stomach! Strips of salt pork were saturated with turpentine, sprinkled with black pepper, then bound on the neck or used as a poultice on the chest.

Onions were used in many ways for treatment of colds and chest congestion and to relieve croup conditions. When onions were cut into slices and sprinkled with sugar, the syrup that formed was excellent for croup. The dosage: a teaspoonful every fifteen or twenty minutes until relief. Onions, boiled and mixed with flaxseed meal and a little vinegar, made an excellent poultice to relieve chest congestion or pneumonia.

An old, old remedy of my paternal grandmother was to roast whole onions, with the skins on, in the ashes in the front part of the firebox in the stove. She broke the onions open so the juice would run out and put them on the chest for croup.

In some parts of the British Isles, a raw onion is still considered a good defense against colds, and a sandwich consisting of bread, butter, and raw onion is not uncommon as a suppertime snack. Hurrah for the British—I think that is a good snack also!

These are some of my parents' old home remedies to help relieve their children of the cold "miseries"—take them or leave them. At least we credit these remedies, partly, for raising a growing family of young 'uns to maturity!

## WORMS BUT NO X-RAYS
### Cecelia Howe

Whatever became of stomach worms, a suspected childhood affliction in the early 1900s? In our neighborhood, no one ever reported seeing one, yet they were a good reliable ailment justifying a battery of home treatments. Mothers constantly scrutinized small faces for the basic symptom, a white ring around the mouth, accompanied by a glassy, feverish glow in the eyes. Or if you displayed feisty spirits or refused to eat those good-for-you vegetables, the treatment began. Out came a large bottle of Jaynes Tonic Vermifuge for a basic assault on the troublemakers.

Now this was a relatively expensive medication and therefore should have restored our energies in short order, but failing this, there was always a militant home remedy so revolting in taste that only the sturdiest worm could have survived it: turpentine and brown sugar. A teaspoonful of this corrosive mixture was gulped, to descend like an avalanche on the worms, done for, we hoped.

Our mothers exchanged preventive worm remedies in their over-the-fence morning visits, then tried them on us, just in case. Most despised was raw garlic buds eaten with dry bread just before bed. My sister and I always sat at our square, golden oak dining room table for this ritual, bread and garlic honored on a plate as though it were an enjoyable dessert. By chewing deliberately I soon discovered that Mother paid no attention to what was swallowed, so when her duties called her elsewhere, I slipped the garlic buds to a supporting board under the table top until I could inter them in our Round Oak Stover. Sometimes Mother would remark, "I think I smell garlic," but no reasonably aware six-year-old would extend that conversation. I fancied that the worms appreciated this delivery from doom.

Winter always brought severe throat infections with no doubts about their reality. In spite of long underwear, leggings buttoned above the knees, mufflers wound to cover noses up to the eyes for our two-block walk to school, we were tortured until May basket time with inflamed throats. Although we had five doctors in our population of twenty-five hundred, none suggested tonsillectomies, possibly because the nearest hospital was seventy-five miles away in Madison.

If we admitted to having sore throats in the first stage of infection, our mother drew dry sulphur through a small paper cone to hit the sore spot. Choking and coughing must have defeated the whole intent of this process to which we submitted without protest. Should your throat remain raspy, the red flannel and salt pork treatment took over. Always on hand was a roll of red flannel strips cut from worn, thin blankets or even Father's discarded red flannel underwear. A thin slice of pork was placed on the sore side of the throat, then the flannel bandage wound to hold it in place, to remain until blisters formed on our skin. This, it was assumed, indicated that the infection had "come out." In warmer weather a pungent ointment replaced the salt pork, but nothing could surpass the curative power of red flannel. Today's child will never experience this miraculous treatment, for who has any red flannel? Rolls of this secured by sturdy safety pins were the first things packed as we lined up our luggage for the annual summer trip to our grandmother's house in Illinois.

When bronchial congestion, known then as "croup," seemed to resist the red flannel and goose grease application, an odoriferous poultice of hot fried onions encased in cotton cloth warmed the chest and soothed us to sleep despite the fumes permeating our entire breathing apparatus.

Occasionally our symptoms baffled that astute diagnostician, our mother, and we visited our family doctor despite the extravagant office call fee of a dollar or at most two, depending on the seriousness of our ailments. Both awe and confidence welled as we climbed the long, steep flight leading to his office above the post office. At least our hearts had to be in good condition to withstand the effort.

Our doctor was considered excellent in the estimation of his patients, and his appearance reinforced confidence. He must have fancied the Kentucky colonel image to be the epitome of professional dignity, for he affected the pointed moustache and trim goatee of southern aristocracy and usually wore a black string tie arranged in a jaunty bow. His gray serge suits could never have been supplied by the local haberdashery, but access to Chicago was no problem in our town, with two trains going and coming each day.

Obeying the Walk In sign on the frosted-glass office door, we would find our respected physician sitting near the window in a battered swivel chair, his feet on another, deep in concentration over a bulky leather-bound volume entitled *Encyclopedia of Modern Medicine*. He didn't look up for a few minutes. If you sidled around a bit you could see the "dime novel" inside. Rumor had it that he favored westerns.

When he finally sensed our presence, he laid aside his research, pushed his gold-rimmed spectacles up on his nose, and greeted us, always by name. Compared with current annual physical check-up routines, the examination was cursory indeed. We just sat in a chair beside him while he took our temperature, counted pulse—always watching his elegant gold pocket watch—then scrutinized our eyes and recorded our answers to routine questions. Mother furnished replies to the more embarrassing inquiries.

Without any laboratory tests, x-rays, or blood count, the diagnosis in my case was probably "kidney complaint," and we left with the usual thick, yellowish medicine, so bitter that it seemed to curdle the water as the five-drops-in-water-after-meals were carefully measured out. Accompanying this medication was the advice to drink two quarts of water daily, and, to encourage this, Mother bought a shiny aluminum quart measure, just for me.

When we were ill we had the special privilege of sleeping with Mother in the downstairs guest room, which boasted a thick goose-feather bed, highly prized and cozy indeed. We couldn't watch TV in the evenings for it had not been invented, but we spent our time profitably doing homework or reading in the golden light from a kerosene lamp. What better time to follow doctor's orders than

during this concentration, so I consumed a quart of the prescription just before the eight o'clock bedtime.

During the night, Mother woke in damp confusion to the realization that she was not having "night sweats" and that her best feather bed might never qualify as an heirloom. Fortunately, innerspring mattresses were coming into use at this stage.

The really big showdown between professional and home remedies came about when compulsory small-pox vaccination was ordered. Doctors did not come to the schools for this first mass inoculation, so we had to climb the steps again for the traumatic ordeal. Instead of injecting the serum with one sharp needle prick, our doctor scratched a circular grille with a small knife, then daubed on whatever-it-was, and taped a celluloid cap over the wound. Plastics were unknown then (1908).

After about a week, my arm was inflamed to the elbow and proud flesh had formed where cap and skin met. Yet our doctor advised leaving it as he had taped it. No longer able to tolerate this ugly wound and fearing eventual amputation, Mother took charge by removing the cap and applying a poultice of sulphur and a patent medicine ointment. Now this heavy, pungent salve had become a cure-all for almost everything, from Grandma's rheumatic shoulder to our cow Goldie's sore teats, so naturally we credited it with saving my arm.

Medications were showing more sophistication as we matured: tincture of iron in solution dropped through a bent glass tube so it would not discolor our teeth; tincture of iodine consumed in the same way or painted on the outside of throats to avoid goitre. A variety of hot teas treated specific minor disorders. Chicken gizzard linings were dried and stored in an empty baking powder can ready for the next sign of nausea.

"Summer complaint" sickened most of our townspeople after every flood rampage of the Pecatonica River. This ordinarily sluggish little river wound a circuitous route around and through our town close enough to the city well to overflow in a vicious flood to contaminate the water supply at least once a year. We had great dosages of boiled milk to cure the dysentery, always part of the agony, but at our house we added mullein tea, which provided some curative agent, we hoped.

Spring usually brought relief from winter's coughs and colds, but it also required a series of tonics to restore lost vitality. Sulphur and black molasses was almost a confection when compared with the turpentine blend, and it seems to have been a national panacea. Spring housecleaning included our interiors as well, with the most revolting of all home medications: castor oil, a sickening horror that orange juice could only faintly disguise. Protest was useless, so we made a rite of taking it alone before a large colored print of St. Anthony, whose compassionate gaze assured us of at least heavenly rewards.

Somehow we survived these primitive dosages, all administered in our best interests, with loving intent. There were no antibiotics, no x-rays, no home-owned temperature thermometers, and, actually, I suspect, no worms.

## GRANDMA'S CURES
*Mrs. Walter Batzel*

Patent medicines and Grandma's home remedies touched the lives of many of us. I know they were a part of mine. Many of these same remedies are a part of my heritage and are used today.

I was skinny, not thin, when I was young. Grandma thought I would catch every bug that came along. To ward them off, I wore woolen vests she so lovingly knit; and long johns—how I hated them. As soon as I came to the corner of our block, I rolled the long johns up above my knees. I always had to remember to roll them back down again before I went home.

Grandma always seemed to know what to do when either my sister or I was ill. She pulled those cures out of her head as if by magic.

When we had infections around our fingernails, Grandma would soak a small piece of bread in cream (real cream), tie it on with a piece of cloth (no bandaid), and in the morning the soreness and inflammation were usually gone. If the remedy didn't cure the first time, we'd try it again. It was cheaper than paying a doctor's bill and much less trouble. In those days, just to get to the doctor was a chore, especially during the winter months or the spring's muddy season.

When winter came, Grandma was kept busy. If we came down with a chest cold, it meant one thing—Grandma got out the goose grease. She raised geese and provided customers with Thanksgiving goose or the proverbial Christmas goose, and we got goose grease. All the extra fat from the geese was melted, some saved for baking, some for Grandma's home remedies.

Goose grease mixed with lard made crisp, rich cookies

and kuchen. Goose grease and turpentine was another story. When the cold settled on our chest, Grandma brought out her goose grease and turpentine, warmed it, and greased our chest and back, then put on a soft, flannel cloth. How we hated that smell, but it seemed to do the job. As she greased our backs, Grandma would say, "The lungs are closer on the back." We always had to lie on our backs for at least half an hour until the grease had a chance to warm up and penetrate.

If we had a persistent hack or cough, we would get a small dose of melted goose grease with the admonition, "Let it go down slowly."

If we ran out of goose grease during the cold season, we suffered through mustard plasters. Grandma made a mixture of dry mustard and flour and added water to make a paste. She put this between two pieces of cloth, put another cloth on our chest or back, then applied the mustard plaster. She kept a close watch to see that we didn't get burned. As it was, our skin was fiery red and warm when she took the cloth off.

If one remedy didn't work, Grandma always had another one ready. If we coughed at night and kept the family awake, she'd be in to see us. She'd bring an ice-cold washcloth, wrap it around our neck, then pin on a turkish towel. The combination must have formed a steam—the cough subsided and we all slept.

"Get that cold away from the head." When Grandma said that, it meant one thing—a mustard footbath. We filled an old dishpan full of *hot* water, added about three tablespoons or more of dry mustard, and slowly inched our feet into the water. We kept them there as long as we could stand it. We had to come up for air once in a while. Our feet were red and crinkly, but oh, how relaxing it was. After Grandma rubbed the bottom of our feet with Vicks,

we put stockings on and went off to bed.

Grandma is ninety-six now and still has her mustard footbaths, and they work—I know.

Patent medicines as well as Grandma's cures were a part of our lives. Dad sold Kuriko, so we all took our daily allowance, but there was also a competitor, Alpenkrueter. One or the other seemed to be a staple in most homes, especially of farm families.

Your sore throat and the chicken's croup could use the same Red Liniment. A drop or two in water for a gargle for us, and a drop and more in the chickens' drinking water were both very effective. It could also be used as a rub to soothe tired and aching muscles.

Watkins Carbolic Salve was another standby. Grease the cows' chapped bags after milking, or use it on your infected or chapped fingers. It healed and softened—good for almost anything.

Some of Grandma's ingredients for her magic cures were raised in her own garden. She enjoyed the beauty of the herbs and flowers and later used them for her concoctions. An article in the December 27, 1900, issue of the *Weekly Chronicle* stated that drug bills would be reduced to the cost of items for soap and other small sundries, and good health would be promoted if people grew their own medicines.

Some of the suggested plants and herbs and their cures were:

The sweet-smelling verbena infusion (steeping in hot or cold liquid) is a cure for sore throat and will also prevent your hair from falling out.

Fennel, an herb used to flavor sauces and meats, makes a man strong, gives him courage, and adds a dozen years to his life.

If you are wanting in common sense, maidenhair fern

will give you some. As a tea it is a cold cure, and the tincture makes one's hair grow luxuriously.

The young shoots of blackberries will harden the gums. A decoction of the leaves is a cure for whooping cough. Blackberry jam is good for a sore throat.

If you cannot sleep, some of the powdered root of a cowslip will send you into the soundest slumber. Boil the roots in ale and your nerves will be strong and unwavering.

Grandma with her "cures," along with the old standby *Doctor Book for Man or Beast*, saved many a life. What else could they do? Her generation was a strong generation and made do with what they had.

## THE ASAFETIDA BAG
### *Pearl Axelsen*

It had been a long, hard winter, with much sickness. Every mother served as the family doctor and nurse, unless the sickness became too severe. Then they called upon the area doctor for help.

Mother, along with the other housewives, had her idea of what to do to prevent or cure any ailment. We were afraid to even cough or show a sign of a sniffle, because here would come Mother with her lighted lamp (she always kept one special lamp for that purpose, as the flannel made the chimney rough), a soft flannel, and the dreaded goose grease bottle. The flannel was warmed around the chimney before being placed on the well-greased chest. We always had a yell ready, whether the flannel was too hot, too cold, or comfortably warm, but nothing changed Mother's idea of the good it would do. I really believe she looked forward to Thanksgiving so she could refill the goose grease bottle, as we always had goose for Thanksgiving. Castor oil was another very important cure-all.

She had struggled so hard to keep us well all through the long winter. Spring was so close, when that terrible news spread through our little town that two cases of scarlet fever had been reported among the school children. In the early 1900s that was a very dreaded disease which usually took its toll in death or left the victims handicapped in some manner. During her early childhood Mother had experienced it with her younger brother, who had defective speech.

Then a very close friend came to her rescue. She was a practical nurse and, Mother thought, an authority on doctoring. She also had a daughter my age. One day she announced to Mother that she knew the perfect precaution to be taken against the disease, and she was using it for her daughter. Mother was elated. She immediately purchased some asafetida salve, which had the most potent odor I had or have ever smelled. This she placed in a small white sack, which we had to wear around our necks like a necklace.

When I was grown up, and medicines had replaced the old home remedies, I once asked Mother, "How could you possibly put that stinking thing around my neck? Do you actually believe it had any value?" She looked at me, calmly smiled, and said, "Well, you didn't get scarlet fever, did you?" That was her theory but mine was different. With that terrible-smelling bag about my neck, no one came close enough to give it to me.

# NO MIRACLE MEDICINES THEN
*Grace Dederich*

When I was a very young child, my home was a one-room log cabin where I lived with my parents and two older brothers and two older sisters. Later another sister and a brother were born. Later still, great tragedy came to our family, but I will tell of that in time.

Memory goes back to sleeping in the cradle at the foot of the big double bed and of trembling in fear in the night when the windstorms would rattle the doorknob. In my mind's eye I see still the room of that cabin with the stairs on one end that led up to the two-room loft. The small room under the stairs had a trapdoor that led to the cellar where provisions were stored. It was a game for me to lift the latch on that little door and crawl through the stair steps and out into the big room. One time I became wedged in—that ended that game!

When I was five years old my parents began building their new house. The first step was to add a parlor and a bedroom to the existing log cabin. Two years later the log house was torn away and the new kitchen was added to the parlor and bedroom and two new rooms were created upstairs. That summer my mother cooked in an open shanty under an apple tree in the front yard, the same apple tree in which bluebirds nested every year. We and the bluebirds shared the tree that summer.

Summer days were long and warm and filled with play—walking on stilts fashioned by an older brother until we walked them into a hornet's nest in the sand, my older sister standing in the creek catching fish with her hands, finding turtle eggs in the sand by the bridge and discovering that they had no shell but a very tough skin, catching turtles when fishing and being thankful that they always fell off the hook.

As clear in mind as if it were yesterday is the picture of my beautiful two-year-old brother Clemens, with his black curly hair and long black lashes fringing violet-blue eyes, holding in his hand a goose egg, the first he had ever seen. My sister Annie would cook him an egg every day, and he happened upon the large pan of goose eggs my mother was getting ready to set under the goose. Though thoroughly astonished at their size, Clemens had selected one, taken it to Annie, and said, "Cook this for me." I see her looking at him with such a fond, amused smile, this beloved little boy who was so shortly to leave us forever.

When I grew older, the happy, carefree days were limited. After rains when the ground was soft I was sent to pull yellow dock weeds in the field. My father took me out to a cornfield that was planted too thick to cultivate and showed me how to hoe there. Summer also found me herding cows for several hours in the morning and afternoon, as there had not been time to build a fence around the cornfield. Still we found time to pick wildflowers in the spring and hazelnuts, sacks full of them, in the fall. My brother would nail a cleat on the shed roof and we would spread them to dry. Strange that today any hazelnuts found seem to be wormy, but they never were then.

The new house was finished the year that I was seven. That fall my younger sister, Christina, started school. She was five years old, so pretty and fair with new red shoes.

That winter and the following spring the dreaded scarlet fever spread through the whole community. The teacher, Nellie Norton, would ask Billy Nachreiner how his little three-year-old sister was and he would reply, "Not so good." Later on she died. My older brother Joe went to what was called the German school and walked there with a neighbor boy. One day Joe came home and told my mother that Frank said that his sister had a fever. A few days after that Joe became ill. He had a headache and was very pale. He didn't want to stay in bed so my mother made up the rocking chair for him with quilts and pillows. The following Sunday both Christina and Clemens became very ill. Scarlet fever! Every family in the community had had it and, though last, we did not escape it either. Soon we were all sick with it, except for my oldest brother, Albert. The two little ones were so very sick. They would not eat a thing. My father would coax them with oranges, a delicacy then, brought out from Spring Green by Aunt Mary, but to no avail. Aunt Mary would come out with Dr. Mahoney, who was the doctor of our sick neighbors, and would stay until he went back. We also had the other doctor from Spring Green, Dr. Bozzard.

My little sister and brother became sick on a Sunday, and two weeks later on Sunday they both died, Christina in the forenoon and Clemens in the afternoon. My father had gone to Spring Green for the casket for Christina. When he came home Clemens was dead also. That was the only time in my life that I heard a man cry. My Uncle Chris came with the wagon and took them to the cemetery. They were not allowed to be taken to the church. We were the last family to have the disease but we had been quarantined! The quarantine placard was nailed to a tree near the road. I remember three neighbors coming and in grief and rage ripping the placard off the tree and tearing it into bits.

That was a very lonely summer for me, wandering around, going to the neighbors, the Trumpfs, who in kindness would give me rides on their horses, playing with their puppy.

I remember the tears the teacher shed for Christina that fall when we went back to school.

The next year I learned to play with my older brother.

# 7 Pranks & Accidents

# A "LIBBER" AT SEVEN
*Verna Maassen*

Women's Liberation has never gotten me too excited, probably because I have always felt that justice and equality are for everybody, white, black, yellow, or brown, girls and boys. I started my own "lib" movement when I was seven. Being the youngest in a family of two prissy teen-aged sisters and three self-centered brothers, I was forced at times to extreme measures just to hold my own.

The only waterhole deep enough in which to swim, during the parched heat of summer, was under the big bridge in front of our house. In cutoffs and t-shirts, we didn't care about swimming suits. My oldest stepbrother and other young men came home from the army that summer and weren't about to wear cutoffs. They swam in the nude. From then on, days as well as evenings, the swimming hole was off-limits to girls. When I complained, my stepmother's only reply was that a little "lady" wouldn't want to swim in cutoffs. I had to wade further downstream where some water had been left in small half-moon ponds, but it was only ankle deep. Then I saw the answer.

The next afternoon I did my chores of drying dishes while an older sister washed, and I gathered the morning eggs. Then I grabbed a pail and a long stick. Scurrying past the sheds, chicken house and barns, I scooted across a patch of pasture that was visible from the house and got out of sight behind a creek bank. The creek bed, between these remaining pools of water, was cracked and dried. Making their way laboriously over this rough terrain were dozens of desperate crabs. Gently I poked a crab with my stick. He angrily grabbed the stick with his claws, and I dropped him into the pail. The sun grew hotter and hotter, but so did my temper when I heard the squeals of delight from my brothers as they hit the cool water after coming in from the field between loads of hay. On and on I worked until the pail was nearly half-full and getting mighty heavy.

Knowing that I would be spotted if I carried the pail across the front yard, I stopped at the barn. The saddle for my horse was kept on the partition so I could slide the saddle on him by myself. As I rode him out of the barn I carefully held the pail low enough on his right side so it couldn't be seen from the house. After I crossed the bridge I turned my horse down into the road ditch behind four big cottonwoods. Dropping the reins, I let him graze while I carefully dismounted and slithered under the barbed-wire fence. The crabs, sensing water, slid quickly out of the pail. I mounted and headed west, away from the house, to drive the cows in for evening milking. Then an afterthought made me head my horse to a far corncrib and fill the pail with corncobs for starting fires. I needed to build goodwill.

The evening meal was finished and chores done. Horses were fed oats, curried, and turned out to pasture; cows were milked and put into their pasture. It was nearly dark before my grown cousin and two other young men arrived and with my three brothers headed for the swimming hole to skinny-dive under the bridge. I hurried through my bath, grabbed a book, and went up to bed.

Pandemonium broke loose when the boys stepped on the crabs and one after another of the crabs attached themselves to exposed flesh. One universal cry went up: "Verna!"

My dad went out to investigate. When he came back, he slowly climbed the stairs. I couldn't help but feel that he, a man with a strong sense of justice, was secretly delighted that I had settled the score myself without involving him.

My sisters had put my bed in an alcove formed by the adjoining closet. A bedstand and lamp were at one end of my bed, and a small dresser at the other. They had looped lace curtains across the opening. It may have been for beauty, but to me it was the "iron curtain" that said that the six-foot-by-seven-foot alcove was all they intended to give me in the sixteen-by-eighteen-foot bedroom. As Dad's footsteps approached the door, I let the book slide half open down the coverlet and closed my eyes, trying to appear as angelic as possible. I think the lace curtains helped, for he stood looking at me a long time, then blew out the lamp and went downstairs.

My stepmother was still angry, but I could hear Dad say, "She's sleeping like an angel. She couldn't have done it."

My only regret was that it was my cousin who had to have three crabs pried off, and not my oldest stepbrother. I had declared war against him, and even as I grew older, wiser, and more mellow, I always maintained a cool, polite relationship. I had made my stand for the principles of universal human rights that would continue throughout my life.

## A DAY I WOULD LIKE TO FORGET
### *Maria Moe*

Parents were grown-ups who lived in the same house that I did. They were a father and a mother. Father did not work like the other men on our street because he was a teacher and went to school. He always had to be dressed up, even on Saturdays.

Mother was home most of the time and wore everyday clothes and aprons because she was a housewife. That meant she did housework. But she did other things too, like bringing us up to be a credit to the family. She did this through discipline that brought punishment if we did not obey. Father taught very little discipline at home because he had enough problems at school. Under severe provocation, however, he did show us he was a man to be reckoned with.

This was my world as I knew it, and I accepted it as a matter of course.

I was generally alert enough to abide by existing rules so as not to provoke either parent, but the one time I did overstep I was to feel in full measure the impact of my father's hand. This was on an Independence Day, a day that supposedly guaranteed me, as well as all others, Life, Liberty, and the Pursuit of Happiness.

Our town made much of the Fourth of July. There were displays of banners and bunting; the band played and people sang; flags waved and decorations abounded. Invariably some high-powered speaker would eloquently proclaim the manifold virtues of our "four fathers" and their place in history.

One thing that had always puzzled me was the reference to only four. Why so few worthy of mention? On our street alone there were twice that many fathers and an equal number of mothers, but these were never mentioned.

All of this was to the good, but what I liked best about the Fourth were the firecrackers, the noisier the better. In our home their use was restricted. Each child was given a quarter to be spent on the afternoon of the third. Under no circumstances were these firecrackers to be fired near the house and definitely not under our parents' bedroom window.

I had the rules in mind when I went shopping the summer I was eight. I took my time about buying because a funny little thought kept nagging at me. Besides that, I had graduated from babystuff and now, being somewhat mature, had other ideas about celebrating.

The idea kept growing and growing.

This Fourth of July I wanted something special, dramatic, really spectacular. I examined everything on display, but nothing suited me.

There were the "penny-poppers," five strings for a nickel, which I had outgrown years before. The "penny-a-piecers" were somewhat on the same order, inclined to hiss and then give up. The "three-for-fives" were not too bad but definitely ordinary. The "five-centers" were nice and noisy but lasted so short a time. All in all I saw nothing I really wanted.

The clerk who waited on me began to show impatience and acted cross because I apparently could not make up my mind. I disliked him because he seemed sort of oily, and I had heard he had a reputation, whatever that was. Finally he asked me what I was looking for.

I told him I wanted something different, something that made a big noise. With that he left the room and returned with a big, fat article enclosed in frilly red paper.

"Now this is what you want," he said.

"Will it make a big noise?" I asked.

"Enough to wake the dead."

I had not planned to go that far, having a great respect for cemeteries, but my funny little idea kept nudging me and I was definitely weakening, especially when he asked, "How much money do you have?" I showed him what I had.

He smiled a little. "This beauty costs much more than you have, but if you really want to celebrate I will let you have it for a quarter."

The exchange was made and I brought the thing home without letting anyone know. Alone in my room, I did some thinking because there were scruples involved. But I was abiding by the rules. I was not going to encroach upon restricted areas, such as too close to the house or under my parents' bedroom window. Nothing had been said about——therefore this could not be counted as disobedience. Besides, it would be such a novel way of starting the day right. No waiting until after breakfast.

At the crack of dawn on that fateful morning I unwrapped my treasure, stole quietly down the stairs, lit the firecracker with a sliver of punk, and slid it cautiously under my parents' bed. Full of giggles I waited in the doorway to join in the general laughter sure to follow.

The ensuing explosion jerked our neighbors out of their sleep, blew out a window, tore plaster off a wall, wrecked the bed, and tossed parents and bedclothes onto the floor. My giggles died a sudden death. Horror stricken, I froze where I stood. Then something rose up from the welter on the floor and looked at me.

It was Father, but not the parent I knew.

He was dressed in a long nightshirt below which were a pair of very white legs, and these began to move in my direction.

Survival is a factor implanted within all of us, and I made the most of it. With a terrified scream I tore out of the house and down the street with Father close behind. Neighbors driven out of their homes by the blast were milling around in their yards. They gaped at the sight of a small girl being pursued by a nightshirt atop of a galloping pair of legs. Some stood stunned but others, sensing the truth, burst out into peals of laughter.

This was no laughing matter for me. Every time I glanced back those legs came nearer, and finally a strong arm reached out. I was firmly grasped, upended, and given the spanking of my life.

With no loss of dignity, utterly oblivious of attire or lack of it, head held high, and image of a scholar and a gentleman maintained, my father propelled me home, accompanied by the cheers of the thoroughly amused neighborhood.

I was immediately sent to my room to repent of my bad behavior. Through the open window came sounds of the celebration—exploding firecrackers, bits of laughter, the band playing the old familiar music, "Columbia, the *Jam* of the Ocean," and "*Bums* Bursting in Air." I could even hear the speaker, although faint and far away, eulogizing the same "four fathers" who had been honored as far back as I could remember. The same four this year as before. No new ones added.

The day dragged to its close. Toward evening I was allowed to come down to watch the fireworks but the magic had disappeared. As with salt that has lost its savor, so had the Fourth lost its appeal.

And it never was the same again.

## THE MOUSE HOLE
### *Lucille B. Engbretson*

There were six of us children, and with six children the disposal of all those baby teeth was a problem! We insisted on keeping them wrapped in tissue and safely stored in dresser drawers, pants pockets, and the fancy teapot that stood on the buffet. That was in the days before the tooth fairy. No, we did not have a friendly little elf to remove our treasured teeth, leaving a coin in return. We had a "mouse hole"! In reality it wasn't a mouse hole at all, but a "doorknob hole," a place in the wall of the front entrance hall where the lack of a doorstop had permitted the brass knob of the heavy outside door to punch a hole in the plaster, exposing and even breaking the lathe behind. It was discovered by our mother when we first rented the house.

Dad, a rural mail carrier, owned and used three driving horses. Each horse worked two days, then rested on the third. Every time we moved to another place, it was because Dad had found a better barn for his horses. It was warmer, it was just the right size, it had a better haymow, or it was closer to the post office! It didn't matter what the house was, the family could get along. But the horses were our lifeblood, so they had first priority. This house was big, cold, and drafty, with no furnace or plumbing, and came complete with our wonderful "mouse hole." A ritual was soon developed for the disposal of all teeth. We all gathered in the front hall while the lucky child dropped the tooth down the hole, saying, "Mousie, Mousie, bring me a new tooth." It worked very well. Sooner or later, sure enough, we got a new tooth!

One day in June Mom received a letter. Her two young lady cousins, Letti and Lulu, were coming to visit for a few days. We didn't have overnight guests very often. I guess it was too well known that Ed and Hulda had a bunch of imaginative children!

Excitement was high, and we were all enlisted to help give a good cleaning and dusting to all the rooms. It was summer and we were using all of the house, so we had plenty of room. The company would have one of the rooms upstairs where we children slept.

Finally the awaited day came, and the young ladies arrived. Oh, but they were pretty! What a flurry of plumes and ruffles, of ribbons and scents. They were so smiling and laughing, teasing and playing with us, reading us stories, and playing the piano and singing. Mother was happy and laughing too, and all dressed up, even if it was only Thursday!

Evening came and as we children prepared for bed, we could hear the girls in their room, laughing and talking, getting ready to go out for the evening.

We did not hear them come in, but it must have been late because in the morning, when we peeked into their room, they were fast asleep. Sis and I saw such beautiful brushes and combs and ribbons on the dresser! We tiptoed in for a better look. As we stood looking at the top of the dresser, there, among the combs and brushes, it lay. At first we thought it was a white marble. I reached out and touched it, it rolled a bit, and there it was, an eye, and looking right at us! Horrified, we backed quietly to the door. Stealing a look at the two heads on the pillows, we noticed that Letti and Lulu had their eyes closed and were sound asleep.

Closing the door softly, we went to our two "little brothers," who were just getting dressed. We told them what we had seen. Of course, they wouldn't believe us. We whispered that if they were very quiet we would show them that it was true. Once again we crept silently to the dresser, and sure enough, there it lay, a blue eye, looking at us! Shocked into silence, we crept back to our room.

In a whispered consultation Bob thought we ought to go tell Mom that either Letti or Lulu's eye had come out during the night. I didn't think it was a good idea. I knew we would be punished for entering their room as we did.

It was then that Bess solved the problem. "I know, when you are little, your teeth come out, and you get new ones. I suppose when you grow up, your eyes are the same. They come out and you get new ones, a different color or whatever you want!" Well, we three thought that she had solved the mystery.

We then decided the best thing that we could do was to get the eye and put it down the mouse hole. Wouldn't she be surprised to find that she had a new eye, and we had helped her get it so quickly!

Once again I entered the room, went to the dresser, and picked up the cold eye. Carefully we all four went down the stairs. At the bottom was the "mouse hole." Before I dropped it into the hole, I cautioned the other three who were gathered around not to tell anyone. It was to be a secret, and then, when the mouse brought Lulu (we had decided the eye was hers, she was our favorite) a new eye we would tell her how we had helped!

So, plunk, down the mouse hole it went! We were eating our breakfast when we heard the screams from upstairs. Following Mother, we all ran up to their room. We found "the girls" frantically dashing about. Lulu was crying, "Oh my eye, my eye, where is it? Children look under the bed. Look under the rug."

We got down on our knees and looked, but we knew it wasn't there. We stole furtive glances at one another.

Finally, "Oh, those horrid children. They took it. I

know they did. I knew we shouldn't have come. Oh, you little brat, what did you do with it?"

We fled downstairs, followed by Mother. Dad was found, and as we gathered around him, we explained how we had dropped the eye down the mouse hole, so the mouse would bring Lulu a new eye.

Mother went up to tell the girls, who soon descended with suitcases and coats and hats. Lulu was wearing a black patch over one eye, visible even if covered by the veil on her hat. They demanded that Dad take them to the train immediately. He obliged.

That was the end of visiting relatives, for many years to come. But after sixty years I can still see that eye, lying among the ribbons and brushes on the dresser top, looking right at me.


## ON ANY GIVEN DAY
## WHEN ONE IS SIX YEARS OLD
*Margaret Doner*

May I tell you about an unusual day in August 1913? I was six years old then. That day stays strong in my memory because often I have been reminded of it.

We lived in a big, white, square house that was built in 1901 from white pine timber purchased in Hermansville, Michigan. The house had been built seventeen years after my father, William Henry Van Zile, had married my mother, Fanny Elizabeth Stickney, in a ceremony on November 24, 1884, in the Town of Antigo, Langlade County. The house, for tax purposes, was described as being on Lot 1 and 2, Original Plat of Crandon.

The home was set back on a corner lot behind two hedges of purple lilacs. The lilacs had been planted to protect us from deep, powdery dust that drifted lazily upward and outward with each plop-plop of horses' hooves and the roll of the wheels they pulled.

My unusual day was a special day for Ma, too, because it was her turn to be hostess to the Woman's Christian Temperance Union. Ma always cleaned and baked the whole week before any kind of meeting, and believe you me, we kids had to toe the mark.

That morning I was sent down to the storm cellar, a small dug-out space off the main cellar, to get a jar of strawberries to be spooned over the homemade ice cream. I hated that place. I was afraid of it, but despite my crying a bit, I had to go. Ma's eyes told me. In my fright I would gather myself into myself and become the smallest human ever, then quietly creep into that place. I was so very sure a giant hand would seize me and I'd be dead on the spot. I always grabbed any jar that I could reach and race upstairs. I put the jar on the kitchen table and started for the door to try to escape before the hired girl would say, "She did it again!"

Ma was on tiptoe speaking into the box phone. Pa was calling from the post office to say that the iceman would be there soon and that Peg Leg, who drove the sprinkler, would do the roads before one o'clock and to quit worrying. I knew Pa didn't think watering the streets did much good because he always said Peg Leg's tobacco juice did a better job.

I had to spread newspapers from the back door to the icebox to catch the wet, sawdusty drips from the iceman's feet and the drips from the seventy-five-pound cake of ice. The iceman always wore a heavy rubber apron and huffed and puffed as he lifted the ice tongs high enough to get that cake of ice into the box without disturbing the cream on the pans of milk.

I scooted up to Wescott's corner to catch the iceman as he turned to go to Ritter's. We little kids always boosted one another up to get chips of ice. The iceman never hollered at us but would snap his whip when the big kids with ice picks would try to get larger chunks.

I was cleanly washed and neatly dressed when Peg Leg turned the water wagon down our street. I had to nod affirmatively again and again, saying, "Yes, Ma said I could ride." Sighing, which was more like grunting, he got down and lifted me up to the wide seat. He said I could ride one block and that was that. The water wagon was a fat-bellied tank that had to be filled often from the water tower close to the "Whiskey" Northern tracks. I hoped some day to be strong enough to push forward the wooden bar that released the valves and let the water cascade down in a wide, fine spray.

Ma told me to stay on the porch and watch for the ladies so I could open the door for them. Most of the ladies tripped lightly on the edge of lawns that framed the roadway. They kept their eyes downward, watching each step, often daintily raising their skirts to avoid dust or mud spatter.

Mrs. Beacon didn't trip lightly. She strode fiercely forward, head up, eyes straight ahead, as if she was forcing backward an enemy that only she could see. She prayed as forcibly, kneeling, arms braced upward on the seat of the rocking chair, pleading in rhythmic voice to save everyone from demon rum and to put poor Peg Leg back on the water wagon.

Women who had been seated comfortably suddenly became restless; heads once meekly bowed were raised; eyes tightly closed, opened; and peculiar looks skittered around the circle from lady to lady as I cried out, "Peg Leg is on the water wagon 'cause I rode with him today!"

Ma's eyes said, "That's enough!" I didn't know what I had done wrong but was glad to get outside when I heard the slap of reins and the soft metal music of harnesses. The big dray had stopped outside the lilacs. Big men, grinning broadly, were rolling two big barrels up on the porch. I was so glad to make amends that I hollered through the screen door, "Ma, Ma! Pa's beer from Milwaukee is here!"

## BRINGING IN THE BEES
*Marjorie Paulson*

In the early 1900s, the comforts of life had improved considerably over those of the pioneer and frontier days. Life was not so completely devoted to survival, and there was time now for relaxation, simple pleasures, humor, and laughter.

The innocent mischief we got into and the small adventures we undertook may seem mild and unsophisticated to the children of today. But if I could leave a legacy to these children it would be that they too would enjoy the freedom, the light hearts and high spirits, and the security of family affection we knew.

I would also have them know that any days can be the "good old days" if the echoes of yesterday's laughter still can be heard.

Instead of eleven children in our family, I suppose statistically there were a dozen. Richard and Robert were twins, but a sister was also half of a set. The other girl-child did not survive.

Our sister's name was Genevieve, but she answered to the name of Moe. Why she was called Moe I do not remember, except that it was short for Moses.

We lived on a farm in Rock County in southeastern Wisconsin where our father grew acres of the sweetest smelling red and white clover that ever filled a hayloft.

The neighbors raised bees.

For the use of our clover we were the recipients of jars of delectable honey. The handle of a wooden spoon would bend as one tried to ladle the heavy nectar onto a stack of golden buttermilk flapjacks.

Eight small-size, six giant-size, or four famished-size pancakes could be browned on the heavy, black cast iron griddle that covered two burners of the big wood-burning stove. The famished-size were the best sellers.

As fast as our mother could pour on the batter, a plate would be ready for her to slide another stack of pancakes on it. If the plate felt sticky to her touch, it was rejected and its owner made to wait until the others had at least one or two pancakes.

After finishing breakfast we were ordered to go outside and play. Our play did not consist of planned, organized activities to expend our youthful energies; we simply inhaled the joy of being young and being alive. We followed the mower trying to catch the fat, slippery frogs that had escaped the teeth of this dangerous farm implement. We picked buttercups to carry home and place in jelly jars to adorn the table.

We roamed the fields and woods. We dug holes at the base of trees and lilac bushes looking for buried treasure. We collected arrowheads on the west forty, a piece of ground that Blackhawk and his fleeing band had reputedly crossed on their way to Illinois. The Indian relics, like the pennies we briefly possessed, slipped through holes in torn pockets and soon were reclaimed by Mother Earth.

We did not know that there were such things as fence lines or boundaries separating farms, villages, and townships. We wandered as far as our sturdy, sun-tanned legs would take us. Thistles, nettles, rocks, broken glass, and rusty nails could do little damage to our calloused bare feet. Stubbed toes and lost toenails were commonplace and ignored.

There was nothing particularly different about the way we spent the day the incident of the bees occurred, except that near the close of the day, we found ourselves with nothing especially amusing to do.

From what sources we accumulated it, I cannot say, but we were storehouses of General Information. We could and did call on this vast reservoir of knowledge to settle disputes, prove a point, or come up with an answer for any problem. On this particular day the problem was boredom.

It was early twilight as we halfheartedly played Duck on the Rock, a game that usually degenerated into what would better have been called Duck the Rock.

The neighbors' bees were homeward bound. Idly we watched them wending their way back from a wearying day in the clover fields. One swarm made it safely across our backyard.

Suddenly a bit of General Information surfaced. "Hey! You know what? You can call in bees by pounding on tin cans and making a lot of noise." We were not a family unit made up of a lot of little units. We were an amalgamated mass with one mind.

Quickly we raced away to raid kitchen, woodshed, and milkhouse. Armed with pots, pans, and tin pails we proceeded to outdo ourselves in noise making. The Apaches could have taken lessons from us.

Bees belong to a highly developed society and are very intelligent. Maybe weariness was a factor, but one swarm of bees like Ulysses heeded the call of the Sirens. They swarmed disorganizedly overhead, confused and indecisive. Slowly they succumbed to the wild beat of the drums, and as if drawn by a magnet they came in for a landing.

But one thing we had not thought out was where they would land. The bees decided on Genevieve. This we had not anticipated but it certainly was making it more interesting and exciting. We increased the tempo.

Starting on top of her head, the bees began to settle down for the night, jostling one another to find a vacant spot. Our mother, long since inured to din, somehow detected a different ecstatic note to the racket.

Glancing out of the window, she appraised the situation instantly. She rushed from the house, untying her apron as she came. Offspring and tinware flew in her wake.

She had no idea which one of her brood was buried under the pyramid, but this was no time to take roll call. She was a small woman and could react with the speed of lightning. Without a thought of self-preservation she went to battle for her young. Flailing away with her apron she attacked the bees, issuing orders as she gave battle. "Go to the garden and get dirt. Somebody get water!"

Previous experience had taught us that when Mother got into the act, it was time to move. Retrieving our strewn buckets, we flew to do her bidding. Even the bees knew they had met their match. Like us they took off.

As fast as we could mix the water and dirt, Mother slapped mud on our sister until she was encased like a mummy in a mud cast. Slowly she was propelled toward the house, the rest of us following and dipping into our buckets to apply fresh mud whenever a piece fell off.

For those whose knowledge of bees is limited, bee venom is the same as the venom of a deadly snake. A single bee sting can send some unfortunate persons into shock and prove fatal within a matter of minutes, although most people can tolerate one or two bee stings, suffering only brief pain and discomfort. But the accumulated venom from a swarm of bees expecting a hospitable reception and then finding themselves the victims of the old Trojan horse trick is something else. Angered, they decided to retaliate before being completely decimated. We knew the bees had suffered considerable casualties; our own were as yet unknown. There could be more than the very real and possible one. If the rest of us did not expire from temporary remorse and fright, we were likely to perish from maternal justice.

The minutes dragged on. After what seemed a lifetime of anxiety, the mud began to cake and fall off. The unveiling was underway. The awful feeling of doom was easing. Our sister was still on her feet.

With eyes puffed shut and lips swollen several times their normal size, she resembled a picture of a Ubangi native we had seen in a *National Geographic* magazine. The rest of her was sort of disappointing. She looked no worse than if she was suffering from a combined case of hives and scarletina.

We had done it again! Our invulnerability to the woes that befall mankind was still working for us. We had made it through another day and there were still eleven of us. A delicious sense of well-being permeated the evening air. It had been a satisfying day!

We had accomplished what we had set out to do. We had brought in the bees. Our ever-reliable Mother had routed them. Even the bees had profited—they had learned a lesson: never to swerve from a prearranged flight pattern. The bumps would disappear and the red color would fade from our sister's torso. Her face would return to normal.

Yes, indeed, it had been a satisfying day!

Life was good and rich, and sweet with a taste of honey.


## THE MOONLIGHT COVER-UP
### Clara Erb Cline

When I was an eleven-year-old child and living on a farm just east of Mt. Vernon in Dane County, something happened that I never forgot. It was in the summer after the First World War ended.

In those days a farm child was expected to help with whatever he or she could besides having regular chores, such as carrying in wood, getting the water for the house, and gathering the eggs. These jobs were most necessary and we seldom got out of doing them. But there were always other jobs. Mine was to divide the chickens evenly among the coops before dark.

Mother always raised a flock of chickens. This year she had over two hundred young ones. They were not just plain chickens but Rhode Island Reds, in her opinion the prettiest and the best kind.

She started early in spring by sending away for especially fine roosters. These she put with the reddest and healthiest-looking hens from her flock in a small shed by themselves. She picked only the best-formed eggs they laid for hatching, kept them in the pantry, and turned them every day. When she had a setting of fourteen, she set them under a broody hen. This year she had about sixteen hens setting on eggs.

It had been a poor year for hay and in spring the barn loft was empty, so in early May, Mother seized the opportunity to put her brooding hens up there. My father sputtered about this. He didn't like his cow territory taken over by a "bunch of lousy, broody old hens."

Mother went to the barn loft every day and took the hens from their nests for twenty minutes so they could eat and drink and stretch themselves. Some of these hens would peck wickedly when you lifted them off their nests and I was afraid of them. Some would "purr" good-naturedly and a few would come flying off the nests, making a squawking noise. Many went back to their nests by themselves. Some had to be chased and caught, and that kind would stand instead of settling down on the eggs. At this point Mother usually would say, "You finish up here while I go and start supper." I would wonder why my sister always got the easy jobs, like throwing down the silage and putting the cows in their stanchions while I had to do this.

When the eggs hatched Mother would take the fluffy little chickens lovingly in her apron to the kitchen for a few days. They got only water at first, then feed from the store, and after that home-baked bread soaked in milk and squeezed out very dry. This gave them the headstart that amazed and puzzled the neighbors. On a sunny day she put them with the setting hens, twenty to a hen, in little coops near the house.

Mother hens had to be cooped up because if left free to roam they would lead the chicks through cold, wet morning dew or take them into tall weeds and lose them or else wander off with them to where foxes and skunks lurked. They had good intentions for their young but not much sense.

The mother hens, or "Clucks," as we called them, could put only their heads through the slats in the coops, but the chicks could go in and come out at will. They "clucked" continuously and at feeding time would make a calling sound at which the chicks would come running to eat. When a chicken hawk soared above, the Clucks would make long, eery, soft trills and then the chicks would rush to the coops or flatten themselves close to the ground.

In the evening when it became cool all the chickens would crowd into just a few coops and then the ones that were in the back of the coops would be pushed and squeezed and would suffocate from lack of air and space and in the morning would be found dead there.

Dividing the chicks was an important job. Much of the feed was purchased and was expensive, and the loss of too many chickens meant that the project might end up in a financial failure. But one night I forgot to divide the chickens.

About twelve o'clock midnight, I was awakened by the dog's barking and suddenly I thought of the chickens. I woke my sister and told her, and together we crept down the stairs in our nightgowns and with bare feet went outside through the wet grass, hushing Shep, and with thumping hearts looked under the coops.

Sure enough, most of those now half-grown chickens had squeezed into only five coops and forty of them were dead. What to do? What would Mama say when she saw all those dead chickens? Should we bury them? We couldn't find the shovel. Should we put them behind the barn? Papa would find them there. My sister had an idea: take them up to the woods. We divided the chickens that were still alive and then put all the dead chickens into a bushel basket we found in the woodshed and started for the woods.

The basket was heavy and we had to stop many times to rest. A cow mooed in the distance, the neighbor's dog barked, a rabbit darted suddenly out of the tall grass ahead of us. It was uphill and the rough weeds along the fence scratched our legs and tore at our nightgowns. Finally we came to the woods and a place where there was a ditch full of last year's old leaves.

We covered the chickens with those old leaves, returned home, put the basket back, and silently went up the stairs and to bed with our scratched legs and wet nightgown hems. We felt lucky that Shep had kept quiet and that there had been moonlight.

The next morning I stayed near Mama when she was feeding the young chickens to see if she would notice anything different. "It seems to me there are not as many chickens here as there ought to be," she said in a perplexed-sounding voice, holding her head to one side and trying to count the lively young things. I kept as still as a mouse and slipped off behind the woodshed before she might happen to look at me and read the expression on my face.

I worried about this for weeks, but she never found out until many years later, when neither one of us had any chickens anymore, young or old. When I told her the whole story she just said, "Well, for goodness sake!"

## THE MURDER OF ELEANOR: A STORY TO MELT YOUR HEART
*Wanda Aukofer*

A beautiful mannequin adorned a purple velvet table in the millinery department of our dry goods store. She had a head and torso to the hips, no limbs. The contours of her body were perfect.

She was lovely. She had waist-length, blonde human hair that Mother would comb into a bun on the back of her slender neck or braid around her head or fix in a Gibson Girl style, which was popular at the time. She had arched, dark brown lashes and deep blue eyes that through the lashes were shining, glowing, and coquettish. Her cheeks, rounded and in perfect proportion to her face, had a faint blush. I loved her straight but dainty nose. Her well-formed mouth and lips had a hint of a smile. Her chin had a tiny cleft of a dimple.

Any hat placed on her head, whether a demure black sailor hat, a feathered, outlandish pillbox, or a flowered straw with roses and a bird, suited her as though her features changed with each style. It was not unusual at times for customers to speak to her and sheepishly turn away, she looked so human. Not only the customers but I myself felt she was human.

On a hot Monday morning I was told to mind the store and turn down the awning so Mother could hang out the wash. The store would be deserted, as Monday was the customary washday in those days. The store was cool and I headed for my lovely mannequin, whom I had secretly named Eleanor. When I was with her, all else was forgotten. She had been on that table all summer, and I felt sorry for her. I would give Eleanor a change and surprise Mother by fixing the window display and putting her in it, as I had seen Mother do many times before.

Starting on her hair, I got the curling iron and made long curls all over her head. They hung to her shoulders. Then I selected a large-brimmed, lacy, natural straw hat and trimmed it with a bunch of luscious red cherries that tipped the brim over her left eye. I added gay red and blue ribbons and pink netting on the crown. To clothe her body, I draped her in blue lace with a multi-colored, sparkling, peacock rhinestone pin at the low neckline. She looked gorgeous.

I carefully carried Eleanor in all her finery to the window. When I opened the door to the window to get out the old display, it was like a hot oven, with the sun beating on the glass. Carefully I placed her in the large window. The sun shone through the latticework of her hat, making a pattern on her face. I trimmed the rest of the space with King Tut chains, bracelets, scarves, gloves, beaded bags, and flowered summer hats on pedestals. I closed the door, feeling smug about my professional piece of work.

About three hours later Mother came into the store and I proudly told her what I had done.

"Did you put the awning down?" she asked.

I said, "Ma, I forgot."

Shrieking, she raced to the window and opened the door. The heat was like a hot blast out of a furnace. She removed Eleanor, her hands sticky and dripping.

I couldn't believe what I saw. The right side of Eleanor's face was stuck with pale gold curls and had sunk into her shoulder. Her neck had disappeared. The hat was askew with the lacy brim resting on her curls. Her eyebrows and lashes stuck into her once-rounded cheeks like fuzzy caterpillars, and the nose rested where her chin had been. The cherries from the hat had sunk to her chin and mouth; the red dye, like droplets of cherry juice on her neck and chest on the blue lace, stuck to her distorted body. The drops resembled human blood. If she were human, as I imagined, her wounds would have been bleeding.

Tears were streaming down my cheeks as Mother scolded me severely.

"But why?" I asked. "Why didn't this happen when you put her in the window?"

Her eyes softened and she replied.

"Because I only put her there in the wintertime. And it wouldn't have happened if you had put the awning down. We could have saved her."

"Why?" I asked again.

"Touch her," she said.

Reluctantly I put out my hand to touch the once-beautiful mannequin. Then I understood. My hands were full of melted, flesh-colored, red-stained, dripping, sticky wax. Eleanor was no more.

In my nightmares after that I would dream I had killed Eleanor.

8 Transportation

# RIDES I REMEMBER
*Blanche B. Lindblad*

"Time flies!" the folks would say. And now, with the allotted three score and ten at hand, I view time as motion, movement. Things making up life become doubly clear when one is transported from era to era—a progress of flight, rides from the old to the new and back again.

Perhaps my earliest rides were in a wicker buggy, bouncing on a buttoned shoe, or shaking on Ma's knee as she fed me mashed potato from her plate.

Better remembered are childhood train trips from Sanborn to Superior, Wisconsin, where Ma shopped at Lightbody Wingate's for silk dresses and picture hats. I would sit stiffly on the DSS&A passenger train, listening to the patterned rumble of wheels beneath, watching the countryside run by. The sleepers charmed me—the polite porter, the mirrorlike wood shining above, following my bed tricks.

There were the usual delights, like soaring into the blue on a board swing, "the pleasantest thing, ever a child could do." And the lawn swing went high, groaning; the seesaw at school had a wonderful bump as it hit the ground. ("I dare you!" and "Fraidy cat," were favorite barbs.) There was the slicky-slide we made by throwing water up the high, muddy riverbank. We'd puff up to the top, then shoot downward, hurting our backs. And oh, across the same Marengo River was *the swinging bridge!* Memory prodded me to write a poem about the bridge in later years. The middle verse runs like this:

*The heave and the sway, and the glorious riding*
*Above an angry stream with its rock and its whirl;*
*Our steps so uncertain, the river bank distant—*
*What venture, and adventure, for each little girl!*

Ma would caution, "Girls, *be careful*," which meant little to us. I recall being thrown from a Shetland pony the Werders owned. (I was safer on a draft horse, my legs straight out because of its girth.) Catching sleighs was forbidden joy, and we'd chase the heavy wood vehicles, with their two sets of runners. Sometimes the sleighs carried hardwood for customers or logs from a lumber camp. Mostly they belonged to farmers coming to the village for supplies from the two general stores, Engleking's and Lampson's.

I used skis some, but sliding lickety-cut downhill on a dark, cold night was more challenging. More romantic was skimming over the frozen millpond. ("Wait, girls, until your father tests the ice," Ma would say.) In my early teens, roller skating to a sweet waltz was the *ultimate*; we didn't mind the choking dust, the garish gasoline light. What riding!

A privileged place was one in the train caboose or the train cab. Another was one on the section car, its tired men hand-pumping us along the rails, pick and shovel aboard. The horse-drawn buggy also fascinated us. I can see the Fullers—he a minister, she a teacher—sitting erect and proper as they rode through the town. In those days, an agony of fear would grip me as we traveled down or up White River's slippery hill on our way to Ashland, horses straining. Dr. Andrus or Hertzman came to the country by horse and cutter from Ashland's livery stable, making new paths around the heavy snowdrifts in order to minister to the sick. This was heroism!

Hayrides, underneath comforters with hot bricks, stars above, were great fun. In the summer we'd ride to the fields on the flat racks, then return perched on a full load of hay. (Taking the monorail or swinging in a cable bucket over Disney World have proved no more enjoyable!

Nor have Chicago's subway and elevated trains.)

Motorcycles had their day, as time sped on. As a young girl, I'd attend the hill climbs. Once, driving down Sweden Avenue, our motorcycle arrowed between two galloping horses as they crossed! I remember how in a sidecar I went through parts of Michigan and Wisconsin— a three-day ride. And I remember how motorcycles with winter runners came to my rescue. There was the journey to a dentist in Ashland. There was the trip to my first teaching position at Provost School, when weather forbade the lengthy walk, and the trip from Glidden to Shanagolden. (That winter, a half-century ago, I'd first take the Soo Line's early Monday train to Glidden.)

I graduated from Ashland County Normal in 1924. To get there I would sometimes take the train from Sanborn to Bibon, there to wait for the Ashland train. Working for room and board, occasionally I would see a silent movie for diversion, with Garbo, Clara Bow, others. Afterward, with a companion, I'd enjoy a hot sandwich from Dolph's cart in the chilly night, then catch the streetcar home. The streetcar traversed Ashland's main thoroughfare and reversed operations at the end of the line. The motorman would get out, pull the trolley rope, take his handle, and open the back door. Fare was ten cents.

No mode of transportation altered my life more than the "Flivver." Pa tried one out, ran in the ditch near White River, and bought the car! (Those side curtains that buttoned on were nifty, I thought.) My rides with Pa bring a smile, *now*! After his depot day he'd hurry to his wild eighty, and I was "chosen" to accompany him. He'd say, "Bunny, hold this dynamite out *far* through the window," and away we'd go, over the rutty road! We'd go to the Delta country for berries, Pa driving off in the brush and felling small trees. I recall the boulders on one sandy road,

Pa proceeding with vigor, the potato salad with fried chicken on top making a high flop to the floor. A hill beyond Mellen presented problems too, in the spring, as I drove the Model T to Gordon Lake. But the car was a miracle—and so much more the modern cars with their comfort, speed, and air conditioners. (Without these I'd never have seen the green gumdrop hills of New Hampshire, historical Cape Cod, a sunset over the Gulf of Mexico. Nor could I have climbed to Buffalo Bill's grave in Colorado. Sightseeing cars at Niagara Falls, Florida "limos" wouldn't have been mine, nor elevators, escalators . . .)

Ma took me on my first ferry boat experience to St. Ignace to cross the Straits of Mackinac. As a young lady, I first rode around Lake Superior — "Gitche Gumee" land — to Bayfield for a ferry ride to Madeline Island. The steam-driven ferries operated among the Apostle Islands, rich in Indian lore, fur trading, and missionary history. A piano was aboard, and the passengers sang together. With the years came a ferry ride across Lake Michigan to Manitowoc, a trip on a bike-beleaguered ferry from Woods Hole to Martha's Vineyard. Rowboats come to mind and fishing trips on Lake Owen, with pancake breakfasts in the woods; a battle with the waves of treacherous Lake Namekagon is relived. Motor boats and marinas came into being. Tours, cruises . . . Knowledge, experience, maturity . . . A shrinking world . . .

I was grown before taking a bus anywhere, and my first plane ride was to Denver in 1947. Bus, plane — each vehicle changed and ordered life in a specific way. Across Florida, past fields of sugar cane and cabbage palms — who *wouldn't* remember? The small shuttle buses, the Greyhound to Key West, and laying my hand on Hemingway's writing table — who could forget! Riding grandly above the clouds from O'Hare and other airports meant being near loved ones, new friends, horizons. Travel was the Bad Lands, *The Sound of Music* at Minneapolis. It was Estes Park and the Passion Play and Canada and history and adventure! (I was there!)

Looking back, I repeat with the old folks, "Time flies!" An era passes; another rushes on. Seeing this flight, experiencing it in rides I remember — moving backward and forward — from the turn of the century, I can say, "It is good, this motion and change!" (An old swinging bridge still lifts me, a whistling train bears me on. I skim over the pond, ride too fast, and court danger anew. "I dare you!" and "Fraidy-cat" still needle me, with Ma saying, "Be careful.") And I still want to move on and up and away.

I ask of flying time: "What next?"


## PADDLE WHEELS ON THE MISSISSIPPI
### *Laura M. Hansen*

One of the pleasures of living in a small, lazy river town on the Mississippi was watching the boats pass and occasionally land at the levee. My home was two blocks from the river and near the levee.

One hot summer day in the year 1906 we heard the low whistle of a paddle wheel packet that echoed through the humid valley. Two long and two short meant that it would land. "Mama, may we go down to the levee?" With permission, my sister and I fairly flew. There was a row of weather-beaten warehouses across the railroad tracks, and we stood near the riverbank and watched the boat land. The levee was located directly in front of the Denniston House at Cassville, which was built in 1836 for the purpose of housing the first capitol of Wisconsin. It was a hotel in 1906.

There on the deck of the arriving boat stood a very large, strong Negro holding a big rope. The other end was wound on a horizontal windlass on the deck. As the gangplank was lowered, he jumped off and ran to a large iron ring embedded in a huge rock and tied the rope firmly.

Along the lower deck of the boat were many Negroes lined up with pieces of freight on their shoulders, sacks of flour, boxes of dried fruit, and canned goods.

One by one they loped down the gangplank and up the shore to the warehouse where they deposited their packages and went back for more. Thus the boat was unloaded. It was then untied, the paddle wheel reversed, and went forward up the river to the next town.

My friend's home was near the levee. The back yard extended to the river where an old flat-bottom boat was usually tied. We sat in it pretending to be traveling. We were not allowed to swim or even wade in the river. When we gazed at the river, it appeared to be peacefully rolling along, but it was actually very treacherous and fickle. Its swift current caused many potholes to develop suddenly. A child could easily be carried away by the current. Therefore we were content to sit and watch the boats pass. There were long barges pushed by smaller boats loaded with coal, lumber, and rafts of logs. The crews always lived on the boats and included a white-clad cook who waved at us as the boats passed by.

My girlfriend's father, who was a Civil War veteran, had a small scow that was used for clamming. The scow held a rack, from which dangled many chains and hooks, that was thrown overboard to drag the river bottom. The clams it collected were boiled on the shore and opened by hand to search for pearls. If alive, they were hard to open.

Occasionally valuable pearls were found and sold for as much as $150 to $1,500. The shells were sold to the button factory nearby. I still remember the large piles of discarded shells perforated by button-size holes.

One day posters announced the coming of the showboat, *Frenches News Sensation.* Our feet fairly danced as we heard the soft musical notes of the steam calliope coming down the river and echoing through the hills. Again we went to watch it land. A band of musicians came off the boat and marched through the streets of town playing popular tunes.

We boarded the boat in the afternoon. Near the front entrance to the left were several bedrooms with beautiful furniture and rugs. The full-length screen doors were locked, but we looked in and assumed that actors and actresses slept there. There was a large auditorium and stage.

In the evening, dressed in our best, we attended the show. The play was *East Lynne,* and the story was very dramatic and sad. At the climax soft violin music was played and everyone took their handkerchiefs out and wiped their eyes, still dabbing them when going down the gangplank. People remarked, "Wasn't that a wonderful show?" *Uncle Tom's Cabin* was another drama sometimes played.

Later, about the year 1915, the *Eclipse* scheduled a daily trip from the upper-river towns to Dubuque, Iowa, and back. Dubuque had a better selection of merchandise and many shoppers used this daily tour. The boat was scheduled for 9 A.M., but was often several hours late because of fog. As my sister and I sat on the levee with our eyes glued to the river bend, our patience became almost exhausted until someone called, "Here she comes!" Then we relaxed.

We rode to Dubuque and walked uptown to visit the stores. Levi, Stampfer, and Rosheks were the leading department stores. After making our purchases and having lunch at a cafeteria, we went to the store office, and because we were from out of town, we received a rebate that was often the full amount of our boat fare. About 4 P.M. we returned to the levee. Once on the boat we relaxed and enjoyed the scenery, arriving home in Cassville tired and happy.

I can never forget the large excursion boats that came several times during the summer. The one I remember most was the *J.S.* It had four decks. All around the second deck was an ornate white wood railing. Small wooden posts extended to the third deck, which had a similar fancy railing. Sixty people standing side by side reached from the front to the back of the boat. Its capacity was fourteen hundred passengers. The ballroom or dance hall was the main part of the second deck. Windows were closely spaced, and there were comfortable seats inside and park benches outside near the railing. The third deck was only partially enclosed. The fourth deck, or the top of the boat, had only a plain, low railing. Two tall smokestacks were near the front, and back of those were the pilot's cupola, which had a fancy dome on top. The large paddle wheel was in back propelled by steam from the boiler on the lower deck. On August 17, 1906, I went on an excursion with my family on the *J.S.*

About 1916, I attended a moonlight excursion on the *J.S.* with a group of college students. I wore a white cotton crepe dress with tiny yellow roses that was quite long and had a gathered puff on each hip. I wore my hair in a Psyche knot on top of my head.

In the back of the ballroom was a slightly elevated platform on which was stationed a Dixieland band that produced harmonious music of snappy rhythm. I can still see the slender Negro man with his long fingers playing chords on the piano while his head was turned watching the dancers. Waltzes, two-steps, and fox trots were played then.

While exploring the decks between dances, we climbed a narrow stairway to the top deck. There were no lights except the moonlight, and the experience was one to remember. The moon was full, reflecting on the quiet water and disclosing the beautiful bluffs on shore. We walked back to the paddle wheel, which sprayed water on us, and as the spray flew out the drops sparkled in the moonlight like jewels.

The *J.S.* had a tragic ending. About the year 1918 or 1920, after taking a moonlight excursion out of Cassville, it moved to Lansing, Iowa. That night, as the dancers were enjoying the evening, the boat caught fire. It quickly landed at the nearest shore where everyone was safely evacuated. The boat, however, constructed mainly of wood, quickly burned up. One death was reported. An unruly drunk man had been placed in the brig and did not escape.

The *W.W.* was also a very elaborate excursion boat on the Mississippi River. Later, the *Avalon* appeared with a capacity of fourteen hundred people. It also had four decks. It was all steel and the railings were plain. It appeared at La Crosse as late as 1958.

I have an old photograph of another paddle wheel excursion boat. It was on the Cassville levee and the photo was taken before the year 1900. It was much smaller than the later boats and had three decks. Although loaded with about a hundred people, it had no railing. It had no gangplank, but a strong wide board served the purpose. The overflow of about fifty people was stationed on an accompanying covered barge. The importance of this gala occasion was revealed by the clothing worn by the people in the photo. About forty ladies wore similar outfits of long, full, white gowns with long sleeves, high necks, and nipped waists. All had fancy, white, high hats. Some were carrying parasols. A dozen or more wore hoopskirts. The men wore dark suits, white shirts, and derbies. One man standing on top of the barge stood with his legs crossed and his derby tipped to one side in a cocky manner. One could just feel the importance of the occasion and the happiness they were enjoying. Could this be a part of the "good old days"?

## TRAINS IN MY LIFE
*Charlotte Knechtges*

The black engine, its evil eye shooting fire, jumped off the track, roared up the street, and crashed through my bedroom window. Three green apples, a dill pickle, and my scariest nightmare.

In our town (the population sign on the village edge showed 300 for years), the railroad was the hub of all activity. Every few hours a train thundered through from far out west on its way to Chicago. Back and forth they boomed on the double tracks, freight trains and passenger trains. Twice a year one of those freight cars carried a magic box with our name on it from Montgomery Ward that held goodies from the catalog — a blue corduroy hat that fell down over my eyes or a tan dress that my sister refused to wear because it looked like a baseball suit. The passenger trains carried relatives from Chicago who were glad to get into the country for a weekend, although one cousin said the whistling, chugging, swooshing trains were noisier than the city elevateds.

When troop trains were scheduled through our town we ran the block and a half to the tracks and waited with a dozen or so other kids to wave to the khaki-clad young men who threw slips of paper out of the windows. The older girls scrambled for the papers because they held the names and addresses of the boys who wanted so desperately to get mail. When the trains were late, the bolder children put their ears to the rails and reported on the vibrations. When the first whistle sounded and the smoke and steam showed up, we'd all yell, "Stand back or we'll get sucked under the wheels." The soldiers were glad to see us.

The tracks were carefully patrolled by men on handcars, but it was not uncommon for cars to derail. After one accident, an engine and a couple of cars stood in the middle of Squaw Hill Road while a frightened runaway horse changed places with them and bolted up the railroad ties with a buggy thumping at its heels.

The railroad divided the town in half. One night about eight o'clock my sister and I begged Mother to let us go down across the tracks to get two of those little Pizo books that Doc Blake was giving away to the schoolchildren. "*Everyone* has one but us," we told her. When we got to the Main Street crossing the gates went up after a freight train passed through, heading north. We didn't move because we saw the lights of another train coming pell-mell down Dane Hill. But Farmer Charlie, on his way home after a drink or two, drove his obedient team straight onto the tracks. The gates went down and locked Old Charlie and his horses in the path of the train. We turned and ran and it was a good thing we did because a leg of one of the horses lit right where we had been standing. Old Charlie wasn't even scratched. The

townsfolk said, "God takes care of the widows and the drunks." We never did get our Pizo books.

The trains took their toll. The father of a boy in my third grade was one of the victims. When the killer train pulled into the station, the brakeman lifted the mangled body out of the baggage car, and the boy, who was waiting to pick up his morning papers, pushed to the front to see what it was. Other victims, or so we heard, were the Belgians who came to town after the war to work in the beet fields and, not knowing American ways or language, would often get into fights in the saloons. Sometimes, so it was said, they were killed and their bodies dragged to the tracks to be run over by one of the many night trains.

An old woman on her way to seven o'clock mass was hit at the cemetery crossing. "I don't know if she had her breakfast or not," a friend of hers said.

There was another victim. My sister came home from school one afternoon and couldn't stop crying because the bank-corner dandies had chased a stray dog onto the tracks where a switch engine sliced it in two and both parts of it squirmed as they lay there before her.

For most of us, the trains were our only transportation. Every day six or seven of us, students and working people, would flag the six-thirty from the Dakotas and climb the high steps with the help of only a "hurry up" from the brakeman. Even on cold mornings we stood and swayed in the vestibule between the two cars because the smell of people just waking up and of the oranges—juicy, dripping-off-the-chin oranges—was too much for us. One evening on the train home a salesman ran down the aisle at the brief stop at Mendota and jumped off, swinging his heavy sample case against the leg of the brakeman. He murmured "Sorry" and ran on. The brakeman shouted after him, "Sorry don't help!"

Every Saturday afternoon Mrs. Hodge would walk three miles up the tracks from her farm to town, do some shopping, and catch the five o'clock to Madison. As the train pelted past her farm she would reach across her startled seatmate, open the window, and hurl a loaf of bread into her back yard. Train people, all of us.

The smell and the noise and the sight of smoke-belching trains were always with me. Even when we moved to Madison the trains followed me. Every morning on my way to work I raced the black engine with its fiery eye to the Mills Street crossing. Sometimes I won. Sometimes I lost and stood while freight cars bumped back and forth in front of me. When a chance opening came, I would gallop the two blocks to University Avenue and then explain to each friend who stopped me, "No, my sick Uncle John did not die. I just have a mean little cinder from the Illinois Central in my watering eye."

## MEMORIES OF THE FASHIONABLE BICYCLE ERA
*May Augustyn*

Bicycling is popular again with both teen-agers and adults. People now bicycle to work and to school, and some teens pedal miles just for the fun of it. Some young people bicycle miles in groups to raise funds for the handicapped.

But bicycling as a sport is not new. I remember, even though a small girl then, the bicycle craze that swept the country in the early 1900s. My father took to the new fad like an old salt takes to the briny deep. He made a special trip to Chicago and bought new bicycles for Mother and himself.

Their bicycles looked much like those of today,

although the tires were not like the balloon tires of today. Dad used a hand pump to fill them with air. The inflated tires today give a much smoother ride.

The sparkle of the new bikes thrilled Dad. Mother's was a low frame with bright metal handlebars and black metal mudguards. Mother's deluxe, streamlined model bore no resemblance to the "old ice wagon" the boys learned to ride on that had pedals so wide they skinned your shins if you got your legs too close to the frame. A small black leather tool case was strapped to the under edge of the new bicycle seats. (Punctures were frequent in the days of unpaved roads.) Both bicycles had shiny bells that rang when a small lever was pushed from side to side.

Dad's bicycle frame was high, built much the same as Mother's, except that a bar extended from the front to the back of the frame.

The bicycles were beautiful, but learning to ride was the immediate problem Dad faced. Mother often said, "Much of Dad's trouble stemmed from the height of his bicycle." He was short but had bought a bike with a high frame, perhaps to boost his ego.

Dad was so thrilled at the sight of the bicycle's shiny splendor that he decided to learn to ride right then. He wheeled his bicycle into the driveway, stepped onto a wooden box, and threw one leg over the bar. He clutched the handlebars and pumped off in a burst of speed. A short distance from the box Dad sailed over the handlebars, and both he and the new bike landed in a heap in the dust of the driveway. Mother watched from a window and laughed so hard she could not go out to see if Dad was hurt.

Dad was surprised at his quick flip over the handlebars but decided it was all in the day's lesson. One fall was not enough to keep Dad from learning to ride. He picked himself up and wheeled the bicycle back to the starting point.

He took the next tryout a little more slowly. Though the front wheel shimmied and he zigzagged across the drive, he managed to hang on half the length of the driveway before he landed in the dust the second time. Dad kept at it despite his numerous spills and many black and blue bruises. He could ride fairly well before too long and was rarin' to go on trips around the area.

Now that both Mother and Dad had learned to ride and had joined the "bicycle crowd," Mother felt that she should dress accordingly. Many of her friends had adopted the new-fangled bloomers, but Mother balked at these. She did consent to wear a divided skirt, fitted jacket, a stiff straw sailor hat, and, of course, gauntlet gloves. Dad told us that she looked as cute in this outfit as she was small.

Dad wore his everyday attire but wrapped metal clips around his trouser legs to keep them from catching in the chain.

One sunny Sunday afternoon Mother and Dad, dressed for the occasion, went for a ride. We lived on the far east edge of Waukesha. During their spin about the countryside, Dad and Mother came to the high Fountain House hill on the opposite side of town.

As they ambled along everything seemed under control, but Dad reckoned without Mother. For some reason, never explained, Mother lost control of her bicycle and started down the long, steep hill like a flash flood. She could not stop or turn off the road, and in her fright and excitement careened into the back end of a loaded hayrack. The force of the collision threw Mother and her bicycle to the side of the road. The large amount of hay dangling from the rack saved Mother from any injury. She was only shaken up but as mad as the dickens when she recovered.

Dad was thoroughly frightened when he saw Mother whiz past him on her way down the hill. He couldn't stop until he reached the bottom of the hill. He coasted past Mother at the side of the road, which was no consolation to her injured pride. Mother let him know about it later. The surprised farmer thought the end of the world had come and wondered what had rammed into him.

Dad talked to the farmer when he reached the foot of the hill and they walked back to Mother. Dad told us long years after that the more Mother thought about her accident the angrier she became. Mother refused to ride her bicycle home, but to walk three miles was out of the question. Dad wondered what to do. The kind farmer came up with a solution. He told Dad, "I'll drive the team home and hitch them to a light wagon." He was back in a short time, as he lived nearby.

Dad and the farmer loaded Mother's bicycle into the wagon, and Mother rode home perched on the high seat beside the farmer. Dad paid the farmer for his trouble and thanked him for his help.

Mother refused to go riding with Dad for a long time and the reason was not discussed. It was a long time before Mother's hurt vanished, but in later years she learned to laugh about her speedy dash down the steep Fountain House hill.

# THE FIRST RIDE
*Alex Gorski*

In the early days after World War I, we lived in the little town of Three Lakes, Wisconsin, in Oneida County. Several doors away from us lived an old teamster by the name of Bill Rexford. Sometimes we called him Wild Bill because of his likeness to the Wild Bill of the dime novels of those days.

Bill owned four or five teams of horses that he used for hauling supplies to the lumber camps in the area. He also hauled logs from the woods to the sawmill. We kids always loved it when Bill would let us help him around the barn, especially when we could groom the horses.

One day Wild Bill decided to buy himself a new Model T Ford. When the car arrived, he excitedly pointed out to us kids all of the fine features of his new toy. Now, in those days you didn't get any prolonged driving lessons when you bought a new car. Ray Barker, the garage man, explained how you started it on battery, then switched it over to magneto. Then you learned what the three pedals on the floor were: clutch, reverse, and brake. There were no gas pedals then. You accelerated with the gas level on the steering wheel.

After Bill had completed his first lesson, he asked me to go out with him to our old farm about two miles south of town to buy some oats for his horses. After a little cranking by us and some backfiring by the car, we got it started and climbed in.

With much ado, Bill got himself adjusted behind the wheel, pulled the gas lever halfway down, stepped on the clutch, and we lurched forward down the road.

I looked over at Bill. He had his corncob pipe gripped firmly straight out from the middle of his mouth. He was holding on to the wheel tightly with both hands. I was hoping that he'd let go with his right hand long enough to push the gas lever to Slow before we hit the first corner—which he didn't. We took it going south on two wheels with me hanging onto the door and wishing he would slow down so I could jump out. No such luck! With a one-mile straight stretch ahead of us, I started to hope that we'd run out of gas or get a flat.

As we passed the Anderson farm about a half-mile down, there were some mares with their colts standing near the pasture fence. Well, sir, they took off across that forty with their tails flying. I think I knew how they felt.

I again dared to look over at Wild Bill, and you never saw a prouder man in your life. Pipe still straight out, pointing to the middle of the road, the look on Bill's face told me that he must be thinking that he's mastered this art of driving a car.

We took the next hairpin turn going east in a cloud of dust and, with another mile of straight road ahead of us, I tried to assure myself that we'd make it somehow and I'd walk home.

We finally got to the farm and, to my surprise, Bill still didn't slow down. The driveway into the yard was pure sand and when we made the turn, the front wheels kind of jackknifed and we headed into the garden potato patch. It slowed the car down enough so that Bill reached down and shut off the ignition. I jumped out on my side, Bill on his. He took the corncob out of his mouth, looked lovingly at the Ford, and then with great pride beamed at me and said, "By dammer, son, she's quick as a cat!"

## BLOWOUTS WITH OUR MAXWELL
### *Jean Lindsay Johnson*

My Milwaukee parents spent their honeymoon in 1906 driving to Fox Lake in their horse and buggy. Mama's arms were so sunburned and swollen that the sleeves of her travel dress had to be cut open. She cried as the cold shears pressed against the tender flesh and swore she would never take a long buggy trip again.

Ten years later, Papa sold his horse and bought a Maxwell touring car. The top folded back exactly like Papa's buggy. Its deluxe snap-on isinglass window curtains were folded neatly in the door pockets. Mama bought a sporty duster coat of tan linen and a blue head scarf that was three yards long. It fluttered wildly as we tore along, and the wind in my hair and the speed were thrilling.

Our first long trip was to our summer place on Oconomowoc Lake. The Watertown Plank Road was graveled, but when the sky darkened, Papa drove off on a side road with grass down its middle. Parking, he yelled, "Get out the side curtains," and jumping on the back seat he yanked up the folding top and pulled long leather straps through rings on the front fenders. Eighteen inches wide, no two window sections seemed to be the same shape. The rain soaked us long before we figured out which section went where and snapped them in place. I had at last stopped sneezing from the first half hour of dusty driving. Like my favorite storybook character, Pollyanna, I said, "Perhaps this good old rain came just to settle the dust." "Yes, dear," agreed Mama. "Now I don't have to worry about getting sunburned either." She looked like a wet hen, but Papa gave her a love pat and said he thought the window curtains made us pretty cozy.

The wheels started spinning on the slippery mud as we crawled up the hill, so Papa backed down and got a running start. We had just made the crest when we heard an explosive blow-out. The Maxwell thumped to a stop. As Papa pulled a new inner tube out from the toolbox on the running board, I asked if it was a Fisk. Magazine ads showed a yawning boy in footie pajamas lighting his way to bed with a candle, an inner tube over his shoulder. It was captioned: "Time to Retire with a Fisk." Tire tubes were very expensive.

Only a strong-armed man could force a tire off the rim flanges easily. My skinny father had little muscle. He used a tire crowbar, and rain rolling down his cheeks made him look like a crybaby. The tire off, he replaced the tube and pumped air into it with a bicycle pump. Slippery with mud, it was not easy to put back on either. He slapped his wet, visored cap against the side of the Maxwell, just the way he used to slap the flank of his horse before getting back on the seat. Brother sat up front helping Mama work the windshield wiper by hand. He also frightened chickens by squeezing the bulb-horn claxon.

We came to a stretch of road under construction and had been bumping over sharp stones and boulders for half an hour before we heard a hissing sound, which meant we had our second flat tire. The rain had stopped, and the storm was now coming from Papa's mouth, in words I didn't understand, as he talked to the iron crowbar. Dipping the inner tube in a puddle of water, he found the tiny puncture by the air bubbles. He lit a match under the patch from his vulcanizing kit and clamped it onto the leaky spot. While this was drying, Mama and I went hunting wild asparagus and four-leaf clovers.

Once at the cottage, we made no more long trips back to the city until school demanded our return in the fall.

Each morning all summer Papa parked the Maxwell under the catalpa at the train depot and commuted to work. Here in the country we went up to bed carrying a kerosene lamp and preferred using the pot beneath our bed rather than run through the rain to the outhouse in the woods. We quenched our thirst from a dipper in a pail of the most heavenly tasting well water. Our canal was polka-dotted with lovely white water lilies, and most all the boats on our lake were the quiet kind with oars.

Yes, those were the good old days. Today I drive a Buick that has had only two punctures in the ten years I have been driving it. When it storms, the press of a button raises the window, and the twist of a knob starts the windshield wiper flopping. Mama and Papa are gone now, but hubby and I have retired at this old summer place. Strolling in the woods or comfy by the fire, we often ponder about the changes we have seen in our lifetime. Mostly we wonder why our government is squandering billions to claim space on that lifeless, desolate moon.

*Soon after the turn of the century*
*Since I joined the human race;*
*Man has gone from horse to car,*
*To plane, and outer space.*

## DAD HAD A DATE WITH LIZZIE
*Anna M. Kortum*

"Did I get any mail today?" asked Dad as he put his empty lunch bucket on the kitchen table.

"There was nothing for you in the morning delivery, but the mailman left this letter for you this afternoon," Mother said as she handed it to him.

Dad gazed at the long business envelope in disbelief. He eagerly opened the letter and pulled out a duplicate copy of a bill of lading dated May 23, 1920, which specified that a Ford car (Model T) was shipped via the Northwestern Railway from Detroit, Michigan. The date of arrival was subject to notice from the local dealer. He read it out loud again and nearly danced with joy. This was our formal introduction to the arrival of our "Tin Lizzie."

We had no telephone, but we did have home delivery mail service twice a day, and so another waiting period began. A second long business envelope arrived one afternoon a few weeks later, advising us that the car had arrived in Kenosha. The excitement this message caused I will never forget, for the purchase of this Model T Ford was the culmination of many years of saving. Most purchases were paid for in cash, and the cash price of Lizzie was $265. The Kenosha State Bank, on the northeast corner of Elizabeth Street and Howland Avenue (now 63rd Street and 22nd Avenue), held our savings for us. Deposits were made faithfully each week.

"I'm going to go to the garage to pick up the car," Dad announced, as he started to dress for his first date with Lizzie. He stropped his straight-edged razor first on one side, then the other, lathered up his face with bountiful globs of suds from his soap cup, and hurriedly shaved. In his haste, he cut himself slightly, but a tiny

square of tissue on the cut stopped the bleeding. He gave his moustache a few quick pats and quickly brushed his wavy brown hair. He had decided to wear his blue serge suit, and when he tried to adjust the hole in the back of his stiff celluloid collar with an opening in the back of the neckband of his striped shirt, he was all thumbs. The gold-colored metal collar button kept falling on the floor, and there we were, on our hands and knees, looking for the missing link under the chifforobe and bed. We finally got Dad together, and after adjusting his cravat he was ready to leave on his important mission. I smiled as I watched him bid us a hasty farewell, with the tiny square of tissue still on his face.

He suddenly returned and announced, "How am I going to get the car home? I can't even drive!"

"You should have thought of that sooner," ventured Mother.

"Put on your roller skates," Dad said to me, "and skate as fast as you can, over to Mr. Erickson's house. If he hasn't started eating his supper, ask him if he could lend me a hand." Mr. Erickson, a painting contractor, was his boss, and having purchased a Ford in 1916, he knew all about cars.

In my excitement, I practically flew up Market Street to Pomeroy Street on my skates. The Ericksons had eaten early, so I had the pleasure of a ride back in their Ford. The back seat of his car was cluttered with paint pots, brushes, and drop cloths, and large splotches of paint were splashed here and there. He used it mainly for hauling his equipment.

Mr. Erickson chuckled as Dad jumped into the front seat and away they went. After what seemed like an eternity, Lizzie in all her black majesty arrived with Dad sitting next to the driver, who was giving him instructions. The car was parked in the driveway, and driving lessons were to begin after work the next day.

Our neighbors were just as excited as we were, and they came to examine Lizzie. Dad raised the hood and, with the Ford manual in hand, gazed at the popcorn popper type of engine. There was no battery or complex wiring system, and the stubborn crank in the front was the thing that decided if it would start. The gas tank was under the front seat, and I noticed as Dad kicked the narrow tires that the front ones were smaller than the rear. That, I found out later, was why he had to carry two spare tires.

According to today's standards, the car wasn't much to look at. It was boxy, tinny looking, and rather awkward, but that car to us was like a black canvas-topped chariot, fit for the gods. I suddenly remembered someone quoting:

*A little gas, a little oil,*
*A little spark, a little coil,*
*A little tin, a three-inch board,*
*Shake it well, you'll have a Ford!*

I wondered how they could ridicule anything so grand.

The next day, driving lessons began, and it wasn't long before Dad was a good driver. Comfort wasn't Lizzie's prime asset, but the views from her high seats made one swell with joy. Her top speed was forty miles per hour, and she seemed to be able to go almost anywhere. If the hill was too steep to climb, Dad turned her around and drove the car up backward. He said that way the gas flowed down to the carburetor. At that time, my nine-year-old mind hadn't the slightest idea what a carburetor was, but the view going backward was just as nice as going frontward. In stormy weather, the canvas side curtains with isinglass windows sewn in would be snapped over the inside frame.

After several months, Dad asked Mother if she would like to learn how to drive. She reluctantly consented, but after running down several rows of a farmer's corn, she decided she'd make a better rider than driver.

The Model T was considered a workingman's car, and the average mechanically inclined man could do his own repairing. It was manufactured with him in mind. Repair parts were often obtained from mail order houses. In addition to your standard repair tools, a shrewd driver often carried along a couple of raw eggs. If the radiator began leaking, the egg was cracked open and dropped in. The leak would be sealed by portions of the egg cooked hard in the hot water of the radiator, and you would be considered somewhat of a mechanical genius. Dad had an old thin dime that he would use to adjust his spark plugs, and when Mother accidentally gave it to me one day, to buy theme paper, Dad followed me to school to retrieve it and exchange it for another. He said he would be lost without it, and so would the spark plugs.

Our mode of living changed with the addition of Lizzie. We looked forward to short afternoon drives in the country. On weekends, Zion City, Illinois, to the south of us, and Twin Lakes, Wisconsin, to the west of us, were the farthest we went. We got to visit friends oftener, and picnics by the beach and in the country were joyful occasions. Today, riding in our modern streamlined luxury cars, I cannot help but reminisce about the good times we had with Lizzie. She was our first love!

## FLYING FEVER CIRCA 1911
### *Henry L. Cotton*

Back in 1911, when I was thirteen and my stepbrother Eddie was twelve, my father took us to Newport News, Virginia, to see our first airplanes. We lived in Portsmouth, Virginia, which was just across Hampton Roads from Newport News and only about thirty miles from Kittyhawk, North Carolina, the site of the first flight of the Wright Brothers, eight years earlier.

About 1909, Glenn Curtiss opened a flying school at Newport News, not only to stimulate interest in flying but to promote the sale of the flying boats he was manufacturing. After hearing of this, Eddie and I bugged my dad until he promised to take us over to see the planes fly. We thought the day would never come, we were so excited, but eventually, one evening, Dad said, "Tomorrow we go."

As you can imagine, a trip like this had to be an all-day affair. First, we took the streetcar downtown where we boarded the steamboat for the fifteen-mile trip across Hampton Roads to Newport News. We arrived at about ten o'clock in the morning on a beautiful sunshiny day. A man on the boat had told us how to find the flying school, so as soon as we got off the boat we walked about a quarter of a mile along the waterfront and there it was. You can imagine the looks on our faces as we gazed with awe at the first planes we had ever seen in our lives. Since they were all seaplanes, some were moored in the water and some were pulled up on land.

We were so excited we just ran from one plane to another, touching them and looking them over. A couple of men were tinkering with the engine on one, so we stood around to see what would happen. Finally, it started with a roar that was deafening and a blast of air that nearly knocked us to the ground and blew Dad's derby hat off his head. I remember that we were impressed with the fact that the construction of the plane's wings seemed to be so simple (or so it seemed to us), just some kind of cloth tacked over a wooden framework. After a while we saw one of the planes take off in the water. We thought it would never lift off but it did, and what a thrill to see a plane actually fly in the air! We decided right there that we would both be fliers, come what may.

All too soon 3 P.M. came and it was time to catch the boat back to Portsmouth. All we could think of and talk about on the way home was flying and those wonderful planes. I'm sure we must have dreamed about them that night. The next day we set about making plans to build our very own plane.

In those days the sawmill would give you all of the edgings you wanted free. (They were the random-width strips left from the saw when they sized the boards.) Mostly they measured about half inch by one inch, which we thought was just about right for our purposes. Also, there was no trouble getting a wooden box for the fuselage of the plane as the grocery stores had lots of them to throw away.

As soon as we had a chance, we went to the mill and returned with all the edgings we could carry. Since Dad was a carpenter, he had lots of nails and tools around home. All we needed now was some sort of cloth for wing covering. We thought of window shades, but we knew our mother would never go for that so we settled for burlap bags (old potato sacks).

Having settled the question of our materials, we set to work to build the plane. We made a wing frame about two feet by twelve feet and nailed this across the wooden box.

Then we added another piece of framework for the tail. We then ripped up our potato sacks so that we had some nice large pieces and proceeded to tack the burlap on the framework. We thought it looked real good. We had an old pair of roller skates, which we fastened to the bottom of the box for landing gear.

After completing the plane, the next thing, of course, was to fly it. Our kitchen was only one story and had a long, sloping roof. We planned to fly it off this roof. Eddie and I drew straws to see who would have the honor of the first flight. Eddie won and sat down in the box while I held the plane. When he said Okay I let it go, expecting to see it glide out into the back yard. To my amazement, when it got to the edge of the roof, it went straight down to the ground, which was about twelve feet down. After the crash I didn't hear anything right away. Looking over the edge, I saw Eddie trying to untangle himself from the wreckage. I'm glad to say he wasn't hurt seriously, but we both learned a lesson about how not to fly. There was more to come a little later.

A few months after this episode, we read in the paper about some flier jumping out of a plane with something called a parachute. It sounded like an umbrella, which gave us another idea.

In our back yard was a small barn with a loft in it. The door to the loft was about fourteen feet from the ground, and we had often been tempted to jump out of this door but just hadn't dared as yet. Now we thought we just might have the problem licked.

We got an umbrella from the house and Eddie got the long straw again. He stood in the door and opened the umbrella and jumped. You guessed it! The umbrella turned inside out and he went down to the ground with pretty good speed. But luck was with him again, and except for a few bruises and skinned spots, he was all right in a few days.

Although we had failed again we hadn't given up. We just needed a better umbrella. A few years before, Dad had owned a fuel oil business which he operated with a horse-drawn tank wagon, selling mostly kerosene for cookstoves. He had what was known as a drayman's umbrella mounted on the seat of the wagon at the time. While rummaging around in the shop one day we came upon this thing stuck back in a corner. Here was the answer to our problem.

We quickly got it out and looked it over. Everything seemed to be in order, so up to the loft we went. I got to try it first and what a thrill! It worked! We almost wore ourselves out jumping that day. We enjoyed that old umbrella for many months with our friends, until the novelty wore off. We had many other projects as we grew up, but I think at this stage of our lives we really had flying fever.

**9 Celebration**

## ANNIE AND THE BASKET SOCIAL
*Lois Laper*

Annie and Herb Werner lived about a mile from the Sand Hill School. Their two sons, Melvin and Elmer, were pupils in that country school, Melvin being in the sixth grade and Elmer in the fourth grade.

One evening when he got home from school, Elmer announced, "Ma, they're goin' to have a basket social in school next month. The teacher says we got to earn some money to buy a curtain for the Christmas program. What's a basket social, Ma?"

Annie explained that the ladies each took a decorated box in which there was a lunch, and the men bought the boxes and ate with the lady whose box they had bought. The school got the money that the men paid for the boxes. Elmer asked some more questions like, "What do you mean, decorated? Why do they call it a basket when it's a box? What kind of lunch is in the box?"

The next morning after Annie had packed three lunches and fed her "men" breakfast, she began thinking about that basket social. She'd like to show those "snooty" neighbors that she could make a beautiful box. Hadn't she seen the box Mrs. Engles had received first prize for when Annie worked for her? Didn't her country schoolteacher used to say that Annie was handy with her hands even though she wasn't so handy with her head? But where would she get money to buy the crepe paper and things? Herbie didn't earn much at the quarry because he was so slow. And besides, he was still making payments on that old truck that he used to get him to the quarry. She knew he was a good man even though people sort of laughed at him, and he gave her all the money he could spare. Then she remembered that Elmer had said that the basket social wasn't until next month. Maybe she could save a little out of the grocery money each week.

So she began to plan and scheme. She found a medium-sized shoebox, not too large to decorate and not too small to hold a good lunch. She thought she would use light blue crepe paper to cover it and then make some white and pink flowers for the top of the cover. She would need some green paper for the stems and leaves. One day she walked to town to see what kind of crepe paper they had. Hoffman's Store had all the colors she needed. But that day she didn't have enough money to buy.

On the way home, when she got within sight of their barn-red house, she felt irritated over her "snooty" neighbors again. Their house was painted barn-red because it was the cheapest kind of paint, and their landlord had had some left over from painting his farm buildings. She had often thought that maybe that was why her neighbors never came to see her or invited her to their parties.

The day of the social finally came. Annie had the box all trimmed a week ago and hiding high in their closet. She had managed to save enough money to buy some green grapes and olives for the lunch. She had spent most of the day baking bread and cake so that they would be fresh. She had bought some powdered sugar so that she could make a nice thick frosting for the cake. She carefully lined the box with heavy waxed paper, which had cost her fifty cents, so that the smell of the shoebox would not taint her lunch.

Herbie, as usual, fell asleep in his chair after supper. Melvin poked him and told him to get ready. Annie said:

"Never mind, Herbie. Go back to sleep. I want to eat with a different man once."

When Annie was seated in the schoolhouse, she looked up at the row of baskets on the shelf and noted to herself that hers was the prettiest one. She hardly listened to the program that came before the selling of the baskets. She knew that Melvin and Elmer were in the line of singing children, but that was all.

Fred Schumacher was the auctioneer, and he took down the first basket.

"We're going to make a lot of money for the school tonight. Look at this fine basket! How much am I offered?"

Two dollars, three dollars, four, five, five-fifty, went the bidding.

"Are you through bidding? Sold to Mr. John Balzac for five-fifty."

Annie's was the fifth box. When Fred took down the fifth box, he said, "My, isn't this a pretty one! How much am I offered for this nice one?"

Then someone whispered loudly, "That's Annie Werner's."

"Come on now. It's for a good cause."

No one said anything. Fred tried again and again. Not one bid, not even a nickel. He put the box back on the shelf and took down another.

Annie felt the tears coming to her eyes. She got up from her seat, grabbed her box, and walked out. Her two boys followed her. They walked down the road in silence. Soon Elmer wanted to know why no one had bought her basket. Melvin gave him a push so that he nearly fell in the ditch. When they got home, Herbie was already in bed, so Annie and the boys ate the lunch.

## SALLY'S PIE SOCIAL
### *Mrs. Vernon Stewart*

Sally hurried home from school as fast as her ten-year-old legs would carry her. She burst into the house, her face flushed with excitement.

"Mother! Mother!" she cried.

Her mother came out of the pantry where she had been busy preparing supper and asked, "Well, Sally, what has happened?"

"Oh, Mother, teacher says we're to have a pie social to raise money for more books, and each one of us may bring any kind of pie we like. Make me a chocolate pie, Mother." Sally spoke so rapidly the words tumbled all over one another.

Every day Sally toted her dinner bucket and trudged the mile and a half to the country school. She enjoyed every minute of her school day, but when the teacher planned the pie social, Sally's joy knew no bounds. All the way homeward she anticipated the event. With every step she bounced with delight. With added vigor her dinner pail swung in perfect rhythm. Her face was beaming with repressed eagerness.

"I'll make you a chocolate pie," said Mother. "When is the social to be?"

Sally clapped her hands at her mother's reply and then said, "It is to be next Friday night."

Now chocolate pie was Sally's favorite kind of pie. Often she would willingly consent to do some unpleasant chore for the reward of a chocolate pie. Sometimes her brother would say she could have his share of the pie if she would fill the woodbox. Sally filled the woodbox.

Those intervening days could not fly fast enough for Sally. All her thoughts revolved around the pie and the social. In school the teacher found her attitude unusually inattentive, for Sally was absorbed in daydreaming. She mused, "Who will buy my pie? Whoever does, I'll have to sit with him! I wish my brother or my Dad would buy it. I hope Walter Hetzel doesn't get it! That would be awful! What would I say to him? I just couldn't sit there! He's a lot older than I am and he's been away to school. I hardly know him. He must be awfully smart! I think I'll show Dad how my pie is wrapped and then maybe he will buy it." So Sally's thoughts ran. They were like mercury in a thermometer, up with joy and elation, then down with fear and worry.

She thought about what she should wear, for in reality, this would be Sally's first occasion to mingle with the grown-ups. "Mother, I must have a new dress for the social!" Sally stated emphatically. "I heard Evelyn and Ruth say that their mothers were making them new velvets and that they have sent to Sears and Roebuck for her cloth-topped patent leather lace shoes. I must have new shoes, too, Mother." Sally's mother was an understanding woman. She didn't want her daughter disappointed, and besides, she had caught the spirit of Sally's eagerness, so she did not hesitate to give acquiescence to Sally's requests.

The evening arrived. At the supper table Sally couldn't eat for she was so excited. On the kitchen table in a box, wrapped in gay colored crepe paper, fringed and scalloped around the edges, sat the famous chocolate pie. Sally had taken particular pains to call her father's attention to it, but somehow he just wasn't any too interested. He even said he hoped no one would buy her pie so she could eat it all by herself.

With the new dress, the new shoes, and the new ribbons tied in her braids, Sally stepped back from the mirror in her room and said to herself, "I'm sure someone will want to buy my pie when they see me."

The family set out for the schoolhouse. All the neighbors were going. Those who lived far drove with horses and buggy; those who lived near walked. Sally rode with her parents in the buggy. She had run out of conversation, like a well suddenly gone dry, and not a word did she say all the way, but her big brown eyes were sparkling with expectation.

They entered the lamp-lighted schoolroom, and Sally hurried to the table to place her pie with its companions. She was so proud of it! Then she settled herself on a bench near her chums as they pushed and shoved to make a place for her. Soon heads bent close together and tongues unloosened as they whispered secret intimacies to one another and cast meaningful looks in the direction of the pies.

At the signal from the teacher, the auctioneer strutted forward. He was the biggest man there that night and his importance loomed before the small country crowd as every eye and every ear strained upon him. He had a loud deep voice and that night he let it boom forth with affected eloquence.

"How much am I offered for this beauty? It's a lemon! Forty-five cents. Do I hear fifty cents? Fifty cents. Who'll make it fifty-five? Fifty-five cents. Sixty? Do I hear sixty? Fifty-five cents once, fifty-five cents twice, and sold for fifty-five cents to the gentleman in the corner!" So the pies went. Each time the teacher came with a new pie, eager, anxious eyes stared at the box. Then with a sigh of relief that it wasn't hers, Sally would again relax. Finally one of the girls nudged her. "She's bringing yours! She's got it!" Sally's heart was throbbing so loud she was sure she wouldn't be able to hear the auctioneer. She sat as tense and rigid as a Greek statue.

"Here's a chocolate pie-um-um!" the auctioneer called. "Who'll open the bidding? Twenty-five cents. Make it fifty. Someone here like chocolate pie? I do. Ought to put this away for myself. Did I hear fifty? Fifty cents!" This came from a voice in the rear. Sally turned diffidently to the back. It was as she'd feared. But the bidding hadn't stopped, and oh, how she hoped, as she clasped and unclasped her hands, that her father would bid for her pie. At seventy-five cents, the auctioneer began his "going, going, gone" and the pie was sold. It was sold to Walter Hetzel! Sally didn't know what to do. All during the remainder of the auction, big lumps kept coming up in her throat. She bravely repressed tears. "What will I say to him? What will he say to me? Everyone will look at us! Where will we sit? I'm not hungry anyway. I don't want any chocolate pie, either." Such harassing thoughts dominated her mind!

The last pie sold, the informality of searching for partners began. Walter unwrapped his beautiful box, found the name, and gazed over the crowd for young Sally. He knew her parents well, but all he knew about Sally was that she was a nice little brown-eyed girl. He thought he had seen her just a moment ago sitting beside his young niece. She wasn't there now. His eyes moved searchingly over the crowd. He approached her parents and Sally's mother said, "She was sitting over there just a minute ago. I have no idea where she might have gone. She will be back, for she wouldn't miss eating chocolate pie for anything." But Sally didn't appear, and the evening wore on. While all the other couples sat chatting idly as they munched their pies, Sally's partner sat alone. "I'll just eat half of this pie," he thought to himself, "then I'll let Sally take the rest home when she comes. I do

wonder where she is. Evidently she's bashful and doesn't want to eat her pie with me."

Soon it was time to go home. The remaining pieces of pie were packed away and people began to leave the school. Sally's parents sat patiently with half a chocolate pie, waiting for Sally.

"I'm getting anxious about her," her mother said. "Something must have happened. She was looking forward to this evening so much. Let's look for her." So they did.

In the boys' hallway, hidden behind the door, stood Sally. Her little frame was shaking with sobs she had tried desperately to still. The eagerness from those teary eyes was gone, and they were downcast with the loss of pride and a feeling of shame. It is true that even to this day Sally shudders at the mere mention of chocolate pie.

## THE MEDICINE SHOW
*Ruth Doland*

Probably the most interesting of childhood memories are those of "making believe." To that end, "The Medicine Show" was a marvel of inspiration for two little girls whose dreams of the moment were centered on The Stage.

Each summer, "The Medicine Show" came to Columbus. The railroad car in which the company lived was switched to a siding just off Birdsey Street, the big tent was pitched, and for six nights the show was on. It consisted of vaudeville acts which were interspersed with hawkers running up and down the aisles shouting their wares. In this case it was bottles of the "Elixir of Youth." Father always bought a bottle, and our mother said it was for this that father took us to see the show at least twice a week. To Eugenia and me, however, though we loved the excitement and the people milling around and the conversation of the men as they left the tent only to return when the skits went on, it was really the acts themselves that held our interest. To these we gave our full attention, laughed loudly, clapped our hands, and pounded our feet along with the rest of the audience. Afterward, as our father guided his excited but sleepy little girls homeward, plans were already forming in our minds for *our* medicine show.

The big barn was our theater. Father moved the buggy, the surrey, and the trap out on the lawn. (I presume that the horses were left in their stalls.) Boards were placed on orange crates to seat the audience, and the stage was marked off with newly cut boughs from the box elder tree. Rehearsals were unnecessary, for the lines were spontaneous and the action was to be exactly like that of the other medicine show. Tickets were made on Mother's sewing machine; no thread was used but the perforations gave a two-part status to the "admit one." The buyer had a stub to keep as proof that he had paid his admission fee. At some shows that fee was ten pins, at others, a handful of rags. I've often wondered what we did with the pins, but how well I remember when the show was over taking the rags to the back door of the Derring Store where they were weighed and exchanged for pennies. We then hurried across the street to Mrs. McCafferty's Candy Shop where we bought jawbreakers and licorice sticks and wandered home happily content with our day's accomplishment.

The particular skit from the show that I am now recalling required a man and woman. Since we were girls, adjustments had to be made. Eugenia was the oldest in our group of neighborhood actors so she always got the most important part, in this case that of the husband. I was the wife. As the medicine show actors had presented the skit, the husband was scolding and belaboring his wife while she was making bread. The wife joined in with harsh words and maddening gesticulations toward her husband. The climax came when she, having reached the boiling point, pounded him on the back and pushed his face down into the pan of flour on the table. When he rose to his full height, sputtering and scolding, his face and hair were heavily coated with flour and much to the delight of the audience he was a defeated man.

Since Eugenia was to be the husband, we needed a pair of pants. We had only one boy in our troupe and he was three years younger and much, much smaller. We borrowed his overalls and, although they were very tight, Eugenia managed to get them on. With the props in place we started the show with much haranguing, many undistinguishable words, and shaking of fists. We talked in what was supposed to be German, but the only real German words that we knew were *"Ach du Lieber Augustine"*; the rest was gibberish. When we came to the place where I was to pound her on the back and push her face in the flour, she couldn't bend! The overalls were too tight. What to do! Try as she would she just couldn't bend over. She hissed at me, "Lift the pan up." I did and pushed her face in it, succeeding in flouring it to quite a degree. The result wasn't bad, but far, far from that of the real skit. The audience, being largely composed of the neighborhood gang and a few devoted parents, cheered and clapped and apparently were completely satisfied. But, you see, they had never been to "The Medicine Show."

## THE DAY OF THE SODA
### *Bert Vawter*

In the spring of 1919 I had just finished the eighth grade. And when I say finished, that was just about it. In our little backwoods country school that was all there was. No promotion. No graduation. We just picked up our books and went home. For most of the kids in the neighborhood that was the end of school.

That year my older sister and her husband were visiting us and she insisted that I go on to high school. The closest high school was thirteen muddy miles away at the county seat. It was a town school, which meant paying a tuition and nine months' room and board. Although my family was neither rich nor poor, five or six dollars a week was quite a burden on the budget. My sister said I should go home with them to Lexington, in the corn belt.

"You're a strong, healthy boy, Bert," she said. "You could work on a farm for wages."

My parents agreed and when Sis and her husband left for home, I went with them. I didn't get a job as easily as she thought I would though, because most of the farmers had large, heavy teams of horses to work and I was too young. A man named "Shorty" Paten hired me finally, and since his horses were more gentle than most, I started to work for him.

My brother, Guy, lived less than a mile away and his wife's younger brother was staying with them. Earl was about my age, and we had known each other all our lives. A routine was soon established. Every Wednesday and Saturday, as soon as we got through with the work in the field, we would eat a big supper, get cleaned up, and go in for a night on the town. Once there, we would go to a restaurant and order a cheese sandwich, a big slug of cream pie, and a bottle of strawberry pop. Then we would go to a movie. After the show we would go to the one store that always stayed open and buy a sack of candy, then head for home.

On the Fourth of July we decided to go to the city and celebrate. We got up early the morning of the Fourth so we could catch the 6 A.M. train. We planned on coming home the next morning. In those days there were plenty of passenger trains so we didn't have to go that early or come back that late but we wanted to make a full day in the city. Since there was only one station between Lexington and Bloomington, we arrived much too early, long before 7 A.M. We went to a little restaurant and had a second breakfast and then to the streetcar line to go to Miller Park.

Miller Park was a beautiful city park with hundreds of lovely, big shade trees, lots of nice green lawn, a little zoo, a small lake with a sand beach where you could rent a suit or a rowboat to take your girlfriend for a ride on a warm afternoon. But we two nitwits got there so early there wasn't a soul in sight. It was pretty dull, so after looking at the animals for a while we decided to go downtown to the square.

Bloomington was a city of twenty-five or thirty thousand and almost all the main business stores were on the square. To our surprise there wasn't too much activity there either. Not too many people on the streets. The displays in the windows were of things we had never seen in the country so we got a kick out of just taking everything in.

Just for something to do, we caught a streetcar that said Illinois Central Depot. We found that the depot wasn't a big fancy establishment, but they did have vending machines. You could get a nice handful of salted peanuts for a penny. So until our pennies ran out we had a third breakfast while watching passenger trains come in and load, unload, and take off. It was exciting to watch the people get off and on and watch them load the baggage on the big iron-tired trucks. When we got bored with this we took another streetcar and went back to Miller Park. Things were still pretty slow but gradually coming to life. The zoo was open and we watched the monkeys. The men in the bandstand were setting up and tuning their instruments.

Downtown the stores were open and we decided to have some ice cream. We wandered into a real fancy place called The Palace of Sweets. It was a combination candy shop and ice cream parlor. We felt doggone awkward and ill at ease. That could be because, while Earl was dressed as an ordinary human being, I had to be a real "Fancy John" dressed in a loud silk shirt with red stripes, a striped silk collar, white pants, patent leather shoes, and a hard straw sailor hat. We found the most secluded corner and sat on chairs made of twisted wire. A pretty young girl came along to take our order. I ordered an ice cream sundae, as did Earl. I knew what a sundae was and that was all I *did* know. It usually consisted of a big scoop of ice cream, some chocolate syrup, nuts, and a big gob of whipped cream. It cost ten cents. But when the girl brought the order it wasn't a sundae at all. It was something in a tall glass with a long-handled spoon and a big straw in it. It was the most delicious thing I had ever tasted in my life. I had never tasted anything that good. We wondered what it was. Somewhere, sometime, I had heard of a chocolate soda and I thought maybe that's what it was.

"Ask the girl," Earl whispered.

"Are you nuts?" I snorted. "She'll think we're a couple of farmers."

That was an unnecessary remark because, if you had thrown both of us into the front end of a thrashing machine you'd have gotten two bushels of hayseed out of the other end.

When we finished this new treat and paid five cents more than expected for it, we walked to a place called the Metropolitan Hotel building. It was a combination cigar store and lunch room with a magazine rack and a soda fountain. It was not nearly as fancy as the Palace of Sweets but we were much more comfortable. We bellied up to the soda bar and I said, "Give us a couple of chocolate sodas," just as though I knew what I was talking about. It didn't seem to jar the man behind the counter any. He just turned over two tall glasses, put two scoops of ice cream in each, squirted in some chocolate syrup, and filled them up with fizz water. From then on we knew what to order. He soaked us more than the other place but they were bigger and better. I think our minds were working on the same channel, because as soon as our straws made that well-known, impolite slurping sound we reached into our pockets for more money and ordered another round. Then with our bellies full and bulging temporarily, we went across the street to the courthouse basement. I know now that there had to be a men's room in that hotel somewhere, but we were two country boys and we were used to the two-holer out in the back yard someplace. At that time of my life I guess I thought that was all the courthouse was used for. Out on the street again we wandered back down to where the fancy theaters were. Douglas Fairbanks and Mary Pickford, along with William S. Hart, were featured that day. We strolled around devouring the movie stars' pictures with our young country eyes for a good half hour, then it was time to go back to Miller Park. First we stopped at the Metropolitan for another chocolate soda. I don't know how many trips we made back and forth that day. But, of course, money was no object. We were both flush. I had shucked the boss down for twenty dollars and Earl was also loaded. Each time we went to Miller Park we would stop in for another soda. At the park we didn't go swimming because we didn't know a thing about bathing suits. Neither of us had ever had one on. But we did rent a boat and take a ride on the lagoon. Then off to the streetcar. A ride downtown. And another chocolate soda.

We managed to take time off between sodas to stand in the middle of the street and listen to an announcer, standing in the second story of a newspaper office, describe the defeat of Jess Willard at the hands of the great Jack Dempsey. The announcer was using a megaphone, talking out the window as it was received by wire. It was hot and dry out there in the middle of the street so after another trip to the basement of the courthouse, yep, we did it—back to the Met and a chocolate soda.

Once, while we were back at Miller Park, we noticed two pretty girls standing in front of the monkey cage. I edged over in their direction. Earl went the other way. He was scared to death of girls. I hadn't any experience with them but I was willing to be introduced. I got fairly close to them, hoping they would speak to me, as I was much too shy to talk to them first, when those damn monkeys decided to make love, right there in the cage. I was never more embarrassed in my life. I pretended to look the other way and not see them, but I managed to take a few peeks at that monkey business going on. The girls must have been embarrassed too, because when I turned around they were gone.

After wandering around the park for a while, listening to band music and some fella sounding off on a soapbox, we again felt the urge to go downtown for another chocolate soda. As I remember, we were in Miller Park until well after dark. They'd had fireworks that night, but we missed them. We were either having another soda or in the courthouse basement at the time.

While we were waiting for the streetcar to make our last trip from the park, we saw a gentleman half sitting, half lying on the grass. He seemed to be also waiting for a streetcar. To make conversation, I said, "I wish that damn streetcar would hurry up."

He looked up and remarked, "Well, son. We're doing the best we can. I think we've given pretty good service today."

He sounded so authoritative that I asked him if he owned the streetcars. He laughed at that and replied, "No I wish I did. I'm the superintendent of the line."

"I'm sorry," I said, thinking I should apologize.

"That's all right," he said. "We hear that all the time." He pulled out his pocket watch and by the light of the streetlamp said, "There'll be two of them here in about seven minutes."

He was right. We got on one of them and took our last trip downtown and—you guessed it—stopped at the Met and had our final chocolate soda. I don't know why we didn't eat any food all day. Guess we just weren't hungry.

We went back to the depot and hung around until 1 A.M. When the big high-wheeled passenger engine came screeching to a stop we boarded and settled down for the long . . . dreary . . . ride home—*sixteen miles at sixty miles an hour!*

That was fifty-seven years ago and do you know what my favorite delicacy is to this day? Yep! How'd ya guess? Chocolate soda.

## THE OLD FOURTH
*Marion Clapp*

John Adams, who died at sunset on the day of the fiftieth jubilee of independence, wrote of the Fourth, "It ought to be solemnized with pomp and parade, with shows, games, sports, guns, bells, bonfires and illuminations, from one end of the continent to the other, from this time forward forevermore."

And so it was in the town of my childhood. The Fourth of long ago had an early and noisy awakening, for the neighborhood boys' giant firecrackers mangled the silence soon after daybreak. Then all over town the church bells rang loud and long. My father would be up and have the large flag waving over our front lawn. At our early breakfast my sister and I begged to be excused after a few nibbles. We failed. On this holiday when he had plenty of time, our father quizzed his daughters about why we were celebrating and told us of the events that led to the first Fourth.

I pictured tea leaves floating in our local lake. King George III was a mean old king, like the ones in fairy tales. Independence Hall recalled the lodge hall where Papa went one night each week. But the names Paine, Jefferson, Adams, Washington, Franklin, Lafayette flickered through my mind and came back with great intensity years later when I studied American history. We were very young; my father certainly did not expect us to remember much that he said. He was relating it for himself. He was recalling our nation's beginnings, he was glorying in its past; in this he impressed us.

Free at last, we brought out our hoard of harmless fireworks and started our own celebration. We would light whole bunches of little "lady fingers," throw them on the sidewalk where they would jump and sputter, unheard in the greater clamor of the neighborhood. The small "salutes" we were allowed to have were our favorites, for they made a big bang. We also feared them a little and tossed them fast, as soon as the fuse lighted. We'd grind some caps under our heels and light some "snakes" and watch them emerge, ugly little things without noise. The odor from the punk and gunpowder, along with the July heat, increased as the morning wore on. The cats and dogs had quiveringly slunk away to quiet cellars to spend the day until the ammunition was spent.

Papa was turning the ice-cream freezer, and we managed to appear as he drew the dasher. What a delicious concoction. No synthetics or fillers in that, just cream, eggs, sugar, and plenty of vanilla. We'd scrape the dasher and also have a few tastes from the can before it was packed in salt and ice.

Now it was time to put on our flower-sprigged dimities and our leghorn hats trimmed with daisy wreaths so Papa could take us downtown on the streetcar to watch the parade. All the way we were accompanied by the noise of exploding torpedoes on the tracks, a racket that would continue all day, or until the neighborhood kids ran out of money with which to purchase more.

It was obvious to any child that this parade was the spectacle of the summer. Flags flying, the color guard led the parade. There were marching patriotic organizations, marching veterans, the cavalry on spirited horses. No advertising anywhere except for our country. Blaring band followed blaring band playing "The Star Spangled Banner," Sousa's "Stars and Stripes Forever," "There'll Be a Hot Time in the Old Town Tonight," "Battle Hymn of the Republic," "The Caisson Song." The caissons were there, carrying heavy cannon. They rumbled and shook

along the pavement drawn by huge Clydesdales, the property of the local brewery. They were handsome, perfectly matched animals, their harnesses decked with red, white, and blue bunting.

Veterans of the Spanish-American War, still young men, marched sprightly, never looking to right or left. The few silver-haired veterans rode in open cars. Some were in blue, some in gray, each to his own conveyance. How wildly the crowd cheered as they passed. The war was half a century in the past. They lived together amiably all year, but on the Fourth of July they were again soldiers of the North and soldiers of the South. At the picnic later in the day they fought the war all over again, displaying more animosity than they had felt toward each other as young men actually fighting the battles.

At home there was company for the big midday meal. We feasted on the first fried chicken of the summer. Accompanying that was a large tureen of new potatoes and new peas in cream sauce that evoked "ohs" and "ahs" when the lid was lifted. There were hot biscuits, crisp crusted, over which we ladled the chicken gravy. At each side of the table sat dishes of wilted lettuce, warm, tart, and sweet, embellished with chopped green onions. To end it all was a banana cake with the homemade ice cream all washed down with iced tea.

After dinner Papa placed a chunk of ice, insulated from the heat with many layers of newspaper, in the back of the buggy. With it went a jar of sweetened lemon juice for the afternoon ade. On top of the ice went the picnic hamper packed with our supper to be eaten in the park.

When we arrived our parents hurried to the oratory and we kids to the playground. I don't know who had the most fun. A good, rousing, patriotic speech delivered by an old-time speaker with arms waving and table pounding was high entertainment in those days, to be read and reread the next day in the newspaper. By the applause and cheers, drifting to us through the trees, some mighty profound sentiments were being expressed that afternoon.

We went from merry-go-round to seesaws, to swings, to slides. By midafternoon the slides were slick with wax after the boys had used the inner boxes from Cracker Jack cartons to coast on all day. We were very apt to land with a thud and a bounce in the dust.

Suppertime came all too soon. We were sighed over for the dirt we had accumulated. We were washed at the faucet, our sturdy little gingham dresses adjusted and sashes tied. Following the meal, with dimes for ice cream in our hands, we went to the refectory to sit among the tree tops in that cool, lovely place of swaying lanterns.

On the buggy ride home, flags were being lowered. Dusk had come to the tree-shaded street. The sun was behind low clouds in the west, and already there seemed to be an afterglow darkening into deep blue-gray. I felt very sad. A happy day was nearing its end, and the timelessness of another year was ahead.

Papa lowered our flag, and the dark grew deeper. We were ready for the last celebration. We fastened pinwheels to the old elm to watch them whirl and spurt sparks and die all too soon. We lit our sparklers, spun them in circles over our heads, and danced like wild men. Over our part of town the sky was aglow with skyrockets. Some of the neighbors strolled over to sit on the porch. Papa added his skyrockets and Roman candles to the collection dazzling in the sky. Someone would say, "That was a beauty," or "What a whiz that was—went clear over Wilson's house."

Then Mama would say, "I'm sure there is enough ice

cream for everyone, if it isn't too soft." Papa had packed it well and there was plenty from the bottom of the large freezer. The ice cream alone made the day a gala one for us kids. As we sat in the cooling night, fireflies flickered on and off in the lilac hedge, as if to add their bit to the now quiet and soft night. Someone would say, "The stars are close tonight." My cat, Lady White Foot, came from hiding, jumped into my lap, and meowed for supper. The neighbors went home slowly as if they, like us children, hated to say good night to a perfect day.

Stripped to our muslin panties, my sister and I got under the hose in the dark backyard and washed the dust and odor of gunpowder from our skin. The river water was warm, and this was the fun way of taking a bath. Exhausted to the point of no return, after a day five hours longer than usual, we donned our soft nainsook nighties and went to sleep.

The world was at peace. The sky was blue. There was great faith in the future of our country. War—something only heard of by us children—seemed as far in the past as shooting with bow and arrow from a pioneer fort. Folks were not cynical of our country's past. They were proud.

## THE CIRCUS AT CLEMANSVILLE
### Ted Irion

The apple crunched crisply, as a fresh-picked apple should. Naturally I picked the largest and prettiest from the "Duchy" tree that stood between the house and the barn. It was the fourth morning of my week's vacation on the farm, it was warm, the bees were buzzing in the garden nearby, and for a small boy everything was just about perfect.

My grandfather had met me at Brooks' Corners where the conductor of the Interurban had helped me off. There was a slight pang of homesickness as I watched the electric car depart for Neenah, but my grandfather put me up on the wagon and assured me that my parents back in Oshkosh would be properly notified by telephone as soon as we got to the farm. I knew, of course, that at the first turn of the crank to get the operator, everyone on the party line would know I had arrived.

It was only a couple of miles to Clemansville, but the horse never moved faster than a walk, contrary to all the stories I had heard of galloping ponies. Besides that, the steel rims on the wagon wheels scraped and jarred over the gravel road, especially where the fresh gravel had just been deposited in the low spots. It seems that each farmer had to maintain his part of the road by hauling gravel from the pit. In most cases, the leveling of the roadway was left to the horses walking over it. But we finally arrived, and the vacation was really underway.

The first days were expended in an intensive exploration of the six-acre farm. It was hardly a farm, but it did have a nice orchard to the side of the house, next to a large strawberry patch. Back of the small barn, which sheltered one cow and one horse, a buggy, and haymow above, was the chicken yard. The chicken house, formerly the Clemansville Post Office, formed one side of the yard.

Towering behind, two rows of stately black walnut trees formed a backdrop to the modest gray board-and-batten farm buildings. The grove extended from the stone pile back of the chicken house, all the way north to the road. The trees were magnificent. The pasture below their branches had already been thoroughly explored during the first days I was there, as well as the red clover field beyond.

The L-shaped white farm house had a curved cement walk connecting the two rear doors; one door opened to the much-used kitchen, the other to the summer kitchen. A pump stood near each door. The iron pump was for drinking water from the well; the other wooden pump, near the summer kitchen, stood over the cistern for soft water. It was on the bench near this pump that my grandfather and I would sit in the evening and watch the sun sink and evening star appear, while the swallows glided noiselessly through the still air. It was then that he told me about Clemansville.

Mr. Clemans came into the area many years before, found the area pleasant, and decided to start a village. At the crossroads, the brick school was built on the northeast, a church on the southwest, while a house and a farm yard filled the other corners. I'm not sure where the small post office was located, but by the time I arrived on the scene, Mr. Clemans had been gone many years, and the post office moved over to my grandfather's place and converted into an excellent chicken house. The school was used each season, but the church only occasionally. Mr. Clemans built the house my grandfather now owned and planted the apple orchard and the walnut trees. Like many of the early settlements, some grew and others didn't.

Clemansville didn't. But it was pleasant, and I thought this was just about the best vacation I had ever had.

I took the last bite of the apple and tossed the core over the grape arbor, into the rhubarb patch, and looked about for some excitement. My glance fell on the little frame church a hundred feet or so away. Here was an area not yet explored. It was easy to climb the fence. I tried looking into the windows, but they were a bit out of my reach. So I watched the sparrows who darted noisily in and out of the faded green wooden louvers in the small, square belfry. Then I happened to look at the wagon sheds in back of the church. A long, low shed with an open front, but with partitions of weathered gray boards, was built to accommodate the horses and buggies of the worshippers. It was useful in rainy or wintry weather. But today my eyes saw not gray boards but a blaze of color! There they were, all across the inside walls, big, bright, and gay— circus posters! I raced back to the shed and with eyes of wonder embraced each stall with complete amazement. I had never been to a circus, never even this close to so many circus posters.

Here were huge elephants standing with one foot on a little keg, tigers growling right at you as they jumped through flaming hoops, acrobats swinging through the air, and all in a riot of color! It was wonderful.

I must have been there a long time, because it suddenly became clear to me that my grandmother's frantic voice was calling my name. I wasn't lost, I was just in a wonderful trance!

Some say the circus never really came to Clemansville, but if they had asked one small boy, he could have told them about the snarling wild animals, the red-nosed clowns, the hippopotamus who could easily have swallowed you if you stood in his yawning mouth, the trapeze performers in their pink tights, and the dashing ringmaster in his shining black boots and long whip.

They didn't believe that the circus came to Clemansville. How could anyone have doubted!

## MY INDIAN DOLL
*Esther Donnelly*

My Indian doll is my oldest possession. She was made for me by Alice Short Bull, a friend of our family, and was given to me when I was four years old. The occasion was a Christmas Eve celebration at a mission church on the Pine Ridge Indian Reservation.

We were the only non-Indian family attending the service and had been seated in a pew not far from the big Christmas tree. From my perch on Mama's lap, I could see laden branches stretching out in every direction. Tall candles flickered on the altar. The delightful fragrance of the newly cut pine tree permeated the air, hiding the kerosene odor of the lanterns which hung from the ceiling.

My little sister, Rose, sat next to me on Papa's lap. We whispered to each other during the singing of the hymns, calling attention to the many unwrapped gifts hanging on the tree. Yards of calico and glistening hair ribbons were draped in graceful fashion on the branches. Bags of tobacco hung suspended at the tips of the branches, and moccasins, made by the Indian mothers, hung closer to the tree's trunk.

"Look up high," I whispered. "There's the doll we asked Santa to bring!"

I was trembling with anticipation. The doll was even more beautiful than her picture, which we had circled in the catalog. Her hair was blonde and curly. Her sheer pink dress had a border of lace. Mama had explained that we would get our presents later at home. But apparently Santa Claus had decided to surprise us by putting the pink beauty on the church Christmas tree.

It seemed that the songs and prayers, most in the Dacotah Indian language, went on for a very long time. At last came the final carol, "Silent Night," sung in English by the pupils of the day school where Papa and Mama taught.

Suddenly there was a blast of cold air across our faces, and Rose and I were instantly awake. There was a jingling of bells, and Santa himself came running down the church aisle. He had on a red suit and a stocking cap with a bell at the very end.

With almost uncontainable excitement, we watched while Santa and his helpers handed out gifts from the tree. Finally, Santa took the big doll out of the branches and lifted it high for everyone to see. Then, still holding the doll he walked on past our pew and called out the name of Victoria Red Bird, a blind girl who lived in a log hut near Buckle Creek. The congregation, which had been silent for a moment, took up a low humming sound of approval as Santa placed the doll in her arms.

I buried my face in the soft folds of Mama's blouse so my tears wouldn't show. Mama patted my back and said, "Look, Esther, here is a present for you." Ellis Poor Bear, one of Santa's helpers, stood in the aisle with an Indian doll in each hand—one for me and one for Rose.

The doll was dressed in buckskin, heavily fringed on the sleeves and hem. She wore amber beads at her throat. I looked under her skirt hoping to find her tiny moccasins. To my horror, she had no legs or feet at all—and neither did she have arms and hands. How could she look so happy without hands and feet?

As we went out into the cold night, I held her close to keep her warm and wrapped her in my own wool scarf. With my free hand I clung to Mama's coat as our family walked slowly home.

In the childhood days that followed I tried to fit the little doll into my playhouse family. But somehow she didn't seem to fit in. I didn't even give her a name. Finally, I put her in a box on the closet shelf and brought her out only to show off her peculiarities.

All of this happened more than half a century ago.

The other day I brought her into the light again. Her face, made of a soft expanse of unbleached muslin with a few ink-drawn lines for features, still bears an expression of peaceful tranquility. And her black horsehair braids are still tied with leather strings.

She has outwaited my childish disappointments—waited until I am old enough to realize that pity, no matter in what degree of concern, is a pathetic substitute for acceptance. Perhaps I, not she, had been the orphan, shutting off the flow of understanding I might have shared earlier of her people's traditions and virtues of acceptance.

## MOTHER WAS A GOURMET COOK
*Erna P. Fenton*

Easily obtained so-called gourmet foods, kitchen appliances of all kinds, and packaged and frozen items make preparations for a holiday dinner a fairly easy task today.

'Twas not so in the early 1920s when my mother and father, immigrants from Norway and Finland, respectively, lived on a small truck farm in Milwaukee County.

Father butchered the hogs and smoked the hams in late fall. Mother made blood sausage, head cheese, and pickled pigs' feet. The geese were fattened. Chickens were kept throughout the year, as also were the cows and the two horses.

Vegetables from the garden and fruit from the trees were placed for winter storage in the basement.

Then Father and Mother took my sister and me on a special trip with horse and buggy into Milwaukee to purchase holiday staples—dried codfish for lutefisk, cardamom seed for the Christmas coffee bread and Norwegian cookies, goat's milk cheese shipped from Norway, round hardtack from Finland, a keg of herring, a bag of flour, a bag of sugar, and the indispensable Domino "lump" sugar. Most often all of these items were purchased at Steinmeyer's, an early version of today's supermarket. Horehound candy was the treat for my sister and me.

Several weeks before Christmas Mother soaked the dried cod in a lye solution and rinsed it thoroughly in preparation for the Christmas Eve lutefisk dinner. Creamed potatoes, carrots, and a dessert of fruit soup or rice pudding plus fattigmann cookies completed the meal.

Although their income was extremely low, Father and Mother made a special effort at Christmas to bring together the relatives and close friends who had emigrated from Norway and Finland to Milwaukee.

Since Father liked to have a full table—enough and a little bit more—for everyone, he helped Mother in the meal preparation. He usually pared the potatoes and other vegetables needing similar attention; he placed the leaves in the dining room table and brought in supplies of water from the well and wood and coal for the stove. Mother did all the cooking and baking on a coal and wood-burning stove which could be temperamental at times.

Mother used her best white linen tablecloth with matching linen napkins for the holiday dinner. On this she placed a white scarf fringed in red and imprinted at either end with a bright red rooster.

A huge goose roasted a beautiful brown and stuffed with apples and prunes rested at one end of the oak dining table. At the other end Father set the baked ham. A platter of thinly sliced, pink, salted salmon bought at a Milwaukee fish market brought pleasant memories of the "old country" to each of these new citizens of America.

Mother served vegetables contrasting in color and texture: a casserole of yellow rutabaga which was mashed and flavored with allspice and ham fat; shredded cabbage butter-browned and seasoned with a sweet-sour sauce; sliced, pickled red beets. Potatoes, mashed or oven-browned, were served with a delicious gravy. Lingonberries from Norway provided tartness to the meal. Mother always made Parker House rolls and served them with her home-churned butter.

Christmas Day dinner ended with a flambéed dessert—baked custard encircled by sauce that was flaming when brought to the table. Norwegian Christmas cookies and slices of Finnish coffee bread were also served with coffee. My sister and I had the privilege of grinding the coffee beans in a small coffee grinder. Mother then mixed the ground coffee with an egg and a dash of salt to make a tasty, clear beverage. In those days real cream was added to the coffee.

Coffee diluted with milk was served in tiny cups to all of us children who learned our parents' custom of balancing a sugar cube on our tongues while sipping the beverage.

So Christmas dinner ended.

I didn't realize until years later the privilege we had of eating holiday dinners prepared with tender, loving care under conditions that today would discourage even the most dedicated cook.

## STARS IN TIM'S SKY
*Olga Wetzel*

It wasn't that the other pupils disliked Tim Reed; they just never even noticed him. He was the last one chosen when games were played. No one seemed to care about his opinion when decisions were made. But he didn't seem hurt; he had reached the point where he expected it to be that way. It seemed the stars had already disappeared from Tim's sky.

Since there were forty-seven pupils (in grades one through eight) and I was the only teacher, he received only average attention from me. None of us guessed that that quiet boy of twelve had as much potential as he really possessed.

Days in a rural school in the 1920s passed swiftly. There was so much to do. A posted program listed the classes in the order in which they were called. No class lasted more than twenty minutes; some lasted only ten. This was not all bad, because then essentials had to be stressed. Even today I feel that if essentials are really understood, the human mind can go on from there—by itself if need be. And my object always was to see that everyone in the class got the essentials; they would all have to make a living.

What a privilege it was to start those little beginners in reading! We used the Laurel Primer. They learned their words first in script. Then print was placed right beneath it, and they soon saw that both are much alike. This was done on the blackboard. Flash cards were also used. For seat work they often made sentences with word cards. At the end of six weeks they were given their first primers. Their eyes just shone when they found they could read the first eight pages. They hurried home to show their parents that they could really read! Tim had a little sister in the first grade. He was very proud of her.

As the weather grew colder, I started planning for our Christmas entertainment. It had meant so very much to me as a child to have an evening entertainment; I would never deny that joy to any group I worked with. There would have to be at least several plays, some songs, a drill, recitations, and motion songs. Tim had a recitation, but he had no part in a play. It seemed he liked it that way.

The week just preceding the entertainment was a very hard one for me. There was so much to arrange for, so much to do.

The older boys built three wooden sawhorses and then nailed planks above them for a stage. They did this on a Sunday afternoon. Other boys went to the woods and cut a beautiful balsam tree. The older girls and I trimmed it. Each year the school bought a few new ornaments to add to the older ones. We put up cedar decorations above the blackboards; cedar was nailed to the front plank of the stage to hide the wooden sawhorses underneath. Tim had remembered to bring small staples to fasten the cedar.

Stage curtains were white sheets that slid along wires on safety pins. Each family furnished a bed sheet. Tim wanted to bring one, but he said his mother felt theirs were not white enough. (They had no well, and had to get their water from a spring, so she never had enough rinse water.)

My tension increased as the evening of the entertainment neared. What if someone got sick? What would we do?

Every recess and a part of the noon hour were spent practicing. We had as many of our regular classes as we possibly could, but toward the last we sometimes practiced during regular school hours. Tim practiced his recitation, and no one paid any special attention. If he got sick it wouldn't upset any of the plays. Through all the practicing Tim was paying attention. He seemed to find a silent joy in drama.

On the morning of the entertainment the ax fell! Soon after I arrived at school there were excited voices in the hall. Something unusual must have happened. Roy Ream was sick in bed, covered with measles! We considered him our best singer, and he took the leading part in our main play.

By nine o'clock gloom had settled over all of us—all but Tim. He said, "I'll take Roy's part. I learned it as they were practicing. I can sing his song at the end too."

Surprise replaced the former gloom.

"We'll practice it and see how it goes," I said.

In this case of need Tim lost all shyness and took the part very well. He was right. He had listened in his quiet way while the play was practiced over and over. He needed no prompting.

I wondered how he would do before an audience.

While I was wondering this, Tim was hurrying home. He had great news for his parents: "I'm taking the leading part in the play tonight!"

"But do you know it?" his mother anxiously asked.

"You'll see! You'll see!" Tim answered.

Imagine Tim's excitement as they neared the schoolhouse that evening. Three big lamps were lighted inside the school, and two lanterns on the outside near the

170

steps. Horse-drawn sleighs were lined up on the sheltered side of the building. Many walked to the schoolhouse.

Inside, the warmth of the room, the beautiful tree, and the expectant faces made all the work seem worthwhile. The Christmas spirit filled the room.

The main play was the last number. The excitement of the evening made Tim forget all fear. He was so sure he knew his part; now was his chance to make his parents and his school proud of him.

And proud they were! Even a professional actor could not have taken that part better than Tim did. It was because he was needed; he was noticed; he was happy! He was so good that he made the whole play come alive.

Interest and intense surprise showed on the faces in the audience. No one had heard Tim sing when he was this happy. He had never been this happy before. This is the song he sang:

*In Bethlehem town on one glad Christmas day*
*The little Lord Jesus so peacefully lay.*
*He came that all people through love should be free,*
*And the joy of Christmas is for you and for me.*

*Merry Christmas for you, merry Christmas for me*
*Merry Christmas, for His great love is around*
*you and me.*

*So sing we His praises with reverent voice,*
*And honor His birthday while nations rejoice,*
*For love sheds its blessings from mountain to sea*
*And the joy of Christmas is for you and for me.*

The applause that followed was like water breaking from a dam. Tim walked to the edge of the stage and bowed to the audience. There was more clapping. Someone called out, "Sing it again!" Tim smiled and repeated the chorus:

*Merry Christmas for you, merry Christmas for me*
*Merry Christmas, for His great love is around you*
*and me.*

Tim's father sat tall and proud and joined in the final applause. His mother did not applaud at all; she sat beside her husband, silently weeping.

And Tim? The stars were back in his sky.


## THE CULOCH
*Roderick MacDonald*

I grew up in a little Scottish settlement in Fremont Township, Saginaw County, Michigan. At the turn of the century, when I was ten, I had my first introduction to an unforgettable celebration called the Culoch. It was an ancient Scottish ritual that took place on New Year's Eve and lasted well into the morning.

The eve of the year 1902 was the happy one for me, for that was the night my father, affectionately known to his neighbors as Beaver Dan MacDonald, invited me to join him in the Culoch parade. He was a giant of a man, and even today, three score years later, I thrill at the memory of seeing him in his feathered bonnet, standing majestically in his family plaid, with what seemed to me at the time to be a giant broadsword at his side. The parade was to start at our home that evening, for this was the night my father was selected to be the leader and sing the hauntingly rhythmic "Dann" (Dew-in), a spirited marching chant. The idea of the Culoch was to parade from home to home, stopping each time to "sip and sup," and then be joined by the grown males of each household to sing and march to the next home, eventually ending the parade at the home of Big Dan MacDonald for a giant feast and party.

The ladies of each household followed the parade in sleighs and cutters after they had treated the paraders.

We started out at seven in the evening, and our first stop was at home of Rory MacIntyre. My father and I stood outside the door, and in a loud clear voice he sang the "Dann." Mrs. MacIntyre then opened the door and extended the traditional greeting, "Welcome in, Highlanders." Then there were hearty greetings from the entire family, and we were led into the cheery kitchen dominated by a gaily set table which practically groaned under the burden of the feast it carried, all good foods of the earth, grown on the farm, and prepared with loving care. I remember that little Katie MacIntyre (she was twelve and beautiful) seemed especially gracious to me that evening, and when I was having a little trouble managing the enormous six-layer chocolate cake she helped me with it and we both laughed heartily.

After a few minutes' visit we stood up, sang a short Gaelic song, and were on our way again, joined now by the MacIntyre males. After several stops, our ranks had swollen almost as much as our bellies, and now our parade included most of the Scottish Highlanders of the area: several families of MacDonalds and MacDougals, MacLeods, MacCormacks, MacCullens, MacInneses, MacPhersons, Steels, MacKays, MacPhees, Grahams, and MacKenzies. There were many others but these are the ones I remember. Some of the homes were too small to accommodate the paraders so we would stand outside as the occupants fed us and visited with us through the windows. By the time we had reached the eleventh or twelfth home some of us were so full we stayed outside by our own option, as the fresh air was by now a greater treat than the smell of good food.

As we neared the end of our trek some of the men were losing their speed and were inclined to stop, but my father started singing a Highland marching song called "The Highland Brigade," and soon everyone was stepping along briskly and happily. Several times along the way old Oak Dan MacDonald would yell "I-dee-ho" and we would all laugh, for this was the day that he had been notified his son had struck it rich in Idaho. Somehow it seemed that the oldsters minded the walk less than the younger ones.

Finally we reached our destination, the home of Big Dan MacDonald. Dan's home was like the man—big. The entrance was in the middle, directly opposite a wide, open staircase that led to many bedrooms on the second floor and a large sitting room called Granny's room. All the women had arrived by now and went directly to Granny's room to take off their wraps. Granny was downstairs with the guests. She had a nickname, Pecky Vorre, the meaning of which was never explained to me. She was ninety-seven years old and the toast of the evening. She was still quite spry and smoked a long-stemmed corncob pipe which she held firmly in her mouth. She greeted me by saying, "Hello, son of Beaver Dan—from the looks of the size of your feet you may grow to be bigger than my son Big Dan." Then she cackled happily and pulled me to her and gave me a big kiss.

John MacDonald, Big Dan's brother, was the fiddler of the evening, and his sister Kate played the organ. Bagpipers played for the special dancing. The Scotch Reel was one of these, danced by four beautiful young girls in special, brightly colored kilts. Another girl danced the popular Highland fling, and Norman Steel drew shouts from all as he whirled through the sword dance. There was lots of singing of Highland songs in Gaelic as well as

English, and even some modern songs of the day, such as "Good-bye, Dolly Gray," "A Bird in a Gilded Cage," and a song of the civil war, "Tenting Tonight."

Most of the eating and drinking was done in front of an enormous fireplace at one end of the room. Many bottles of Scotch sat on the table, along with another giant feast of food. I have a hazy memory of Murdoch MacGuiness sitting in a corner of the kitchen trying to get his bagpipes to work. He didn't know Bogey Dan MacDonald had poured beer into the pipes to stop the sour notes Murdoch had been hitting as a result of too much sour mash.

It must have been three in the morning before we went home, full and happy. But I have one more happy memory of that New Year's Eve. That was the sight of Crooked John MacGuiness staggering through our back yard at noon the next day, holding a lantern high and looking for the Culoch parade.

## MY FATHER'S VIOLIN
*Beatrice Derrick*

My most cherished memory of my childhood is of our fireplace and my father and his violin. He had built this fireplace out of beautiful red brick, which he had manufactured himself, and he was so proud of it. This fireplace was the focal point of our life. We actually lived in front of it, studying our lessons there, playing checkers, popping corn, reading, doing fancywork. My mother did her knitting there. When friends came to call, another log was laid on the fire, tea and some of my mother's freshly baked bread or cookies were served, and everyone sat around that fireplace visiting or spinning yarns which sometimes were a little out of perspective.

Best of all was when my father would take his violin down off the shelf, at our urging, of course, and play. This violin was a Stradivarius, and he dearly loved it. It had the most beautiful rich tone, and he loved to play it. He could play for hours without tiring. It was only after working all day in the cold that his fingers would get quite stiff, but as he continued to play his violin, gradually his fingers would limber up. Then he'd swing into his repertoire, always beginning with "The Blue Danube Waltz," then going through the wildest two-steps, jigs, and waltzes you ever heard.

We always delighted at "The Old Man and His Wife." He'd start the Old Man off by playing very quietly and slowly and, on all the low notes, hesitating occasionally like a man who is considering and weighing every word carefully. Then he quickly brought the Old Lady in, rudely interrupting the Old Man with all the shrill high notes, increasing the tempo, never even stopping for a breath, which went on for quite a spell, as she had a lot to say. When she had finished her tirade, we waited with bated breath for the final act, when the Old Man comes in with a resounding "No" or "Yes, dear." This piece sent us into peals of laughter. My father could imitate just about anything with his violin: a train coming down the track, approaching or leaving the depot, blowing its whistle, and engines chugging away. You'd swear the birds were coming down out of the trees in that violin, with the winds actually whistling, horses trotting or galloping, wolves howling, and many other sounds. He could make that violin talk.

My younger brother and I would vie with one another for a place as close to our father's knee as we could snuggle, there on the floor, while he played. We were completely happy and contented and could listen to him play his violin forever.

But as the evening wore on, the flicker and the heat of the fire in the fireplace cast a spell on us until our eyes would droop with sleep. Our father would then swing into a medley of lullabies and send us off to bed. This would go on and on during the long winter nights and we never tired of it.

But my father's violin suffered a sad fate at one of the innumerable dances that were held at our house. One of my older brothers, who by then had taken up violin playing too, had been accompanying one of our neighbor boys with the violin and laid it down on his chair during intermission for lunch. Someone came in, removed his wraps and laid them over the chair, covering the violin. Someone else came in and promptly sat down on this chair. Crack it went. You could hear it way across the room. Everyone suddenly stopped laughing and talking. You could hear a pin drop. It seemed as if a pall had settled over the room. Everyone dreaded to remove the wraps. My brother, white as a sheet and with big tears rolling down his cheeks, rushed back into the room. That episode tempered the merriment for that evening.

Repeated efforts were made to find someone who could repair and restore this precious violin, but to no avail. They all shook their heads sadly.

My brother did obtain another violin for his father, but it wasn't his old violin, his first love. It didn't have the same rich and deep tone, and as my father played by ear entirely, he just was unable to coax the music out of it. The performance didn't meet his satisfaction, so soon he laid it away dejectedly and never could be persuaded to play a violin again.

The old violin was stripped and laid up on a shelf to gather dust and was forgotten. Many years later, the brother who played a violin died, and his home was being sold. When I asked his grandsons about the violin, they were all surprised to hear about it. It was discovered in the attic, wedged between two two-by-fours and covered with dust and cobwebs. No one would give it a second look and questioned what I wanted that old piece of junk for. It was a sorry sight indeed. Besides its face being cracked, half of its back was also gone.

Again I searched for someone to repair it, with no success. Almost no one was interested and those who were would charge exorbitant fees that were discouraging.

But one day, Heaven opened up for me. I was with a busload of senior citizens at a craft show in Duluth, and at one of the many tables there sat a sweet little old man and his wife, displaying several old violins that they had restored and repaired. I could hardly believe that such luck had come to me. I turned to them with tears in my eyes. My prayers had been answered, but I was apprehensive that they could repair this violin. With all my past disappointments it was almost too much to hope for. But the man quickly put me at ease when he said, "Don't you fret. We get some of these violins in shoe boxes and all in pieces. I'm sure we can repair it for you. I haven't seen a violin that I couldn't repair. Send it to us and we'll let you know." I was almost afraid to ask him his price, and my mouth fell open with shock at his low fee. I couldn't wait to get home. I felt as if I was floating on air and told everyone on the bus of my good fortune.

I carefully and quickly packed and mailed the violin out the next day. A month later, the violin was returned, and it was impossible to see where it had been glued and pressed together so perfectly. It had a new back, and it was also gilded. But best of all, it played. It has that same beautiful, rich tone that I remembered. I'll always remain eternally grateful to this sweet little old couple.

It graces my wall now in an old-fashioned shadow box frame lined with red velvet, with an old music sheet my father used to play and his picture. It is simply exquisite! I can close my eyes and hear again those old medleys my father used to play.

## THE SEARS ORDER BOX
### *Jean Bunker Schmidt*

I sometimes wonder if parents realize the utter delight their children sometimes experience with some event or happening in the home that their elders may consider more or less routine. I have in mind an event that took place annually when I was a child, usually after Christmas when prices were marked down in the mail order catalogs.

We lived on the Dakota prairies back in the pre-World War I days, and because of the distance to town and the lower prices, most all "store-bought" articles were ordered from Sears, Roebuck. This particular order for Sears was not a matter of individual families sending in their separate lists. It was, instead, a community affair.

The orders were made out by the mothers of each family and handed, together with a personal check, to whichever "Head of the Family" gave his address that year for the items sent for. The entire listing was sent by this neighbor in one envelope. In due time all items arrived in a single large crate.

How well I remember the year my parents' address was given for "the box." For days after the order was sent in, my mother was asked over and over, "Have you heard anything from the box? Hasn't the box arrived at the freight depot yet?" Even we children waited impatiently. When the notice finally came, it was like telling us a favorite aunt had arrived in town, waiting to be brought out to the farm home. My mother rang up each family on the telephone and set a certain evening for the neighboring families to come and claim their individual orders.

This particular Saturday evening our house began to fill with men, women, and children. The large crate was brought in from the coal shed and placed exactly in the center of the living room. Papa brought the crow bar from its nail in the entryway and then *Crack!* went the rough top boards. Mama, a systematic woman, carefully removed a layer of packing paper, folding it carefully, its future use in mind. Then she made sure she had found the invoice before any of the articles were removed.

My father lifted out the first article. Mama peered into the package, then checked with her invoice. "I think this is yours, Lizzy," she said. Her neighbor, with a smile, exclaimed, "Oh, yes, my wool dress goods. Isn't it pretty, though!"

Aunt Mary hovered over the box. "Is my crinkle crepe there?" She lowered her voice to a whisper. "My nightie is getting pretty threadbare!" When the desired package was discovered, Aunt Mary showed the material to all the other ladies, who in turn showed their own different pieces of yardage.

Together, Papa and Mama removed and handed over the articles to the owners. There were such things as a large box of Rub-No-More, a dozen bars of Lennox soap, barber shears, rick-rack, a curling iron for my eldest sister's chum who had "hateful" red hair and tried to compensate with curls. My sister, who could play the organ, gleefully accepted from Mama's hands the three or four sheets of music she had been allowed to order. I still remember the titles: "Bird of Paradise," "Silver Sleigh Bells," "Carry Me Back to Old Virginny."

There was one whose title I didn't understand. To me, it read "Minute in G," pronounced as a "minute" of time. I asked my mother why it was given such a puzzling title. "Does it take exactly a minute to play it?" I asked. Smiling, she explained that the word was pronounced "min-u-ett." The memory returns whenever I hear the piece played.

One particular package piqued my interest. I noticed Mama had slyly set it aside, near the organ. I pretended I was weary of watching the activities (far from it!) and sat myself down beside the organ. Silently, I read the words on the package: Lydia E. Pinkham's Compound.

I supposed it was some kind of medicine. I squinted my eyes into the smaller print. Surprisingly, the description seemed quite flowery. "Revives the spirit," I read. "Restores a natural luster to the eye." Fascinated, I read on. It seemed whoever drank this liquid would find roses planted on his cheek.

I looked around the room at the cheeks of the ladies present. My mother's cheeks were quite tan from the wind and sun. Perhaps, I reasoned, Mama had ordered the compound with the hope that after drinking it, her cheeks would be rosier than Aunt Mary's. Or, perhaps, to please and surprise Papa. I wondered for a long time just why she ordered it.

As the items were lifted from the order box, the piles of goods placed on the floor became higher. Each family piled their own articles nearby so that they might occasionally tear off a wrapper and examine what they had ordered. There were shoes for the children (squeals of delight!); one pair for an older girl had laces and cloth tops.

There were black cotton stockings; union suits of all sorts and sizes; leggings; serge, flannel, wool, silk, and chambray yardgoods. Mama had four girls, so naturally many of her items included needles, J&P Coats thread, and thimbles.

One sizable package came up out of the depths of the box. Mama looked at the invoice, then smiled. "This seems to be yours, Grace," she told the woman who had ten children. Her neighbor took the package. Unabashed, she exclaimed, "Oh, yes! I'd forgotten I ordered it. We do need another one. I've only got four now. I've forgotten what the price was. Look on the list, Ila."

"White enameled chamber pot," Mama read. "Medium size, sixty-five cents. Cover, thirty cents."

"Well, it's a dollar well spent," the woman said. "No one will have to run outside at night in forty below. Now, our family'll be all set for the rest of the winter!"

I noticed the twinkle in Papa's eye even before he spoke. "Don't you mean you'll all be setting?" he said, as everyone broke into laughter. No one could ever say things were dull when Papa was around.

As the box became more and more empty, the conversation became more animated. I tried to listen to everyone, but I could gather only fragments of sentences.

"Plaster? I didn't order—oh, castor—castor oil. Half a gallon—"

"Isn't this sateen lovely? I can get two or three petti—"

"Lookee my new stocking cap! An' I got—"

"This 20 Mule-team boric acid—twenty cents. A real bar—"

"Did you hear that, John?" I heard Papa say. "Boric acid costs a penny a mule!" I remember how the men roared with laughter.

A few of the women had received all the items they had ordered and were talking of what they intended to order next year. "I want a carpet sweeper," one said. "They have a Colonel in the catalog for only two dollars and ninety-five cents."

"You might as well say three dollars," Mama remarked. "I think a broom sweeps just as well, myself." (She was the practical one.) "But I do need a new coffee mill. That Family mill prices all the way from thirty-nine cents to seventy-six cents."

She changed the subject. "We're close to the bottom of the box. Pa, you'd better handle this last package."

"You bet your boots," Papa said cheerfully. "Now, what in the sam hill is this thing, anyway?"

"Hey," one of the men called from across the room, "that's my horse collar!" He took it from Papa's hands. "How do you like it, everybody? It's an Emory, made for buggy harnesses."

"Pretty swell," Papa told him. "Now your roan will be the best-dressed horse in the county! Well, that's all, folks. You can go home now!"

Of course everyone knew that Papa was only joking again. Even now, my eldest sister and her school friend were bringing in a huge dish of apples to pass around. Papa had brought a bushel basket of them from town when he drove in to pick up the order box.

Finally, someone noticed the lateness of the evening and reminded the others that we must all get up early to get to church on time. The families gathered up their separate bundles and packages and scrambled into their long warm coats, overshoes (and leggings for the children), mittens, scarves, and muffs. Mama handed each family their own-kept-warm and newspaper-wrapped flat-irons they would be placing at their feet as they cuddled comfortably under thick lap robes in the bobsled.

The exciting "order box" event was over for another year.

# 10 The Good Old Days

## THOSE "GOOD OLD DAYS"
*Bert Vawter*

I suppose I am one of the first and one of the worst to complain about taxes, inflation, the high cost of living, and high prices in general, but when people start talking about those good old days, I wonder just how good those good old days really were. I have heard people talk about the good old days as long as I can remember, and I can remember so close to three score ten years that it scares me. But if you really want the good old days, you can still have them.

When were the good old days? For this yarn I am going to go back to the years before World War I. At that time everything was smooth and calm. The world was pretty much at peace. (Since then, we have been involved in four wars, the Great Depression, assassinations, political scandal, and other upheavals.) The location will have to be central Illinois, as that is where I was raised. I want to pick a rural area because I didn't see a large city until I was fifteen years old. For the occupation of the person involved, let us go to the semiskilled, common laborer, that is, the handyman who could do almost anything pretty well although he was not a master at any one trade or profession. That is the background of my family.

If you wish to enjoy the good old days, you can first look around and find a place to live, a house or some kind of building. Working people did not live in fancy homes, so the price you may pay to rent cheaply will not be for a very fancy place. It will probably need a little repairing. You will have to patch the roof or maybe fix the door or window, do some painting and paperhanging. But it would be a place in which to live and as good as a lot of people had in the good old days. You won't get wall-to-wall carpeting, but you can pick up some runners and pieces of carpet at Goodwill, the Salvation Army, or rummage sales. You can get by. You won't have running water in the house, but you'll probably have a well in the backyard. You can carry the water to the house in buckets. There won't be any electricity in the house, of course, but you can use kerosene lamps or candles. There won't be any furnace or a central heating plant, but you can pick up a couple of stoves, a heating stove for the living room and a cookstove for the kitchen. Now, a wood-burning stove for the kitchen may be a little hard to come by, but they are available. You will find wood to cut. There's lots of timberland where the owner will let you have the dead and down trees for cleaning up and at little or no cost. You'll be rather busy, of course, because you are back in the good old days, and you'll be working on your job six days a week, ten hours a day. Cutting wood will be quite a chore. Naturally, you won't have a chain saw. You will be using an ax and a one-man saw the way we did in the good old days, but you won't have the expense of a fancy chain saw and the oil and gasoline it takes to run them.

If you need a pound of coffee or something from the store, you won't go out and crank up a six thousand or eight thousand dollar automobile and use seventy cents a gallon for gas. You will walk. That's the way they did it. You can still walk. Of course, you won't have the expense of a bathtub or expensive water heater because you can carry the water in from the well, heat it in pots and kettles on the cookstove, and take your bath in the kitchen in a washtub. You won't have the expense of an electric washing machine or dryer. You can always use a washboard or manual-powered washing machine. They're not very much of a wifesaver, of course, but they're cheaper. That's what they used in the good old days. You won't have to buy expensive detergent and washing aids. You can always use cake laundry soap because it's cheaper, or you can make your own soap. It just takes grease, lye, and water to make soap. If you don't have enough grease around the house, the local butcher will give you all of the beef tallow you need to make soap for practically nothing.

For its size, the electric iron is the most expensive appliance to operate in your home. But you did not have any of those in the good old days. You can get a couple of flatirons and heat them on the cookstove, although it may be a little rough in the hot summer. Another problem you may encounter will be having no sink in the house that you rent, but you can set a five-gallon bucket under the table or a bench where you keep the water bucket and the washbasin. When the bucket is full, you carry it out and dump it.

Of course, we know it's impossible to duplicate the good old days 100 percent, but if you could avoid working for anyone who takes out for Social Security, that would save you the trouble of going down to the post office and picking up your Social Security check when you become sixty-two or sixty-five years old. If you didn't get involved with an employer that offers unemployment benefits, you wouldn't have to fool with unemployment compensation in the event that you were laid off. That is also true if you worked for a company that had unemployment insurance. In the good old days very few companies did, so very few people ended up with a pension. If you do get involved with a pension plan, you will gain a little bit of weight from the good old days.

After a hard day's work you may occasionally enjoy a couple of beers. In the good old days you could walk into a neighborhood bar and get a large stein of beer for a nickel. Today a large glass of beer would cost you about fifty cents. Of course, in the good old days people were working ten hours a day for about $1.50 a day. Today if you were good at working at an odd job, you would be making $5 per hour. In the really good old days you could buy three glasses of beer for only fifteen cents, or one hour's work. Today, three beers would cost you $1.50, or about twenty minutes' work.

My father was a kind of country butcher. In the winter he would dress the beef and then cut it up and peddle it from house to house throughout the countryside. Hindquarter meat was fifteen cents a pound. Forequarter meat was ten cents a pound. A forequarter weighs, as a general rule, a little more than a hindquarter and would average out to about twelve cents a pound. Of course, they started at one end and cut through to the next. If you were unlucky, you would get a neck. If you were lucky, you might get a center cut porterhouse or T-bone piece of loin. In the good old days, a five-pound chuck roast for your Sunday dinner would cost you about sixty cents, averaging twelve cents a pound or four hours' work. Today meat averages over a dollar a pound, but in most stores a five-pound chuck roast would cost you about $4.50. That would be three days' work in the good old days or forty-five minutes' work today.

You could raise chickens for eggs and meat, but you would have to raise the feed that you use. If you have to buy the feed, the eggs and meat would cost you more than they would in the supermarket. If you have room, you could also raise some pigs for meat. Again, you would have to raise all of their feed. Of course, you wouldn't buy any prepared food. You would make bread and everything from scratch.

Most of the old-timers didn't have health or life insurance. Naturally, no one had radio, TV, or anything like that in the good old days. You would buy your perishables every day to avoid spoilage because you wouldn't have a refrigerator or a freezer. You would hang your butter or your milk in the summertime in the well to keep it from spoiling. We used to do it. It works. You shouldn't have to buy very much canned food because you could raise and can or dry most things yourself. Of course, you would be quite busy working ten hours a day six days a week cutting wood for one stove the year round and two stoves in the wintertime and raising a garden and feed for chickens and pigs. But that's the way they did it in the good old days. Clothing would not be too big an expense, as you would probably have only one suit, and you could wear that for six or eight years. In the good old days there wasn't any withholding, so you went up to the boss on Saturday night after working ten hours a day six days a week and you got your full pay, all of it. The full nine dollars. Today after you have worked sixty hours, Uncle Sam has his hand in your pocket before you even get your check. He can take as much as sixty dollars and leave you standing there with only about two hundred forty dollars left after a week's work.

So there you are if you want the good old days. They aren't too hard to come by. But as for myself, I think I'd rather sit down in this nice comfortable chair in a nice robe and slippers after a nice warm bath and watch Lawrence Welk on a twenty-five-inch television set. At the same time, I'll just keep on griping about taxes, inflation, and high prices for gasoline.

## YARNS OF YESTERYEAR
*Floyd L. Smith*

There it still stands, the L-shaped frame house, three miles east of Lime Ridge, where I was born eighty-five years ago.

As I look, it is almost as I remember when I was a small boy. There is the upstairs window I looked out of every morning as I awoke from my bed, which had a straw tick. An enclosed porch has been added to the front of the house. There are a few of the Norway spruce my father planted for a windbreak west of the house. Across the road south stands the old red barn. The silo was added after I left. Silos were not commonly used then.

My eyes look north to the path up the hill. I walked this path many times in my young, carefree days. This path led past the old lime kiln where we boys worked and played. Weather has nearly destroyed the kiln.

Limestone burning was a new and fascinating industry. Not only was our farm blessed with an outcropping of excellent limestone, but there were also many loose cobblestones in the fields on top of the hill. We boys learned to hate those smaller stones because every spring before planting time we had the back-aching job of picking stones from the field and carrying them to the edge of the field to make fences. One spring after a very cold winter when the frost had "heaved" a large amount of stone to the surface, we hitched a horse to the stoneboat to haul the stone and relieve our backache.

My father was a good stonemason. He conceived the idea of making good use of troublesome limestone, also turning a profit on the labor of us four boys. He made plans to construct a lime kiln using the bedrock for the wall and burning the limestone for commercial use.

There was a good market for lime among farmers who used it to make mortar for stone walls. It was also used instead of paint to whitewash the inside of log houses, barns, and chicken coops. Paint was very expensive.

With picks and shovels we leveled a twelve-foot circular area in the fifty percent slope of the hillside. This made room to build a round lime kiln nine feet high and eight feet in diameter of limestone bedrock. Dad then built a firebox of limestone on the floor seven feet long by two feet wide. This connected to an outside door.

Now came the boys' job of hauling and filling to the top that huge opening with smaller limestone. We hauled and hauled stone for several days.

The winter before, we had cut ten cords of seven-foot-long cordwood to burn in the kiln. Everything was ready to start the actual burning of the limestone. Fire was started in the huge firebox. It was to burn continually for eight days. This meant that two boys formed two teams to fire the kiln night and day. We erected a tent near the kiln and equipped it with a straw tick and an alarm clock. Each team fired the kiln for twenty-four hours. What a beautiful sight to look down from the top of the pit into that burning mass of stone. The colors waved and changed from red to purple, green, yellow, and violet, then combined and danced in unison.

After eight days we let the fire die. When the stone cooled we had a mass of nice, white, commercial lump lime. Farmers and builders for miles around came with horse-drawn wagons to buy lime to use for its many purposes. For all our labor each of us had money to buy a new suit and to buy Mother a new hat.

Another standard industry for every family when I was a boy was soap making. We saved the hardwood ashes from the heating stove and placed them in an upright wooden barrel three feet high and two feet in diameter. The barrel, with small holes in the bottom, was mounted on a large flat stone. A sheet of tin was placed between the stone and the barrel bottom. When the barrel was full of ashes I carried water for two weeks, one pailful a day, and poured it into the top of the barrel. This caused the lye to leach out of the ashes to the tin at the bottom of the barrel. The lye was caught and saved for soapmaking. The liquid lye was mixed with fat trimmings from butchering beef. This mixture was placed in a large iron kettle outside. The kettle was mounted eight inches off the ground with five stones. Fire was kept burning under the kettle for two days. With occasional stirring to prevent burning we then added a little rosewater for perfume. When cooled it was cut into squares and stored in a dry place. If the mixture failed to harden when cool, we had soft soap, which some women preferred for washing clothes.

The medical profession was in its infancy when I was a boy. The average span of life was about forty-one years. I often think of the dreaded disease diphtheria, very common then. My parents told me how this dreaded disease spread through our neighborhood when I was one year old. I got diphtheria as did two of my older brothers. A third brother never got it. Being the youngest, I was dangerously sick. Some called it black diphtheria. Dad ran to our neighbor and asked him to race on horseback ten miles to Reedsburg to ask Dr. Edwards to come quickly. My parents thought I was dying because I could hardly breathe and my throat was closing. In four hours Dr. Edwards came and administered the newly discovered antitoxin. After treatment I began to revive. Two of our neighbors' children died of the disease. They took them in the night to bury them. No one dared to accompany them as the surrounding country was strictly quarantined.

Many families lost one or two children to diphtheria. That was the winter of 1893.

Most ordinary sicknesses Mother cured with epsom salts given once a week. In spring we got three doses of sulphur and molasses to cleanse our blood.

Despite all the work children did, they also had lots of fun. Mother tried to have us attend Sunday school at United Brethren Church. Afterward we walked one mile to the old swimming hole where we swam and dived with all the boys of the countryside. Bathing suits were not worn then, so we swam in the nude. Cartoonist Clare Briggs, who was born in Reedsburg and got his start there, made "The Old Swimming Hole" famous. The *Reedsburg Times Press*, our local weekly paper, recently printed a series of Briggs's famous cartoons of 1920 and 1930.

On the Fourth of July we really had fun. We tiptoed downstairs before daylight to explode a hoard of firecrackers and announce the big celebration. After breakfast we helped our parents hitch the horses to the wagon and packed plenty of homemade ice cream, together with a three-layer cake with inch-thick coconut frosting. We journeyed two miles to my grandparents' farm where we met and played with our "kissin' cousins." After dinner we often went to Goodell's Grove at Lime Ridge to enter the foot races and hear patriotic speeches.

My grandparents, the Ephriam Smiths, had migrated in 1853 from Morrow County, Ohio, and settled on 160 wooded acres of land in Ironton Township. My father was then six months old. They made the trip with ox team and wagon, stopping at night with farm families. When they came through Chicago it was a small, dingy-looking village with the houses and buildings standing on marshy ground.

Three years later and after clearing seven acres of wild land, Grandfather decided to return to Ohio to get more supplies. He left the wife and eight children in Wisconsin while he and an older boy went back to Ohio. This time they traveled with horse team and wagon. They brought back two barrels of apple butter and a barrel of cider. Apples were plentiful in Ohio because Johnny Appleseed had migrated westward through Ohio laden with apple seeds which he gave to settlers to plant. He supposedly planted apple seeds along the road as he traveled on foot.

## A SPRING GROWL
### Harry A. Friedman

Spring fever!

A feeling of indolence overcomes me—indolence coupled with an impulse to go somewhere, just anywhere, as far from home as I can get.

My wanderlust is not inspired by romance. It is a passion aroused by a desire to escape from the ordeal of spring house cleaning. This domestic horror burst into my awareness more than three score years ago and remains a traumatic experience.

During the Easter vacation of 1916 I first emerged from the cocoon of subconscious observation into reality. The memory is vivid. It was the spring before America entered World War I. The following year our home was converted to electricity, which did little to alleviate the unwelcome servitude but provided hilarious moments as I went from room to room switching lights on and off.

That morning I returned from Bechstein's Swimming School on the Milwaukee River to find furniture pushed aside. Beds were piled with clothing that had been removed from the darkness of gaping closets. Pictures and wall hangings were down and wrapped in old bed sheets on the floor.

In retrospect, the disarray surely represented some kind of task order. I saw only organized confusion giving way to disorganized chaos.

My beloved mother and sister, attired in dust caps and aprons, stood like sentinels in the midst of it all. My first reaction was one of excitement.

"Are we moving?" I may have blurted.

"Yes. We're moving the rugs to the back yard and you can practice batting."

Out of nowhere there materialized what became a familiar wire rug beater. My moment of excitement turned to sheer dismay.

Somehow we managed to roll up the rugs. They were either Wilton or Axminister. I favor Wilton because no boy was more wilted than I when the task was done. Size nine by twelve is burned deep in my memory. It must have been a monumental effort to carry the rugs outside and hang them on ropes strung between acorn-topped clothesline poles.

Being a dutiful son, you start to pound the walls of cloth. Each rug becomes a huge ball hurtling toward you. The beater is now your favorite bat. You are having fun. (Wait, innocent youth! Wait!) Soon there is a sensation of heat. Your arm feels like lead. The beater weighs a ton. The steady rhythm of the beat becomes irregular and falters for longer intervals. It is no more a game. Dust clouds the air. It penetrates nostrils, eyes, and mouth. Did I neglect to mention that my head also was adorned with a dust cap? Oh, shame!

Finally, the chore is done. Rugs are rerolled, brought into the house, and deposited in their respective rooms. What I would have given for wall-to-wall carpeting! We were blessed with wall-to-wall floors. The rugs would be relaid after all the interior cleaning had been completed. *That* was explained.

Cleansed of grime, you have a youth-size lunch, your munching interspersed with fruitless griping. "It's time you helped," you are told by the dear One Who Cares. Mama's boy suddenly has become a big man. How quickly we grow old in times of travail.

Next you help to take the wearing apparel outside to be aired, but not until the lines have been wiped clean of the rug debris. While the clothes are airing, feather beds and pillows are carried to the back porch and draped over the railings. Blankets are strung on clotheslines in the yard. "No. You don't have to beat them! Do you want to get the clothes full of dust?" Thank goodness for that!

Armed with a flannel-covered broom, you are given the dubious honor of wiping down walls in the bedrooms and closets. "Don't forget to watch for cobwebs." So you watch and wipe and wonder. Where do cobwebs come from? We don't have spiders.

As you finish each bedroom, the bucket brigade enters with mops, rags, pails, and hand wringers. Floors, woodwork, and furniture receive the benefit of a thorough cleansing. Woman's work is never done. Also a boy's work.

You help when and where you are recruited. All this takes time, but you are cautioned not to take your time doing it. As the afternoon wears on, scrubbing and polishing come to a halt. The clothes have been brushed down, removed from the outside, and restored to individual closets.

When the coast is clear, blankets are given a good shaking, folded, and carried back into the house. Now you go to the porch. With some assistance from your sister you shake out the bedding and bring that back. Beds are remade while you take a half dozen throw rugs outside and shake them. You yourself are beginning to shake. Replaced in the bedrooms, the small rugs are given a treatment with a Bissell carpet sweeper.

And thus endeth the first day.

Now cometh the second day. You and sister are summoned to the front rooms. Mama hops up and down on a step-stool from window to window, removes the delicate marquisette curtains, and deposits them on your outstretched arms. You carry the gossamer lace gently through the house into the yard where two large wooden frames lean against the building. "Don't get caught on anything!" You are careful not to.

You are about to get a lesson in curtain-stretching. Two round galvanized washtubs stand on the grass. The curtains are dunked one-by-one in soapy water and rinsed repeatedly in clear water. Dripping wet, they are hung over towel-covered washlines to await impalement.

Curtain-stretching does not require that fingers be punctured by the sharp prongs protruding from every inch of the frames. For a novitiate it becomes an occupational hazard. Admonitions are plentiful. "Don't pull too hard! Don't drop it! Be sure it's even! Get the ruffles straight!" Thankfully, the ordeal terminates. You await a miracle to bring surcease from your labors. No miracles are in sight.

Once more in the house, you again become a dust-broom wielder with exclusive rights to wall-brushing operations in the front rooms. Yes, you watch out for cobwebs. Where *do* they come from? Finished, there is a welcome lunch break. You learn cobwebs come from dust. You don't believe it.

Energy restored, you are handed a bar of Bon Ami soap, a damp cloth, a dry cloth, a small pail of water.

Instructions are brief. "Rub the soap on the damp cloth. Not too much. Rub the cloth on the windows. When the soap dries, wipe the windows clean with the dry cloth. Get into the corners. Don't get any on the wood." It's easy. As the white film dries it becomes a canvas challenging your artistic talents. The temptation is strong. You draw pumpkin faces with your finger. The One Who Cares is watching. The hazy masterpieces vanish in a flurry of arm movements. The windows sparkle.

One more task awaits. The object of your doubtful affections is now the huge parlor stove. After a detailed verbal rehearsal, you remove every vestige of dust from all the black sections of the stove. The heavy nickel trim is rubbed and polished until it glistens. Isinglass windows on the doors are wiped inside and out. The metal-covered asbestos pad on which the stove stands is doused with Fels Naphtha soap, rinsed, and wiped dry.

As you rise from a torturous kneeling position to admire your work, two loving arms enfold you and a kiss is planted on your cheek. "It looks beautiful! You're the best helper a mother ever had!"

That was my treasured reward. All the agony became ecstasy. An anticlimax was a great piece of marble cake, as only she could make it, and a cup of hot chocolate.

There was much work that I was spared at the time, but not in the ensuing years. Floors were scrubbed and polished with O'Cedar Oil. Furniture received the Wizard Oil treatment. Heavy, overstuffed mohair sofas and chairs were brushed and washed with ammonia. Company dishes and knickknacks were washed and returned to cabinets. Tarnish was removed from 1847 Rogers silverware. Later I learned to use all-day sucker sticks tipped with cotton to get into the nooks and crannies. Rugs were relaid and given a once-over with the Bissell sweeper. All the furniture was put back into position. Curtains and pictures were rehung. The house was filled with an aromatic mixture of soap, ammonia, oils, and moth flakes. But, it was *clean.*

I was ten then. Youth and a habit of obedience had made me captive in an atmosphere of love and cooperation. Now, in the golden years of retirement, I have become a housework captive in a more mature environment of devotion and submission. The burdens have been eased considerably by modern conveniences, but I have serious problems. I cannot remember whether the green Endust cloth or the blue one is used on the furniture, or whether the yellow cloth is used for high or low dusting.

The reward is as precious today as it was long ago, however, when another dear One Who Cares tells me, "I don't know what I would do without you."

Can fall cleaning be far behind?

## THE BUTCHERING
### *Betty Wetzel*

In the spring when the first litter of little pigs were fighting greedily to be head of the line at their mother's cafeteria, my father started appraising each one shrewdly.

My brothers and sister and I liked to name these first little pigs. Neither of my parents, however, ever referred to any animal by the names we children gave them.

My brothers preferred a big, noisy aggressive pig they called a shoat. They named him Aberhart after the biggest boy in school, who was also the neighborhood bully.

My sister and I named our favorite Cedric. Our friend Cedric was a somewhat dandified older boy who had a knack of telling things so as to make everyone laugh, even Miss McGilvary, the teacher.

I was reading a library book one night when Dad said, "I'm going to cut that boar out of the herd tomorrow, Elsie. The one with the good conformation the girls are always talking about."

"Elizabeth'll have a fit when it comes time to butcher," Mother objected.

"We won't mention it when that time comes," Dad said. "Have you noticed that his shoulders are the same width as his hindquarters? His chest is full, his rump rounds toward his tail—"

"And his tail is curly," I finished triumphantly. It had just dawned on me that they were discussing Cedric.

"Humph!" A man of few words, Dad grinned at Mother. That look frequently passed between them whenever one of us said or did anything that pleased or surprised them.

"Are we going to take Cedric to the fair?" I demanded.

Dad muttered something about chores and ducked out of the house. That was another trick of his. But Mother was more than equal to coping with whatever he shirked.

"We must have good pork for the winter, Elizabeth," she said reasonably. "You're old enough to know that. Your dad figures that animal will make the best meat for us."

"But Dad said he was well formed," I argued. "That's what it takes for a prize winner. We could brush him real pretty—"

Mother had closed her lips firmly. I knew there was no use of further begging.

But my parents did discuss the subject that night. Alice and I shared the bedroom next to theirs. I was just imagining parading Cedric past the judge's stand, a blue ribbon dangling from his red collar, when I heard my name again.

"Elizabeth is determined to groom that animal for the fair," Mother said.

"I told you before, Elsie, he's the prime hog in the yard. We've got to feed the best for the winter's meat."

"But couldn't we show him at the fair, then butcher him?" You had to give Mother credit for trying.

"And have the kids raising the roof? Can you imagine the fuss they'd all make if we butchered their prize hog? No, Elsie—leave it alone."

After that they just whispered. But I lay awake a long time entranced with my vision.

The way Dad pampered Cedric after that it was almost as if we *were* getting him ready for the fair. He put Cedric in a separate pen at the side of the pig lot. (Everyone else called it the hog lot, but Alice and I didn't like the word "hog.")

There was a little gateway in the fence so that Cedric could go back and forth into a fenced-off section of the clover lot all the pigs grazed in. The fence kept him from mingling with the other pigs, and he had his own private patch of clover.

Alice and I felt sorry that he was isolated from the others. We used to visit him to talk to him. We'd brush him with an old broom and he seemed to like that. At night Dad would give us a half pail of milk, from the separator, to take down to him.

Dad said that keeping him apart from the rest was the only way that Cedric (only Dad called him "that boar") would get all the proper things he needed to make the tastiest pork.

There were troughs with several partitions in the pen.

One partition was for rye, one for oats, and one for soy beans. There was another that was used for either tankage or linseed oil, both of which Dad said cost like the dickens. There was a tank that was always filled with fresh water.

By August, Cedric looked like a picture. Even Charlie whistled approvingly.

"Man, did you ever turn into a brawny, bonny swine!" he exclaimed. Charlie was my second older brother and he always talked like a book. But then, so did the rest of us. Mother said that was because we were such avid readers. Well, so was she. Fortunately there was no television then!

Even the bully Aberhart came to look Cedric over. When he said, "Ed, you'd better take that boar to the fair. He'll take first prize sure," Dad only grunted.

"This one's for butchering."

We all gasped to think Aberhart would call our father Ed.

September drifted into October. The older boys whispered together. They made sly remarks about tragedy stalking our family.

My oldest brother, Obbie, said one day we'd come home and find no Cedric, only a pile of pork chops and spare ribs.

Charles crowed gleefully, "I'm going to make me a whistle out of his tail!"

In November the weather turned cold as Antarctica. Dad said, "Time to close off the parlor, Elsie."

The parlor was our deep freeze in the wintertime. I was engrossed in *The Tale of Two Cities*. Alice was completing a doll's outfit. But we pricked up our ears when the older boys smirked knowingly.

Next day Obbie and Charlie left school at afternoon

recess. Albert, Alice, and I didn't notice they were gone until after the bell rang.

At four o'clock we three little ones stumbled and ran all the way home. The air stung like needles with cold and my lungs were bursting. Mother wasn't in the house. But someone was moving in the corncrib.

An open driveway separated the two huge bins that made up the corncrib. Sawhorses had been set up with planks laid across them to make a scaffold at the far end, away from the house. Just like in *Tale of Two Cities*, I thought.

The scaffolding looked as if it had just been washed, but the ground beneath it was red. Forming a yardarm between the sides of the cribs was a stout pole with pointed ends. Suspended from the pole was a clean, white carcass, split neatly down the middle, with ribs and backbone exposed.

Appalled, Albert whispered, "It's Cedric! They've gone and butchered Cedric."

"Yes, and Obbie and I helped scald him," Charlie boasted. "Mother heated a whole boilerful of water. When it was boiling we poured it into the hog barrel."

"First, Dad slit the boar's throat," Obbie said importantly. "Then after it had bled awhile, he stuck the ends of the pole through the tendons of his legs. Then we helped douse him up and down in the water with the hoist."

"His bristles came off just as easy when we scraped him," Charlie added. "See how nice and white he is? I guess you can call us men now."

Suddenly both Obbie and Charlie seemed bigger and older.

"Dad's a fine butcher," Obbie said. "He's going to let the carcass hang right here tonight so it'll freeze good and hard. Then tomorrow he'll cut it up and put it on the table in the parlor."

"We helped good, didn't we, Dad?" Charlie looked anxious.

"That you did!" My father's words were sparse, as usual, but he grinned at Mother, so I knew he was pleased.

We stared at the neat, white carcass. It didn't look like anyone we had ever known, certainly not Cedric.

Mother held a stone crock. Steam rose from it, but she was wearing mittens.

"That isn't your pet, children," she said gently. "It's an animal we raised to use for food to put on our table, when it was ready. The older boys knew that when they helped with the butchering. Come, let's go to the house. I made an apple cake."

We were always hungry after school and especially after that hard run home. As we followed her she called over her shoulder, "We're going to have fresh liver for supper. That's your favorite, Elizabeth."

We were not allowed to complain about our food and I wasn't going to. I'd have some of the apple cake. But I knew I couldn't eat one single bite of that liver.

## THE CORNER GROCERY STORE
### *Margaret Kennedy*

What a fascinating place the grocery store was for the children growing up in the 1920s. I lived with my family on South Orchard Street between Mound and Chandler streets in Madison, Wisconsin. Our neighborhood grocery was in a stucco building on the corner of Mound and Orchard streets that also housed a bakery, shoe repair shop, and a plumbing business. Mr. Croft was the owner of the grocery and Mr. Koepcke was his butcher. Later, Mr. Koepcke took over the whole store.

I remember the front door of the grocery was right on the corner and the other stores fronted on Mound Street. On the cement stoop in front of the grocery were three machines popular with all the children. First there was a peanut machine with a glass top filled with peanuts—insert a penny in the slot and get a handful. Another penny could be spent in the gum machine for a single stick. Our favorite was the movie machine. For one cent, you looked through the scope and viewed a two- or three-minute movie.

In the grocery store, under the big plate glass window looking out on Mound Street, was a slanting shelf that held the produce in season. Just inside the front door on a large hook was hung a big bunch of bananas. Once they found what was thought to be a tarantula in a newly delivered bunch, and it was put on display in a jar for a couple of weeks.

The grocer or his clerks personally waited on each customer and you waited your turn. The women exchanged the latest news and gossip while waiting. I remember one day overhearing a woman asking Mrs. Koepcke what kind of laundry soap my mother used. She remarked how white my mother's wash always looked. In a very short time Green Arrow Naphtha soap was the choice of most of the women. These bars of tan-colored soap were shaved with a sharp knife, put in a pan with a little water, and melted on the stove before being put in the washing machine.

Many things were sold in bulk and the grocer weighed and bagged your purchases. He had a long pole with a clawlike contraption on the end to grab packages and cans on the highest of the shelves that lined the side wall. The two name brands of canned fruits and vegetables that I remember were Monarch and Del Monte. Coffee beans were bought in bulk and ground as needed in coffee grinders at home. Most people bought flour in twenty-five-pound sacks.

The only night the store was open was Saturday, and it stayed open until nine. A few stores were open on Sunday, but Mr. Croft's was always closed. Many people charged their groceries and paid for them on payday. There was a long, narrow box on the counter next to the big cash register which held the individual tablets of charge slips of the customers. The cash register was gold colored and it had a crank on the side that had to be turned to open the cash drawer.

The cookie cases on the floor had glass doors that swung back. The grocer opened them, dropped your choice of cookies in a brown bag, and weighed the amount on the scales. My favorites were the ones with vanilla-waferlike bottoms on which sat a glob of chocolate-covered marshmallow topped with a walnut half or candied cherry. Other marshmallow cookies were covered with white- or pink-tinted coconut instead of chocolate. We were allowed to have these only occasionally. Most of the time our mother bought ginger snaps, windmills, or fig cookies.

The meat department was at the back of the store. There was a big walk-in refrigerator in which hung a beef carcass on a hook. The door was a heavy wooden one with a big black handle. There were no plastic-wrapped cuts of meat in the display case and no packages of cold cuts. The butcher sliced off the amount of cold meat you wanted from large rolls of sausage. The hamburger was individually ground at the time of purchase. I don't remember having fried chicken when I was a child.

Chickens were bought whole and roasted for Sunday dinner. The chickens were larger and fatter then. In fact there was much more fat on all the meat in those days. Most of the roasts and steaks were really tough too. The floor of the meat department was always covered with sawdust to help keep it clean. Our meat purchases were wrapped in heavy, salmon-colored paper torn from a large roll on the edge of the counter.

The favorite place in the store for all of us youngsters was the glass case up near the front of the store where the penny candy was displayed. We must have tried the patience of the grocer many times as we pressed our noses against the glass and took ages to decide what we wanted. There were two-for-a-penny caramels, vanilla, strawberry, or banana flavor, and chocolate-covered toffee dumb-bell suckers (a sucker on each end of the stick). Then there were licorice sticks, boxes of licorice cigarettes, or white cigarettes with red tips, chocolate cigars with a band around the middle like real cigars, jawbreakers, and gumdrop balls on a rubber band. Sometimes we would spend the whole nickel for a chocolate-covered Holloway sucker or a good-size candy bar. Mmmm, I can taste them yet.

The ice cream container was near the candy counter, and the luscious smell of that bulk ice cream still lingers in my memory. The grocer scooped the ice cream into heavy paper cartons with wire handles. There were half pint, pint, and quart sizes. My sisters and I always tried to have Mrs. Koepcke wait on us because, knowing we had a big family, she packed it down to give us a heavy quart. A five-cent ice cream cone on a hot summer day was such a treat. Mrs. Koepcke always pushed the ice cream down into the cone and often put an extra scoop on top. She genuinely liked children and called all of us honey and sweetheart.

All the kids loved her, too.

The grocery stores of the twenties were very different from today's supermarkets. I think we've lost something in the transition. I guess it's the personal touch.

## REWARD
### Lucille B. Engbretson

I pulled the stocking cap down tight over my ears as I turned the corner. The north wind flung icy bits of snow into my face. The cap did much to keep the ears warm, but the wind bit at the space around my knees between the too-short maroon coat and the gray, many-buttoned, high leggings. The unshoveled snow crunched under my feet as I made my way down the narrow path.

I could hear someone approaching in the snow and, lifting my face to the biting wind, I saw a shape bundled into a long flapping coat, muffler, and fur cap. He stepped into the snow to let me pass.

Soon I reached the bit of shoveled walk directly in front of the butcher shop. The sidewalk there was scattered with sawdust carried out of the shop on the boots of departing customers.

I passed the shop, came to another path of snow, then saw the lights of the general store shining out onto the walk. The lights of the windows reflected on the bright bits of metal fastened here and there on the harnesses of the many teams tied to the hitching rail in front. The wagons behind them were loaded with large bags of ground feed, flour, sugar, and boxes of groceries.

The horses, cold and impatient while their masters sat at the bar in the saloon across the street, pawed at the frozen snow and pulled at the traces. Their frost-rimmed nostrils sent trails of smokelike frost floating into the air. They terrified me, these huge, powerful animals, kicking and pawing impatiently at the snow. Once in a while they succeeded in freeing themselves and, rearing and plunging, they would race down the rutted street. The familiar cry of "Runaway!" brought men dashing from the stores and saloons. It struck terror in my heart.

Upon reaching the store, the jangle of the bells on the door announced my entry. The warmth of the store mingled with the smell of moth balls, prunes, peanut butter, kerosene, and the many smells of leather.

Approaching the high wooden counter with its little windows showing rice, navy beans, coconut, prunes, dried apples, and raisins, I timidly asked for a pound of peanut butter. The clerk reached for a stack of wooden "boats," cupping one in the palm of his left hand. He turned and grasped the flat wooden paddle in the wooden tub of peanut butter. Oil ran down his hand as he scooped up a glob of the rich spread and slapped it into the boat. He flipped the boat deftly onto the scale and squinted. "Little over a pound, all right?"

I nodded, thinking of the money I hotly held in the palm of my hand, still encased in the fuzzy woolen mitten.

"Anything else?" he asked.

Meekly I asked for "a pound of soda crackers, please."

Reaching over his head he pulled a paper bag out of the rack hanging there. This time he had to round the end of the counter and approach the barrels and boxes lined against the side of the wall. A large black and white cat jumped out of the sugar barrel as he passed. Reaching the cracker box, he had first to grab the hammer and "rip off" another board from the side of the box. Reaching in, he succeeded in filling the brown paper bag with huge squares of white, unsalted crackers.

Returning to the scale, he again squinted at the gauge, then removed a few crackers to the counter beside the scale. He reached for the string and slipped it around the bag, top to bottom, several times, as he clutched it to his once-white apron. Tying the string in a knot, he gave it a jerk. It came loose, once more to dangle overhead from its little metal cage.

Pushing the packages together on the counter, he lifted his brows and I stammered, "A spool of white thread, please, number fifty."

Again he rounded the counter, this time making for the table in the aisle between groceries and dry goods. There, among the stockings, mittens, tape, and wool yarn, stood the cylinder with the colorful columns of thread. He gave the apparatus a quick half turn, and a spool of thread dropped into the palm of his hand. He returned to stand behind the tall counter, his hands spread wide as he leaned forward to look down into my face. When I said nothing he took his pencil in hand and figured on the cracker bag.

"That will be twenty-four cents."

The red mitten came off and a hot, moist hand laid a quarter on the counter.

"And a stick of licorice, please, sir."

That was my reward for making the long frozen walk and facing the terrors of the snorting horses and the unknown in the growing darkness.

## OUR VILLAGE BLACKSMITH
*Herbert W. Kuhm*

The compact, German-oriented neighborhood in Milwaukee in which I lived as a boy at the turn of the century was, like a young village, sufficient unto itself. It centered at the six-point intersection where the old Fond du Lac Road crossed Lloyd and Eighteenth streets. To us youngsters the exciting nucleus of this ethnic microcosm was the blacksmith shop. Over the double doors fronting the smithy was the weather-worn sign lettered Otto H. Dobbratz—Blacksmith. Surmounting it was an oversized wooden horseshoe for the benefit of the immigrant German *Landsmann* who could not read English. Its open end was down, as was customary with blacksmiths, so that it "would pour good luck onto the forge."

At the time of my boyhood, in the opening decade of the 1900s, there was no "spreading chestnut tree" in front of the Dobbratz smithy, but to my six-year-old eyes Dobbratz nevertheless was "a mighty man with large and sinewy hands" who, like Longfellow's smith, "swung his heavy sledge with measured beat and slow." The thick leather apron that went down to his shoes to protect his clothes from flying sparks was cloven to allow for his holding a horse's hoof in the vicelike grip of his knees.

The broad folding doors of the smithy were almost always open so we youngsters could stand there staring bug-eyed into the cavernous interior which was dark even on the sunniest day because its rippled glass panes were turned to black silk by their sooty patina. From the shop came the heady aroma of harness leather, soft coal smoke from the forge, the ammoniacal smell of horses, and the acrid pungence of singed hoofs. The heavy plank flooring, rough and scarred, was littered with a debris of old nails, hoof parings, and spent coals from the hearth. Deep in the shop was a pile of worn-out horseshoes and a jumble of wagon parts and farm equipment waiting repairs. Overhead on the crossbeams hung a store of shining horseshoes ranging in size from dainty ones for light racers to sturdier ones for farm work horses, or the stout Percherons and Clydesdales that drew the barrel-heavy brewery wagons.

Lucky for us youngsters the work area for shoeing was in the front of the shop where the smith could get the most light on his work. The respectful distance we kept from him was determined by the distance sparks would fly from red hot metal as he tempered it on the anvil with blows from his sledge.

Suspended from the ceiling was a huge bellows, the "leather lungs" that pumped air into the forge. From the rafters overhead the smith chose a blank shoe of the desired size. This was placed in the glowing coals of the forge with long pliers. When the iron was "het up" to his liking, he laid it on the anvil and with ringing blows hammered it to the pattern of the worn out shoe, then plunged it in the scummy water of the tub at his elbow. Brackish steam billowed to the rafters. After again heating the shoe, he placed the horse's foot between his knees and pressed the hot iron against the hoof. Into the holes of the iron he then drove home the square-headed nails. Twisting off the protruding ends, he filed them smooth, and the foot was shod.

More fascinating than a chestnut tree could have been in front of Dobbratz's smithy was the large cast-iron water trough that bifurcated the road between his shop and the corner saloon across the street. It held cold running water for city horses and for the cows brought in by farmers and dealers to the cattle market. We youngsters would scrounge for long horse hairs on the floor of the smithy and dunk them in the basin to see if they really would "turn into snakes" as we had been assured by the older boys. "Nary a snake" did we see, but it was fun trying.

In seventh heaven was the boy who, after "rushing the growler" (that is, fetching a tin bucket of beer from the saloon) for one of the smiths, was rewarded with a ring made from a shiny horseshoe nail rounded on the tapering end of the anvil so that it would encircle a finger. Pride in its possession transcended the discomfort of its sharp edges.

While the mare was being shod or a wheel re-tired, there was time for talk between the waiting patrons and the habitual loafers who slouched on the long bench in front of the shop or on empty nail kegs within. The talk ranged from good-natured banter and random gossip to politics or the standings of the baseball players in the Western League whose ballpark was just down the street. Even some horse trading was done by the glow of the forge. The clientele of the smithy was strictly stag, the men often punctuating their remarks with a spurt of tobacco juice aimed at some dozing horsefly or grasshopper. We generally steered clear of the hangers-on, for their corncob pipes reeked putridly from their stokings of strong Peerless, Giant, Nigger Hair, or Eight Brothers tobacco.

But dark clouds were increasingly glooming the horizon of blacksmithing as the newfangled automobile and the gas-powered tractor replaced the horse. The once-familiar smithy that inspired Longfellow's rhymed tribute gradually went into oblivion along with the livery stable and the apothecary shop. The deserted smithy was either torn down or converted into a garage. As the fires died in his forge and cobwebs gathered on the rafters where the shining iron once had hung, the blacksmith became a legend, a symbol of the past.

## TIN PAIL REFLECTIONS
*Evelyn Cameron*

Just an old-fashioned syrup pail, the kind with a pressed-down cover and a wire handle . . . As I touch it, years drop away and I am a child again in our little village on the river.

These tin pails were a part of our way of life in the early 1900s—buckets to be filled at the fountain of early youth. They enriched our learning, stimulated our curiosity, and indirectly taught us the joy of being useful. With pails we walked through seasons making keen observations of the commonplace.

A pail like this held molasses, Red Hen or Brer Rabbit, Karo Syrup, light and dark. Varying in size from a pint to a gallon, they served many purposes. After the original contents had been used for pancakes, gingerbread, scalloped spice cookies, or spring tonic laced with sulphur, the pail was scrubbed and, because the rim always retained some rinse water, put on the back of the kitchen wood stove to dry. Then it was stored on an attic shelf along with others to await service.

In early spring we tapped the maple trees that surrounded our yard and hung pails on wooden spiles to gather sap. This we poured into big kettles to boil down on the kitchen range until we had syrup, generally enough to fill a small earthen pitcher. The flavor of that fresh-from-the-tree sweetness on Mother's buckwheat pancakes is still a special breakfast memory.

When watercress was its tenderest, we took pails to the brook and filled them with these tangy greens. In salad or between fresh slices of buttered bread, cress carried its own taste of spring. I still savor that first crisp, peppery sandwich. When the cress flourished we increased our coffers by selling it to neighbors for ten cents a pailful.

Often we took pails to the river near our grandparents' home to get white sand, small shells, and pretty stones. Sometimes we found tadpoles, crayfish, or turtles and took them home with us. These weren't always appreciated, especially a pet turtle that crawled under the furnace woodpile in the basement and died. We had to repile the wood until we found the turtle, which we gave proper burial, complete with music and clover blossoms.

On hot summer days Grandmother, who lived across the road, made lemonade or rhubarb shrub and sent pails of it, along with tin cups, to men working in the fields. I remember how they mopped sweaty brows with red kerchiefs and drank deeply of the tart goodness.

Her special vegetable soup found its way to ailing neighbors in a syrup pail. She sent her Danish sweet soup to new mothers by the same method. The lid protected these gifts of the heart and hand, and the trustworthy pail made delivery easy for us children.

To keep her churned butter fresh, Grandmother placed it in a syrup pail, pressed the cover tight, tied a small rope to the handle, lifted a platform board, and lowered the bucket into the chilly depths of the pump pit. Outside, hanging on the spout, was another pail that proved convenient for priming the pump, filling the chicken trough, washing vegetables, or offering a refreshing, long cool drink.

From our garden we heaped pails with new peas, snap beans, golden plum tomatoes, and ground cherries. Did you ever taste ground cherry pie topped with whipped cream? A delicious dessert!

Using small pails we picked raspberries, gooseberries, and currants in Grandmother's garden. Little hands found the biggest berries near the bottom of the bushes. It took longer to fill our pails with strawberries because we popped most of them into our mouths—a little sand improved the flavor. Somehow we never thought of these tasks as work. Sights and sounds filled our hearts and minds—chattering squirrels, cooing doves, blue skies, splashing water from the gristmill flume, and happy voices made helping a pleasure.

These pails found service for gathering eggs, scattering chicken feed, and gathering windfall apples in the orchard to be fed to the pigs that were being "finished." Grandfather believed that apples, along with apple wood smoke, improved the quality and flavor of pork.

Brown sugar was stored in these air-tight containers as were lard, dried herbs, salt, popcorn, and moth balls. For paint pails they had no equal, and at our general store, pails hung on kerosene pumps and vinegar barrels to catch drips from spigots. On a hook near the tobacco counter, another pail held Adam's Standard or Plowboy tobacco—handy for filling pipes of farmers who smoked and exchanged news while their wives traded crocks of butter and crates of eggs for groceries.

In autumn we found hazelnuts along dusty roadsides and spread them on the strawshed roof until their brown ruffles dried. Then we shucked and stowed the nuts away for winter cracking. The firm, round nuts were good to eat but even better in Mother's hazelnut torte.

School was within walking distance, but on stormy

days Grandfather had a hired man take us and the neighbor children to and from school in a horse-drawn bobsled—a primitive taste of busing. Mother packed lunches for my brother, sister, and me in pails on which she had painted our names for easy identification. Along with others, they were placed on a rack in the cool hall until twelve o'clock dismissal. We endured the morning classes in anticipation of the surprise we knew we would find at the bottom of our pails.

When ice covered porch steps we sprinkled them with sand kept in pails for that purpose. We scooped snow for cooling bowls of Jell-O and testing the consistency of candy and frosting. These testings were almost as good as the finished confections.

Christmas trimmings were stored in the pails. Long strings of candy beads, red-sugared strawberries, and shiny cherries were kept looking bright from year to year. To help trim the tree, we were allowed to loop the beads on the lower branches and twist the wired berries on green tips, but we weren't entrusted with the old, more fragile baubles.

The tin syrup pails served well . . . The one I now hold is a mirror reflecting cool water, summer sun, burnished leaves, winter stars, and the fleeting, irreplaceable years of a happy, happy childhood.

## THE ROLL BASKET
*Edna Hoeller*

Back in the dear dead days of old I carried lunch to my father, who was a city fire fighter. Mother would pack the lunch in a wicker basket that was slightly larger than the ones children get at Easter. They were a great deal stronger, and we used them when we went to the bakery for rolls.

Every Milwaukee family had a roll basket. You went to Jaeger's bakery in the early morning hours and asked for six rolls or a dozen hard rolls. The clerk would take your basket and count into the basket the amount you asked for. The clerk did not wear gloves, nor did she handle the rolls with a piece of wax paper as they do now. This was a no-nonsense deal; you asked for rolls and got rolls. They tasted very good. I am sure there was no thought in any customer's mind that such a thing as germs was being passed along.

My brother and I would go to the bakery when it was barely daylight. Many times the streetlights would still be lit and we could see the smoke curling up into the skyline from the factories near by.

My aunt Annie worked at Jaeger's bakery. I remember her telling that she had to get up at four o'clock in the morning and catch the "owl car" (the streetcar that ran every hour on the hour after midnight) to get to work. My aunt had the key to the store. She unlocked the door, put on the lights, got the rolls from the back of the bakery, and arranged the baked goods on the shelves. Then she checked the route slips of the drivers, counted out the number of rolls, and put them in the large wooden baskets that each driver had for his truck.

Usually the drivers arrived about five o'clock and sat

down and had a cup of coffee and a sweet roll at the small tables. Sometimes customers came into the bakery on their way to work and ordered coffee cake and a cup of coffee, which was the custom of that day. The drivers would tease my aunt and joke with her about being sure to count right or favoring one driver over another. After the baskets were filled the drivers carried them out to the trucks and placed them on shelves in the wagons. The sweet rolls on the pans were placed directly on the shelves in the trucks and the next day the drivers returned the pans.

My brother and I were always surprised about the way the drivers bantered with Aunt Annie. To us she was always a very strict person and there was no way we would kid around with her. She wore a large white granny-apron and a white cap of the type that French chefs wear.

At the bakery we asked for rolls, sweet rolls (sometimes called crullers), schneckens, fry cakes, or doughnuts. We usually also took home with us some good Old Milwaukee rye bread. My mother made white bread but would never go to the bother of making the rye bread.

Our roll basket was used at noon also when my brothers and I took our dad's lunch to the firehouse where he was on duty.

We attended St. Joseph's school on Eleventh and Cherry and we passed the firehouse on our way to and from school. Sometimes Dad would take us in the back of the firehouse to let us pet the horses and feed them cubes of sugar. It was then that he mentioned what he would like to have Mother pack for his lunch. We would scamper home to get our meal and Mother would pack the roll basket for Dad. Sometimes Mother got the beer bucket, which was a tin bucket with a tight-fitting lid. She put in

good old-fashioned noodle soup or would heat up the sauerkraut and pork that we had from the night before. You must remember that we did not have thermos jugs in those days.

When Mother filled the basket she would first put in a big linen napkin, then the clean plate, and then the silverware. One of my fondest memories of my dad is that he always used a linen napkin at the table and he never ate a meal that he would not remark, "Gee, that was the best meal I ever had" and say "Thank you." Perhaps the fact that he was raised in an orphanage made him so appreciative. In the basket that we took over would be a few nice big slices of caraway bread or Old Milwaukee rye bread, buttered and wrapped, in another napkin. Sometimes a slice of Mother's homemade pie was added.

My mother had been a cook at the Pfister Hotel. She was the best cook and could make the most delicious lemon pie I ever tasted. She would hand us the basket when we were ready to return to school and always warned us not to spill the soup and not to tarry on the way.

My brother Henry earned a few pennies during summer vacation by sitting around construction sites where tunnels were being dug and pipes laid for the gas and electric company. The workmen would ask him to go to the saloon to get their beer buckets filled. He had an old broom handle on which he hung the tin beer buckets. A bucket of beer cost about ten cents. A great many of the men who worked at the construction sites or for the sanitation department told us not to drink the city water but to drink beer as they did. That way, they assured us, we would grow up to be strong and healthy. When I asked my mother if this was true, she agreed with them.

She had been born on the farm and raised there and

would not allow us to drink city water. Whenever we went to visit Grandmother we would fill up jugs full of spring water from the farm and bring them back with us to drink. When that was gone we had boiled water in the form of coffee for breakfast. This was freshly ground every morning, put in the big coffee pot with an egg, and shaken up well. The boiling hot water was added. At noon we had hot chocolate made from Baker's cocoa, and at supper "green tea." She couldn't tolerate the idea of drinking water from a lake that sewage was being dumped into. It was repugnant to her. To this day I still don't drink water except to take medicine.

We would carry the basket to the firehouse, being sure not to let any of our classmates upset the basket, as they frequently wondered what we had. When we got near the firehouse we could see the men sitting in their captain's chairs, sunning themselves.

Across the street was the "detention home," an old red brick building with bars on the windows where children who were law offenders were placed. Occasionally the children would be looking out of the windows and would call to us. Usually their language was not complimentary. Many times my father remarked to us that if we didn't behave ourselves we could find ourselves in that very same place.

The firehouse was an interesting place to see. Many times the firemen showed us the projects that they were working on. Some of the men would be building doll houses or rocking horses as gifts for the poor children at Christmastime. Some of the houses for the dolls were so pretty that I would have liked to have had one for myself, but I was always told that they were for these children.

On occasion when we were present an alarm would come into the fire station. As soon as the bell rang, the ticker tape started typing out the number of the alarm box. The firehorses would come out of their stalls and stand in front of the engine that they would be pulling. Their muscles quivered, and they literally danced with impatience. My father prided himself on being the only man in that station who could put the bit into the horses' mouths without the horses rearing up on their hind legs.

Above the spot where the horses stood hung the harnesses, resembling huge spiders. As soon as the horses were in place one of the men released a lever and the harness fell over the horses' backs. One fireman strapped the buckles under the bellies while another one got the doors open. My father always preferred to put the bit into the horses' mouths as he did not like to have the horses hurt.

Many years later when my father visited the firehouse near our home he would tell the firemen that the mechanized engines could not get out of the firehouses in less time than the horses did.

Sometimes when we did not have school, we could stay and wait for the firemen to return. Usually the horses would be steaming and blowing from the exertion of pulling the engines. Sometimes their nostrils would be bloody from running so fast and working so hard. The engines would be backed into the firehouse and the men would release the horses from the harnesses. The horses then would be rubbed down and walked to calm them down. They were just as excited as we were when we watched a fire.

When I was older I heard my father tell how the city sold one of the firehorses at an auction to a rag picker, and every time the horse heard the fire sirens, he started running as though he was still in service. Finally the poor man had to sell the horse back to the city, and the horse was retired to pasture. Sometimes we got to go upstairs in the firehouse. The cots that the men slept on were made up so tightly that one could, as my dad would say, "bounce a fifty-cent piece off of it." We would get the chance to slide down the brass pole, and my dad would be there to catch us as we hit the floor.

The firemen had tasks to do, just as they do now—brass to polish, harnesses to check, and stalls to clean. At times the men relaxed with a game of skat and sheepshead. I still have a picture of my dad in a gym suit, boxing with another fireman.

## THE CENTER OF OUR HOME—THE DINING ROOM
*Catherine W. Lewis*

I was musing yesterday about the passing of the family dining room. Ours was always a combination dining room, sewing room, study hall, birthday and wedding center, as well as a homey sort of kennel for our pet cats and dogs. Comparable to today's family room, it—unlike our living room or parlor—was the center of our home.

It was the place we tossed our school books on the big dining room table and hollered, "Mama, I'm home. Can I have a piece?" "A piece" was a slice of homemade bread, slathered with butter and topped with brown sugar, home-baked beans, or perhaps fresh homemade peach jam. Grandfather Whittier always declared Mama's bread was better than angel food cake any old day.

The first dining room I remember in Kaukauna was in our little cottage at the foot of the hill leading up to St. Mary's Catholic Church. A base burner with isinglass doors brightened and warmed the room during the winter months. Sunshine streamed in during the winter days, and a hanging lamp cast a warm glow by night. Papa would sit with us while Mama, flushed and rosy-cheeked, brought in steaming hot bowls of her homemade noodle soup, a plate of hot johnnycake, a ring of hot bologna, plus thick slices of American cheddar. On special days we had dessert served in Mama's beautiful footed dishes—little red ones trimmed with gold. Alas, the serving bowl long ago vanished, but I have the heirloom dishes that I use lovingly on extra-special occasions. We drank milk that had been delivered to our back door, the milkman ladling it into one of Mama's pitchers.

There were no fast-food services around the corner, no supermarkets. There *was* Julius J. Marten's Grocery and Department Store, Lehr's Butcher Shop, and Kalupa's Bakery. The groceries were delivered in a horse-drawn cart or carried home. Telephones were not common in Kaukauna when I was growing up.

Our tablecloths were real linen—Mama's best on Sundays and holidays, and carefully mended ones other days. The world of plastics hadn't engulfed us then. We had "everyday" dishes and Mama's best china. Like the linen tablecloth, the best ones were used on Sundays and holidays only. I can remember a special cake, a Lady Baltimore, that a friend of Mama's made. It was a picture as it rested resplendent on one of Mama's Bavarian china plates that had been a wedding gift.

Family dinners were held regularly several times a month at Grandfather Whittier's home, way across town in those days, today just a hop and a jump. His dining room was one of the exciting rooms in his ten-room house, which he had had built in 1895. A friendly side porch adjoined the dining room and led out to spacious lawns surrounding the house.

We children were very solemn at Grandpa's house.

"The Old Gentleman," as Papa called him, served us our dinner from the head of the table. He'd cut my boiled potatoes in large chunks and put gravy on my meat. His hired girls couldn't cook as well as Mama. Grandma had died before the house was completed, although Grandpa had taken her over in a livery stable hack to see it shortly before she died. Hired girls, a whole procession of them, helped to run the house. Later, Mama and Papa were invited to live with Grandpa in the old home. I remember Papa saying, "I'll not serve the way Father does, I can tell you that. I like the way you have everything for us to help ourselves, Alice."

Years later I had a chance to go to Grandpa's old home. There were now plastic doors closing off the dining room from the living room, and the spacious hallway and winding staircase were all closed off. Where, oh where, were the wonderful sliding doors of my youthful memories? A thousand poignant memories were evoked as I walked through the once familiar house. How could I tell the curious woman walking so quietly beside me of the fun I remember when Mama and Papa had let us stay up to greet the new year, and we sat in the dining room and giggled over Mama's mince pie and glasses of cold milk.

Grandpa's dining room was Mama's sewing room, too. Aunt Ruth, Aunt Mamie (she later became Aunt *May*), Aunt Maude and Uncle John Greenleaf Whittier, and Uncle Ed all spent vacations with us. Ah, that tape recorders were in vogue then. How the walls reverberated with joyous visiting, geat arguments, all tempered and adorned with Mama's great cooking. What a turn-of-the-century novel I would have had—look out, Eugene O'Neill! Mama's homemade bread, sliced raw onions in vinegar (Uncle Ed's favorite), mounds of hot mashed potatoes, and great roasts of pork and beef graced that board that truly "groaned," all topped off with whichever fruit pie was in season. Nothing ever topped Mama's lightly browned apple pie with a thick slice of American cheese. No a la mode—ice cream was reserved for birthdays, and it came complete in a freezer and all the neighborhood kids were invited over. The neighborhood always seemed a little larger on our birthdays, but Mama made it stretch. The birthday person got to lick the scoop at the end.

I digress. We really had one of the first Holiday Inns of this century. And the prices *were* reasonable. Free board and room in exchange for good company, sparkling stories, all laced together with family love. Who helped Mama with the dishes while the men repaired to the front porch, we kids lit out for the neighborhood playgrounds, and my graceful aunties went out to the lawn swing to exchange youthful gossip? No wonder Mama had many "sick headaches," as migraine headaches were once called. After all, it was home to all Papa's brothers and sisters—and it was fun to get boxes of candy from New York and brooches from Chicago when our aunties and uncles came visiting. If Mama ever complained, I was unaware. Mama managed to keep four restless, growing kids happy and contented, and Papa was inordinately proud of his Alice.

Aunt Ruth spent every weekend with us since she was attending Bushey's Business College in Appleton. Once she brought us all a good case of measles. Mama took care of us all. Her tasty foods worked their special magic, and before long we were back at the dining room table, able to sit up and take nourishment.

Our third dining room in Kaukauna was in a pretty little house not too far from Grandpa's. I got to the house ahead of Mama and I had put up her pretty plates on the handsome plate rail in the dining room. "Did you wash the rail, child?" "No, Mama, I wanted to surprise you. Should I have?" "No matter," Mama said, "the plates look mighty pretty." I was thrilled to turn on the dining room lights and watch them sparkle on the hand-painted dishes.

Mama always had our teachers from Nicolet School over each fall for a good supper. It was the custom in those days to entertain the teachers and the pastors, too, at a family dinner. We'd exchanged a ten-room house for an eight-room house, but Mama had a linen closet off the dining room and we could still come in to our dining room from the outside and holler, "Mama, I'm home. Can I have a piece? I got to go to the liberry." "Yes," Mama would call out, "you may have a piece, but it is *li-brar-y*, dear. *Library!*"

Soon Papa, who was a machinist for the Chicago and Northwestern Railroad, was transferred to Ashland, Wisconsin, and I began a succession of meals in other dining rooms.

I've had meals at palatial private homes, plush restaurants, supper clubs, farm kitchens, elegant hotels, city apartments, dining rooms in Canada, Great Britain, France, and Belgium, on ocean liners and planes, at truck stops, diners, carnival hash houses, ranches in Wyoming, church suppers in Illinois, PTA suppers in all the towns in which I've taught, in ethnic restaurants. Really, I've rarely missed a meal, but none of the exotic places have remained as vivid and cozy and downright loving in memory as the dining rooms of my home when I was growing up. I really think our family dining room cast a special aura on us all.

One time, when we had moved to Ashland, my older brother Ed and my younger brother Bob had a quarrel at the table. Ed got up and started striding from the dining room, announcing loudly, "I'm going to leave home!"

Mama said gently, but loud enough to be heard, "Bob, then you may have Eddie's pork chop." Eddie was back in a flash and speared the chop off the serving plate. "No, you don't, not on your tintype, Bob. It's mine." Peace was restored and Eddie never ran away from home.

We had a beautiful built-in china cabinet in that home that was the reason Mama wanted to buy the house, but she loved the chandelier there, too. The chandelier was missing when we took possession of the house, but the cabinet remained. Mama always had difficulty saving enough meat loaf for the following day's sandwiches. One night she hid the remainder of the loaf in the cabinet. Bob had searched for some meat for a sandwich and settled finally on a three- or four-egg sandwich which he proceeded to eat in the dining room.

Suddenly he began to sniff and, straight as an arrow, dashed to the sideboard and drew out the meat loaf that Mama had sought to save for another day. Bob just added the meat loaf to his egg sandwich and looked around for a slice of pie to finish off his Epicurean feast.

## SILK IS FOR ROYALTY
*Anna M. Kortum*

During the middle of the Roaring Twenties, our junior high school class was preparing for spring graduation, and with it came the traditional class play. All who were interested stayed after school for tryouts, and by class time the next day, you knew if you had made it or not. That was the beginning of the end—I made it!

The part of Susan, the maid, was assigned to me. She was a strait-laced character, prim and proper. She was also a friend of the morose undertaker in the play, but that made no difference to me, for I was elated! We each received a copy of the three-act play, and many sessions of memorizing and practice followed.

A few weeks before opening night of the performance, we had to start gathering our costumes together. My black servant dress, white starched apron, and headpiece were to be furnished. Three things that I had to supply consisted of a teapot, black shoes, and a pair of black silk stockings. The teapot and black shoes posed no problem, but the thought of black silk stockings loomed before me like a dark threat. None of my friends wore silk. Mom wore a fine lisle hose, so I had to find some other way to obtain them.

Out of character, I had never worn anything but long, tan, cotton stockings, secured with round, white, elastic garters. In my transition from elementary to junior high school, I had graduated from the long, white, elastic side garters that were pinned to a vest or to small side tabs sewn to the union suit.

No amount of pleading could change Dad and Mother's insistence that I wear long, heavy underwear. The baggy surplus of material near the ankles had to be folded over neatly while adjusting the long, cotton stockings. If you weren't careful, the lumps wouldn't fit very well into the high, laced, low-heeled shoes. As I grew older, often I would roll the long, bulky union suit legs up over my knees. Anyone viewing me from the back would wonder why I suddenly appeared to be slightly bowlegged. With the coming of spring, one graduated to short, lighter apparel. I was thankful that graduation would take place in warm weather.

During that period of time, my father was in the process of building his first house on the edge of town. Many nights he sat at the round, oak dining table with stacks of papers, trying to figure out his finances. To ask him for money for a pair of black silk hose at this particular time was inconceivable. After much pondering and soul-searching, I decided I would have to drop out of the play. That was the beginning of the end!

Dejectedly, I approached the teacher and said, "I am unable to furnish the black silk stockings needed in the play, so I'm afraid I'll have to drop out."

"Nonsense," said Mrs. Chambers vehemently, "you'll do no such thing. I'll see to it that you will get the hose, and please forget about dropping out."

Afraid that the tears I was trying to hold back would start falling, I meekly said, "Thank you," and walked to my next class as though I had wings on my feet.

What a strange coincidence that we should be studying about China at that time. Oh yes, for centuries their silkworms had been munching on mulberry leaves and producing cocoons from which the Chinese wove their precious silk. Cloth of the kings, they called it, and all I needed was one little pair of black silk hose! The thought of silk became a regular obsession with me.

Time passed by swiftly, and suddenly, the day before the matinee arrived. After class, Mrs. Chambers presented me with a gaily wrapped package.

"Please accept this with my compliments," she said. "It is a graduation gift for you."

Again I offered my thanks with a lump in my throat.

I knew what the gift would be, but nevertheless I could hardly wait to unwrap it. There in the soft folds of tissue paper was a pair of genuine black silk hose and a lovely pair of black silky round garters, trimmed with black lace and tiny pink rosebuds. The full-fashioned stockings had a black seam running up the middle of the back, and the two rows of fashion markings set on either side of the calf of the leg were indeed marks of distinction. How fine and soft they were, and to make them even more elegant, a diamond-shaped design was woven into the hose, near the top. I felt like royalty already.

The play was a huge success, and Susan, the maid, got a roaring laugh when she lifted the teapot too high and poured the liquid next to the cup as she gazed down at her sleek, silken legs.

The gift was treasured for a long time, and accidently, when a small run developed into a long ladder in one of the hose, the repair was made for a small fee in a little shop that specialized in that type of work. A needle, similar to one of a knitting machine, was mounted onto a thin, wooden handle. As if by magic, the run disappeared as the needle was adjusted, and the hose was as good as new.

Since that time, stockings have been made out of lisle, rayon, nylon, and other new fibers, but I can truthfully say that none have ever given me more pleasure than my first pair of sleek, soft, silk stockings.

## 11-11-11 AND ELEVEN
*Verneil Berard*

It was 6:25 P.M. that cool night when my sister, Cicely, and I headed for the Palace. We lived a little more than four blocks from the theater. I was skipping with joy, hugging my music, and thrilled that it was to be my debut as a part-time silent movie piano player that night. Cis had invited me to play the piano pieces that I knew.

Cis was almost eleven years older, and we took music lessons from the same teacher, Evelyn Ward Rosebush, in Port Edwards. I'm sure they planned this because my music books were missing from the pedestal the night Cis went for her lesson. All week, she'd say to me: "Do you remember 'Twittering of the Sparrows'? Play 'Dance of the Marionettes' for me. Do you know 'Crazy Bone Rag'? What is the name of that piece in 6/8 time? Play it!" I sure had a workout that week.

When we turned off Goggins Street onto Third Avenue I could see the lights on the marquee, and the first thought that came to me was: "Am I going to play and not make any mistakes?" I stopped skipping and matched my sister's steps, which were lengthier than mine and hurrying to make it on time.

I took a deep breath when the right door was pulled open and we were in the lobby. The lady who sold tickets and her husband, the ticket taker, greeted us. Perhaps it was their smiles, whether quizzical or not, and their good wishes that freed me from my doubting thoughts. He held open the inner door.

The theater lights were on and a few steps to the right we looked and then trotted down the aisle. It was downhill. My heels would bury in the carpet, but it took forever for my toes to land on it. Was it so slanting? I know it was the longest aisle I ever remember.

Across the entire front of the stage, a metal railing with its colorless, dusty, scollop-topped curtain enclosed the orchestra pit with entrances on each end. I was so excited to see what it looked like on the other side of the curtain, I didn't notice Cicely taking a step down into the pit. My entrance was something else. I sailed into a couple of music stands and chairs on my way down, landing on my knees. I held on to my music for dear life. It had tabs extending past the edges of the books with labels on them, such as Horses, Storm, Dance, March, Sad. Sad was always a piece in a minor key. My rag, "Crazy Bones," matched the motions of the saloon's piano player on the screen. Lucky for me, I could go flying, but not the music. I knew I'd be sent home if it was not in order. I hurt a little and limped behind Cis to center stage in the pit. She turned on the piano lamp.

What a piano! It was a huge Kimball upright with battered, yellowed keys and a few noticeable burn marks. Its height reached the floor of the stage. It was positioned a little left of center stage and at a slight angle to ease the frequent glimpses of the piano player at the recessed movie screen. Our screen was at the back of the stage, so people could perform in front of it on special occasions. Center top of piano was adorned with a long, horizontal, metal lamp with its adjustable, rounded shade that illuminated the tiered, open music books which were sprawled across the piano for easy access. It would also silhouette the piano player's head above the curtained railing.

On the high front corners on each end of the piano, rearview mirrors were mounted that, when focused right, pictured about the top third of each aisle next to the exit doors. These enabled you to see if the aisles were still crowded with people or contained just a few stragglers headed for the exits. We were to play until the theater was nearly empty after the first show. Remember, we went to shows, not features.

The chair was a medium high-backed, straight chair, cushioned according to the height and length of the legs of the pianist. Better make yourself comfortable, for it would be at least two hours before you had a break between shows.

We took off our coats, turned them inside out, and put them over spare chairs. Cis went around the end of the piano and returned with a spotted white rag. This was a dust rag, first. The lamp, front of the piano, keys, and two chairs rated the rag in motion. I wondered why the rag had black, circled spots on it. Much to my surprise, she sat on the chair, wound a clean part of the rag around her forefinger, and proceeded to give the necessary keys a spit bath. The finger turned black.

My music was arranged first that night. I struggled to find a comfortable height on that chair. I wound up in a slanting position, on one cushion, and being short legged, only used the front fourth of the chair seat so I could reach the pedal.

I could see very little of the screen, but it wasn't necessary, because Cis had the pieces I could play lined up with the cue sheet. These sheets were just "one line" from the suggested selection that was suitable for the upcoming action on the screen. The approximate time was given, such as two and a half, four, or five minutes. Cis was my cue director. From my Oliver Ditson Music Series Books, I would play "Love's Oracle," "Light of Heart," "Remembrance," and "Bonjour," which was my "horse" music, written in 6/8 time. Once I told her, "You've covered up my horse music." But she yelled, "Keep right on playing, they can't hear you anyway." I was sure everyone was standing. All were shouting, yelling, and screaming. By the time the disappointing "oh's" were audible, the kids were searching and slumping into their seats.

Wednesday through Saturday nights, the piano was the solo instrument in the theater. The newsreels first, then a serial that enticed you to come back week after week, and last, the movie. The theaters competed to have the best show for Sunday matinee, Sunday, Monday, and Tuesday nights with a string quartet or a small orchestra in the pit. They rated Marion Davies in *Yolande*, Colleen Moore in *Sally*, or Harold Lloyd in *The Freshman*, but the other, less expensive shows filled in the remainder of the week. Westerns and comedies were very popular.

My repertoire kept me on the chair until eight o'clock. Cis took over as I packed up my music, put on my coat, and left the pit, a lot smarter than when I had entered. That flop was the only one I made that night. I leaned forward, trudging up the aisle. It was not nearly as long as I thought, for I was in the lobby in a few seconds.

I lingered there to look at the pictures, hung very high, and two deep around the walls of the lobby. I didn't know all of them, but later I learned who they were. You remember the most famous ones, but have you thought about Vilma Banky, Marilyn Miller, Mae Murray, Mabel Normand, Nancy Carroll, Bebe Daniels, Bessie Love, Corinne Griffith, or Lili Daminta? Remember the famous sisters: Gish: Lillian and Dorothy; Talmadge: Norma and Constance; Bennett: Barbara, Constance, and Joan; Costello: Dolores and Helene? Now, the handsome men: three Richards: Arlen, Barthelmess, and Dix; Monte Blue, Charles Farrell, Reginald Denny, John Gilbert, Ben Lyon, John Boles, Tom Meighan, Gilbert Roland, and the not so handsome but so lovable Harry Carey, William S. Hart, Hoot Gibson, Buster Keaton, Jack Holt, Lewis Stone, Tom Mix, George Arliss, Victor McLaglen, and the Berry brothers, Noah and Wallace.

I pushed open the outside door and stood in the limelight of the marquee. I walked toward home and the brightness at my back gradually faded.

The one, dim arc light on Goggins Street induced fear first, and then lightning speed. I welcomed the little white porcelain, center-screwed knob on our screen door. Opening the door just a crack, I squeezed through onto our porch. As I stood there catching my breath, Mama opened the living room door. "How did it go tonight, Punkie?" "I didn't make any mistakes, but I played too loud to suit Cis," I answered as I released my music on the pedestal and walked to the foot of the stairs. It was a school night and bedtime.

The Sleeping Fairy passed me by so I could relive the grand and glorious night. My heart was still pounding with excitement. Would I be invited to play again? Cis said yes the next morning, and I knew Mrs. Rosebush agreed when she opened her door for my next lesson.

My title is a tattletale. It is my birth date and I was eleven.

## MY FATHER, THE TRAVELING PREACHER
*Mattie E. Lynch*

My father was a traveling evangelist, called by the Lord to preach the gospel.

He held his meetings in the summertime, and he bought his own tabernacle and the lumber to make the seats, which consisted of planks two inches by twelve inches and twelve feet in length. Under the seats was spread wheat straw.

He always pitched the tabernacle up in a small clearing of timber by the side of the road. He drove his own team, hitched to a lumber wagon, and took along a man to help him set up the tabernacle. He carried along food for the horses and food for us.

I was ten years old and always went along with my father on his circuit. We carried a small tent of our own and I did the cooking (most of it) on a two-burner coil oil stove.

The meetings sometimes lasted a week. They were held in many different places near little towns in Kansas, some of which are not there any more: Vineland, Eudora, Blackjack, Clearfield, Lawrence, and Overbrook.

I remember well the meeting held at Overbrook. It was in 1900 when William Jennings Bryan was running for president the second time. People were handing out caps for the campaign with Bryan's name printed on them, and they put one on me, over my long brown curls. I wore it the evening of the meeting.

It was a very exciting spiritual meeting and there was a large crowd. My father never believed in a mourners' bench nor in a collection. He felt the good Lord would provide, which He did. Father would ask the people to come forward, shake their hands, give a prayer, and say, "May God bless you real good."

One man was so spiritually moved that he took off his hat and passed it through the crowd for a collection. There were many dollars in the hat, and he brought it foward and handed it to my father, but he would not accept it. Then the man asked me to hand him my Bryan cap. Not knowing what he wanted, I handed the cap to him and he poured all that money into it. My father gave me a scolding for letting the man do it. I said, "Well, Dad, what should I do with it?" He told me to give it to the Bryan campaigners. I did, and it was readily accepted.

It seems strange to me now that the word of those camp meetings got around so fast. There were no autos or phones, just horses. The news traveled by word of mouth and we always had large crowds.

I remember another meeting vividly. It was held at Clearfield, Kansas, one of those places that isn't there anymore. Only a little Evangelical church stands there and the cemetery where my parents, two sisters, a little brother, and my paternal grandparents are buried. A brother preacher of my father's, another man called by the Lord to travel and preach the gospel, was holding a meeting there. His name was Milt Hughs. They were having a great spiritual meeting there—women were praying, shouting, twirling until exhausted, and falling in the aisles. The men were all standing, shouting, "Amen, Amen. Praise the Lord!" The preacher called out, "Now let's all get up and tell what the Lord has done for us."

When my father stood to testify, he was so spiritually overcome he began to preach, forgetting that it was not his meeting. After a little while, my father was asked to sit down, but he preached all the louder. Then my father was carried bodily across the road by three men—there were a lot of stumps left from clearing the timber. I followed them, crying, "Don't you dare hurt my dad!" They sat him down on a large stump and said, "There, now you can preach from there!"

Father stood up on the stump and began to preach, louder and louder. People from the other meeting began to swarm across the road, until my father had the entire crowd listening to him. He preached fire, hell, and brimstone. There was a full moon, and the night was still. The crowd was crying, shouting, and saying, "Praise the Lord, Glory Hallelujah, Amen, Praise the Lord, Oh, My Soul." Many people gave their hearts to the Lord that night by that stump!

My father, John L. Kramer, was a small man. He was born in Wurttemberg, Germany, and came to America when he was three years old. He was self-educated, having had only seventh-grade schooling. He always read the Bible, the only book he had to read. He homesteaded at Clearfield, Kansas, and when not traveling and preaching the gospel, he ran a blacksmith shop. My parents lived above the shop, and that is where I was born. There were thirteen children and I was the fifth one.

Father made and repaired harnesses for all of our neighbors. He did smithing, cobbled shoes, and dehorned and branded cattle for all the neighbors. He also made hand-hewn pine splints for broken arms, legs, and fingers and even set the fractures for our neighbors.

He bought pasture land near Ottawa, Kansas, and herded our neighbors' cattle to that pasture thirty miles distant with horses and a chuck wagon.

Father and Mother were married when he was thirty-five years old and she only seventeen. Mother died at age eighty-two, father at age eighty-one.

## THE OLD HAMPDEN CHURCH
*Walter Wright*

The old Hampden church, a pioneer landmark for nearly a century, is gone. It was built in 1883 as a replacement for the older "Gravel" church, the original church of the early settlers, a mile or so northeast. It served the Methodists and other Protestants of the area as an "outer appointment" of the Fall River church for about forty years, when it was closed and the congregation scattered, most of them going to Fall River.

For over fifty years, it stood empty, a scarred and battered memorial to the "faith of our fathers." Sold to a neighboring farmer who used it for machinery storage, it was invaded by passing vandals who littered its floor with cigarette butts and beer cans and even punched holes through the ceiling. In concern for the safety of the trespassers, its owners, the Helgersons, arranged to have the Portage Fire Department (with Columbus Fire Department standing by) burn it down, and this was done on Saturday afternoon, January 10. It took less than an hour to obliterate this famous landmark. An attempt was made to salvage its lumber, but it had been built too well. Held together with square, old-fashioned nails, its fine, full-measure lumber splintered before the nails could be withdrawn. It is gone now, but it will not be dead as long as it lives in the memory of a single person who attended it.

I went to Sunday school and church there until I was thirteen years old and entered high school in Fall River. Although my memories are necessarily childlike and, perhaps, frivolous, they are vivid. The church shared its pastor with the Fall River church (or the other way around) and he drove out every Sunday afternoon with horse and buggy or horse and sleigh. The service was long and tedious to a child of eight to twelve years, in stiff Sunday shoes that were never worn out but only outgrown and worn long past the time they even approximately fit.

Only three preachers—the Reverend Mr. Collinge, Bennett, and James—made any lasting impression on my boyish memory. The Reverend Mr. Collinge and Bennett had some depth of character, some inner glow, that was recognizable even to a child. The Reverend Mr. James is remembered for a different reason. It was he who, despairing of his flock's salvation, brought in traveling evangelists to show them the way to redemption. One of them, a tall, cadaverous individual with a rasping bass voice and a style of delivery that required excellent physical condition, ranted and raved and stormed and pounded the pulpit in a way most impressive to a boy of eight or nine. I remember thinking that the words and eloquence were very similar to those used by our hired man the time the cow kicked him into the gutter, but I presume the construction was different. Another time, a team of two evangelists, who believed in the hard sell for salvation, was brought in. A male quartet came once, but I do not remember if it was to supplement some of these evangelists or on their own. They sang beautifully and they sang one song that frightened me for days. I don't know that I ever heard it again, but I have never forgotten it. It started out moderately enough, reporting a dream:

*I dreamed that the great Judgment Morning*
*Had dawned, and the trumpet had blown . . .*

From there, it went on to the inexorable, climactic conclusion:

*And, oh, what a weeping and wailing*
*When the lost were told of their fate;*
*They cried to the rocks and the mountains,*
*They prayed, but their prayers were too late!*

It scared the daylights out of me, and for the next two or three days I pondered over my puny collection of sin-sick secrets. But the sun came out again and all—or most—was forgotten. The net result of that experience on me was a permanent and abiding allergy toward professional evangelism.

On the bank of the benches was a long, corrugated space in the wood that presented an inevitable temptation to a restless boy to scrape his stiff shoes across it and make a noise like a Halloween tic-tac. I always tried to do this noiselessly, but it was one of those things that could not be done noiselessly, and my father would put a restraining hand on my knee and offer me a clove, or a piece of stick cinnamon, or, rarely, a peppermint to suck on and keep me quiet.

There was an elderly man, Dave James, with an impressive red beard. When the sermon bored him, which was frequently, he slept. And when he slept, he snored very softly, and when he snored his beautiful red beard waggled in a most fascinating manner.

A big arch was painted on the wall back of the pulpit, and within this arch was a picture of an opened Bible, and above the Bible, some words in Old English script. I found out later that these words were "Search the scriptures," but at the time I thought the first word was "Sarah." As my stepmother's name was Sarah, I spent many a Sunday afternoon trying to figure out what that last word was, to indicate what she had done to merit such public recognition.

Then there was the music. I don't know whether the choir was as good as I remember it, but it sounded beautiful to me. They sang the old hymns which, for some reason, are seldom sung anymore: "No, Not One," "Softly and Tenderly," "Stepping in the Light," "True-hearted, Whole-hearted"—the basses could roll out on that one—then, the one affectionately known as "Cwm Rhondda" for short—any Welshman can tell you which one that is. There was one I particularly liked, with the title, as I understood it, "The Calf Has Never Yet Been Sold." I discovered later that the title actually was "The Half Has Never Yet Been Told," but the discovery removed some of the charm.

I should also like to submit that I had one of the prettiest Sunday school teachers that ever was. I have read somewhere that several movie stars teach Sunday school classes regularly. Nevertheless, I will enter my Sunday school teacher against all comers. She was an eighteen- or nineteen-year-old girl named Maude Zink. We learned Bible verses from colored picture cards and were supposed to memorize the text. I can still tell you what John 3:16 says, without looking it up.

The congregation of the Hampden Methodist Church was a close-knit group of families, second generation from the original settlers, who were Anglo-Saxon migrants from New England and York State, with a strong residue of Puritanism. They carried names like Taylor and Henton, Goodman and Wright, King and Matthews, Sample and Sowards, Tillotson and Edwards. The church was the center of not only their religious life but also their entertainment. Lawn and box socials were held on its grounds; "Skip to My Lou" games were played there on warm summer nights, with fireflies and whippoorwills in the background. And real homemade ice cream!

The old Hampden church is gone and it leaves an empty place against the sky and in the hearts of those who remember. No longer are we admonished to "search the scriptures." Its virtues were the simple virtues of friendship and compassion and concern. And—despite the evangelists—its God was not the jealous, angry, vindictive God of the Old Testament, but a God of love and mercy.

## THE LYDIA PINKHAM LADIES
*Ann C. Haller*

My childhood bloomed, withered, and passed into adolescence in an age that firmly believed children should be seen but not heard.

The result was that a quiet child, seemingly engrossed in a storybook, could store up masses of information culled from the conversation of unsuspecting adults.

Some of the richest prospecting took place at my grandmother's. Twice weekly she gathered together a clutch of female family members, friends, and neighbors. To avoid the appearance of idleness or frivolity, the ladies brought their "fancywork." French knots were scattered like measles on pillowcases. Pure linen towels were relentlessly monogrammed. Miles of crocheted lace resulted from those sessions. And as the busy fingers flew, the busy tongues kept pace.

There was no radio or television in those days. The newspaper was gravely read by the man of the house, and carefully selected tidbits might or might not be passed on for the delectation of the distaff side. But gossip, news of a personal sort, flew by a sort of osmosis from one lady to another with incredible speed. It was not all idle or unkind. Their world was small, people lived in the same houses for years, and they took an intense interest in each others' lives and activities.

I have come to believe that some of these ladies assumed that the child, seen but unheard, in turn did not hear. Wrong! Others assumed, because they laced their conversation with euphemisms, that the same child would not understand. They were both right and wrong. Taking their words literally frequently led to misunderstandings on my part that kept me puzzled until I worked their meanings out or forgot them as new grist came to my mill.

A lady uninvited to the gatherings because she was "fast" and because she "painted" puzzled me for days. Since the lady described as "fast" usually moved with a sort of languid waddle, I was not much better informed when a more sophisticated cousin informed me that this naughty lady had daringly invited the frozen postman in for coffee on a bitter winter morning. I also knew that she refrained from the acceptable exertion of china painting or watercolors. I failed to link the fact that she "painted" with the same cousin's information that she actually applied rouge to her cheeks and lips. Since I did not know what rouge was, the matter remained incomprehensible.

Sex was never discussed, and I was in my teens before a more enlightened aunt publicly used the word "pregnant." Ladies presenting their spouses with an heir were described in whispers as "expecting" or by the more

timid as being "you know!"

New arrivals were presented to the children as accomplished facts and never mind the preceding nine months. Questions as to where we ourselves came from were met with fanciful tales. By pooling our information my cousins and I discovered we had all arrived from widely varied sources. I was a no-nonsense delivery by the stork. One introverted cousin was squelched early in life by being informed that he had been found in a plebeian cabbage patch. One immaculate, blonde-curled child maintained a haughty superiority because she had been found by her doting mother in the heart of a rose!

Taking the term "drink" literally also caused me problems. Alcohol was, in our family, reserved for medicinal hot toddies and used sparingly in the creamy bowl of Christmas eggnog. I knew nothing of its evils. I therefore found it hard to understand why the fact that one of the ladies' husbands "drank" should be a cause for sympathetic commiseration. Didn't everyone "drink," I thought innocently as the ladies sipped their tea?

Oddly enough, many of these same ladies who loudly proclaimed that "lips that touch liquor shall never touch mine" consumed astonishing amounts of a universal panacea called Lydia Pinkham's Compound. Warranted to soothe or cure almost any "female complaint" or "female trouble" (two phrases that long lay unresolved in my mind), the familiar brown bottle was a part of nearly every well-equipped home. What was never mentioned was that because of the high alcoholic content, the little brown bottle was first cousin to the little brown jug the ladies so loudly condemned in public.

Time went by and the ladies continued to gossip, and my young mind continued to translate their words in a literal theater of the absurd. The guarded disclosure that one lady's husband was "running around" inevitably gave me an astounding picture of that corpulent gentleman running in endless circles. I could not understand why the young man who had been discharged from his position because he had "sticky fingers" hadn't simply washed his hands.

All things end, and the day came when I was firmly banished to the company of my contemporaries. Childhood lasts a long, long time. The years flew by and my memories of the Lydia Pinkham Ladies faded.

Then one day I looked across a crowded room at a small girl child seated in a corner. She looked up and, across the room and across the mists of time, briefly the eyes of the Young Child and the Old Child met. She smiled shyly, then dropped her eyes to the picture book in her lap. I gently lifted my cup in salute and took a sip of my slightly bitter tea.

11 Going Home

## DOWN MEMORY LANE
*John W. White*

The man is poor who has no hometown. You need a hometown to store away your memories and your dreams. If you have no hometown, if nowhere there is a place that you belong and that belongs to you, then memories float aimlessly in time.

What you need to pin down memories is a tree-lined street you walked down as a kid, or an old house that once was home. You need people who call you by name and who see a little boy standing behind the man you are now. This is a hometown.

So I am home again and the streets I walk are the streets I walked when I was a boy in Rockton, Wisconsin.

Most of the buildings I knew so well then are now gone, but in my mind's eye they are still there. I clearly see Adler's Saloon, with a dance hall upstairs, which was about half a block from our home. At every opportunity, when I could get a lead on Ma, I visited the saloon, much to her chagrin. I don't think I went there for a nip but, rather, to view the upright slot machines, which made noises and flashed lights.

Across the street from the saloon was the blacksmith shop. My brothers and I spent lots of time there watching the blacksmith, Jean Marshall, shoe horses, make plowshares, and so on. Sometimes he let us work the bellows for the forge, and we thought he was wonderful. Several years later I read "The Village Blacksmith" by Longfellow, and there was an accurate description of Jean.

A block west of the blacksmith shop was the cheese factory. We kids made many trips there to ask for curds, which generally came out "turds," much to the glee of the genial cheesemaker, Blaine Kennedy. He sat us down and gave us curds and coarse salt, our manna from heaven.

One half block north of the blacksmith and about halfway to the cemetery was the Newcomb House (so called because it was owned by Burt Newcomb) where we lived when I was a small boy. Many things happened while we lived here. For instance, a cyclone suddenly hit our town, and were we frightened! It was dark as night and the air was full of flying debris—shingles, boards, limbs. The winds were fierce and made monstrous noises. Everytime the tempo of the wind increased our house seemed to rise and then it would settle back on the foundation. When the holocaust was over we were limp. The inside of the house was full of water that had come in around the windows and doors. A short two miles away the winds struck Uncle Charley Ericson's farm, blew down the barn, and killed many cattle and horses. A great tragedy indeed.

Uncle Charley (who was really my dad's Uncle Charley) was some man. One time he and Aunt Rose came to Rockton, via horse and buggy, to do some shopping. On the way home, the young horse became frightened crossing the bridge across the Kickapoo River and bolted down the bank into the river. At this point the water was deep and turbulent, and how they survived is a miracle. Uncle Charley, who must have been in his sixties, swam and struggled until he caught up with Aunt Rose more than a hundred yards from where they went into the river. He held her up and eventually was able to wade ashore with Aunt Rose in his arms. He carried her home through the pasture some three quarters of a mile. The rescue proved that he was a worthy representative of the early Vikings.

We used to go to the cemetery, only a few feet away,

to visit the graves of our ancestors and neighbors. Some people are afraid to visit cemeteries, but not us. It always seemed to me that there were friendly spirits there who were pleased to hear the voices of little people.

The school was only a little over a block south of our home past the saloon, but when Mother took me there to start the first grade, it seemed miles away. As if this was not enough to scare me to death, the teacher assigned me to a double seat with a girl as a partner. I didn't recover from my fear of girls for some twenty years.

A half block south of the school was McVey's store. I remember well the time mother sent me there with a quarter to buy some clothespins. The temptation for chocolates, with filled centers, was too great, and when Mother eventually came looking for me I was sitting on the front steps of the store, eating chocolates at a great rate. To say that Mother was displeased is probably the understatement of the year.

Another house I remember well is the so-called Randolph House, across the street from the community hall, where my oldest sister was born. What I'd like to do is go up on the front porch of this house, open the door, and call out, "Ma, I'm home." But you don't dare push your dreams too far. You can go home again. The fellow was wrong when he said you couldn't. You can go home again, only just part way.

# MADISON IN THE EARLY 1900s
*Josephine Baltes*

My early memories date back to Madison as it was in the early 1900s when the city was young and ended on the west side at Monroe Street.

Vilas Park was evolving from a park to include a zoo. Collecting animals to show the public was in its infancy. I remember the first cars and the last rides in horse-drawn carriages in the city, early streetcars ridden for a nickel, homemade remedies for illness, and walking "uptown" and back to my home near Vilas Park. We saved nickels and I guess it was part of our entertainment.

Another form of entertainment was parking on the Square in our Model T and watching the Saturday night shoppers. Many times there were other forms of entertainment. One night there was a Ku Klux Klan parade with full regalia and flares. Very frightened, we all wondered who was under the white sheets. We were sure there were local people. I don't remember finding out.

Since my dear Dad was city park superintendent in those days, we were the caretakers of small animals such as monkeys and alligators. They were sometimes housed in the basement while their cages were being built. That had to be in the very early 1900s because we moved to a new home on Erin Street when I was ten years old.

One of the mysteries of my early childhood was a squat green building at the end of Erin Street at the entrance to Vilas Park. One day the green building was gone and there was a beautiful marble fountain. Graceful figures looked as if they had risen from the sea and water flowed over shells and rocks. It cost some six thousand dollars in 1925.

We children played across the street on the Indian

mounds that overlook peaceful Lake Wingra and picnicked there. The decision was made to open a road through the area so cars could travel into the park at that entrance. What excitement we had when diggers found the artifacts of Indian lore in the mounds. I wish I could remember what happened to them. For a long time we children approached the area with fear. Were the ghosts of the past still there?

In the early 1900s Fred Winkelman came from Chicago as the first zoo superintendent. I fondly remember visiting the Winkelmans' home on West Lawn Avenue and playing with the tiny lion cubs they carefully raised following their birth at the zoo. There were always two at a time. While they looked like kittens, they were already vicious, so I was closely supervised while I attempted to hold them. I remember it was hard for Mrs. Winkelman to give them up when they were turned over to the zoo.

A big change came in the park during the Depression when WPA helped build sturdy cages of heavy rock and steel. Some of those cages are still in use.

Hospitals then offered very simplified care. My sister was born in a private maternity hospital in a home on Wisconsin Avenue near the present Masonic Temple. Then eight years old, I was allowed in the nursery where I could hold my sister and view the other little charges. I guess germs were not feared then.

My tonsils were removed in a small brick building on the corner of Brooks and Mound Street, the beginnings of Madison General Hospital, across from Longfellow School. My father was allowed to sleep on a cot at my side. The work must have been done in June or July because the hospital closed for vacation in August. I remember wondering what sick people did in August. That must have been in 1922 or 1923.

My first school days were spent at Longfellow School until I entered Edgewood Academy and became a "day boarder." Only a few girls came each day for lessons and returned home at night. Most of the students were boarded and were from far away. They had to wear uniforms. We did not wear uniforms and were stamped differently in our academically run world.

One benefit was receiving daily lessons in proper eating during the noon meal. I vividly remember being told to break my bread into small pieces and to butter them as I ate.

Learning to dance with each other at the noon recess also kept us occupied. There were no gym classes for proper young ladies. Walking about the spacious grounds was the extent of our exercise. Gum chewing was frowned upon, as was leg crossing. Dresses were safe calf-length; no earrings were allowed, and hats and gloves were ordered when shopping.

I walked to school most days. No one had heard of busing. The streetcars traveled on Mills Street to University Avenue. A transfer at Mills Street to a Wingra Park streetcar meant a long ride, so I walked, usually through the park. It was perfectly safe then. On inclement days my parents were waiting for me after school.

We must have "broken the trail," so to speak, for present-day travelers. Our family camped in a tent and took a trip each summer. We went as far as Niagara Falls and Mammoth Cave in Kentucky. It took two days to get to Vandalia, Ohio, where my father took part in the national trap shoots. We often camped in some congenial farm yard come evening. I remember meeting some very nice people and once being awakened by turkeys outside the tent.

Our mother made traveling knickers for herself, my sister, and myself. Since we were all females, we were often a free sideshow on city streets when we shopped. Friendly and unfriendly stares greeted us. One time so many people stared at us that we returned to our large Buick sedan without shopping. Dad had outfitted the car with extra luggage carriers at the side and back, so we must have been quite a sight.

For medicinal purposes, my mothers always prepared sandwiches of sliced onions on bread, generously spread with butter and heavily salted. It is still my remedy when I am exposed to illness. My family jokes that no one, even a virus, can get near me then.

The use of boiled onions and turpentine pressed into a bag and worn around the neck to ward off the dread flu of 1918 is still vivid in my mind. It must have worked for me because I am still here to tell the tale. I remember so many people around me were very ill, including my mother and father. There were many deaths.

There was also the spring tonic each year when Grandmother came to visit. Down went the sulphur and molasses to clear out the winter poisons.

Those were good days and difficult times. The Depression brought families close together in their financial struggles. Many homes housed more than one family. Entertainment was simple and usually centered around home activities like checkers, puzzles, and card playing. Tomorrow was another day to cope with, and held a promise of rosier sunsets. But it was a time of simple living and unhurried days. Days to be remembered.

## TELL ME THE TALES THAT TO ME WERE SO DEAR LONG, LONG AGO—LONG AGO
*Dorothy Inbusch*

Crank. Ring. "Central, I want Main 527." Does that sound familiar? It was in the 1900s.

Do you remember when you visited Grandma, there were so many wonderful things to do. She had big stone crocks of spiced crab apples, pickled peaches, cucumber gherkins, and mincemeat. It was always my task to chop the suet, seed the raisins for the mincemeat, and scrub the cukes. What a heavenly aroma when I ground the coffee beans in the square mill with a drawer in the front. She had two big barrels in the pantry, one for sugar and one for flour. I almost fell in the sugar barrel, scraping it. She always did her own baking and often she ran short of bakery goods. She sent me down to a shop with fifty cents. I bought a loaf of bread, five cents; a dozen doughnuts, twelve cents; a dozen cookies, twelve cents; a cinnamon coffee cake, fifteen cents; and brought back change! It was awfully hard to fill up four small children.

Grandma grew up in Vermont and frequently we had New England boiled dinners — codfish balls or salt mackerel and boiled potatoes for Sunday breakfast. Once in a while she made baked beans and brown bread for supper. The bean pot was filled with beans, molasses, salt pork, and I don't know what else, and cooked for twenty-four hours on a shelf inside the coal stove.

Do you remember school days at Milwaukee Downer College, looking for the "hat"? The sorority and fraternity dances at the Town Club with refreshments of ice cream and cake? The benefit roller-skating parties for some charity?

Early school was Miss Treat's, held in the Parish

House of All Saints Cathedral. We loved to be chosen to pump the chapel organ — which had a long wooden handle that went up and down, because then we didn't have to attend the service — or to toll the bell in the spire. It had a long rope, and as the bell swayed, it lifted me off my feet.

The boys went to Dr. Pratt's or Country Day. Their school clothes were knickers, long black stockings with leather kneecaps, and blouses — white at one time.

Do you remember our pompadors? We pinned some soft material called rats to our heads, combed our hair over to make the "pomps," and topped it with a big black taffeta bow, plus one at the back to get our hair out of the way. Do you remember the boudoir caps we wore and the black velvet ribbon tied around our necks, with a white tulle "pom" at the nape?

I had long, curly hair, and Mother dampened it and brushed it around a long stick.

Do you remember sliding down the cellar door and getting your panties dirty? "I don't want to play in your yard — I don't like you anymore. You'll be sorry when you see me sliding down the cellar door."

We could hardly wait until the Little Colonel, Elsie Dinsmore, and the St. Nicholas came out, and the boys anxiously awaited the next Alger or Henty book and *Youth's Companion.*

The band concerts at Lake Park and Soldier's Home? Snitching ice from the big wagon? Talking to the policemen with their tall derbies and billy sticks?

In winter driving up Humboldt Avenue in a jingling cutter, wrapped in a fur robe, and the blowing snow stinging your face?

Do you remember squinting between the planks in the wooden sidewalks, hoping to spy pennies or nickels? You chewed a wad of gum, put it on a long stick or string, praying it would adhere to a coin. Sometimes it did.

Do you remember whenever there was a heavy rain the wooden block-paved streets would swell and float away? The tooth fairy who left a nickel?

The gas lamp-lighters, the amusement park wonderland; its roller coaster and bump-the-bumps? The open streetcars, Daisy and Marguerite in electric lights?

And the theaters; Rose Melville in *Sis Hopkins,* John Drew at the Davidson in *Trelawny of the Wells.* Sarah Bernhardt and Lillie Langtry at the Majestic or Palace, the German Stock Company at the Pabst?

The Deutscher Club, which had been the Mitchell Mansion?

The Palm Garden. The huge wide-bladed overhead fans making a wonderful breeze as they whirled?

Do you remember the Salvation Army bands in the summer, their money kettles and bells at Christmastime?

The little girls with their jump ropes and jacks, the boys shooting mibs or spinning tops?

Do you remember when the streetcars went only as far as the car barns at North Avenue, and the farthest north you could go was Hampton Road? If you lived farther, you had to walk.

The unpaved dirty and dusty road, Lake Drive now, where fees were collected as toll from people riding bicycles or surrey driving? A long wooden bar blocked the road and lifted after the ten-cent fee was paid.

Do you remember going to the corner candy shop and having a hard time choosing among the yummy sweets displayed in jars; the fluted tin dishes filled with pink candies that came with their own spoons; the licorice whips; the lollipops with real licorice root handles which we chewed afterwards; sucking a jaw breaker and forever spitting it out to see what color it had become; the surprise when it got small to find an anise seed at the center; and the awfully chewy caramels that loosened your braces, much to the annoyance of the dentist?

Do you remember the clanging bell on the fire truck, the one stack engine belching black smoke while two men at the water truck pumped up and down? The chief dashing up in a runabout with a fast-pacing horse; the fire bell at the engine house ringing 1-2—1-2-3-4, and you knew just where the fire was? Do you remember St. John's Cathedral bell clanging six o'clock, and the booming bell on the clock tower of City Hall?

Do you remember the ten-cent movies? We cried with the Gish sisters to the tune of "Hearts and Flowers," sighed with the lovers, thrilled while the cowboys galloped by looking for rustlers to the tune of "William Tell."

We had a ballroom on the third floor of the house, and many a dance was held to the tunes on the phonograph with the morning glory horn. Refreshments of punch and cookies.

There were few automobiles but we had a Tin Lizzie and a Kissel Kar, and Mother had a Rausch and Lange electric coupe. No TV, thank goodness, and not many radios, but we did listen to "Amos and Andy."

Do you remember Mr. Bournique's dancing class at the Atheneum? The little girls in long-waisted dresses with very short skirts, big hairbows, wide sashes and gloves. The little boys in Eton suits, gray-striped trousers, short black jackets, turned-down collars, and flowing black ties—gloves, of course. The boy bowed to the girl. She smiled, curtsied, and away they galloped or waltzed. Mr. B. clacked his castenet, a long line formed, and we tried to follow his intricate steps. The papas and mamas seated on a raised platform at the end of the hall proudly watching their darlings.

Do you remember the huge cloud of steam from the Northwestern locomotive as it shrieked to a halt, disgorging passengers who rushed to the Tallyho for a citywide sightseeing trip, or to the small Parmalee bus for the Pfister Hotel or Plankinton House for a seventy-five-cent Sunday dinner?

Do you remember the excursion ship *Bloomer Girl* that docked at the Pabst Whitefish Bay Resort where wonderful fish dinners were served and Swiss yodelers entertained?

If you lived in the city you went out on the dummy line, a small locomotive on tracks, pulling little passenger cars. Dinners sometimes got served outdoors on tables and chairs in the form of toadstools. The Christopher Columbus whaleback ship came up from Chicago and docked in the river just south of Gimbel's.

We spent several summers at a working farm resort, White's on Nagawicka Lake. It was thirty miles west of the city and we went out in the surrey. To lighten the load, we got out of the vehicle and walked alongside the horse up the hills. It took us all day. We slept in cottages lit with kerosene lamps and walked to another building for meals. Room and board was fourteen dollars a week and the meals were wonderful — all homemade farm produce. I gathered eggs, and the boys cranked the ice cream freezer, with the reward of licking the ladder. I loved to go to the hayloft looking for kittens, and I usually found a litter or two.

The man who milked the cows watched for the cats that usually came at that time, and he squirted milk in their direction. For amusement we had dancing parties in the pavilion, sailboat races, corn and marshmallow roasts, hayrides, swims, walks to the village.

Our pleasures were innocent — we never thought of

sex, though we did neck a bit. Crime was low, and we could go for strolls at night. No one even locked doors. Charity did not chill, and poverty was no disgrace.

If time would only turn back, and make us young again.

## A PLACE TO REMEMBER
*Harry A. Friedman*

Blessed is the magic of nostalgia and the power it gives us to probe the elusive shadows of the past.

I remember a terrified four-year-old sitting rigidly as his long curls were snipped so that he could go to school like a little man. I remember the first fish caught on the end of a line tied to a finger; the joy of chasing the ice-wagon man for cool chips; the sawdust on the butcher shop floor; the six-cent weekly allowance — five cents to see Charlie Chaplin and a penny for a mysterious grab bag; open-air streetcars; helmeted policemen; the first long pants; steaming fire engines.

Oh, I remember many things, but most of all I remember Lapham Park.

Near Eighth and Walnut in Milwaukee, there was a hill with a thick stand of elms and oaks. There was a trail to the top and on all sides shrubs growing to provide hiding places. In the summer a host of wildflowers carpeted the grassy slopes, and on the summit one could stand like a Balboa and with young eyes survey a small world. There were games to play—run-my-good-sheep-run, hide and seek, cowboys and Indians with pretend bows and arrows and hand-hewn guns made from fallen tree branches. I can still hear the cries of "bang-bang" as we dashed from one street to another. High sport was rolling down the hill in the cleared areas.

North and west of my hill was a wide expanse of playground. It really was a complete outdoor gymnasium equipped with parallel and horizontal bars, leather horses, giant swings, ladders for climbing, basketball courts, and baseball diamonds. Here "chicken muscles" hardened and prize-winning athletic skills were developed.

Sunday morning handball games, where a hand was the bat and tennis balls the missiles, drew crowds of spectators. Playing baseball with the Lapham Athletic Club was a great thrill because this twelve-year-old could hit the ball into the treetops that bordered the field.

There was keen competition in the frequent stunt meets promoted by the playground supervisors, many of whom were students attending Marquette University and the old Milwaukee Normal School, now UW-M. The all-city playground and gymnastic tournaments and daily personal contacts gave everyone an opportunity to profit from the character-building benefits of lasting friendships and displays of good sportsmanship.

When the hill became a gigantic mound of snow, a ski and sled slide was constructed. This was an icy trough that extended downward for a considerable distance from the top of the hill around the edge of the playground. For skis we used old barrel staves tied to the shoes with leather thongs or rope, and often enough, we just slid down on our shoes or belly flopped helter-skelter on garbage can covers. The playground was surrounded by a low, rounded snow fence inside of which was a very large ice rink.

On the south side of the hill was my favorite relaxation place, the library and social center. Here it was that a nine-year-old approached Miss Zolon, the librarian, and hesitantly asked for a library card. In due time it was presented and for all these years I have cherished the

Under the guidance of that understanding woman, I was introduced to a beautiful realm of fantasy. I went along with Marco Polo on his perilous journeys. Stanley had me as a wide-eyed companion when he found Livingston in the African jungle. I suffered with Peary at the North Pole, sailed the seven seas with Magellan, and marched through Mexico with Cortez. The Orient with its mystery and intrigue; the glamorous South Seas; pirates, soldiers, explorers, inventors — all existed vividly in my book world. But the library is gone, together with all of the historical and fictional characters that beckoned to me from its shelves.

The social center was an integral part of my second home. Robert Witt—"Daddy Witt" to me and hundreds more—was the director. That gentle, great-hearted man was my mentor as I entered young manhood. It was he who assisted and encouraged and introduced us to the real meaning of a social center. Game rooms, club rooms, handicraft areas were packed daily, winter and summer, with boys and girls of every race, creed, and color in the neighborhood. To us, Daddy Witt and compassion were synonymous. The center is still there, housed in a bleakly gray building, and I am sure that it includes the various activities that drew us there.

West of the hill there was a huge, octagon-shaped building which we knew as "the pavilion." This was the center of all indoor sports activities, especially during the winter months. Basketball, wrestling, boxing in the main hall, and foot races on a wide balcony that circled the interior were popular. On a broad, deep stage were presented pageants, musicals, and amateur plays by various neighborhood groups.

The pavilion had been built on heavy girders that rested on many wooden pilasters sunk into the ground. This provided an area of great adventure as we crawled on hands and knees to fathom the mysteries of a narrow gauge railroad track, abandoned little open cars with rusted wheels, parts of what appeared to be old lampposts, wooden frames with the last vestiges of gilt paint clinging to their decaying surfaces — and just "things and stuff." We didn't know then that all of these "things" were the remnants of a glorious era in the park's history.

Milwaukee always has been famous as a beer center, and until World War I it also was nationally known for its beautiful beer gardens, some of which dated back to 1848. Lapham Park once was a beer garden. Known as Schlitz Park, it was famous throughout the country as a place to visit.

The site, originally the homestead of pioneer Garrett Vliet, was purchased by Charles Quentin in the 1850s and known as Quentin's Park until the mid 1870s, when it was acquired by the Schlitz Brewery and converted into a lavishly appointed amusement park.

A wide, terraced stairway was constructed on one side of the hill, which was believed to be an old Indian mound. On the top was a large observation tower and from it one could look upon the whole city. The stairway was illuminated by gas light which gleamed from large glass globes mounted on gilded lampposts. Altogether more than two hundred of the gas-light globes had been mounted on terraces and grounds. Toward the end of the century it was the boast that the park was "ablaze with thirty-two electric lights."

Under the many trees were rustic tables and benches and vine-covered pergolas. Bridle paths traversed the area; children romped on the playground while all popular lawn games were offered. It was the place to visit on starry summer nights and the hub of the city's *Gemuetlichkeit.*

A featured attraction for the children was a miniature railway which girdled the park and ran under the girders which supported a great, octagonal theater with a seating capacity of more than one thousand.

Here Milwaukeeans were introduced to opera, first Gilbert and Sullivan and later the Italian and German operas. These were presented almost every week and starred famous singers from all over the world. Local musical societies and orchestras performed daily during the summer, many of the performances also being offered outside.

The war brought a halt to Schlitz Park's attractiveness. For a few years it was the center of political rallies, wrestling bouts, and prize fights. Finally, the site was purchased by the city and Lapham Park was established in honor of Increase A. Lapham, a noted Milwaukee scientist.

The Schlitz Park embellishments were removed, except for the hill and pavilion. Now the hill is gone and the pavilion is gone. The flat areas where they stood shimmer with the reflections of cherished memories as the tumult of expressway traffic bursts into the reveries with a disturbing roar.

But it truly was a place to remember.

## GRAND FORKS DAYS
### *Robert G. Anderson*

Every time I get a whiff of a pipeful of Prince Albert I'm carried back to my boyhood in Grand Forks, North Dakota, fifty-some years ago. I can hear Pa sucking on his blackened corncob as he toasts his stockinged feet on the oven door of the kitchen wood stove. Ma has bread and three-day biscuits rising, and soon the house will be permeated with a heavenly aroma. And I know that when Ma draws the fragrant loaves and biscuits from the oven, my brother Arvid and I will shoulder each other for first crack at an end crust or hot biscuit.

We were a big, harum-scarum family in those days, teetering on the brink of poverty but not quite slipping over. Of seven kids, Arv and I fit somewhere in the middle. He was twelve and I was ten. One older brother clerked at the Golden Rule and another worked after school at the Lion Drugstore, so you can see that not much money was coming in to our family.

The trouble was that Pa was a little of everything — plumber, carpenter, ditch digger. A handyman. But there wasn't enough work available for him to be handy at. Consequently, except for an infrequent odd job, Pa's activity consisted mainly of swapping stories with his Norwegian cronies at Olsen's Plumbing Shop.

At first we lived on Second Avenue where most of our neighbors were Jewish — many of them Orthodox. According to their religion they were forbidden to light their own fires on Saturday, their Sabbath. So Arv and I spent many a chilly Saturday morning making the rounds of the Blums, the Greenbergs, Baums, and Hochmans where paper and kindling were already neatly laid. All we had to do was strike the match handed to us and touch it to the paper. Sometimes we got a cookie and sometimes a nickel.

Almost every summer Sunday some civic organization had a picnic, complete with games, races, and contests. Prizes consisted of boxes of chocolates or merchandise certificates worth two or three dollars. Arv entered the dashes because he was fast as a hummingbird and won many races. We kids ate the candy but Ma cashed the certificates.

One hot Sunday afternoon, however, Arv overreached himself. He'd just won a three-pound box of candy in the hundred-yard dash and looked about for more worlds to conquer. He entered the Catch the Greasy Pig and Climb the Greasy Pole contests. Much to his credit, he was the first to come within an agonizing inch of the dollar bill waving cheerily from atop the smooth, greased pole. But it eluded his grasp and slowly he slipped down — down to defeat.

Arv was also one of the first to catch the greasy pig, but the outraged, squealing porker was a living dynamo and my brother couldn't hang on long enough to flip it over on its back, which was a condition of winning.

The lanky, farmboy winner smiled as he gave Arv some advice. "This is where it don't pay to be first — let the others wipe most of the grease off before you step in and make your play."

My brother stuck to the dashes after that.

Then our family moved closer to the river, which gave Arv and me greater opportunity to explore and fish. If a composite picture of Tom Sawyer and Huck Finn were made, it would mirror my brother. I can see him now, hand poised above his jerking fishline. "I got a bite!" he whispers fiercely, bare toes dug into the sandy clay shore. A snap of the line and he sets the hook, then reels the catfish in hand over hand.

Our method of fishing needs explanation. A limber green twig is pressed into the soft clay, and a forty-foot line, complete with baited hooks and heavy sinker, is tied to the end of the twig. Then the line is coiled into loops, much as a cowboy gathers a lariat. Then the heavy sinker end is twirled above the head and cast far out into the river. As the line sinks and the sensitive end of the twig rights itself, all that remains is waiting for the bite.

My brother disdained the pale, listless garden variety of earthworm that was commonly used as bait. We dug beneath the loading platform of a grain company where moist piles of chaff yielded hundreds of manure worms. As I scooped them into a can I noticed they stunk like a pride of skunks but the little red rascals made more gyrations than a belly dancer in a hive of hornets.

"Put a couple—maybe three on a hook," Arv advised me. "More ends wiggling, more bites."

And he was right. We pulled a lot of tasty catfish and bullheads out of the Red River and it was a good thing because Ma counted on those fish to fry or make Norsk fiske suppe for the family. But I wasn't the fisherman my brother was—I'd soon lose patience and wander off below the wooden bridge that arched to the Minnesota side. Or I'd wade into the shallows out to the island to watch the frogs and crabs and darting birds.

Sometimes we'd catch enough fish that he could sell some to the Greek for ten cents. Then we'd have to scrounge another dime so we could go to the show. We were movie buffs and as often as possible we'd be in the front row when the rangeland heroics of Tom Mix or William Desmond were unreeled. My one fall from grace in Arv's eyes came when I let my sister talk me into attending a stageshow of the "Butterfly Kiddies" when I could have seen Dustin Farnum in *West of the Catalina Mountains* with him.

One summer day Arv and I were fishing a deep bend in the river with two friends, Myron and Titten Hauge. Titten and I didn't get any bites so we wandered downstream. We found a decrepit raft tied to a crumbling pile and climbed aboard. In our play we didn't notice the slow swing of the craft toward midstream until the frayed rope parted. Titten jumped for the shore and made it, but the force of his jump tumbled me into the deep water.

I threshed awkwardly; I could not swim. After a few moments, as in a slow dreamlike movement, I bobbed up and down, up and down, helpless in the murky water. Curiously, after the first sharp stinging in my nose, the feeling of drowning was not unpleasant.

Meanwhile, Titten had raced back upstream to fetch Arv, and in a minute my brother sliced into the water after me. Vaguely I felt his hands clutch my arm and shirt before he boosted me to the surface and the precious air. Dragging me to the shore, he dumped me onto the grassy bank. I coughed and gagged and retched for a quarter of an hour.

Arv was mad and scared, giving me a stiff bawling out before he returned to his lines. As I slowly returned to even keel he cooled off, and four catfish later he took me home. He told Ma what had happened in such a matter-of-fact manner that Ma made nothing of my close call.

I must have looked entirely normal.

On another occasion a ragged tramp stepped out from under the big wooden bridge while Arv and I were fishing. Ma had warned us to be wary of strangers, but it was too nice a morning for suspicions and this man had nice eyes.

"Hello," the seedy character called as he approached the small fire we'd built against the chill river mist. "Nice mess of fish you've got there. Ever bake 'em?"

"No," Arv's answer was guarded. "We fry them. That is — Ma does."

"Look here, if you can spare a few I'll show you how to bake them. Real good eating."

Since he had a sizable stringerful, my brother agreed after a thoughtful pause.

The tramp set right to work and neatly filleted several nice catfish. "Got any heavy paper and some grease?"

We'd brought sandwiches from home and now the stranger rubbed the butter on the heavy butcher's paper they'd been wrapped in. Then he put the fillets inside the paper, scooped clay from the river's edge, and formed a ball around the whole. Finally he tossed it into the fire and piled dry sticks around it.

For an hour or so he told us stories of far places like Spokane and Sacramento and Albuquerque — until he prodded the hard-baked ball from the fire and cracked it open. I'll never forget the wonderful taste of that baked fish.

And as the taste of heavenly catfish lingers on my tongue, so do the other memories linger in my mind. It was a sunny time of pure and innocent joy.

## BACKYARD MEMORIES
*Dorothy Vogl*

By today's standards, the backyard of my childhood would be considered a blighted area. But it was like all the others in a typical small town: The things we needed were kept in easy reach and were utilitarian rather than beautiful. And as I think of the hours a little girl spent there, I remember the fun, security, and contentment of plain, unpretentious family life.

Our back door opened onto a good-sized, weathered, wooden stoop with a handy bench at one end. In the center stood a pump for cistern water — that soft rainwater so wonderful for washing clothes or bathing, but not for drinking. Against the house was a woodbox containing the fuel for our kitchen range. Pans and tubs hung on the clapboard siding, and a broom and mop stood in the corner.

Three steps on one side of the stoop led down to a narrow boardwalk that we followed to the big woodshed and, beyond that, to the privy. Three steps on the other side led to the vegetable garden. To the north was the slanting outside cellar door and a good patch of lawn, dominated by an old wooden clothes-reel. Our hammock hung between its center pole and a corner of the house. A box elder tree shaded the stoop and offered a convenient limb for my rope swing with its notched board seat, made for me by Papa. Another pump near the house gave us well water for drinking.

In the summer, Mama did the family wash on the back stoop. In rainy weather, or in winter, operations were transferred to the kitchen. Clothes were always sorted on Sunday evening and the whites put to soak. A stand held two galvanized tubs, one with the washboard for rubbing the dirty clothes and the other for rinsing. Between them was the wringer, turned by hand. The clean clothes were hung on the squeaky revolving clothes reel and on extra lines that Papa always put up.

The hammock was one of my favorite spots on drowsy summer days, the best place for reading Elsie Dinsmore, Mildred Keith, and my many books about the Campfire Girls. If it was Tuesday morning, I was lulled by the steady chug-chug-chug of the gasoline engine that generated the town's electricity. It was located in the machine-shop-smithy next door. "Charlie" provided power from dusk until ten at night and also on Tuesday mornings for women fortunate enough to own electric irons. Mama didn't have one, and we had no electric lights or telephone either in the nice, big, two-story house Papa rented for ten dollars a month.

Sometimes, through the open window, I'd hear my mother playing the piano: "Silver Threads among the Gold," "Red Wing," "Over the Waves," or "After the Ball." Often Mama brought out a kitchen chair and joined me in the backyard with a pitcher of "ginger tea." (We had no ice cubes, and not even an icebox, but our well water was clear and cold.) Dear, fun-loving Mama, in her neat, ankle-length housedress, her hair pulled softly back into a pug, and eyes smiling through rimless glasses!

My friends and I often played house in the woodshed. On one side was the coal bin, filled with hard coal in anticipation of winter. The coal stove with its isinglass windows and shiny nickel trim stood nearby and would be transported to the parlor in the fall. On the other side of the shed stood piles of neatly stacked firewood, split with an ax by Papa and Grandpa, for our kitchen range. In the fall, one section of the wooden floor was strewn with walnuts and hickory nuts in their green husks, in the process of drying. The woodshed was also a wonderful place for finding newborn kittens, regularly supplied by my beloved black cat. The gunny-sack ragbag yielded all manner of cast-off clothes which childish imagination transferred into costumes.

In summer the privy was shimmering hot and buzzing with flies. One or two cats usually followed me to the outhouse and contentedly rubbed against my legs as I sat on the little hole made especially for me. Oh, the contentment of it all — buzzing flies, purring cats, and even the human odors tranquilized me as I paged idly through the torn Sears, Roebuck catalog.

Beyond the privy was my pet cemetery. Here lay ill-fated kittens, baby chicks from my aunt's flock, dead birds found by chance, and even mice from the traps at school. Wooden cigar boxes from Papa's barber shop made ideal coffins, and a big stone pile behind the woodshed was my source of headstones.

Edging our garden, a three-board fence separated our lot from our neighbors' shedlike, dirt-floor garage Papa rented to house our 1915 Ford. He had to drive in carefully on two planks, one for the right and one for the left wheels, to avoid making ruts.

Here and there were other delights. The tree that bore Duchess apples I was so fond of in their tart, green stage. Mama declared I'd get cholera morbus (whatever that is) but I knew she was joking. In early spring I watched for the pieplant to poke its red shoots through the ground. There were flowers, too — peonies, cosmos, phlox, golden glow, and lilies of the valley. Oh, yes, and those delicate, romantic bleeding hearts. If you pulled one apart carefully, you'd find a pair of slippers, scissors, and a needle.

No vacation elsewhere could rival those childhood summers spent in that old, shabby, lived-in backyard I remember so well.

What can a backyard tell about history? Politically, probably nothing, but in changing lifestyles it can tell a great deal. For the same type of middle-class family, the slamming back door is now a thermopane that slides open onto a concrete patio, perhaps covered with indoor-outdoor carpeting and furnished with chairs and recliners designed for the purpose, not cast-offs from the house.

Daughter suns herself in a swim-suit — good riddance to black sateen bloomers, petticoat, gingham dress, and apron! Mother wears shorts and halter. Their music comes from a transistor radio.

The privy has moved indoors and is becoming the most glamorous room in the house. Water comes magically, hot or cold, from shiny faucets.

The "Tin Lizzie" in its dirt-floor garage has given way to one or maybe two sleek automobiles in an attached-to-the-house garage with overhead doors, most likely equipped with automatic opening devices.

The cool dark place called the cellar, with its outside door, became more elegant as a basement, and the basement has often become a "rec" room. Who needs a cellar when there's a beautiful refrigerator-freezer dispensing ice cubes and cold drinks!

The washtubs, wringer, and clothes reel are replaced by an automatic washer and dryer. The house has central heating, gas, oil, or electric, and few of today's children have ever seen a coal bin or a coal scuttle.

The backyard is still a pleasant place, with patio, colorful chairs and umbrellas, perhaps a swimming pool, playground equipment, well-cared-for lawn. We wouldn't want to go back to the old ways. But I'm glad to have been a child in my own backyard of long ago.

# MY RECOLLECTIONS OF EARLY FARM LIFE
*Mrs. John Novak*

Our family had been renting farms for some years in southern Wisconsin. We were immigrants, and as did most immigrants, my dad's one aim in life was to own a plot of land he could call his own.

New Holstein was a German-Dutch community, we being the only farmers of Czech descent living there. My mother could speak German, so she had no speech problems, but Dad had a hard time making himself understood, and on many occasions I had to translate for him.

When Dad heard there was cheap, undeveloped land to be had in northern Wisconsin, he decided to go prospecting. I can still remember how elated he was when he came back from his trip to announce he had bought a little forty-acre farm in a Czech community near Neva Corners. Now he would not have a language barrier.

The spring of 1924 found us settled on this little farm. The log barn had room for five cows. It had two small windows which didn't let in much light. The cows all wore around their necks bells that tinkled merrily as they munched their hay or chewed their cud.

The house was a small frame building with two rooms and an unfinished upper story. There was a cream separator in one corner of the kitchen. It became my duty to turn the flywheel every day after milking to separate the cream from the milk and also to keep it immaculately clean.

Dad delivered the cream to the Neva cheese factory every day with one horse and a milk wagon. This was our only income, and the family had to practice thrift, buying only the bare necessities.

The farm had small patches of clearing, these being divided by pine stumpage, and each little clearing had a few of the largest pine stumps still standing, some being two and a half or three feet in diameter. These would all have to be dynamited before they could be removed, as this was in an era before the bulldozer came into the picture.

I can remember one old settler telling Dad, "Buy your dynamite right away, Joe, while you still have some money left. Most of these people ran out of money, and that's why the biggest pine stumps are left standing in the middle of each clearing. You cannot clear this land without dynamite."

So Dad purchased a large amount of dynamite, and one of the settlers taught him how to lay it, so that the blast would split the stump for easier removal.

I soon found out how hard it was to clear a small plot of land. Dad would spend one day laying the dynamite and blasting, and the next few days would be spent removing the stumps. Dad would hook a chain around the uprooted sections and drag them away with a team of horses. This was dangerous work, as some of the long pine roots still adhered tightly in the soil, and the whole thing would sometimes turn over.

My job was to fill in the crater that was left after the stump was removed. This crater was about four or five feet in diameter. My dad's instructions were, "First throw in the stones on the bottom, then dig out all the roots that are left, and fill the hole with soil as smoothly as you can."

This was no easy task. Some of the roots were long and stuck fast. I had to pry them out with a pick and then shovel the surrounding soil into the crater. It was back-breaking work, as I was a young girl weighing around one hundred fifteen pounds.

Our cows had no end of pastureland. Our forty acres bordered with the high hills north of us, which was wild forest country and unfenced. I often walked along the old "logging road" left by the lumberjacks in years gone by before I could find them for milking. No one told me there were wolves and bear in this part of the country. I doubt that I would have been brave enough to go so far alone if I had known this.

Some summer days, after the evening chores were done, the young folks of the neighborhood would gather at our place to pile the half-rotted pine logs around the stumps in our pasture. Someone soon built a fire, and the young folks would each in turn add their contribution of pine roots, brush, or other waste wood lying in the pasture.

This was fun! Then, as the evening wore on, the fire illuminated the area and seemed to spread cheer among us. One of the boys would bring out his accordion and the group would join in singing the old Czech songs to his accompaniment. Later we had lunch and lemonade to enjoy right there under the stars with the glowing embers of the bonfire fading into a last, slow-burning pine torch. This sort of entertainment was not only fun but served another purpose, that of getting another little piece of land cleared.

I was happy to be in this kind of environment, which held a feeling of togetherness among friends and neighbors. With the back woods all around us I felt I was living a pioneer story.

Our firewood came from the huge stump piles Dad had made during the summer when blasting. This wood gave out an excellent source of heat, but brought out the blackest smoke through the chimney.

Our hogs and chickens supplied us with meat and eggs for the coming winter, and our variety of garden vegetables, our skim milk, and the wild blueberries we picked supplied us with a diversified diet that was very satisfactory. Mother also made cottage cheese and an aged cheese from our plentiful supply of skim milk. Coffee, flour, salt, and sugar, besides kerosene, were about the only other staples Mother would buy to supplement our menu, and the only things she could afford.

Dad built a smokehouse and smoked all our bacon and hams and sausage that winter in a way that withstood the next summer without becoming moldy or rancid. These hung up in the attic and ensured a good supply of meat.

Dad was a basket weaver by trade, which he learned in the Old Country, and every spring we would help him cut the long, slim willows and store them for winter basket weaving. He could make baskets, hampers, ferneries, or cradles of any size or shape ordered. His finished products were well made and durable and brought extra cash during the winter months when the cows went dry. Dad passed away in 1938, but some of his baskets are still in use today.

Almost every Saturday night there would be a potluck social. During the summer the men would sit outside with their pony of beer and discuss farm problems or politics, the women would rule the kitchen, and the young folks would dance to the tune of the Victrola. Sundays would be spent as an outing or picnic near someone's woodlot, and the summer just slipped away into happy memories.

Winter was a time for box socials, pie socials, dancing, and sleigh rides. The drama club would meet for rehearsals and put on quite a program, both comedy and serious drama, giving its members a wonderful outlet in which to express their art.

Life was beautiful in this Czech community. The women worked as hard as the men, but the weekend of togetherness within the community more than outweighed and compensated for any inconveniences there might have been, and everyone was ready to face another week of hard labor.

All in all this was a very satisfactory and full life. We were never bored, as there were so many diversified outlets in our work as well as in our social life, which gave us a feeling of fulfillment, a happy, healthy mind and body, and a healthy home life atmosphere. Now in my aging years I can only reminisce, but I still get a sense of enjoyment out of reliving every precious moment of my youth in those North Woods of Wisconsin.

*List of Participants,*
*1976-1978*

Nearly one hundred stories are included in this volume of *We Were Children Then;* many more were contributed to the Yarns of Yesteryear Program in the years 1976-1978. In recognition of the great contributions of all the participants, the name of each writer is listed here.

# A

Ethelyn Aanrud
*Amherst Junction*

Mona Aanrud
*Amherst Junction*

Elizabeth Abbott
*Marshfield*

Hilda Abegglen
*Racine*

Grace Aberg
*Shell Lake*

Loretta Ackerman
*Milwaukee*

Gertrude Adams
*Madison*

Mattie Adams
*Oregon*

Mildred Adams
*Montello*

Mrs. LaVerne Ader
*Menomonie*

Sr. M. Adrian
*Sinsinawa*

Letitia Albrecht
*Augusta*

Anne Allen
*Milwaukee*

Clinton Allen
*Viroqua*

Margaret Allen
*Baraboo*

Ruth Allschwang
*Milwaukee*

Mrs. Ross Alm
*Argyle*

Conrad Amrhein
*Milwaukee*

Katherine Amunrud
*Hixton*

Adella Andersen
*Milwaukee*

Mrs. Eugene Andersen
*St. Germain*

Gladys Andersen
*Oconomowoc*

Amelia Anderson
*Ellsworth*

Emily Anderson
*Madison*

Esther Anderson
*Rio*

Marie Anderson
*Woodville*

Mary Anderson
*Bloomer*

Robert G. Anderson
*Milwaukee*

Stan Anderson
*Dodgeville*

Ella Andre
*Kewaskum*

James Andre
*Kewaskum*

Marguerite Arndt
*Barron*

Mrs. Frank Arrigoni
*Auburndale*

Delores Aspenson
*Viroqua*

Arvid Asplund
*Two Rivers*

Florence Atkinson
*Albany*

R. Boyd Atkinson
*Albany*

Frances Atwell
*Fond du Lac*

May Augustyn
*Fond du Lac*

Wanda Aukofer
*Milwaukee*

Juanita Austin
*Brandon*

Pearl Axelsen
*Marshfield*

Lindsey Ayers
*Menomonee Falls*

Webb Ayres
*Kenosha*

# B

Ethel Babcock
*Burlington*

Edmond Babler
*Waupun*

Mrs. Henry Baebler
*Monticello*

Melba Baehr
*Eau Claire*

Clara Baerwald
*Hartford*

Selma Bagan
*Black River Falls*

Helen Bagdonas
*Oshkosh*

Beatrice Baker
*Lake Geneva*

Dorothy Balcom
*Eau Claire*

Josephine Baltes
*Middleton*

Letha Bannerman
*Wausau*

Trudy Bard
*Clintonville*

Allan Barnard
*Monroe*

Arthur Barnhart
*Menomonie*

Eva Barrick
*Milwaukee*

H. T. Barry
*Whitewater*

Mrs. Walter Batzel
*West Salem*

Christine Bauer
*Mondovi*

Esther Bauer
*Wauwatosa*

Lillian Bauer
*Colgate*

Fred Baumann
*Milwaukee*

Ann Baumgard
*Waukesha*

Henriette Baumgartner
*Wausau*

Mrs. Ray Baxandall
*Oshkosh*

Mrs. George Baxter
*Milwaukee*

Robert Baxter
*Boyceville*

Robert Beard
*Green Bay*

Ruth Beardsley
*Waupaca*

Violet Beck
*Genoa*

Sr. Mary Alfred Becker
*Fond du Lac*

Maude M. Becker
*Fish Creek*

Viola Beckman
*Appleton*

Barbara Beecham
*Phillips*

Florence Beecroft
*Waukesha*

David Behling
*Mequon*

Leo Behrens
*Sheboygan*

Mrs. May Bell
*Milwaukee*

Carl Bellman
*Amery*

Mrs. Ann Bengert
*Wisconsin Rapids*

Victor Benson
*Clear Lake*

Lillian Benway
*Lake Geneva*

Verneil Berard
*Wisconsin Rapids*

Kenneth Berdan
*Whitehall*

Alice Berg
*Milwaukee*

Thea Berg
*Milwaukee*

Wanda Bergen
*Sheboygan*

Augusta Berges
*Edgerton*

Nellie Berget
*Argyle*

Ben Bergor
*Madison*

Martin Bergsjo
*Eagle River*

Mrs. O.M. Best
*Madison*

Helen Bethel
*Spooner*

Josephine Bethke
*Richland Center*

Rosemary Betz
*Fond du Lac*

Caroline Betzold
*Lake Mills*

Frank Bialek, Sr.
*Green Bay*

Jessie Biegemann
*Waukesha*

Beulah Bills
*Neillsville*

Alvina Bindl
*Plain*

Hannah Bindschaedler
*Monroe*

Mrs. John Bingenheimer
*Greendale*

Frances Bintz
*Berlin*

Roger Birdsell
*Janesville*

Melva Birkholz
*Milwaukee*

Florence Bischel
*Middleton*

Gladys Blahnik
*Ashland*

Nettie Blair
*Manitowoc*

J. Floyd Blakeley
*Walworth*

Vivian Blakeley
*Walworth*

R. H. Bleasdale
*Janesville*

Everett Blether
*Madison*

Mildred Blink
*Oshkosh*

Esther Bloch
*Hamburg*

Martha Bloom
*Rhinelander*

Marcia Bloomfield
*Marshall*

Ernst Bluedorn
*Eau Claire*

Ruth Blumer
*Kewaskum*

Mrs. Ruth Blumer
*Kewaskum*

Esther Bock
*Appleton*

Mary Bodenburg
*Phillips*

Evaline Boeck
*Mayville*

Florence Bohn
*Milwaukee*

Marylin Boinski
*Milwaukee*

Dorothy Boisen
*West Bend*

Walter Bolander
*Amberg*

Francis Bolda
*Milwaukee*

Frank Boldt
*Sheboygan*

Harriet Bombera
*Stevens Point*

Elna Bonell
*Altoona*

Mrs. Dalton Booher
*Fond du Lac*

Della Bopf
*Wausau*

Lucille Bork
*Oshkosh*

Mae Bork
*DeForest*

Betty Bosche
*Milwaukee*

Mina Bosshard
*Janesville*

Winifred Bourdeau
*Waterford*

Mrs. Arthur Bourke
*Green Bay*

Rose Boutin
*Eau Claire*

Lavona Bowar
*Cross Plains*

Beulah Bowden
*Brodhead*

Margaret Boyne
*Milwaukee*

Margaret Bradley
*Kenosha*

Clara Bragg
*Milwaukee*

Helen Brandemuehl
*Cross Plains*

Marian Brandt
*Fennimore*

Edna Braun
*Reedsburg*

Lucy Braun
*Monona*

Sr. M. Carlotta Breister
*Fond du Lac*

Mrs. Irv Brekke
*Monroe*

Frances Brennan
*Rhinelander*

Marjorie Brescia
*Baraboo*

Lilly Brettin
*Fall Creek*

Thomas Brever
*Rhinelander*

Violet Brewer
*Richland Center*

Ferne Bridge
*Juda*

Clarence Bridges
*Two Rivers*

Elsie Briggs
*Fond du Lac*

Myrtle Briggs
*Winneconne*

Angelia Brill
*Wauwatosa*

Wallace Brockee, Sr.
*Clayton*

Mabel Brommer
*Durand*

Hazen Brooks
*Green Bay*

El Brothers
*Gilman*

Earl Brown
*Amery*

Frances Hogg Brown
*Neillsville*

G. Frank Brown, Sr.
*Fond du Lac*

Genevieve Brown
*Fond du Lac*

Harry Brown
*Madison*

Vaughn Brown
*Fredonia*

Josephine Brozek
*Gillett*

Mary Bruce
*Wauwatosa*

Irene Brun
*Baraboo*

Queen Brunette
*West Allis*

Ruth Brye
*Ettrick*

Estella Bryhn
*West Salem*

Lauretta Buboltz
*Brillion*

Francis Bucholz
*Sheboygan*

Edith Buckmaster
*North Freedom*

Ererine Buckner
*Oshkosh*

Dorothy Buhr
*Clear Lake*

Clara Buley
*Oconomowoc*

Joyce Burg
*Milwaukee*

Mrs. Clarence Burling
*Colfax*

Lynn Burlingame
*Black River Falls*

Erna Burmeister
*Cedarburg*

Ruth Burmester
*Reedsburg*

Gen Burns
*Kenosha*

Ardell Burress
*Madison*

Mrs. Armand Burt
*Pigeon Falls*

Pearl Busby
*Milltown*

Edith Busch
*Wautoma*

Grace Busse
*Birchwood*

Maybelle Bussian
*Milwaukee*

Alice Butke
*Milwaukee*

Frieda Butler
*Jacksonport*

Al Butor
*Madison*

Nellie Butt
*Bowler*

Mae Buyeske
*Milwaukee*

Lois Byrns
*Dane*

Mildred Bywater
*Delavan*

# C

Mrs. Willie Calhoun
*Milwaukee*

Evelyn Cameron
*Oshkosh*

Mabel Cameron
*Oshkosh*

Alice Campbell
*West Allis*

Adele Carlisle
*Milwaukee*

Laura Carlsen
*Spooner*

Marguerite Carnachan
*Two Rivers*

Maurice Cash
*Milwaukee*

Mary Ceci
*Milwaukee*

Helen Chamberland
*Spencer*

Florence Chance
*Madison*

Sarah Chance
*Amery*

Daisy Chapin
*Beloit*

Josephine Charlier
*Green Bay*

Ray Chester
*S. Milwaukee*

Mrs. Herman Christ
*Fond du Lac*

Roszella Christensen
*Monroe*

Edwin Christenson
*River Falls*

Ruth Bunker Christiansen
*Frederic*

Amelia Christianson
*Viroqua*

August J. Christianson
*Grantsburg*

Anton Chudy
*Greendale*

Rosalie Cicero
*Racine*

Arnold Claire
*Greenwood*

Marion Clapp
*Verona*

Dorinda Clark
*Milwaukee*

Julian Clark
*Waunakee*

Marie Clark
*Janesville*

Myrtle Clark
*Hancock*

Paul Clemens
*Manitowoc*

Clara Cline
*Janesville*

Mrs. John Coates
*Colby*

Jerry Condon, Sr.
*Mosinee*

Helen Condry
*Platteville*

F. Rogers Constance
*Westfield*

Alice Converse
*Whitewater*

Etta Cook
*Oregon*

Gwendolyn Cooper
*Richland Center*

Eve Corkery
*Three Lakes*

Robert Corliss, Sr.
*Wautoma*

Melissa Cornelius
*Oneida*

Leota Correa
*Kenosha*

Lillian Corrie
*West Allis*

Edith Corsario
*Janesville*

Henry Cotton
*New Richmond*

Velma Coulthard
*Platteville*

Hazel Hackett Cox
*Beloit*

Bing Crapser
*Madison*

Carla Crass
*Madison*

Robert Creek
*Janesville*

Edna Crist
*Wisconsin Dells*

Edward Cronquest
*Cadott*

Barbara Crossman
*Madison*

Lydia Crowley
*Fond du Lac*

Alice Cummings
*Endeavor*

Alwyn Curran
*Eau Claire*

# D

Bernice Dahl
*Cottage Grove*

Clifford Dahlin
*Palmyra*

Clara Damm
*Racine*

Margaret Damp
*Gillett*

V. Daniels
*Black Creek*

Ottillie Danielson
*Neillsville*

Thelma Davies
*New Lisbon*

Helen Davis
*Oxford*

Selma Dearth
*Blanchardville*

Mildred DeBeck
*Madison*

Grace Dederich
*Baraboo*

Wenonah Deffner
*Madison*

Ernest Dehorn
*Rhinelander*

Alma Deischer
*Prairie du Sac*

Gretchen Deiters
*Marinette*

Paula Delfeld
*Brownsville*

Emily Delsmann
*Manitowoc*

Richard Delwiche
*Green Bay*

Mabel Dencker
*Sun Prairie*

Ethel Denison
*Ashland*

Beatrice Derrick
*Webster*

John Desmond
*Appleton*

Agnes Dettmann
*Colby*

Lydia Dettmann
*Neshkoro*

Russell Devitt
*Madison*

Walter Diedrick
*Edgerton*

Kathryn Dierbeck
*Milwaukee*

Mrs. Lloyd Dieter
*Muscoda*

Jessie Dietrich
*Madison*

Sr. Catherine Dietzler
*Milwaukee*

Florence Dillett
*Shawano*

Margaret Dillon
*Janesville*

Hazel Disch
*New Glarus*

Mrs. Ingeborg Disch
*Madison*

Albert Dobrient
*Milwaukee*

Esther Dodte
*Neillsville*

Lydia Doering
*Abbotsford*

Leonora Dohm
*Sun Prairie*

Ruth Doland
*Columbus*

Celia Dombrowski
*Westfield*

Florence Domer
*Oshkosh*

Margaret Doner
*Appleton*

Esther Donnelly
*Waupaca*

William Donnelly
*Waupaca*

Gladys Doran
*Fontana*

Ethel Dorn
*Appleton*

John Dorn
*Waunakee*

Sr. M. Adrienne Downey
*Sinsinawa*

Laura Doyle
*Fond du Lac*

Elizabeth Drabek
*Stone Lake*

Richard Drakos
*Oak Creek*

Hugo Drechsel
*Milwaukee*

Edna Dretzka
*Cudahy*

Mary Dries
*West Allis*

A. Ward Drill
*Greendale*

Harold Duckert
*Monona*

Carey Duddleston
*LaValle*

Cornelia Dudley
*Whitewater*

Helen Duerr
*Neshkoro*

Bryan Dugdale
*Madison*

Ethel Dunham
*Baraboo*

Anne M. Dunst
*Glendale*

Harriet Durand
*Webster*

Frances Dvorak
*Francis Creek*

# E

Pauline Easterson
*Eau Claire*

Catherine Eberle
*Wauzeka*

Bertha Ebneter
*Pardeeville*

Harry Ecklund
*Racine*

Bess Edmark
*Gillett*

Catherine Edson
*Eau Claire*

Myrtle Edwards
*Pardeeville*

George Egan
*Waukesha*

Caroline Eggebrecht
*Milwaukee*

Emily Ehrenberger
*Racine*

Vera Marie Ehrlich
*Milwaukee*

Hulda Eid
*Madison*

Mrs. Herbert Einerson
*Mt. Horeb*

Caroline Eisold
*Sheboygan*

Erna Elliot
*Springbrook*

Marjorie Elliott
*Monona*

Burr Ellis, Sr.
*Appleton*

Ernest Elmer
*Greenwood*

Vera Ender
*Onalaska*

Lucille Engbretson
*Wild Rose*

Myrtle Engen
*Frederic*

Evelyn Engeseter
*Packwaukee*

Arline Ensenbach
*West Bend*

Clara Equitz
*Princeton*

Amanda Erickson
*Hixton*

Eileen Erickson
*Stevens Point*

Albert Esch
*Edgerton*

Anne Esch
*Edgerton*

Verna Ethier
*Butler*

Hubert Evers
*Merrill*

Frieda Eversum
*West Allis*

Cora Ewers
*Soldiers Grove*

# F

Alma Fabisch
*Beaver Dam*

Mrs. H. E. Fahrman
*Oshkosh*

Clara Fairman
*Brodhead*

Edna Fairweather
*Milwaukee*

Nellie Falkofske
*Ellsworth*

Edna Farrell
*Kenosha*

Ada Federman
*Sauk City*

Marian Felder
*Bloomington*

Sr. Claude Feldner
*North Fond du Lac*

Gertrude Felker
*Camp Douglas*

Marie Felzo
*Sheboygan*

Milda Fenner
*Milwaukee*

Erna Fenton
*Shawano*

Verona Fink
*Shawano*

R. G. Fischer
*Manitowoc*

Cora Fisher
*Reedsburg*

Margaret Fisher
*Ft. Atkinson*

Mrs. Stephen Flaherty
*Montello*

Marjorie Flegel
*Racine*

Sr. M. Plato Fleischmann
*Campbellsport*

Mrs. Edwin Fleming, Sr.
*Bagley*

Alvina Floistad
*Scandinavia*

George Fohey
*West Allis*

Lucille Fons
*Menomonee Falls*

Leigh Ford
*Twin Lakes*

Laura Forsmo
*Middleton*

Joy Forster
*Poynette*

Ruth Fosdick
*Green Bay*

Margaret Foss
*Waukesha*

Mrs. Stanley Fouks, Sr.
*Deer Park*

Mrs. Anthony Fox
*Fond du Lac*

Sigmund Frankowiak
*Winnebago*

Harry Fricke
*Stoughton*

Bonnie Friday
*Madison*

Harry Friedman
*Milwaukee*

Virginia Fries
*Oshkosh*

Bertha Friske
*Mellen*

Leo Friske
*Milwaukee*

Jack Fritz
*Rhinelander*

Emma Froiland
*Viroqua*

Ernst Frost
*Green Bay*

Vlasta Furlich
*Racine*

Anastasia Furman
*Oshkosh*

# G

Ted Gall
*Madison*

Elaine Gardner
*Racine*

Florence Gardner
*Milwaukee*

Sophia Gartler
*Milwaukee*

Edna Gates
*Reedsburg*

Eugene Gauger
*Wautoma*

Annie Gawlik
*Whitewater*

Wilbur Gay
*Washburn*

Mary Gaylord
*Balsam Lake*

"Gene"
*Neillsville*

Marjorie Gensicke
*West Allis*

Charla George
*Gleason*

L. D. George
*Cumberland*

George Gerbing
*Sheboygan*

Blanche Gerend
*Kaukauna*

Rose Gerstenberger
*Milwaukee*

Clara Gerth
*Oshkosh*

Melvin Getlinger
*Rudolph*

Annie Geurink
*Ringle*

Ray Gibbons
*LaValle*

Winifred Gibbons
*LaValle*

Esther Gibbs
*Spooner*

Victoria Gibson
*Delavan*

Carrie Gilbertson
*Avoca*

Martha Gilkerson
*Milwaukee*

Belle Gill
*Sheboygan*

Thora Gillette
*Madison*

Mary Glavin
*Milwaukee*

Amelia Glemboski
*Kenosha*

Mary Gmoser
*Milwaukee*

Lois Gollnick
*LaCrosse*

Gladys Goodburne
*Milwaukee*

John Goodman
*Belleville*

Hilda Goodrich
*Green Bay*

Alex Gorski
*Milwaukee*

Inez Gorsuch
*Pardeeville*

Stuart Gorsuch
*Pardeeville*

Marie Gottschalk
*Wauwatosa*

Edith Gotz
*Pittsville*

Frances Goulais
*Racine*

Dorothy Grabinski
*LaCrosse*

Verdon Grabinski
*LaCrosse*

Cora Graham
*Webster*

Mrs. Joseph Graham
*Augusta*

F. E. Granros
*Green Bay*

John Grant
*Racine*

Evelyn Grassel
*Sturgeon Bay*

Mrs. M. Grawin
*Racine*

Arthur Gray
*Madison*

Violette Grayson
*Amherst*

Lizzie Greeler
*Neillsville*

Mrs. Frank Green
*Oshkosh*

James Green
*Wales*

Marie Green
*Edgerton*

Wilma Green
*Madison*

Irma Greenthal
*Milwaukee*

Leroy Grenawalt
*Beloit*
Daisy Grenzow
*Monroe*
Mrs. Stanley Grienier
*Appleton*
Fern Griffin
*Shell Lake*
Esther Grimm
*Marshall*
John Grimm
*Marshall*
Thelma Grimm
*Janesville*
Julia Grosse
*Appleton*
Rose Groth
*Appleton*
William Groves
*Viroqua*
Irene Grunden
*Madison*
Esther Gustafson
*Elkhorn*

# H

Dorothy Haas
*Racine*
Lorenz Hackbarth
*Tomah*
Catherine Hacker
*Milwaukee*
Alice Hackett
*Lake Geneva*
Katherine Haefliger
*Janesville*
Helen Haefmayer
*Waukesha*

Mrs. John Haeuser
*Fountain City*
Louis Hagengruber
*Schofield*
Arline Hahn
*Reedsburg*
Sue Haines
*Milwaukee*
Ethel Hale
*Milwaukee*
Elsbeth Halin
*Viroqua*
Les Hall
*Arcadia*
Margaret Hall
*Richland Center*
Ann Haller
*De Pere*
Angeline Hallman
*Berlin*
Ellouise Halstead
*Union Grove*
Eva Halstrom
*Two Rivers*
C. O. Halverson
*Neenah*
Maxine Halverson
*Mt. Horeb*
Margaret Hammons
*Clear Lake*
Gordon Hampel
*Madison*
Emma Hansche
*Kenosha*
Laura Hansen
*Rhinelander*
Alice Hanson
*Racine*
Clara Hanson
*Deerfield*

Eugene Hanson
*St. Croix Falls*
George Hanson
*Brookfield*
Mrs. Harold Hanson
*Ft. Atkinson*
Helen Hanson
*Viroqua*
Ida Hanson
*Richland Center*
Nettie Hanson
*St. Croix Falls*
Rolfe Hanson
*Stoughton*
Ruth Hanson
*Kenosha*
Cecile Hardie
*Taylor*
Dorothy Harmer
*Black River Falls*
Helen Haroldson
*Mt. Horeb*
V. M. Harris
*Argonne*
Harold Hartline
*Lancaster*
Arnold Hatch
*Eau Claire*
Joyce Hathway
*Waukesha*
Marian Haucke
*Algoma*
Eva Hauge
*Black Earth*
Sadie Hauge
*Mosinee*
Mildred Havlick
*Green Bay*
Romana Hayes
*Madison*

DeLorr Hayward
*Green Bay*
Cecelia Hebal
*Stevens Point*
Louise Hebenstreit
*Milwaukee*
Wilma Heberlein
*Milwaukee*
Louise Heeter
*Racine*
Hila Heffernan
*Kewaunee*
Anna Hegner
*Appleton*
Mabel Heian
*Stanley*
Mrs. Edward Heideman
*Clintonville*
Marguerite Heiden
*Milwaukee*
Julia Pfund Heike
*Eau Claire*
Olivia Mueller Heike
*Durand*
Eleva Heimbruch
*Royalton*
Ida Heitkamp
*Cuba City*
Stanley Held
*Alma Center*
Roy Helgerson
*Mt. Sterling*
Bergloit Helgestad
*Edgerton*
Irene Helker
*Platteville*
Dorothy Helmke
*McFarland*
Doris Hendersin
*Sparta*

Faye Hendricks
*King*
Mrs. Henry Hendricks
*Sturgeon Bay*
Erleen Hendrickson
*Watertown*
Mrs. Joseph Hennes
*Appleton*
Neoma Herber
*Berlin*
Sr. M. Martine Herbert
*Fond du Lac*
Clara Hermann
*Oregon*
Erna Hermann
*Black Earth*
Sr. Lucia Herr
*Fond du Lac*
Cecilia Herreid
*Madison*
Elizabeth Herritz
*Baraboo*
Ben Hersch
*Milwaukee*
George Hetchler
*Cornell*
Wilbur Heuer
*Madison*
Gertrude Hewitt
*Hixton*
Mrs. Charles Hicks
*Shullsburg*
Eleanor Higgins
*Fond du Lac*
Kathryn Higley
*West Allis*
Carlton Hill
*Schofield*
Gladys Hill
*Presque Isle*

Helen Hill
*Schofield*
Mrs. James Hill
*Glidden*
Alice Hinrichs
*Madison*
Lucille Hirsch
*Milwaukee*
Nan Hirsch
*Medford*
Gordon Hoard
*Fond du Lac*
Edith Hockrack
*Milwaukee*
Myrtle Hoeft
*Madison*
Edna Hoeller
*Milwaukee*
Gertrude Hoffman
*Appleton*
Veva Hoffman
*Clintonville*
Irma Hoffmann
*Fond du Lac*
Walter Hoffmann
*Mazomanie*
Christine Hofman
*Appleton*
Irvin Hofschild
*Port Edwards*
Cora Hoiby
*Madison*
Floyd Holden
*Arkansaw*
Nathan Holesovsky
*Wauwatosa*
Ethel Hollander
*Milwaukee*
Lillian Hollander
*Fond du Lac*

Lloyd Holliday
*Gays Mills*
Orpha Holliday
*Gays Mills*
Etheline A. Holmes
*Mt. Horeb*
Marjorie Holmes
*Madison*
Mathilda Holt
*Hager City*
Gertrude Holtman
*Kenosha*
Julia Holverson
*McFarland*
Dorothea Holz
*Green Bay*
Catherine Holzman
*Fredonia*
Otto Holzman
*Menomonie*
Ethel Hooks
*Platteville*
Gladys Hooper
*Waukesha*
Evelyn Hoppe
*Columbus*
Elfrieda Horlamus
*Madison*
Alfred Horn
*Milwaukee*
Eva Hougum
*Stratford*
Hazel Housel
*Green Bay*
Jack Houston
*Manitowoc*
Marjorie Howard
*Janesville*
Cecilia Howe
*Janesville*

S. Marge Hrebenar
*Campbellsport*
Freda Huber
*Milwaukee*
Mrs. George Hudson
*Milton*
Cynthia Huenink
*Monroe*
Vera Huffman
*Warrens*
Mrs. Cleo Hughes
*Dodgeville*
James Hughes
*Kenosha*
Julia Hultman
*Menomonie*
Emma Hunt
*Rhinelander*
Melvin Huset
*Black Earth*
Grace Huybrecht
*Green Bay*

# I

Edwina Ihlenfeld
*Jefferson*
Dorothy Inbusch
*Milwaukee*
Ted Irion
*Oshkosh*
Annie Israel
*Marshfield*
Marie Iverson
*Sun Prairie*

# J

Olive Jablonske
*Gleason*

Dolores Jack
*Bagley*

Sr. Eileen Jackman
*Fond du Lac*

Ralph Jacobs
*Verona*

Sigurd Jacobsen
*Milwaukee*

Beulah James
*Rewey*

Mrs. Perry James
*Darien*

Lucy Jo Jarstad
*Green Bay*

Alfred Jasperson
*Viroqua*

Helen Jelinske
*Shawano*

Paula Jenkins
*West Allis*

Edith Jens
*Stoughton*

Clara Jensen
*Montello*

Ellis Jensen
*Kenosha*

Ruth Jensen
*Green Bay*

Walter Jenswold
*Humbird*

Gladys Jepsen
*Milwaukee*

Genevieve Jepson
*Manawa*

Ruth Jesse
*Crandon*

Grace Jessel
*Wauwatosa*

Ida Jessel
*Elk Mound*

Lucy Jewell
*Norwalk*

Amie Johnson
*Tigerton*

Mrs. Arnold Johnson
*Osseo*

Mrs. Bert Johnson
*Pardeeville*

Eunice Johnson
*Sturgeon Bay*

Eva Johnson
*Minocqua*

Isabel Johnson
*Milwaukee*

Jean Johnson
*Oconomowoc*

Karen Johnson
*Chippewa Falls*

Margaret Johnson
*Scandinavia*

Gladys Johnsrud
*Dodgeville*

Gussie Johnston
*Fond du Lac*

Cecilia Jones
*Janesville*

Emily Jones
*Madison*

James Jones
*Rosendale*

Lawrence Jones
*Black River Falls*

Mrs. Leslie Jones
*Holcombe*

Mildred E. Jones
*Minocqua*

Mildred R. Jones
*Baraboo*

Mabel Jonkel
*Baraboo*

Jennie Joos
*Verona*

Pearl Jopke
*Milwaukee*

Almeda Jordan
*Radisson*

Evelyn Joslin
*Rhinelander*

Mrs. Rudolph Jungemann
*Arlington*

Dorothea Jurgensen
*Gays Mills*

# K

Harriet Kaestner
*Wauwatosa*

Mildred Kain
*DePere*

Therese Kaiser
*Milwaukee*

William Kaitschuck
*Neillsville*

Safira Kallio
*Owen*

Mrs. Art Kanaman
*New London*

Sr. Lauretta Kane
*Manitowoc*

Mrs. Otto Kangas
*Milwaukee*

Verge Karow
*Tomahawk*

Becky Kasten
*Milwaukee*

Emma Kauffman
*Neillsville*

Esther Keilholtz
*LaCrosse*

Edna Keller
*Milwaukee*

Loretta Kemnitz
*Milwaukee*

Charles Kendall
*Kenosha*

Evelyn Kennedy
*Shullsburg*

Margaret Kennedy
*Dane*

Olive Kepler
*Richland Center*

Annette Kerlin
*S. Milwaukee*

Vieno Keskimaki
*Withee*

Helen Kessenich
*Spring Green*

Emma Ketelboeter
*Madison*

Theo Keysers
*Wrightstown*

Thelma Kiger
*Montello*

Ethel Kimpel
*Milwaukee*

Bernadyne King
*Neenah*

Lucille Klauke
*Fish Creek*

Julia Klein
*Milwaukee*

Hobart Kletzien
*Madison*

Josephine Klotz
*Milwaukee*

Mary Klune
*Neillsville*

Olga Knapp
*Bear Creek*

Charlotte Knechtges
*Madison*

Helen Knight
*Dalton*

Letta Knoble
*Gays Mills*

Emma Knoebel
*Glenwood City*

Kathleen Knutson
*Berlin*

Evelyn Koch
*West Bend*

Gertrude Koch
*Madison*

Fred Koehler
*Horicon*

Robert Koehler
*Bear Creek*

Albert Koenig
*Loganville*

Ruth Koepke
*Oconomowoc*

Mary Koestler
*Cudahy*

Mrs. Chester Konkol
*Wisconsin Rapids*

Anna Kortum
*Kenosha*

Babette Kovacs
*Milwaukee*

Jewell Kraemer
*Marshfield*

Glenn Kramer
*Eastman*

Marie Kramer
*Eastman*

Enid Kraus
*Brown Deer*

Eva Kriewaldt
*Shawano*

Anne Krueger
*Greenleaf*

Avis Krueger
*Wautoma*

Clarence Krueger
*Oshkosh*

Hanette Krueger
*Little Chute*

Sulvia Krueger
*Fond du Lac*

Molly Kruse
*Neenah*

Jan Kubitz
*Janesville*

Ida Kuehnast
*Stevens Point*

Gus Kuenster
*Lancaster*

Mrs. Ben Kuenzi
*Waupun*

Herbert Kuhm
*Wauwatosa*

Ottillie Kunkel
*Neillsville*

George Kupkovits
*Milwaukee*

Mrs. Hubert Kurkowski
*Menasha*

# L

Twen LaBreche
*Milwaukee*

Margaret Laehr
*Watertown*

Elsie Lajcak
*Oshkosh*

Melva Lamich
*Kenosha*

Marjorie Lamm
*Durand*

Charlotte Lanham
*Danbury*

Mary Lanphere
*Beaver Dam*

Lois Laper
*Rock Springs*

Paul Lappley
*Madison*

H. K. Larimer
*Shawano*

Mrs. L. Larmon
*Hannibal*

Lawrence Larmon
*Hannibal*

Charles Larson
*Port Washington*

Emma Larson
*Waupaca*

Lela Larson
*Chippewa Falls*

Marjorie Larson
*Green Bay*

Sylvester LaRue
*Neenah*

Mrs. L. P. Lathrop
*Boscobel*

Lois Lauper
*Hollandale*

Helen Law
*Madison*

Verne Lawler
*Mazomanie*

Evelyn Leach
*Saukville*

Victor Leahy
*Soldiers Grove*

Myrtle Leatherman
*Monroe*

Sophie Lebowsky
*Milwaukee*

Mary Lechleiter
*Oshkosh*

Mathilda Ledvina
*Butternut*

D. D. Lee
*Sparta*

Mrs. Earl Lee
*Black Earth*

Mrs. Jesse Lee
*Blair*

Mrs. Jessie Lee
*Milwaukee*

Margaret Lee
*Dodgeville*

Sr. Amor Lehn
*Milwaukee*

Maurine Leischer
*Oak Creek*

Beatrice Leisk
*De Pere*

Earl Leland
*Madison*

Ruth Lembke
*Sussex*

Grace LeMense
*Casco*

Mrs. Erwin Lemke
*Beaver Dam*

Eva Lemke
*Oconto Falls*

Mrs. Albertus Lemmenes
*Waupun*

Edith Leppla
*Mosinee*
Anna Lester
*Hudson*
Modest LeVeque
*Milwaukee*
Blanche Levy
*Milwaukee*
Catherine Lewis
*Fond du Lac*
Blanche Lindblad
*Ashland*
Berniece Lindholm
*Darlington*
Katherine Lindner
*Greenwood*
Eleanore Little
*Wisconsin Dells*
Philip Litzkow
*Milwaukee*
Mabel Longley
*Oconomowoc*
Gladys Loomans
*Ripon*
Harriet Loomis
*Waukesha*
Florence Lorence
*Racine*
Isabel Lowe
*Washburn*
Edith Lowery
*Lakewood*
Irene Luchsinger
*New Glarus*
Mrs. Floyd Lucia
*Milwaukee*
Margie Luebke
*Baraboo*
Marion Lund
*Boscobel*

Lillian Lundin
*Kenosha*
Iva Luther
*Poynette*
August Luttig
*Richland Center*
Arthur Lyle
*Pell Lake*
Eva Lynch
*Oak Creek*
Mattie Lynch
*New Glarus*
Russell Lynch
*Wauwatosa*
Ellen Lyons
*Birnamwood*
John Lyons
*Phillips*
Rachel Lysager
*Stoughton*

# M

Hazel Maas
*Adams*
Verna Maassen
*Kenosha*
B.W. Mabbott
*Unity*
Hazel McDonald
*New Glarus*
Roderick MacDonald
*Madison*
Hazel McDowell
*Waukesha*
Nellie McDowell
*Montello*
Dorothy McEachron
*Whitefish Bay*

James McGaw, Jr.
*Milwaukee*
Ruth McGibeny
*Madison*
Helen Machovec
*Hillsboro*
Molly Macisak
*Pardeeville*
Cora McKellips
*Winneconne*
Floyd McKensie
*Rhinelander*
Dorothy McKiernan
*Monona*
Ada McKnight
*Stoughton*
Ambrose Mackowski
*Neshkoro*
Mary McLaren
*Racine*
Evelyn McLean
*South Byron*
Daniel McLeod
*Stone Lake*
Mary McMahon
*Portage*
T.A. McNeil
*Ladysmith*
William Madison
*Kewaskum*
Arthur Maegli
*Milwaukee*
Helen Magee
*Prescott*
Margaret Maier
*Racine*
Agnes Maltz
*Oak Creek*
Wilma Maly
*Muscoda*

Agnese Mann
*Racine*
Ethel Manthey
*Waunakee*
Luella Marit
*Algoma*
Emma Markgraf
*Fall Creek*
Adele Marquardt
*Milwaukee*
Evelyn Marsh
*Milwaukee*
Gordon Marshall
*Oshkosh*
Mrs. John Marshall
*Gillingham*
Lella Marshall
*Oshkosh*
Phyllis Marshall
*Racine*
Mary Martelle
*Edgerton*
Henry Martin
*Iola*
Sr. M. Faustine Masanz
*Fond du Lac*
Bertha Mason
*Shorewood*
M. Luella Mason
*Milwaukee*
Sr. Marian Massart
*Kaukauna*
Eleanor Mathison
*Phillips*
Eunice Mattakat
*Evansville*
Lue Mattern
*Kenosha*
Ruben Mauer
*Fennimore*

Mildred May
*Hayward*

Lulu Mayer
*Slinger*

Ruth Meagher
*Milwaukee*

Georgia Medley
*Gillett*

Roy Meier
*Ogema*

Howard Meiller
*Madison*

Angela Meis
*Fond du Lac*

Sr. M. Paulina Meis
*Fond du Lac*

Blanche Mendl
*Deerbrook*

Jerry Mendl
*Deerbrook*

Emmalyn Menssen
*Burlington*

Edward Menz
*Sheboygan*

Harvey Mercer
*Prairie du Chien*

Clara Merrifield
*Platteville*

Irene Messman
*Two Rivers*

Sarah Metcalf
*Stone Lake*

Mrs. Fred Meuer
*Milwaukee*

Anne Meulemans
*Downing*

Lillian Meyer
*Cable*

Marie Raschka Meyer
*Eau Claire*

Mary Meyer
*Prairie du Sac*

Myrtle Meyer
*Brookfield*

Myrtle Meyer
*Berlin*

Wilma Meyer
*Sheboygan*

Beatrice Michaels
*Oconto Falls*

Mrs. P. H. Mickle
*Madison*

Margaret Middleton
*West Allis*

Bertha Mikkelsen
*Janesville*

Alice Miller
*Boscobel*

Edna Miller
*Neenah*

Elonore Miller
*Mequon*

George Miller
*Milwaukee*

Helen Miller
*Kenosha*

Josephine Miller
*Sparta*

Lee Miller
*Shorewood*

Loretta Miller
*Milwaukee*

Sr. M. Hermana Miller
*Kaukauna*

Sabrina Miller
*West Salem*

Marion Mills
*Madison*

Willis Milne
*Sparta*

Karl Mimedime
*Waukesha*

Mabel Minkebige
*Kaukauna*

Della Mitchell
*Oxford*

Carol Mittelstadt
*Phillips*

Johanna Mittmann
*Milwaukee*

Maria Moe
*Madison*

Sr. Agnes Therese Moeder
*Fond du Lac*

Concetta Molina
*Brooklyn*

Marguerite Mollett
*Peshtigo*

Genevieve Molthen
*Milwaukee*

Blanche Moltoni
*Hurley*

Olivia Monona
*Madison*

Doris Montfort
*Ashland*

Clarice Moon
*Delavan*

Mrs. Frances Moore
*Racine*

Alvin Morgan
*Kenosha*

Eleanor Morgan
*Kenosha*

Lenore Morgan
*Winneconne*

Lois Morgan
*Phillips*

Lillian Morke
*Cable*

Lucinda Morken
*Ettrick*

Ethel Morris
*Weyerhaeuser*

Kenneth Morris
*Manitowoc*

Leslie Morris
*Madison*

Mary Morrison
*Madison*

Agnes Hope Morrow
*Bloomington*

Margaret Mosuch
*Madison*

Elma Mots
*Milwaukee*

Mark Movrich
*New Richmond*

Ethel Moyer
*Madison*

Mrs. William Moyer
*Union Grove*

Elizabeth Mrkvicka
*Plainfield*

Mrs. Al Muckerheide
*Kewaskum*

Augusta Mueller
*Milwaukee*

Ida Mueller
*Oshkosh*

Cyrilla Mullen
*Dodgeville*

Jeannette Mundstock
*Madison*

Dorothy Murphy
*Shawano*

Vera Myers
*Milwaukee*

# N

Melvin Nack
*Siren*

Walter Naef
*Madison*

Norma Nate
*West Bend*

Edna Nauman
*Sparta*

Kathryn Nawrocke
*LaCrosse*

A. A. Nebish
*Phillips*

George Neckerman
*Madison*

Jennie Neerhof
*Cedar Grove*

Ida Nehls
*Neillsville*

Catherine Neilson
*Fond du Lac*

Alma Nelson
*Janesville*

Ellis Nelson
*Ashland*

Mary Nelson
*Waupaca*

Nellie Nelson
*River Falls*

Olive Nelson
*Blanchardville*

Signe Nelson
*Phillips*

Sr. M. Susanna Neubauer
*Sinsinawa*

Mrs. Harvey Neuman
*Appleton*

Dorothy Neumann
*Algoma*

Mrs. Franklin Neuschafer
*Fremont*

Louise Newman
*Milwaukee*

William Nichol
*Milwaukee*

Clara Nicholson
*Racine*

Grace Niehoff
*Fall River*

Edna Nielsen
*Racine*

A. M. Nilles
*West Bend*

Hermine Nimmow
*Rock Springs*

Nina Nixon
*Neenah*

Marcia Nobel
*Richland Center*

Mrs. Dagmar Norman
*Fontana*

Alfred North
*Fond du Lac*

Frank Northrop
*Luck*

Laura Norum
*Amery*

Jack Norwood
*Stratford*

Matilda Notham
*Durand*

Mrs. John Novak, Sr.
*Deerbrook*

Mary Novotny
*Walworth*

# O

Helen Ochsner
*Middleton*

Ethel Odegard
*Whitewater*

Clara Oesau
*Kiel*

Alice Oetting
*Menomonie*

Nettie Ohl
*Elkhorn*

Cleo O'Kane
*Boscobel*

Ine Olmstead
*Orfordville*

Mrs. Nile Olmstead
*Beloit*

Reynolds Olsen-Tjensvold
*Mequon*

Bessie Olson
*Mauston*

Carl Olson
*North Freedom*

Evelyn Olson
*Appleton*

Hazel Olson
*Milwaukee*

Louise Olson
*Spring Valley*

Marguerite Olson
*Theresa*

Martin Olson
*Stoughton*

Mona Olson
*Chippewa Falls*

Elizabeth O'Neal
*Milwaukee*

V. C. O'Neill
*Elkhorn*

Rae Onstine
*Prairie du Sac*

Carl Opelt
*Neillsville*

Walter Oppermann
*Port Washington*

Elizabeth Ortman
*Ashland*

Esther Oslage
*Rothschild*

Dorothy Osner
*Portage*

Florence Osterloth
*Clintonville*

Catherine Otten
*Milwaukee*

Minnie Owen
*Middleton*

# P

Vernon Palms
*Augusta*

Ruth Parent
*Milwaukee*

John Parker
*Hartland*

Robert Parkin
*Black Earth*

Johanna Parris
*Milwaukee*

Roy Passineau
*Wisconsin Rapids*

Magdalene Patterson
*Superior*

Florence Patton
*Lake Geneva*

Bee Paulson
*McFarland*

Marjorie Paulson
*Milwaukee*

Mrs. Martin Paust
*Columbus*

Mrs. Arthur Pearson
*Aurora*

John Peckham
*Hortonville*

Vivian Peik
*Chilton*

Elizabeth Perry
*Eau Claire*

Lee Perry
*Oshkosh*

E. E. Person
*Cecil*

Anita Peters
*White Lake*

Bertha Peters
*Milwaukee*

Florence Petersen
*Racine*

Sylvia Petersen
*Owen*

Mrs. Arie Peterson
*Sharon*

Conrad Peterson
*Gurney*

Harold Peterson
*St. Croix Falls*

Mae Peterson
*Onalaska*

Mildred Peterson
*Lodi*

Oliver Peterson
*Washburn*

Sylvia Pfaff
*Sparta*

Sr. Dionys Pfefferle
*Campbellsport*

Ruth Phelps
*Oconomowoc*

Elizabeth Philleo
*Wisconsin Rapids*

Flora Phillips
*Rhinelander*

Mary Phillips
*Sun Prairie*

P. C. Phillips
*Sun Prairie*

Edith Pier
*Madison*

Ann Pierce
*Sauk City*

Ignatius Pietrzak
*Stanley*

Lois Pink
*Waupaca*

Mrs. Frances Pohlman
*Green Bay*

Dora Polanski
*Bloomer*

Catherine Pollen
*Manitowoc*

Viola Polodna
*Prairie du Chien*

Alonzo Pond
*Minocqua*

Dorothy Pond
*Minocqua*

Hazle Poole
*Richland Center*

Luella Pope
*Franklin*

Adelia Portwine
*Sun Prairie*

Carolyn Potter
*Black River Falls*

Ellis Potter
*Madison*

Greta Potter
*Superior*

Ralph Potter
*Oshkosh*

Ella Poulsen
*Racine*

Anna Pressler
*Madison*

Roland Priem
*Menomonee Falls*

Anna Prine
*Baraboo*

Lisa Proctor
*Appleton*

Angeline Proudlock
*Menomonie*

Charlotte Pruess
*Tomah*

Helen Prutz
*Plover*

Mrs. Saima Pudas
*Iron River*

Kathleen Purtell
*Wauwatosa*

# Q

Irving Quale
*Stoughton*

Esther Quinn
*Columbus*

Lillian Quinn
*Wausau*

# R

Anna Rabe
*New Holstein*

Nellie Ranney
*Menomonie*

Lurlyn Rasmussen
*Campbellsport*

Fritz Rathmann
*Milwaukee*

Marjorie Rawson
*Poy Sippi*

Catherine Raymer
*Ashland*

Gladys Rebelein
*Platteville*

Linda Rebenstorff
*Caroline*

Grace Reed
*Richland Center*

Freda Reichert
*Milwaukee*

Bernice Reideman
*Lake Mills*

Lois Reine
*Wausau*

Sr. M. Ernesta Reinhardt
*Sinsinawa*

Mrs. Harold Remmel
*Milwaukee*

Marjorie Renner
*Hartland*

Vern Reuter
*Walworth*

Reuben Rex
*Spencer*

Charlotte Reynolds
*Cable*

Mrs. Clarence Rhode
*Neshkoro*

Verona Rhode
*Appleton*

Carl Rhody
*Ogema*

Hazel Rice
*Madison*
Florence Richards
*Rice Lake*
Mrs. Paul Richeson
*Lake Geneva*
Erna Richter
*Milwaukee*
Lucille Richter
*Milwaukee*
Mrs. Andrew Riedl
*West Allis*
Esther Riedner
*Nekoosa*
Mrs. Jake Riegel
*St. Croix Falls*
Mrs. Robert Riegert
*N. Fond du Lac*
Marie Rienks
*Sparta*
Estelle Riepe
*Oconto*
Greg Rinzel
*Pewaukee*
Edna Risch
*Franklin*
Naomi Ritchie
*Rice Lake*
Ella Ritland
*Chippewa Falls*
Vivian Roberts
*Elroy*
Sr. Kevin Robertson
*Milwaukee*
Clara Roblee
*Neenah*
Anne Rockwell
*Oshkosh*
Molly Roehrich
*Sturtevant*

Mae Roets
*Milwaukee*
Dorothy Rogers
*Oshkosh*
Edith Rogers
*Lake Geneva*
Lilas Rohloff
*Janesville*
Dorothy Root
*Fond du Lac*
Evelyn Rose
*Watertown*
Ray Rose
*Watertown*
Erma Rosenbaum
*Fond du Lac*
Carl Rosenberg
*Danbury*
Leona Rosenow
*Coleman*
Mildred Rosenthal
*Fond du Lac*
Irene Ross
*Tomah*
Flora Rossdeutscher
*Richland Center*
Iva Roundy
*Portage*
Gertrude Rowe
*West Allis*
Madaline Roycraft
*Omro*
Jack Rudolph
*De Pere*
Leora Rudolph
*De Pere*
Irene Ruffing
*Hilbert*
Coca Rundahl
*Coon Valley*

Emma Rupp
*LaCrosse*
Lillian Russell
*Westfield*
Ernest Ryall
*Kenosha*
Henrietta Ryall
*Kenosha*
Marie Ryan
*Sparta*

# S

Lee Sackett
*Waupaca*
Selmer Saeter
*Ellsworth*
Minnie Safford
*Port Washington*
Mrs. Fred Sager
*West Bend*
Genevieve St. Clair
*Fox Lake*
Norman Sainty
*Eau Claire*
Ione Sallander
*Madison*
Zeminia Samson
*Milwaukee*
Grace Samuelson
*Sturgeon Bay*
Phil Sander
*Kenosha*
Mrs. Berget Sandstrom
*Milwaukee*
Verna Saniter
*Watertown*
Mrs. Adolph Sauer
*Neenah*

Mary Sauer
*Menasha*
Mrs. Frank Sawle
*Vesper*
Leone Schaaf
*Mineral Point*
Sr. M. Ignatius Schaefet
*Campbellsport*
A. G. Schaeffer
*Milwaukee*
Esther Freund Schaerff
*Madison*
Cecelia Schallhorn
*Milwaukee*
Luella Scharlau
*Arcadia*
Gertrude Schaub
*Chilton*
Helen Scheynost
*Cameron*
Luella Schiedermayer
*Kaukauna*
Helen Schlough
*Mazomanie*
Eunice Schluenz
*Cudahy*
George Schmeling
*Sheboygan*
Elsie Schmidt
*Rib Lake*
Genevieve Schmidt
*Madison*
Jean Bunker Schmidt
*Siren*
Leona Schmidt
*Winter*
Nelle Schmidt
*Fond du Lac*
Ruth Schmidt
*Merton*

Dorothy Schmitz
*Middleton*
Eloise Schnaitter
*Beloit*
Elizabeth Scholz
*West Allis*
Dorothy Schrader
*Evansville*
Irene Schreiter
*Appleton*
Grace Schroeder
*Spooner*
Laura Schroeder
*Appleton*
Mabel Schroeder
*Wisconsin Rapids*
Sr. M. Angelus Schroeder
*Fond du Lac*
Mildred Schroeder
*De Forest*
Thelma Schroeder
*Warrens*
Virginia Schroeder
*Horicon*
Herbert Schueppert
*Wauwatosa*
Elsie Schultz
*Clintonville*
Iva Schultz
*Waukesha*
Mildred Schultz
*West Allis*
Vernon Schultz
*Madison*
Ilse Schultze
*Milwaukee*
Hattie Schumacher
*Dorchester*
Agnes Schumann
*Mazomanie*

Mary Schuster
*Madison*
Ellsworth Schutte
*Wausau*
Elsie Schutz
*Portage*
Freida Schwamb
*Neillsville*
Marguerite Schwandt
*Wautoma*
Mary Schwartz
*Menomonie*
Evelyn Schwebke
*Beloit*
Douglas Schwefel
*Fox Lake*
Kathryn Schwirian
*Madison*
Mary Scopetta
*Kenosha*
John Seaquist
*Sister Bay*
Kenneth Searles
*Union Center*
Mary Secanky
*Racine*
Margaret Sedbrook
*Lancaster*
Nellie Seeburger
*Phillips*
Hulda Seeger
*Racine*
Elgie Seeman
*Madison*
Joseph Seiler
*Algoma*
Mrs. Murle Seitz
*Janesville*
Selma Sellnow
*Albany*

Arnold Semrau
*Peshtigo*
Elizabeth Severson
*Monroe*
Mrs. G. A. Seymour
*Marshfield*
Elizabeth Shackley
*Mineral Point*
Margaret Shale
*North Freedom*
Lillian Shaw
*Viroqua*
Emma Shepard
*Baraboo*
Betty Sherman
*Oconto*
Evelyn Sherwood
*Gays Mills*
Harvey Sherwood
*Whitewater*
Nell Sickler
*Edgerton*
Dick Sigl
*Marshfield*
Casmer Sikorski
*Stevens Point*
Mrs. Roland Sikorski
*S. Milwaukee*
Margaret Sime
*Boscobel*
Alyce Siminow
*Sheboygan*
Edith Simmons
*Rhinelander*
Mrs. Elmer Simoneau
*West Bend*
Bessie Simpson
*Gillingham*
Merle Sinclair
*Milwaukee*

George Sisson
*LaCrosse*
Roy Sisson
*Sheboygan*
Clara Skott
*Madison*
Benita Slattery
*Manitowoc*
Edith Slette
*Racine*
Carl Slipper
*Milwaukee*
Georgia Smart
*Waukesha*
Alicia Smith
*Menomonie*
Beatrice Smith
*Westfield*
Esther Smith
*Pardeeville*
Fay Smith
*Shawano*
Floyd Smith
*Reedsburg*
Lylia Smith
*Sparta*
Marion Smith
*Frederic*
Myranda Smith
*Sheboygan*
Olivine Smith
*Milwaukee*
Rosa C. Smith
*Milwaukee*
Sylvia Smith
*Sparta*
Vivenne Smith
*Belleville*
Juanette Solberg
*Eau Claire*

Selma Solie
*Menomonie*

Mrs. Alex Sommer
*Mineral Point*

Mrs. Ernest Sommer
*Neshkoro*

Alice Somodi
*Milwaukee*

Margaret Sonnentag
*Neenah*

Olive Sorensen
*Kenosha*

Leo Sorenson
*Manitowoc*

Mabel Sorenson
*Manitowoc*

Clai Spaulding
*Oconomowoc*

Henry Spear
*Beaver Dam*

Mrs. Jessie Spector
*Appleton*

Beth Spencer
*Madison*

Marion Spencer
*Balsam Lake*

Mary Spindler
*Grand Marsh*

Lorena Splittgerber
*Clintonville*

Madeline Spoerl
*Milwaukee*

Telmes Staaland
*Brodhead*

Elmer Stadtler
*Greenfield*

Thelma Stafford
*Eagle River*

Ruby Stamstad
*Black River Falls*

Adolph Stangel
*Manitowoc*

Clarence Stangel
*Manitowoc*

Cecilia Stanke
*Phillips*

Mary Agnes Starr
*Madison*

Geraldine Stavrum
*Cable*

Lillian Steenis
*Appleton*

Bertha Steensrud
*Black Earth*

Viola Steeps
*Eureka*

Vina Stefonek
*Rhinelander*

Esther Stein
*Sheboygan*

Max Stein
*Milwaukee*

Clara Steinberg
*Oshkosh*

Irene Steinberg
*Eau Claire*

P. Steinberger
*Sun Prairie*

Mrs. Arnold Steingraber
*New London*

Mrs. Fred Steinke
*Sparta*

Lillian Stelter
*Montello*

Hazel Stenseth
*Verona*

Amelia Stenulson
*Black River Falls*

Marie Stern
*Gillett*

Mrs. Blodwen Stevens
*Menomonie*

Mrs. Carl Stevens
*Oshkosh*

Gladys Stevens
*Neillsville*

Helen Stewart
*Eau Claire*

Margaret Stillmak
*S. Milwaukee*

Doris Stone
*Madison*

Marcella Story
*Milwaukee*

Cal B. Stott
*West Bend*

Mabel Strait
*Sparta*

Mrs. Reinhard Stuewer
*Bonduel*

Martha Styer
*Colfax*

George Suchy
*Waukesha*

Esther Sullivan
*Williams Bay*

Sidney Svenson
*Middleton*

Robert Sweetman
*Racine*

Cal Swenson
*Waupaca*

Eleanor Swinsky
*Neshkoro*

# T

Elfrieda Taeuber
*Madison*

Lillian Taggert
*Milwaukee*

Will Talsey
*Wood*

Marie Teegarden
*Kenosha*

Gustave Telschow
*Fountain City*

Anna Terry
*Baraboo*

Nell Teschke
*Oconomowoc*

Edith Tesser
*Wisconsin Dells*

Kathryn Theiler
*Racine*

Sr. Mary Theodore
*Jefferson*

Sr. M. Agnes Therese
*Fond du Lac*

May Thibaudeau
*S. Milwaukee*

Jeannette Thiede
*Briggsville*

Ada Thiers
*Mazomanie*

William Thies
*Reedsburg*

Elva Thomas
*Tomah*

Lydia Thome
*Portage*

Dorothy Thompson
*Kenosha*

Earl Thompson
*Richland Center*

Frances Thompson
*Lodi*

Mrs. Marshall Thompson
*Milwaukee*

Ruth Thompson
*Richland Center*
Rena Thorpe
*Boscobel*
Mildred Thut
*Madison*
Samuel Thut
*Madison*
Alice Tibbetts
*Shawano*
LaVerna Tinkham
*Ripon*
Marguerite Tirk
*Greenwood*
Alice Tobin
*Adams*
Elizabeth Tock
*Appleton*
Alma Tollefson
*Menomonie*
Ida Beth Tompkins
*Horicon*
Louie Tornowske
*Patch Grove*
Maryadelle Tornowske
*Patch Grove*
Mabel Traiser
*Appleton*
Ellen Trapp
*Milwaukee*
Mrs. Henry Traut
*Poynette*
Beatrice Trefren
*Viola*
Agnes Troeger
*Milwaukee*
Clarence Truttman
*Ellsworth*
Mary Tutkowski
*Milwaukee*

Anna Tydrich
*Bloom City*
Howard Tyrer
*Mineral Point*

# U

Alice Ubert
*Milwaukee*
Harold Uehling
*Waupun*
Clementine Ujazdowski
*Milwaukee*
Chester Ulezelski
*West Allis*
Cecile Ullrich
*Milwaukee*
Marie Urbanek
*Cashton*
Mrs. Nels Urness
*Black Earth*
Selma Urness
*Madison*

# V

Grace Vachon
*Rhinelander*
Mary Valiquette
*Ladysmith*
Mary Van Den Bosch
*Kaukauna*
Agnes VandeWall
*Cedar Grove*
Herschel Van Gilder
*Birchwood*
Kathleen Van Gordon
*Black River Falls*
Norma Van Hekle
*Madison*

Frances Vannix
*Tomahawk*
Marjorie Van Ouwerkerk
*Sheboygan Falls*
Lulu VanVuren
*Chippewa Falls*
Thomas Vaughan
*Madison*
Bert Vawter
*Trego*
Edna Veale
*Kenosha*
Florence Veek
*Windsor*
Marion Viertel
*Berlin*
Eloise Vlasak
*Eagle River*
Sarah Voeks
*Sheboygan*
Dorothy Vogl
*S. Milwaukee*
Mathilde Voigt
*Racine*
Vanita Volkert
*Reeseville*
Ivan Von Berg
*West Allis*
Gladys Vorpagel
*Grafton*

# W

Edward Wagner
*Omro*
Esther Wagner
*Elkhorn*
Louis Wagner
*Madison*

Monica Wagner
*St. Nazianz*
Mrs. Otto Wagner
*Chilton*
Ellen Wagoner
*S. Milwaukee*
LaVeda Wahlberg
*Beloit*
Marie Wahlen
*West Bend*
Carol Wait
*Clintonville*
Catherine Walborn
*Racine*
Marjorie Walker
*Edgerton*
Margaret Walter
*Lake Geneva*
Dorothy Walters
*Milwaukee*
Hazel Wampler
*Wisconsin Dells*
Leone Wandrey
*West Allis*
Kerner Ward
*Milwaukee*
Dorothy Warren
*Oxford*
George Waste
*Mondovi*
Isabelle Watson
*Shawano*
Florence Watters
*Appleton*
Harold Wautlet
*Algoma*
Josephine Wautlet
*Algoma*
Mamie Weber
*Pembine*

Gladys Weborg
*Ellison Bay*
Ellen Weddig
*Fond du Lac*
Marie Welch
*Stevens Point*
Arthur Wellnitz
*Lac du Flambeau*
Berkeley Wells
*Ashland*
Gale Welsh
*Darien*
Isobel Welter
*Solon Springs*
Leona Wendland
*Sheboygan*
Violet Wendt
*Helenville*
Alice Werndl
*Hayward*
Aurelia Werner
*Hartford*
Bessie West
*Luck*
Gene West
*Wautoma*
Harriet Westphal
*Sturgeon Bay*
Ottila Wettstein
*Fond du Lac*
Betty Wetzel
*Milwaukee*
Olga Wetzel
*Shawano*
Evelyn Weyh
*Portage*
John White
*Eagle River*
Mamie White
*Milwaukee*
Ralph Whitehead
*Appleton*

Marion Whitworth
*Mondovi*
Cletus Wickens
*Sarona*
Hylda Wickus
*Wisconsin Dells*
Lauretta Wieland
*Pewaukee*
Mrs. Antola Wilburn
*Milwaukee*
Arnold Wild
*Campbellsport*
Joseph Wildenberg
*Little Chute*
Edna Wilke
*Milwaukee*
Ruth Wilkinson
*Black Earth*
Rudi Willert
*Pewaukee*
John Willey
*Burlington*
Mrs. Edgar Williams
*Dousman*
Helen Williams
*Milwaukee*
Olive Williams
*Oshkosh*
Pearl Williams
*Middleton*
Myrtle Williamson
*Verona*
Helen Willmes
*Racine*
Clarence Wilsing
*Sheboygan*
George Wilson
*Delafield*
Mary Wilson
*Cuba City*
Warren Wilson
*Medford*

Charles Winans
*Scandinavia*
Grace Winkler
*Hiles*
Leona Winter
*Eau Claire*
May Wirkuty
*Neillsville*
Mrs. Herman Wirtz
*Mt. Calvary*
Elsie Wohlust
*Oak Creek*
Evelyn Wolfe
*Kenosha*
Betty Wolfgram
*Milwaukee*
Louise Wolfgram
*Milwaukee*
Elizabeth Wood
*Appleton*
Mrs. Norman Wood
*Two Rivers*
Lora Woodard
*Appleton*
Delma Woodburn
*Madison*
Sylvia Worden
*Plover*
Mrs. Edward Worringer
*Lodi*
Caroline Wright
*Columbus*
Charles Wright
*Columbus*
Gertrude Wright
*Milwaukee*
Walter Wright
*Columbus*
Ted Wurtz
*Kenosha*
Adell Wutke
*Green Bay*

## Y

Alexa Young
*Madison*
Ruth Young
*Baraboo*

## Z

Anita Zahn
*Lomira*
Lucille Zais
*Stanley*
Germaine Zareck
*Milwaukee*
Lola Zautner
*Elkhorn*
Gladys Zeasman
*Madison*
George Zeller
*Milwaukee*
Sylvia Zellmer
*West Allis*
Genevieve Zenner
*Milwaukee*
Catherine Zenz
*Lancaster*
Elmer Ziegler
*Madison*
Mrs. Harry Zielinski
*West Allis*
Glennie Ziemann
*Balsam Lake*
Alma Zillmer
*Marion*
William Zillmer
*Marion*
Dorothy Zimdars
*Green Bay*
Elizabeth Zimmerman
*Babcock*
Sr. Jane Zurbuch
*Fond du Lac*

*Clarice Chase Dunn received a Bachelors of Education degree from Eau Claire State Teachers College and a Masters degree in journalism at the University of Wisconsin-Madison. She has taught in high schools, junior college and in a Japanese Relocation Center. She has also taught English to foreign students. She spent ten years developing programs in special education.*

*As a writer, she has published articles, essays, plays, juveniles and short stories. She and Robert E. Gard began the Yarns of Yesteryear Project in 1974.*

*Gen Lewis has been Director of the Yarns of Yesteryear Project for the past five years. In her position with the University of Wisconsin-Extension Arts Development Unit, she handles various publishing projects and serves as Coordinator for the Reminiscence writing course.*

*She has a journalism degree from the University of Wisconsin and two degrees in education: B.S., Edgewood College, Madison, Wisconsin; and M.A., St. Joseph College, West Hartford, Connecticut.*

*She has also had experience in the sales promotion, publishing, advertising and public relations fields.*

*Marian Lefebvre is a well-known Midwestern illustrator and designer. She is best known for her illustrations in WE WERE CHILDREN THEN, VOLUME I. One critic commented that these illustrations "are like the memories of the writers, distorted somewhat by the years, romanticized a little by imaginations that seek to love the past, yet full enough to bring reality to what might be thought of as a dream." In her art, she continually recreates the past, both in mood and historical detail.*

*She is also an award-winning designer, most notably for THE ONLY PLACE WE LIVE.*